THE NORTH - WESTERN PROVINCES OF INDIA

THE NORTH - WESTERN PROVINCES OF INDIA

THEIR HISTORY, ETHNOLOGY, AND ADMINISTRATION

W. CROOKE

WITH SIXTEEN ILLUSTRATIONS AND A MAP

GYAN

Published by

Gyan Publishing House
5, Ansari Road
Daryaganj, New Delhi-110002
Phone: 011-47034999, 9811692060
E-mail: books@gyanbooks.com

Distribution Network
gyanbooks.com
India, USA, Canada, UK, Australia, France

ISBN : 978-81-212-3829-8 (PB)
First Published, London, 1897

2nd Impression 2020

Printed at: Gyan Press, Delhi.

THE NORTH-WESTERN PROVINCES OF INDIA

THEIR HISTORY, ETHNOLOGY, AND ADMINISTRATION

BY

W. CROOKE
BENGAL CIVIL SERVICE (RETIRED)

WITH
SIXTEEN FULL-PAGE ILLUSTRATIONS AND A MAP

METHUEN & CO.
36 ESSEX STREET, W.C.
LONDON
1897

Frontispiece. THE PILLAR OF THE STATE. A JÂT CULTIVATOR.

PREFACE

THIS book is an attempt to tell the story of one of the greatest of our Indian Provinces from the social point of view. If some space has been given to the geography of the country, it has been intended to explain the environment of the people. The sketch of the history up to the establishment of our rule has been written with the same object. I have then endeavoured to discuss briefly some of the chief social problems which the Government has attempted to solve—the repression of crime, the crusade against filth and disease, the relief of famine, of the depressed classes, the development of agriculture and trade.

This is followed by an account of the people themselves, largely based on information collected in the course of the Ethnographical Survey of the Province, which has been recently completed under my superintendence. I have tried to describe briefly the more interesting tribes, and to show what are the religious beliefs of the peasantry. This is a subject which I have dealt with more fully from the standpoint of Folklore in another book. Lastly, I have described how the revenue is "settled" and collected, how the peasant is protected from extortion, how he farms the land and makes his living.

I have used throughout information stored in a mass of

Blue Books—Census, Settlement, and Administrative Reports, a body of literature practically beyond the ken of English readers; and I have largely used information derived from Sir W. W. Hunter's *Imperial Gazetteer*, and those of the North-Western Provinces and Oudh prepared under the orders of the Local Government. For access to many of these, I have to thank the authorities of the India Office Library.

For the illustrations I am indebted to Mr J. O'Neal and Sergeant Wallace, R.E., of the Rurki College.

Since this book has been in type the true site of Kapilavastu, the birth-place of the Buddha (p. 66), has been discovered by Dr Führer, in the Nepâl Tarâi.

CONTENTS

CHAPTER I

THE LAND IN ITS PHYSICAL ASPECT

CHAPTER II

THE PROVINCE UNDER HINDU AND MUSALMÂN RULE

CONTENTS

CHAPTER II—*continued*

CHAPTER III

THE PROVINCE UNDER BRITISH RULE

CHAPTER IV

THE PEOPLE: THEIR ETHNOLOGY AND SOCIOLOGY

CONTENTS

CONTENTS

CHAPTER VI—*continued*

CHAPTER VII

THE PEASANT AND THE LAND

LIST OF ILLUSTRATIONS

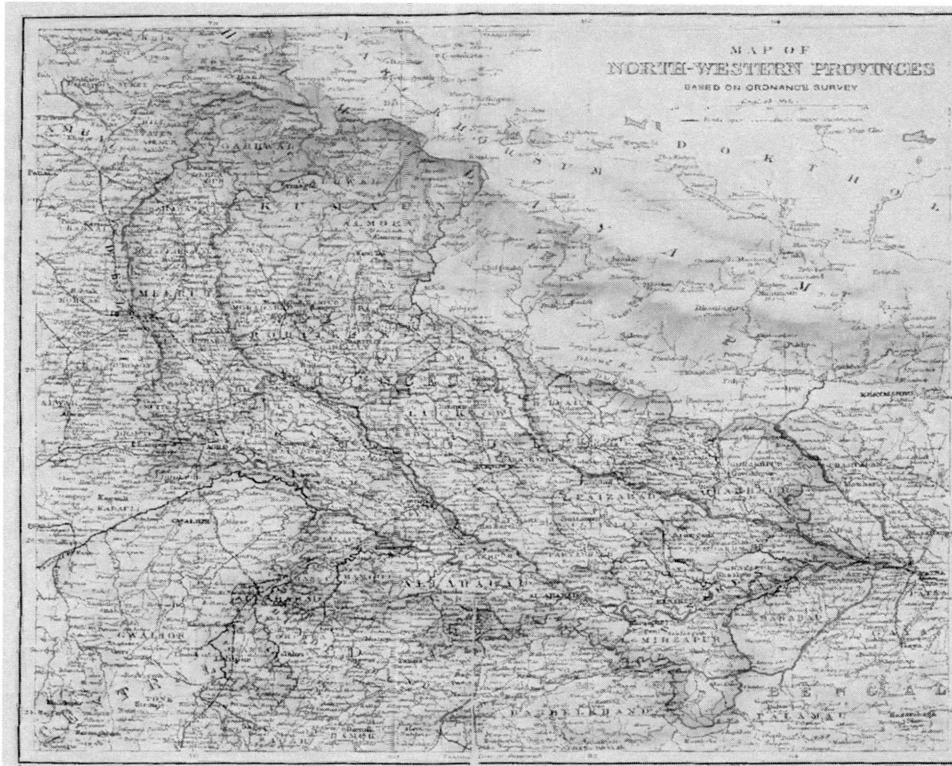
MAP OF
NORTH-WESTERN PROVINCES
BASED ON ORDNANCE SURVEY
GARHWAL
ALMORA
MEERUT
ALLAHABAD
FAIZABAD
MIRZAPUR
GWALIOR
SHAHABAD
BENGAL
PALAMAU
BAGHELKHAND

THE NORTH-WESTERN PROVINCES OF INDIA

CHAPTER I

THE LAND IN ITS PHYSICAL ASPECT

A WIDE open Plain, the alluvial valley of the Ganges, Jumna and their tributaries, with a slight uniform slope to the east and south in the direction of the course of the great river seaward towards the Bay of Bengal; a tract to the north including some of the highest mountains in the world, and separated by a series of valleys from a lower range which bounds the alluvial Plain; to the south of the Jumna a poorer country, rising from the river bank to the edge of the Vindhyan plateau, part of the backbone of Central India —such is the country known by the clumsy and inappropriate name of the North-Western Provinces and Oudh.

This is a name which comes down from the time when our arms had not yet crossed the Jumna and the centre of gravity of our power in northern India lay in Bengal and Calcutta. Times have changed since then, and now the official title of the Province is more unsuitable than ever.

We have been, in truth, unfortunate in our provincial nomenclature, in so far that it has little historical continuity. It is only natural that the name of Assam, for instance, a newly occupied country, should be little more than three centuries old. But Panjâb, though it represents the old Sanskrit Panchanada, "the land of the five rivers," is a Persian word. Bengal, the land of the Vanga tribe, is not found in common use before the eleventh century; Bombay, the shrine of the goddess Mamba Devi, is at least as old as the middle of the fifteenth, and Madras, the original meaning of which is obscure, dates from the middle of the seventeenth century. While Wessex, Sussex and many other English localities hand down the names of early colonists, there is here no trace of the kingdom of Panchâla in the centre or of Kosala to the east. It was the Muhammadans who for religious motives were most anxious to discard the old Hindu names. In some cases, as when they re-christened the old Prayâga as Allahâbâd, they succeeded in obliterating the ancient title save in the lips of priests and pilgrims; but few would now recognise Agra in Akbarâbâd, Delhi as Shâhjahânâbâd, or Gorakhpur as Muazzamâbâd. With us the loss of the old names has been more the result of lack of historical instinct than from any desire to widen the gulf between the past and the present.

Yet it would be hard to find a really suitable name for this rather heterogeneous slice of the Empire. It occupies pretty much the same area as that which the Musalmâns called Hindustân, the seat of the early Hindus, who knew the land between the two rivers as Madhyadesa, "the middle land," or Mesopotamia. The western part and the adjoining portion of the Panjâb they called Punyabhûmi, "the holy land": Aryavarta or Brahmavarta, "the land of the Aryans and their gods." The term Hindustân has now been extended by the geographers to denote the whole north of the peninsula, as contrasted with the Deccan (Dakkhin), the southern country, or even to all that we now include in India, exclusive of Burma. In the early days of our occupation we called it the government of Agra after the Mughal capital; and if we were now to rename it it would be difficult to suggest a better title. The more ancient Hindu names are too indefinite and have passed too completely from the memories of the people ever to be again revived.

Of all the provinces of the Empire none is of greater interest than this. It is the veritable garden of India, with a soil of unrivalled fertility, for the most part protected from the dangers of famine by a magnificent series of irrigation works: occupied by some of the finest and most industrious of the native races: possessing in its roads and railways an unusually perfect system of internal communications. Within its borders or close to its western frontier was the earliest settlement of the Hindu race, and here its religion, laws and social polity were organised. Beneath the ruins of Hastinapura and Ajudhya lie the remains of the two ancient capitals commemorated in the two famous national epics. Here Buddhism supplanted Brâhmanism, only in its turn to succumb to the older faith, and to sink into such utter insignificance in the land of its birth that it has hardly retained a single adherent, while it has given a religion to half the human race. Here are nearly all the shrines of the discredited creed, the scenes of the birth, the preaching, the death of the Teacher. But since they were visited by the old Chinese pilgrims they have fallen into utter neglect, and it is only within the last generation that the sites of most of them have been identified. The interest which some of the modern Buddhists have recently shown in the temple at Gaya may perhaps by and by extend to places like Kusinagara, Sravasti, Sarnâth or Sankisa.

In later times the country was the prize of one conqueror after another—Ghaznivide, Pathân, Mughal and Sikh, Marhatta and Englishmen. Agra yielded to none of the other Mughal capitals in magnificence ; at Jaunpur and Lucknow two subordinate Musalmân dynasties reigned, which profoundly influenced its history. This was the ground on which the final struggle for Empire took place, in which the British came out victorious. Here was the chief scene of the Sepoy Mutiny which resulted in the final downfall of the royal family of Delhi, in the course of which Englishmen and Englishwomen shared a common fate at the hands of a faithless soldiery, and the heroism of the imperial race, suddenly driven to bay, was most nobly displayed. Yet curiously enough, except where Jay Chand of Kanauj fell at the hands of the invading Musalmân, Shihâbuddîn, the battle near Agra where Dâra Shikoh was defeated by Aurangzeb and the fights of the Mutiny, there is no important battle-field within its boundaries. The rout of Humayun by the Afghân Shîr Shâh occurred just beyond its eastern limits ; the historic field of Pânipat, where the fate of India was thrice decided, lies a short distance beyond its border to the west.

Mere figures and small scale maps do little to help us to realise the importance of the charge which the conditions of our Indian Empire impose upon a small body of English officers. It conveys little practical information to be told that the area of the province is 107,503 square miles, and the population 47¾ millions. To put this in another way—the total population is about the same as that of the whole German Empire in an area rather smaller than that of Italy. Its area is slightly less than that of the Transvaal, but between black men and white men President Kruger governs only 800,000 souls, which would be smaller than the average charge of an Indian Collector. The North-West Provinces alone have a population little less than that of the United Kingdom; Oudh includes twice as many souls as Belgium, which, again, has less people than one division, that of Gorakhpur. The Lucknow division alone contains more people than Ireland or Scotland, Sweden, Portugal or Holland, Canada or Ceylon. One district, Basti, exceeds in population New South Wales and New Zealand put together.

Geographically speaking, the Province may be said to include the upper basins of three great rivers—the Ganges, Jumna and Ghâgra, and their tributaries. The two former rising in the Native State of Garhwâl at the extreme north-west corner from the snows of the inner Himâlaya, debouch at once into the open plain through which they pass till they join at Allahâbâd. Just beyond the eastern frontier, in the province of Bihâr, the united stream, henceforward known as the Ganges, is met by three other great rivers. Of these two, the Ghâgra and the Gandak are also snow-fed, and after passing through Nepâl, pour their waters into the lower Plain, the Ghâgra with its tributary the Râpti draining Oudh and Gorakhpur, while the Gandak only just touches the Province to the east and then trends away through Bihâr. The third important river, the Son, is not like the others fed by the snows. It drains part of the Vindhyan plateau, and after passing through a part of the Mirzapur district to the south-east, sweeps round to meet the Ganges further on in its course.

The boundaries of the Province nowhere exactly agree with the physical conditions by which it is dominated; its limits, in fact, everywhere indicate that it was formed not on ethnical or geographical considerations, but was the result of historical influences. It does not follow to the north the natural frontier of the lower Himâlaya, because to the north-west it includes a portion of the inner and higher range with the intervening valleys, and on the extreme east it has surrendered a part of the Tarâi or malarious jungle at the foot of the hills to Nepâl. To the west and south its natural limits would have been the Jumna; but opposite Mathura and Agra it includes patches of territory, which from a geographical point of view should form part of Râjputâna, and further south the Bundelkhand country, which on physical and ethnical grounds would naturally be included among the States of Central India. Its proper frontier to the east would be either the river Ghâgra or the Gandak. With the former as its border it would lose a valuable part of Oudh and Gorakhpur: with the latter it would gain from Bengal a rich piece of Bihâr.

Before long some readjustment of the Provincial administrations of northern India is inevitable, if only to relieve Lower Bengal, which has an area equal to that of the United Kingdom with the addition of a second Scotland, and a population as great as that of the United States and Mexico combined—a charge quite beyond the powers of any single governor. Bengal will probably be relieved for the present by combining the division of Chittagong to the east with Assam. But sooner or later a more radical redistribution of territory must be effected, and this will probably result in the addition of the eastern districts of the North-West provinces to the new Province of Bihâr, which would then be as large as a quarter of the German Empire with a population as great as that of England and Wales. This tract will then be physically and ethnically homogeneous and administered under the same revenue system, that of the Permanent

Settlement. We shall lose, by the severance of Benares and the neighbouring districts, some of the most fertile parts of the Province; but the relief to the already overburdened Local Government will be welcome.

The present frontier, again, is neither ethnical nor linguistic. To include all the Hindi-speaking peoples it would be necessary to absorb the eastern Panjâb and Bihâr with a still larger area annexed from Râjputâna and Central India; and men of the same race are found both east and west of the Jumna and Gandak and north and south of the Ganges. But it is only in newly settled countries like Canada and western America that administrative divisions can be marked off by straight lines on a map, and the limits of a Province formed on the ruins of ancient empires must conform to historical or political considerations and to none other.

Looking at the country merely from the physical point of view, it may perhaps be best compared with Egypt—the river system of the Jumna and Ganges representing the Nile, the Arabian and Lybian hills, the mountain barrier to the north and the Vindyan and Kaimur ranges to the south. But the Nile valley with an area of 11,000 square miles is only about the size of the division of Rohilkhand and its population is about equal to that of the Faizâbâd division. In other respects the contrast is no less striking. The Indian province is ours whether for good or ill by right of conquest; no foreign power can or does claim rights of co-dominion with us. We have no frontier to guard against a Khalîfa and his Dervishes; there are no jealous neighbours and we are quite beyond the dangers arising from European statecraft. But in the antiquity of the relics of an ancient civilisation there is no comparison. The monumental history of Egypt begins some forty centuries before the beginning of our era; the oldest building in northern India cannot be fixed with certainty before the time of Asoka, who lived about the era of the first Punic war. We have nothing which can be compared with the Pyramids, the temples like those of Karnak or the rock sepulchres with their wall paintings and sculptures which so vividly represent the life of those early times.

THE LAND IN ITS PHYSICAL ASPECT

The Province, as a whole, includes perhaps greater diversities of physical aspect, scenery and climate than any other country of the same area on the face of the earth. The only country with which a comparison is possible is Peru, with its Sierra or lofty mountain tract and the Montana, or region of tropical forests in the valley of the Amazon. To the north are stupendous mountains covered with eternal snow; beneath them a lower range with a more equable climate, clothed with dense jungle and abundant vegetation; below these, again, a line of malarious woodland and vast savannahs of grass and reeds. Passing these we reach the alluvial Plain, populated almost up to the limits of subsistence by a most industrious population, subject to a tropical climate, swept by winds at one time of the year whose breath is as the breath of a furnace, at another gasping under the damp heat of the rainy season, at a third chilled by the sharp touch of frost; and beyond these, again, clusters of low hills covered with scrub jungle and exposed in summer to the fiercest heat of the sun.

The Province may then naturally be divided into three tracts—the northern mountain region: the central Plain: the southern hill country. The following table illustrates their varied conditions:—

Tract.	Districts.	Area in Square Miles.	Density of Population per square mile.	Rainfall in inches.
Himalayan, ...	3	13,973	81	62".13
Plains—				
(*a*) Submontane, . .	7	18,202	486	46".43
(*b*) Upper Duâb, . .	5	10,133	509	31".25
(*c*) Central Duâb, .	6	10,139	470	28".38
(*d*) North Central, .	7	14,166	499	38".29
(*e*) South Central, .	15	25,300	652	38".42
Plains, Total,	40	77,890	—	—
Southern, ...	6	15,639	221	37".51

These figures bring out the enormous predominance in area and population of the Plains as compared with the rest of the Province. Some of the southern districts, such as Mirzapur and part of Bundelkhand, include a hilly tract on the skirts of the central Plain; but this fact does not to any considerable degree affect the figures, which show that the Plain tract includes about 72 per cent. of the area and 89 per cent. of the total population.

This enables us to dispose of a misapprehension which very generally prevails among English people, and is mainly based on the inexpressive title of the province. It is very commonly supposed that when an officer is lucky enough to escape the Bengal delta, or the less favoured Presidencies of Madras or Bombay, he necessarily spends most of his time in the Hills. The globe-trotter sees him here in the cold weather enjoying an excellent climate and pleasant surroundings, and wonders what is the justification for the higher rates of pay which the Anglo-Indian enjoys as compared with officials of a similar grade in Europe. But as a matter of fact, the average official has little concern with the Hills. The mountainous tract to the south contains no health stations, and the heat of Bundelkhand is even more trying than that of the Plains north of the Jumna. In the Himalayan tract there are two leading health resorts, Mussoorie and Naini Tâl, the latter the headquarters of the Provincial Government during the more unhealthy season. Besides a small number of Secretaries and the normal civil staff of these Hill districts, there is a considerable influx of visitors, ladies and children, and those officers who can be spared from regimental duty, or civil officials who are unable to utilise short leave for a visit to England. But the number of officials who are able to retire to the Hills periodically, or are permanently posted there, is very small.

The ordinary servant of the Crown, military or civil, spends most of his time in the Plains or in the southern hill country. Most of the European and native troops are posted in the Plains, at great cantonments like Meerut, Lucknow, Bareilly, or Allahâbâd. The High Court sits permanently in the Plains, and there the chief offices of the Provincial Government are established. Only a very small proportion of the executive staff, magistrates, police officers. engineers, school inspectors, Custom officers, and so on, serve anywhere but in the Plains. It is, in short, the great tropical Plain which dominates everything; those parts of the territory ruled by the Lieutenant-Governor which lie beyond it are in all but mere area inconsiderable; from the political and executive point of view they are distinctly a negligeable quantity. Any candidate for the public service who selects this Province in the expectation that he will spend most of his service in an excellent climate will be sorely disappointed.

Taking up these three physical divisions of the Province, we have first the Himalayan tract, which includes three districts—Garhwâl, Almora and Naini Tâl, all under the charge of the Commissioner of Kumaun. Of these, two districts, Garhwâl and Kumaun, are well within the higher mountain zone; while Naini Tâl includes the tract of malarious swamp and jungle at the foot of the lower hills, and between them and the Plains, which is known as the Tarâi and Bhâbar, and must be separately described. Of the purely mountainous districts, a mass of tangled peaks and valleys, it is difficult to give a general sketch. It includes some of the most lofty mountains in the world, clothed with eternal snow. Nanda Devi, consecrated in the Hindu faith as the guardian goddess of the range, soars to a height of 25,661 feet; Kamet and Badarinâth are respectively 25,413 and 22,901 feet above sea level. These are a little lower than Mount Everest, the giant of the eastern part of the range. But they are slightly higher than the South American Andes, and we have to go to the Pamir or Karakorum range to find a worthy rival to these magnificent peaks.

This region roughly falls into three divisions. First, we have the outer Himâlaya, with a height of from 5000 to 8500 feet, which rise abruptly from the lower Plain, and then sink sharply to the north into deep and narrow valleys. Here the clouds rising from the ocean first strike the mountain barrier and produce an excessive rainfall, the general average being from 80 to 90 inches, about the same as that of the Scotch Highlands, but all concentrated within little more than a quarter of the year. There is little arable soil, and the climate, except on the breezy summits of the hills, is malarious and unhealthy; population is scanty, and the country is mostly covered with dense forest. Behind these heights are lower hills and wider valleys, receiving a rainfall little more than half that of the outer barrier. Here cultivation is more dense and cultivation more extensive. Behind these, again, are the giant peaks and higher valleys, which during the winter are impassable from snow, and in the summer are inhabited by a scanty nomadic population of cowherds, wood-cutters, and Tibetan traders, who barter wool and borax, and take back in exchange salt, cloth, and metals, which are hauled up with infinite labour to these higher levels from the marts in the lower country.

The mineral resources of this inaccessible land are probably great, but have been as yet imperfectly explored. In Kumaun iron and copper abound, but the competition for labour on tea-gardens and agriculture has nearly doubled the price of grain; hence the local iron is no longer able to compete with imported supplies. The same is the case with the copper mines, from which much was at one time expected. The rude indigenous system of finding and refining the ore has given way before the cheaper article from Europe. The mines are too much isolated, too far from profitable markets, worked by too inefficient methods, to make the industry remunerative. It will need a more advanced plan of working cheaper and more abundant labour, improved communications, before mining in Kumaun or Garhwâl can be carried on with success.

Gold in small quantities is found in the sands of the Alaknanda and other tributaries of the Ganges; but as yet the matrix has not been reached, and the process of collection is extremely primitive and laborious. There is a small quantity of gold imported by Bhotiya traders from the Tibetan hills, a fact which was probably the origin of the fable of the gold-

BHOTIYA BUDDHISTS.

bearing ants told by Herodotus and other early writers. The trade is checked by the prevailing superstition that no large nugget should be removed because it belongs to the genii of the place—an idea which crops up everywhere throughout the whole range of folk-lore.

The European tea-planter has gradually forced his way some distance up the lower slopes; but, as regards climate, this region is distinctly inferior to Assam: and it is highly improbable that in the tea industry it will ever secure a leading position.

The inhabitants are few; but they thrive because their wants are simple, and they derive some income from employment as wood-cutters, and bearers of litters for the European visitors to the health resorts, and from the adventurous Hindu pilgrims who throng to the famous shrines along the upper course of the Ganges and its tributaries. A simple-minded, hardy, cheery fellow, the hillman is in decided contrast to the menial village serf of the Plains, debilitated by fever and the rigour of his environment. But he has little of the courage and martial spirit which makes the Gurkha of Nepâl one of the best of our native mercenaries. We meet occasionally, at the foot of the hills, the quaint figures of Bhotiya wanderers from Tibet, with their Mongoloid faces, squat figures and grotesque dress. These are about the only adherents of the Buddhist faith likely to be met with within the boundaries of the Province.

The scenery is everywhere beautiful in the extreme. No one who has ever seen them will forget the view of the snows at sunrise and sunset, as they glow with all the tints of opal and of pearl against the northern sky. Bishop Heber writes of the view from Bareilly: "The nearer hills are blue, and in outline and tints resemble pretty closely, at this distance, those which close in the valley of Clwyd. Above them rose what might, in the present unfavourable atmosphere, have been taken for clouds, had not their seat been so stationary, and their outline so harsh and pyramidical, the patriarchs of the continent, perhaps the surviving ruins of a former world, white and glistening as alabaster and even at this distance, probably 150 miles, towering above the nearer and secondary range, as much as these last (though said to be 7600 feet high) are above the Plain on which we are standing. I felt intense awe and delight in looking on them; but the clouds closed in again, as on the fairy castle of St John, and left us but the former grey cold horizon, girding in the green plain of Rohilkhand, and broken only by scattered tufts of pîpal and mango trees."[1]

Reaching the heights themselves, the view is not less beautiful. From the top of Chîna, which rises over the lake and station of Naini Tâl, we look over the lovely wooded mountains of the Gâgar range, clothed thick with oak and pine, mingled with the gorgeous flowers of the rhododendron, and thence to the forest of the Bhâbar, which lies almost at our feet; beyond it the swamps of the Tarâi, and then in the dim distance the green plain of Rohilkhand. Turning to the north we have a scene which only a poet or painter could depict—a chaotic mass of mountains, thickly wooded hill sides seamed with deep ravines, dark blue ranges piled one beyond another; and, as a background to the landscape, the immense snowy peaks, never trodden by the foot of man; the evening falls and they fade slowly into the darkening sky, peopled by innumerable stars.

So from Mussoorie, as the mists dissolve from the lowlands, we have an unrivalled panorama of wood and silver streams encircled by rocky or forest-covered hills, now glowing with the amber tints that accompany the fall of the leaf, now at night lit by the fierce glare of a jungle fire, and here and there in the distance the emerald green of rice or wheatfields. Grander still is the first burst of the monsoon, when the water-laden clouds from the ocean impinge on the mountain barrier and pour a deluge over the lower hills, setting every rivulet in flood, and sometimes bearing down the wooded hill sides in a chaos of ruin. By and by the damp billows of fog roll up from the valley and shroud the landscape in an impenetrable pall of vapour.

All this, to the Hindu of the Plain, is the land of myth

[1] *Journal*, i. 248.

and mystery, associated with the most ancient and sacred traditions of his race. Here live his deities, each in a paradise of his own, on the summits of the trackless peaks. Here the Pândavas sought a way to heaven amidst the eternal snows, and in dark caves and secluded hermitages the sages of the old world puzzled out the secrets of life and time. In sequestered valleys, deep amid the bosom of the hills, were shrines, like Kedârnâth and Badarinâth, which were far beyond the range of the Pathân and Mughal who raided and ravished in the Plain below; here for many ages the indigenous Hindu civilisation was permitted to develop, safe from foreign influence. Every rock and spring and stream is the home of some legend told by the forefathers of the people. Beyond the eternal hills lay Uttara Kuru, the paradise of the faithful—"the island valley of Avilion"—

> "Where falls not hail or rain or any snow,
> Nor ever wind blows loudly; but it lies
> Deep-meadowed, happy, fair with orchard lawns.'

Flanking this mountainous region is the lower range, known as the Siwâliks, the home of Siva or Mahâdeva, behind which lies embosomed the fertile valley of Dehra Dûn. It is only quite within recent years that this fair territory has been opened up. Here a connecting ridge forms the watershed of the Ganges and the Jumna. It was here, at the siege of Kalanga during the Nepâl war, that we gained our first real experience of Gurkha gallantry. After our occupation the experiment of colonisation through the agency of European grantees was tried, with little practical result. But, as the jungle is gradually cleared, with diminishing malaria and extension of irrigation, it is sure to become the seat of a thriving agricultural peasantry; and once the railway is pushed on to the base of the hills, Dehra and Mussoorie will certainly become important European colonies.

While the higher ranges behind consist to a great extent of crystalline, metamorphic rocks, the sub-Himâlaya is built up of soft sandstone, but all so broken and disturbed by the action of cosmic forces that there is little continuity of structure, and the stone which it supplies is of small value for building purposes. It is broken into sharp, rugged peaks, with precipitous ravines, and clothed so densely with jungle that it affords a safe asylum for the larger fauna, the wild elephant, the tiger and the sâmbhar stag. This forms the most valuable part of the forest tract protected by the State. Here, during the hot season when the scrub and undergrowth are as dry as tinder, a spark let fall by some careless cowherd or traveller may result in a serious conflagration, and the forest officer must ever be on the alert to hasten to the scene of danger and isolate or extinguish the flames.

Beneath these lower hills and separating them from the plain lie the tracts known as the Tarâi or lowland and the Bhâbar. This is the ethnical frontier between the low and the upper country. The Bhâbar is a tract of waterless jungle, where the underlying clay stratum extending to the foot of the hills has been overlaid by a mass of gravel and boulders, the detritus of the overhanging hills, washed down by the streams which drain them. In the rainy season the numerous torrents cut into the upper soil, and in the ravines thus formed the characteristic features of the region become apparent. The splendid trees of the forest derive their support from only a scanty layer of earth above the underlying mass of shingle. It is from the vapour-laden air that they receive the moisture which promotes their growth, but even here there is not that lavish luxuriance of growth which is found in the damper tropical life of the South American forests. Through the shingly subsoil the drainage rapidly percolates, leaving the upper surface arid and waterless, only to appear again lower down the slope, and after passing through the marshes of the Tarâi, to feed the rivers which traverse the Plains, and end in the system of the Ganges and its tributaries. This tract is colonised in an intermittent way by emigrants from the hills, who retire periodically to the higher levels when malaria is most prevalent.

The Tarâi thus becomes a region of marsh and fen, a land of sluggish streams and water-choked morasses, the soil a moist alluvial formation which encourages the growth of coarse grasses and thickets of reeds, in which in the hot weather the tiger, wild buffalo, and swamp deer find a congenial home. This tract is called in popular parlance the Mâr, which the people interpret to mean "the land of death," but which may be better explained as "the wilderness." Here the water is so near the surface that wherever a buffalo rolls in the mud or a stick is pushed into the clammy soil a spring gushes out. At nightfall the mists raised from the saturated ground by the fierce heat of the sun collect like a pall over the landscape, and bring the justly dreaded jungle fever in their train. In some places the patient labours of the marsh-dwellers, the Thârus and cognate tribes, have pushed the sheet of cultivation right up to the foot of the hills, and the land is covered with a rich harvest of rice. But they do this at the sacrifice of health and strength, their stunted frames, swollen spleens, yellow skins and diminished families tell the tale of their struggle with the unhealthiness of the climate. It is one of the current fictions which swarm in the records of Indian sociology that the Thâru is proof against malaria. As a matter of fact, it has been shown in Bengal, where he lives under pretty much the same conditions as in this Province, that he stands much lower, as might have been anticipated, in the scale of fecundity and average duration of life than other castes who enjoy healthier climatic conditions.

It is remarkable that this tract, which is now exposed to malaria in a most dangerous form, was once the seat of an opulent and advanced civilisation. The Tarâi is full of ancient ruins, fine old mango groves, sculptures and wells, the remains of thriving cities. We know from the evidence of the Chinese Buddhist pilgrims that the Gorakhpur jungles contained flourishing towns before the fourth, while showing signs of deterioration in the seventh, century. The failure of the Muhammadans to extend their conquests to the hills shows that in their days the country was quite as unhealthy and impenetrable as it is at present. Hence perhaps from sheer necessity it was chosen as the site of cities of refuge, where the persecuted Buddhist or the Râjput chieftain, dispossessed by the Musalmân invader may have sought shelter. When we see in recent years the effect of a sudden outbreak of fever in some of the flourishing districts of the Ganges-Jumna Duâb, we can understand that a calamity of the same kind may have wrecked the civilisation of the Tarâi. Perhaps the cosmic forces of elevation and depression, which have not as yet exhausted their energy, may have altered the condition of things.

We come next to consider the lower hills south of the rivers Jumna and Ganges. Here the conditions are very different from those of the northern region. The hills here are known as the Vindhyan and Kaimûr ranges and are part of the mountain system stretching right across the centre of the peninsula, the home of scattered Dravidian tribes such as Santâls and Gonds, Bhîls, Kharwârs, and their kinsfolk. The word Vindhya means "the divider," and this range was for many ages the political as well as the ethnic frontier between Hindustân, or the land of the early Hindus, and the Deccan (Dakkhin) or south country. It was across this range that adventurous Hindu missionaries in ancient times forced their way and brought the knowledge of the faith into the southern parts of the peninsula. But after that it was permitted to work out its social development undisturbed by the lords of the Ganges valley until its conquest was undertaken in earnest by the Musalmâns.

In direct contrast to the northern tract, we have here hills of only moderate height, rising to the elevation of about 5000 feet—little more than that of Ben Nevis. The jungle is much scantier and less luxuriant, the water supply almost everywhere limited, in some places so insufficient that the village women have to go miles to find a spring, or draw their supplies from fetid water holes which they share with the cattle and the beasts of the forest, and a traveller must carefully select his halting-place in some favoured spot amidst the arid wilderness. On these low, bare, stony hills the heat of the summer sun beats with terrific force. Parts of the country in drought and desolation vie with the rainless peaks which surround the Gulf of Suez or line the Arabian desert.

This deficiency of the water supply is the main cause of the curious scarcity of animal life. It is only in the recesses of the heavier jungle that the tiger, the sâmbhar stag and the spotted deer find a home. A few ravine deer occupy the broken sides of the lower hills, and here will be sometimes seen a sounder of pig of a leaner, gaunter type than the heavy beast of the Plains which battens in swamp and cane brake. The graceful black buck is occasionally seen, but his horns never reach the length of those of his brethren in the neighbourhood of Mathura or Bhartpur. Even the hill tiger is a different animal from that of the Tarâi. He is a shorter, fiercer, and more active brute, trained to greater endurance, his muscles toughened by the long range of country he must cover nightly in search of prey. The leopard, too, from his environment, is distinguishable from the Bengal species. In the damp Himalayan forests he is darker and redder in colour, and has larger spots than in the Central Indian hills. Some naturalists have gone so far as to separate the two varieties; but the best authorities are disposed to consider them identical in species—the difference being due to the fact that one is the denizen of thick, marshy swamps or damp jungle, the other inhabiting the rock caves or the bamboo clumps and stunted thickets of the waterless hills.

Were the water supply more abundant this country would be the sportsman's paradise. In some favoured spots the tiger and leopard abound, and find plentiful supplies of food in the droves of half-starved cattle which are driven up from the Plains to eke out a precarious subsistence on the scanty herbage, which, poor as it is, is more abundant here than in the home pastures, burnt brown by the fierce heat of summer. When the hot west wind blows strongly the herdsmen set fire to the crisp undergrowth, and with the first shower of the rains, the hills are again green with fairly abundant grasses. In this land of drought the absence of bird life is specially noticeable. While in the Plains they nestle in every grove, and the morning air rings with the notes of innumerable birds, here they follow man, and are found only in the neighbourhood of water, round the scattered patches of cultivation or in a few of the moister ravines or valleys. Here the oak, pine and deodâr of the north are replaced by a scanty jungle of gnarled and stunted trees, the bastard Sâl, the catechu acacia and the cotton tree. The bamboo abounds, but seldom attains much luxuriance of growth; it is only in favoured spots that the more valuable Sâl and teak are to be found.

But it is where water combines with woodland, hill and ravine that the scenery really becomes lovely. Such is the valley of the Son, which drains the central plateau into the Ganges. Towards the Ganges the Vindhyan range slopes down to the valley in successive terraces or gradual declivities. We are led up to the first complete view of the rich Plain below by occasional glimpses of the greenery of grove and field scattered here and there along the descent, with the grey sands and silvery waters of the great river on the northern horizon. But where the plateau meets the Son the more stable sandstones form a sheer precipice a couple of hundred feet high, an almost perpendicular wall of rock, from which, as from the battlement of a great fortress, you look down on sheets of virgin forest, and beyond this on the yellow sands which fringe the river. Hence the old Sanskrit poets gave it the name of Hiranya-vâha, "the gold bearer," and the modern Hindu calls it Sona, "the golden." In earlier times considerable quantities of gold seem to have been found in Chota Nâgpur, and recent discoveries make it possible that gold mining may be largely revived in this part of the country. As it is at present, the only mining industry is a little iron manufacture carried on by the Agariyas, a tribe of Dravidian smelters who carry on their occupation in a most primitive way. This and a little agriculture, the collection of silk cocoons, lac, catechu, gums and other jungle products are the only industries of the dwellers in the forest.

In the way of forest scenery it would be hard to find in India anything finer than the valley of the Son; but it can

AN AGARIYA METAL SMELTER WITH HAMMER AND FOOT-BELLOWS.

be reached only by a long and tedious march from the Gangetic Plain, and is as yet quite unknown to the tourist. While along the Ganges you meet wide stretches of grey sand and beyond it a sheet of cultivation, here the jungle extends right down to the rocky bank and clothes the rolling hills to the south, supremely lovely in its vivid greenery at the close of the rains, and in its tints of crimson or amber at the approach of early summer. Dominating over the whole landscape is the sombre, buttress-like peak of Mangesar, the mountain godling of the jungle people. Here and there, as at Agori and Bijaygarh, are seen the ruins of the rude strongholds, built by the early Râjput settlers to overawe the aborigines, now a placid, timid race, in whom it is hard to recognise the successors of the wild, independent savages, who, if the local legends are to be trusted, were once cannibals, eaters of raw flesh, and carried on a fierce guerilla warfare with the invaders throughout this rude borderland.

But, on the whole, these southern jungles will disappoint the visitor who expects to meet a world of tropical vegetation, immense trees crowded together in a damp fertile soil, the festoons of creepers, the choking undergrowth, the abundant animal and vegetable life. The jungle is in most places hardly more than patches of scrub, the trees of small size, their trunks gnarled and twisted, their leaves green only when moisture prevails in the rainy season, and parched to a dull, dusty brown, as the sky clears and they are baked by the sun. Some of the trees add to the dreariness of the landscape—the cotton tree with its gaunt, grey trunk, the Salâi rising with its ashy, leafless branches, above the undergrowth, give the forest a bleak and wintry appearance. The Kulu, to quote Captain Forsyth, "looks as if the megatherium might have climbed its uncouth and ghastly branches at the birth of the world."

So far we have spoken chiefly of Mirzapur. Further west in Bundelkhand, from an eminence you see nothing but the rugged crests of innumerable hillocks, from which all culturable soil has been washed into the ravines, and which roll towards the horizon like the waves of a troubled sea. In some places immense masses of rock are piled together in the wildest confusion. Up to their very base extend patches of the richest black cotton soil. This soil is, as will be shown later on, probably composed of disentegrated laterite, poured out in ancient times from the crater of some vast Central Indian volcano, of which no trace can now be found. Many of the Vindhyan hills are tipped with a reddish ferruginous substance, the detritus or scoriae which resulted from igneous action. In some instances this is replaced by veins of quartz, which traverse the gneiss or tip the low sandstone hills, as in Mirzapur. These Vindhyan sandstones are of immense geological antiquity, perhaps pre-Silurian. But as they are devoid of fossils, their precise age cannot be determined with certainty. They produce an admirable building stone, which formed the material of all the ancient stone buildings in the Gangetic valley, and quarries near Agra, Allahâbâd, and Chunâr are still extensively worked. The marble of the Tâj, and the palaces of Agra and Delhi, was procured at an excessive cost of labour from Makrâna in the Jodhpur Sate, far to the west in Râjputâna.

From these two areas, which may be termed the Himalayan and the Vindhyan fringes, we pass to the great Plain itself. This is only the upper portion of the alluvial valley of the Ganges, which extends from Hardwâr to the Delta, where the river finally joins the ocean. As a river it ranks high among the rivers of the world. In historic interest and in its services to agriculture it may be compared with the Nile. There is, however, this important difference—from the Atbara to the Mediterranean, a distance of 1200 miles, the Nile does not receive a single brook: the Ganges all through its course is constantly reinforced by tributary streams. The length of the Nile, again, which is estimated at 3400 miles from Lake Victoria Nyanza, is about double that of the Ganges, 1557 miles; but the maximum discharge of the Ganges at Râjmahâl is five times that of the Nile at Cairo.

As to the origin of this vast Plain there has been much speculation; but the problem cannot be completely solved until much deeper borings are made. According to one theory an Eocene sea once extended like a great estuary through the middle of the Peninsula, its waters lapping the rocky barrier to the north and south; subsequently the silt-bearing waters of the rivers, laden with the detritus of the Himâlaya, gradually filled up the depression. According to another account its depression was contemporaneous with the disturbance and contortion of the Himâlaya. Messrs Medlicott and Blanford, the best and most recent authorities, incline to the latter view, and suggest that "the crust movements, to which the elevation of the Himalayas and of the Panjâb, Sindh and Burmese ranges are due, may have also produced the depression of the Indo-Gangetic Plain, and that the two movements may have gone on *pari passu*," both being to some extent still in progress. Borings, so far as they have been made into the deeper strata in the course of the erection of bridges and other buildings, show only successive deposits of sand and clay; and the only thing in the nature of a rock which the soil contains is patches of what is called Kankar, a nodular carbonate of lime, most valuable for building purposes, and admirable as road metal. This is, of course, quite a recent formation, and its deposition continues at the present time.

Through this unstable alluvium the rivers have cut their present courses. Their task is one of constant demolition and reconstruction. At one spot, as the current impinges on the friable bank, it gradually undermines it, and by and by immense masses of the upper surface soil come toppling down into the current, only to be dissolved at once in the water and carried along and deposited on some new site further down the course of the stream. In such seasons at night camping near the river bank, you will hear the sound as of distant artillery, when tons of stuff at a time plunge into the river. Occasionally the damage done is really serious, when ancient mango groves, temples and homesteads are swept away. A year or two ago, from danger of this kind, it became necessary to abandon Ballia, the headquarters of the most eastern district, and it was considered hopeless to attempt to save even the public buildings and the residences of the officials. If you desire a really exciting life, you have only to purchase one of these riverine properties. If the current sets against your lands you may be made a beggar in a single night; or, perchance, the stream in a more genial mood may pile rich banks of silt along your border, which may continue stable for years and grow magnificent harvests; or the fickle current may sweep it all away again with some of your own best land in the bargain. In any case whatever land you gain you will have to hold through vexatious civil, criminal and revenue suits, and by the time the final decree is issued the whole face of the neighbourhood may have changed. No more arduous task falls upon the district officials than the investigation of cases such as these. A claimant will sometimes appear and assert rights dormant for a generation over a patch of sandbank which now occupies the assumed site of a village long since demolished. Possession is here more than the proverbial nine points of the law. The rude bludgeon-men of the riverine villages need little provocation to turn out and resist rival claimants; serious riots and loss of life have often occurred in quarrels of this kind.

Another difficulty which meets the investigating officer is that of comparing ancient maps. Where the whole surface of the neighbourhood is completely changed from year to year, it is extremely difficult to find any certain point from which to commence measurements. Often he has to abandon the river bank altogether, and go some distance inland to find an ancient temple, or some tree or boundary pillar, from whence he can with some degree of confidence start the survey.

One thing is certain—this periodical movement of the great rivers, which seems to be in some degree influenced by the revolution of the earth, will not be checked by the feeble hand of man. However cunningly he designs an embankment, however deep he plants his piles and ranges his fascines, the subtle genius of the stream will find a means to evade or undermine them: or it gaily works its way through the friable alluvium behind them and leaves them high and dry as a proof of its contempt for humanity and all its works. So is it ever with him who essays to draw out Leviathan with a hook or push back the ocean with a mop.

These variations of the river's course may arise from the most trivial causes. A snag gets safely anchored in the mud, becomes the nucleus of a shoal and diverts the current; a sunken boat, a deposit of Kankar, a bed of stiff clay will produce the same effect. But some rivers are more sedate than others. The Jumna, for instance, maintains a fairly definite course. Writing of Farrukhâbâd, Sir C. Elliott tells us that "the Ganges, as becomes its great age, keeps sedately within its bed, and only rolls wearily from one side to the other. But the Râmganga is a gambolling vagabond, and wanders at its own sweet will over many miles of country, carving out beds capriciously for itself, and leaving them as illogically; so that it becomes quite exciting to watch it in its frolics and to mark off on the map, as one inspects villages day by day, the different past courses of the river."

Hence in many places we find that the river has completely abandoned its ancient course and carved out a new channel for itself many miles away. Such is what is known as the Bûrh Ganga—"old lady Ganges"—which can be traced in a line of swamps from the Aligarh district down to Farrukhâbâd. That this was the ancient course of the stream is shown by the shrines and hermitages which stud its banks for close on a hundred miles. From the Musalmân chronicles it would seem that this change in the river's course occurred in the time of the Emperor Akbar, in the middle of the sixteenth century. More than twenty years ago the Ghâgra performed a similar feat in the Gorakhpur district, severing during one rainy season some forty square miles of country from one of its baronies.

A fickle stream like this is the worst enemy of the peasant. He never knows when it may sweep across his fields in destructive floods; as Virgil says—*Pluvia ingenti sata laeta boumque labores diluit.* Or it may carry off all the arable soil and leave only sterile sand, or it may deposit valuable silt.

Under such conditions agriculture is a simple lottery and this in a great measure accounts for the recklessness and improvidence of the riverine proprietors.

Connected with this kind of fluvial action is the well recognised distinction between what are known as the Khâdir and the Bângar,—the former the lands close to the river bed which are liable to annual flooding with the resultant alluvion or diluvion; the latter the stable uplands, which though themselves the gift of the river in ancient times, are now no longer exposed to its influence.

The Khâdir of the larger rivers has something of the same character as that of the Lincolnshire Fens. In the rainy season much of it is for a time submerged. Sometimes the retreating floods leave behind them a deposit of rich silt; sometimes arid sand. Trees are few and lose their vigour as they force their roots deep into the sloppy subsoil. Here and there patches of tamarisk give shelter to sounders of wild pig, which boldly ravage at night the crops on the adjacent highlands, and with the first flush of dawn cautiously retreat into the thick covers on the edge of the river. Their incursions impose a heavy burden of field-watching upon the peasant, and check the production of the more valuable crops, such as the sugar-cane, which these animals specially love. Here British officers of the Tent Club make their annual outing and enjoy the most manly and exciting sport which the country affords. Their visits are, it is needless to say, welcome to the people, who will gladly turn out to beat the covers and assist in the hunt. The clean-feeding jungle boar is in quite a different category from the foul domesticated pig which swarms in the hamlets set aside for the village menial races, and deserves the abhorrence which is felt towards it all through the oriental world. But for the wild boar the peasant has a healthy respect. He has little confidence in his old musket and rusty sword as weapons of offence against him. If no Sâhib cares to spear him he will employ a gang of Kanjar gypsies or wild-eyed, savage Banjâra nomads to thin their numbers. But if there is a chance of sport he will not take active measures against them for the same consideration that makes the English farmer's wife tolerant of an occasional raid by Reynard into her poultry yard.

From the verge of the uplands the Khâdir in the cold weather presents the appearance of a flat desolate expanse. The grass has by this time lost its autumn greenness and assumes the brown tint which characterises the landscape. In places there are sluggish streams and reedy marshes where wildfowl of all kinds abound—snipe and teal and ducks of many varieties, kingfishers and waders, contemplative paddy birds immersed in the stalk of the wary frog ; a line of grey geese appears through the mist as with the approach of day they leave the gram field and seek shelter on some open sandbank amidst the stream. A jackal gorged with carrion creeps into the shade of the sedge ; a stealthy wolf, his jaws red with the blood of kid or fawn, sneaks through some thicket. Villages are few save where some eminence affords a site raised high above flood level and gives a chance of saving the cattle when the floods are out. Usually there is only a hamlet of makeshift huts which can be easily abandoned in time of danger. Cultivation is scanty : but the soil, if not so deep and strong as that of the uplands, has at least the vigour of freshness ; the population is so sparse and rents so low that new land can be selected yearly and the crops which can be saved from pigs and wild geese are often highly remunerative.

The Khâdir, again, supplies excellent grazing for large herds of cattle, for buffaloes in particular, and the Ahîr and Gûjar speculate extensively in the production of ghi, the only nitrogenous food which the orthodox Hindu can use. They seal it up in the empty kerosine oil tins which have become such an essential in rural life, and export it to the larger cities. This, except some secluded valleys in the Himalayas, is the last part of the Province where the absence of the men of these tribes for months at a time in charge of their cattle permits the domestic institution of polyandry. Damp and malaria work here as in the Tarâi, and the herdsman of the Khâdir is a poor, anemic, fever-stricken creature, a shy semi-savage, whose hand is against everyone ; ready, if chance allows, to drive off the cattle of his wealthier neighbours and pass them on from one receiver's stall to another till all trace of them is lost. There are special local industries, the cutting of firewood, the collection of thatching grass, fibres for rope, reeds for matting; and here the Kanjar digs out the fragrant roots of the Khaskhas of which he constructs the fragrant screens with which the European cools his house when the hot west wind blows.

In some places, again, and in particular along the Jumna, the Khâdir is replaced by a tangle of wild ravines which slope from the uplands to the river's bank. Such is the rough country along the Chambal, which drains the Native States of Gwâlior and Dholpur and finally joins the Jumna below Etâwah. Here from an eminence you see as far as the eye can reach a labyrinth of rugged ravines and green valleys covered with acacia jungle, every prominent bluff showing the ruins of some robber stronghold of the olden time. This was for centuries a No Man's Land, an Alsatia occupied by wild Râjput tribes, robbers and raiders by profession, who settled on the flank of the Imperial highway through the Duâb, and were a thorn in the side of the Musalmân administration. Many a tale is told of raid and rapine committed by these sturdy caterans. Armies often retired baffled before the difficulties of their fastnesses, and native rule could never maintain that steady pressure upon them which the condition of the country and its people necessitated. This was left to British law to effect, and now the land has peace. The descendants of these freebooters draw a scanty livelihood from terracing their sterile ravines. They are always ready to negotiate a loan with a moneylender, but it is hard to serve a writ on a defaulter, still harder without risk of life or limb for an outsider to eject them from their paternal acres and hold it in defiance of the opinion of the country side. The experience of the Mutiny showed that they are as ready as ever to give trouble if they dared.

Above the ravine country and the riverine Khâdir is the Bângar or old settled alluvium which long ages of patient tillage have raised to a state of extreme fertility. Here again we must distinguish the tracts into which this region naturally divides itself.

We have, first, the Duâb, the Mesopotamia, or land between the Jumna and the Ganges, which without the territory south of the Ganges and Jumna included in its districts, has an area of about 22,500 square miles, two-thirds of Ireland; secondly, the northern tract, including Oudh, Rohilkhand and the Gorakhpur and Benares Divisions—about 50,000 square miles, a quarter of France.

The Duâb is the fertile, thickly-populated tract extending between the rivers Ganges and Jumna from Sahâranpur to their junction at Allahâbâd. In the western part it is widely irrigated by the Upper and Lower Ganges Canal. Through it the East Indian and North-western Railways provide the main line of communication between the Bengal Delta and the Panjâb. Junctions at Allahâbâd, Cawnpur, Tûndla, Hâthras and Aligarh link it with Oudh, Bombay and Central India. Its chief cities and commercial marts are Sahâranpur, which commands the Dehra Dûn valley: Meerut, a large military cantonment: Aligarh, the seat of a flourishing Anglo-Muhammadan College: Hâthras, an entrepot for cotton and other country produce: Etâwah, one of the Central Indian frontier posts: Cawnpur, an important trading mart and the seat of prosperous manufacturing industries; Allahâbâd, the Provincial capital, the headquarters of the High Court and the chief public offices. Only the stream of the Jumna separates it from Delhi, now included in the Panjâb, from Agra, the Mughal capital, now a large and flourishing commercial city, and from Mathura, one of the holiest places of Hinduism. The railway has now quite displaced the rivers as a highway of commerce. This is shown by the decadence of two once flourishing centres of trade—Farrukhâbâd in the Central Duâb and Mirzapur, formerly a great trade centre, to which large gangs of Banjâra merchants in the old days conveyed the products of Central India and received in return iron and brass ware, cloth and salt. This region has now been tapped by direct railway communication with Calcutta and Bombay, and the once famous bâzâr of Mirzapur is deserted.

The richest portion of the Duâb is that to the west, where, aided by an abundant water supply, the Jâts of Sahâranpur, Muzaffarnagar and Meerut are about the finest yeomen in India. Here will be seen the results of the labour of a most industrious, sturdy peasantry, vast sheets of wheat and barley, sugar-cane, cotton, millets and maize. Here the plough cattle are of the finest breed, and most thriving yeomen own a brood mare or two, the produce of which find a ready sale at the agricultural fairs as remounts for our cavalry or for private use. It is only towards the lower apex of the Duâb that the opium poppy is largely grown; all along it and more particularly towards the east indigo is an important staple. More especially at Cawnpur and Agra, just beyond the Jumna, there is an extensive factory industry, supplied with the best modern machinery and largely interested in the manufacture of cotton and woollen goods, and articles of leather. Everywhere we find indications of an active industrial, commercial and agricultural life.

The aspect of the country is that of an unbroken flat, "spread like a green sea the waveless plain of Lombardy" which Shelley saw from a nook in the Euganean hills. It is drained by the Hindan, Kâli and innumerable minor streams which find their way sooner or later into the Ganges or the Jumna. The scenery is monotonous in the extreme, but has a quiet rural beauty of its own at certain seasons. In the early cold weather you can march for weeks through an almost unbroken stretch of the richest cultivation, wheat, barley or other cereals, the Arhar fields yellow with blossom like an English gorse brake, thick masses of sugar-cane, tall fields of tufted millet, the cotton with its white bolls, and an infinity of garden crops, poppy, pepper, mint, anise and cummin, the cucumber trailing over the brown house thatch, the castor with its purple bluish leaves and stalk. Cultivation is too close to allow much woodland or culturable waste to exist. At every mile or so you meet a village nestling in the shade of its mango groves or pîpal trees: its tank and rustic shrine glittering through the rich foliage; the huts covered with brown thatch or reddish tiles. When the crops are cut in the early spring the scene changes as if by magic. The country now looks dusty, baked and cheerless to a degree. This is specially the case in the rice-bearing tracts. The hot wind blows like the blast of a furnace; the sky resembles a great copper bowl; the horizon is narrowed by a thick haze of dust; the cattle cower for shelter in the scanty shade, and all nature gasps with thirst. Then after a time the wind lulls, the heavy clouds gather on the horizon, and the monsoon bursts with a roar of heaven's artillery. The herbage revives at once, the trees are green again when the grime is washed from their leaves; the ploughing and sowing of the rice and millets, the patient tillage which the coming spring crop needs call the peasant from the torpor of the hot weather. Then succeed weeks of drenching rain with intervals of damp relaxing heat. The rivers are all in flood, the country presents the appearance of a marsh; fever and cholera, the pestilence that walketh in darkness, the destruction that wasteth at noonday, claim their victims. At last the rains are checked, a cold chill rises with the dawn, the soft mist collects in the lowlands. Then the peasant cuts his autumn rice and millet and begins to collect the swelling cotton bolls. His oxen, refreshed by the enforced rest of the rains, and strengthened by the fresh store of herbage, are ready for the hard work of the early winter, the continuous series of ploughings for the wheat and barley, the severe exertion of hauling the laden water buckets from the depths of the well. The jaded Englishman looks up his rifle and cartridges and soon the white tents are pitched near his house, and all is made ready for a start into camp. In a day or two, as he rides on his first march from headquarters he will find his tents pitched in some shady mango grove, the horses tethered a short way off, the servants cooking in the shade, the village magnate awaiting an audience, a crowd of suitors ready for the opening of the court, a bare-legged runner hastening up with a bag of papers which will keep the Collector busy till the afternoon is well spent. Then tea and chat, a stroll with gun and dogs, or a visit to the school or police station. After dinner all but the sleeping tents are struck, laden on a string of camels and carried ten miles forwards, where their owner meets them ready again next morning. And as he starts to join the fresh encampment nothing is left on the site of the place where he has halted for the day but the mouldering fires, the piles of straw and rubbish to tell of the busy crowd which occupied it only yesterday.

But no map or figures or description can give any real idea of the teeming village life through which the official thus makes his annual progress; the sheet of growing corn crops, the peasant laboriously turning up the rich brown soil, the oxen labouring at the well to the creak of the pulley and the driver's song, the children leading the cows and goats to pasture, the Brâhman ringing his little bell to call his god to attend the service, the women cooking, gossiping, squabbling, all in the open air; the old crone grumbling as she works the spinning-wheel; the brown faces, black eyes, bright dresses, and tinkling bangles of the girls as they laugh and chatter at the well; the grey-beards settling village politics under the pîpal tree. Life may be hard and sordid, but these careless souls somehow manage to enjoy it to the full, and no murmur of discontent at their meagre lot rises to the gates of heaven from the lips of these toiling millions.

The difficulty is in this continuous Plain to get anything like a bird's-eye view of the general aspect of the country. There is no really lofty eminence from which the glance can sweep and take in its salient features. The oldest village mound, an accumulation of the debris of countless generations, is only a petty hillock, and the view from it is everywhere bounded by the green masses of the mango groves which surround it. Here and there is an open vista which stretches out to the horizon in an unbroken expanse of rice cultivation or barren, salty plains. In the rains the rice tract is a sheet of greenery; in the summer it resembles a grey, brown chessboard, broken up for convenience of irrigation into a maze of minute plots; the salt waste has few trees, except an occasional acacia or a patch of scrubby thicket.

It is from some of the higher buildings in the cities alone that in the clear air of the cold weather, beneath a sky of cloudless blue, an extensive survey can be made. Thus, in all the Plain there is perhaps no pleasanter view than from the battlements of the Fatehgarh fort, whence are seen the pleasure house of the Nawâb, the minarets of the Karbala mosque, the rich greenery of the hunting preserve, and far in the distance the faint silver line of the Ganges. So, from the summit of the graceful clock-tower at Mirzapur you look down on the ceaseless movement of the gaily-dressed crowds, and the whole city resembles a forest, the white houses with their red-tiled roofs showing at intervals through the trees which shade every bâzâr and courtyard. Or from one of the minarets of Aurangzeb's mosque at Benares you can watch the troops of pilgrims, the bathers at the Ghâts, the glittering spires of a myriad temples, the sacred bulls moving ponderously along the crowded alleys, the monkeys playing on the roofs. A colder and sterner landscape unfolds itself from the ramparts of a fort like that of Awa in the Central Duâb. Here we see the narrow border of wheat and tobacco fields encircling the grey mud bastions of the Râjput stronghold, and beyond a wide dreary expanse of salty barren waste, over which the torrid wind of June blows with pitiless, scorching vigour.

But hitherto we have spoken of life in the more favoured villages and cities. In the Central part of the Duâb, where a series of years of excessive rainfall, insufficient drainage, and wasteful use of canal water have raised the subsoil level, malaria is endemic, and wide tracts of new waste, the pallid frames of the people, all speak eloquently of the losses caused by fever. But this will be discussed more fully later on.

There are, again, many places where the soil is little better than sterile sand, growing nothing but poor autumn millets, and unfit to produce sugar, cotton or wheat. The more industrious peasant classes avoid lands like these, and cling to the rich loams and fertile clays. The sandy tract is the heritage of the more restless and lazy Râjput, the Ahîr or Gûjar cattle breeders, where inefficient tillage and squalid homesteads are in direct contrast to the thriving agricultural settlements of the Jât or the Kurmi.

Far worse than these unfertile lands are what are known as the Ûsar plains, of which there are between four and five thousand square miles in the Province, at present absolutely sterile. If this area could be brought under the plough, and support five hundred souls to the square mile, not under present conditions an excessive average, it would feed a couple of million mouths, about as much as the total increase of the population in the period 1881-91. The reclamation of Ûsar is thus an economical question of the greatest importance, and a small literature has been devoted to it.

Reh, or the saline deposit which is brought up to the surface by the combined action of water and the sun's heat, is not of uniform character. "Most generally carbonate of soda is the prevailing ingredient; at other times sulphate of soda; but both occur together, and associated with them in more or less quantity are common salt and salts of magnesia and lime. Of the origin of these salts there is no positive certainty, but they are most probably the salts which are dissolved out on the gradual decomposition of igneous rocks, and are subsequently deposited when the water that holds them in solution evaporates."[1] So long as the surface remains covered with trees or vegetation these salts do little harm; but with any rise in the subsoil water level, caused, for instance, by excessive canal irrigation or natural saturation, there would be a tendency for these salts to rise to the surface by the action of the sun's heat, aided by the capillarity of the clay subsoil.

The appearance of Reh is unmistakeable. It shows itself either as a snowlike deposit on the surface, or as a puffy crust of brownish efflorescence which crackles into dust as you walk over it. No better or safer riding ground can be found than a plain like this, as there are few depressions and no holes concealed beneath the surface. Most Ûsar will produce in the rains some kind of herbage, generally of a very coarse and innutritious description; but in the dry

[1] Voelcker, *Report*, p. 51.

season it is almost completely bare. The worst point about it is, that in moist tracts, notably those in which saturation is due to excessive use of canal water, it shows a decided tendency to spread and infest land hitherto free from its influence.

The result of a long series of experiments has been to show that Ûsar may be reclaimed. If fenced in, and for a time protected from grazing, the coarser grasses gradually gather strength, and spread more and more over the surface; the dust blown by the wind from neighbouring fields collects round their roots, and their periodical decay produces a thin layer of richer mould. With the increase of herbage the power of the sun in drawing up the salts from the subsoil becomes weaker, and in time the inferior vegetation is, to some extent, replaced by more nutritive grasses. This, the natural, is also the cheapest mode of reclamation. A similar result, at a larger expenditure of capital, is produced by a deposit of silt or rich manure, or by flooding and embanking the surface water. But such methods, except under specially favourable circumstances, can hardly be remunerative. It is enough that the experiments hitherto made show that the reclamation of Ûsar is possible; that no great financial results have been attained is only what might have been expected. But it should be different in the case of peasants devoting their surplus labour to the improvement of small patches in the neighbourhood of their own fields, and even if the land thus recovered from the waste never reaches a high point of fertility, it would at any rate grow wood and fodder, which they sorely lack. But the Indian cultivator is so conservative, so wedded to traditional methods of farming, that it is difficult to induce him to undertake a task which cannot be immediately remunerative. It is something to have shown that the attempt is not quite so hopeless as has hitherto been believed. As matters stand, all that the Ûsar plains produce is a little coarse grazing, and some of the salts and silica is worked up into the common glass bangles which the village girl so dearly loves.

This leads to another question on which much discussion

has taken place—the provision of fuel and fodder reserves. It is needless to say that under the native administration the forests were utterly neglected. Much land fitted only to grow trees was allowed to pass into private hands, and the existing forests were ruthlessly destroyed. The jungleman, as he wanders about, axe in hand, is an unmerciful wrecker of the forest, which he makes his home. He hacks and hews without the slightest discrimination, and, from sheer recklessness and want of thought, will destroy a promising sapling which, when cut, is quite useless to him. In the earlier period of our rule we were equally apathetic about forest conservation, and it was not till increasing pressure on the waste, and the new demand for wood, which arose with the development of the railway system, attracted attention, that the Government was roused to a sense of the danger. Since that time forest conservation became an important business of the State. Between reserves and State forests the Indian Government now owns 108,000 square miles, and this will be extended as soon as Burma and Madras are fully dealt with. In forests alone it holds nearly the area of Italy—a property of enormous and yearly increasing value. The increased demand for fuel on the railways has again been met by the opening out of extensive collieries in various parts of the country. But these sources of wood and fuel do little to help the peasant of the Plains to find a rafter for his thatch, or the wherewithal to cook his cakes and boil his rice.

In the earlier days of railway enterprise many splendid groves, particularly in Oudh and Rohilkhand, were cut down. This destruction of the woodland drew attention to other dangers. It became apparent that the loss of trees was likely to affect the annual rainfall; and where the railway passes close to the Siwâlik hills the denudation of the slopes rendered them unable to absorb and retain the rainfall which, pouring all at once into the lower level, produced dangerous floods. In this Province the pressure of a dense population soon reduced the woodland area. Had the State interfered at an earlier period, the condition of things would be very different from what it is at present. The hilly tracts of

Mirzapur, for instance, might have been saved from absolute denudation of the more valuable trees, and would have, for ages to come, provided an ample supply of timber and fuel for large cities like Allahâbâd and Benares, and for the dense population of the adjacent valley. In spite of this period of neglect, it is no small matter that the Provincial Government has now about 4,000,000 acres of reserved forest, somewhat less than the area of Connaught, under conservancy.

But the management of these forests has been an uphill task. It was only in the more secluded places that much valuable timber remained uncut; the existing trees needed careful nursing, and much replanting was inevitable. Now the department is beginning to pay; in 1893-94, the surplus revenue was about R.x. 70,000.[1] The chief danger to the timber is from forest fires. When all the undergrowth is parched in the fierce heat of an Indian summer, a spark from a herdsman's pipe, or even the very friction of the branches against each other by the wind, is sufficient, on the authority of Thucydides, if it were not corroborated by Indian evidence, to start a destructive conflagration. No more awful sight than a mountain side, on the Vindhyan or Siwâlik range, in the grasp of the fire demon can well be imagined. In 1893-94 attempts were made to protect 2807 square miles, of which 186 were burned. It has been more than suspected that some of these fires were caused maliciously by villagers in the neighbourhood, smarting under a sense of wrong at the restrictions imposed upon them; but, as a rule, there is not much tension between the Forest officer and the villagers on his border.

The form of conservation now in force provides for the survey of each block of forest, and the preparation of a working plan for future action. Open paths are cleared so as to isolate the blocks and reduce the area of fires; communications are opened up for the utilisation of produce, such as building materials, bamboos, fibres, and the like.

[1] Here and elsewhere I use the convenient formula—1 R.x. = Rs. 10. The real exchange value of the rupee in English money is now only about 1s. 3d.

Lopping and felling are carried on as required, and nurseries are established for the propagation of the more valuable trees. That these reserved forests will in time become a most valuable State property is certain.

But the preservation of these forests does not much relieve the lack of fuel and fodder in the villages at a distance from them. That part of the reserved area in which grazing is allowed supplies grass to about three-quarters of a million of cattle, merely a drop in the ocean as compared with existing stocks. As regards fuel, again, the peasant of the Plains depends on the twigs which his children collect in the small village waste, on the dry stems of some of the crops which he raises, and, in particular, on the dung of his cattle. Hitherto the comfortable theory has been widely accepted, that this had little influence on the manure supply, because most of the nitrogen passed away into the air and was washed down again into the soil by the periodical rains, while a large proportion of the other valuable constituents survived in the ashes. Dr Voelcker has clearly shown the fallacy of this belief; as a matter of fact, by the burning of manure 97 per cent. of the nitrogen is absolutely lost, besides the physical and mechanical effects which the manure, in its natural state, produces on the soil.

Except where casual grazing is supplemented by the growth of fodder crops and stall feeding, the scantiness and lack of nutritive qualities in the food, which the ordinary Duâb bullock can pick up, are shown by its emaciated condition. The margin of waste available is diminishing yearly with the extension of cultivation, and much of the waste shown by statistics is really salt-infested plains, or other lands which produce little fodder. The suggestion has been made that the State should compulsorily acquire patches of land and conserve them as fuel and fodder reserves. But the difficulties attending such a measure are immense, and the advantages doubtful. It would involve the wholesale ejectment of people whom it would be impossible, without a system of emigration which the peasantry show no inclination to adopt, to settle elsewhere; the prevention of trespass would be a very serious task, and lead to much irritation; and, lastly, there seems reason to believe that the present stock of cattle is excessive. A people who revere the cow as a godling will not send useless beasts to the shambles, and thus their numbers tend to overpass the fodder resources. On the other hand, a first-class agriculturist, like the Jât, finds no difficulty in growing an ample stock of artificial fodder and in stall-feeding his cattle. A smaller area, treated in this way, will supply a larger amount of food than a grazing ground, which all may use. It is obviously to the reduction of useless animal mouths, and to the extension of stall feeding, that we must look for an improvement in the existing state of things.

We have thus dealt with some economical problems which specially affect the Duâb before attempting to describe the special character of the remainder of the Plains.

The chief distinction between Oudh, Rohilkhand, and Gorakhpur, as compared with the Duâb depends upon the fact that they are, on the whole, cooler, damper and better wooded, and that the saline area is less extensive. The population is more distinctively Hindu than in the Upper Duâb, which also suffers much less from congestion. These districts grow less fine wheat, more rice and sugar. This part of the country does not possess and does not so urgently require those immense canals which with so much advantage irrigate the Duâb. Here the risk of a failure of the annual rains is much more rarely felt; with water much nearer the surface wells are more efficient and easily worked, and irrigation from tanks is more common. Rohilkhand, eastern Oudh, and the adjoining districts are the main seat of the very profitable and rapidly-increasing sugar industry, and the climate and the habits of the people render the important State monopoly, the opium poppy, workable. No peasant can surpass the western Jât as a grower of wheat and cotton, and this mode of agriculture suits his broader style of farming. Poppy, on the other hand, is more of a garden crop, requiring a vast amount of careful, minute industry which the Jât does not care to bestow upon it, and much female and child labour which only the Kurmi or Kâchhi, who is more of the market gardener type, can supply. Poppy, too, is extremely sensitive to cold, and cannot be grown with success in the harsher western climate. Besides this, it thrives better on well irrigation than on the water of the canal.

It is in the extension of the cultivation of sugar that the best chance of an improvement in the agriculture of Northern India probably lies. In 1891-92 this crop occupied 1,363,000 acres, or about 6 per cent. of the area under autumn crops. The average outturn of irrigated cane calculated in Gur, or coarse sugar, in preparing which the juice is simply boiled down and inspissated without removing the treacle, may be taken as varying from 2400 to 1600 lbs. per acre. After supplying local wants of a people among whom sweets of various kinds are an essential article of food, the exports from the Province amounted to 180,000 tons, of which over two-thirds went to the Panjâb and Râjputâna. That the demand is enormous may be concluded from the fact that in 1889-90 sugar to the value of R.x. 1,900,000 was imported into India from Mauritius. Enquiries in Calcutta show that the average consumption of sugar is about 60 lbs. per head per annum. It is the main support of the pilgrim on his travels, and in places like Allahâbâd and Hardwâr, at the periodical bathing fairs, the sales of sweetmeats are immense.

Sugar production must have been a very ancient Indian industry. This is proved by the names for its preparations, and by the references in the Institutes of Manu, which exempt the weary traveller from punishment if he plucked a cane or two from a roadside field, a picture of rural life which in its reality and vividness recalls the prevailing custom in modern times. But it is probable that much of the sugar in ancient times was obtained from the juice of the palm. It is as difficult to imagine how the Indian peasant could ever have existed without sweets as to conceive what with him could have taken the place of tobacco.

But it is not only from an economical point of view that the sugar industry is of prime importance. It demands the highest skill of the farmer, and its culture is itself a lesson in the higher art of cultivation. If the crop is to succeed the soil must be repeatedly ploughed and heavily manured; the weeding, hoeing and protecting it from its numerous enemies involve constant toil. Manure follows the cane, and where the crop is grown it is more evenly distributed over the village area. The crushing and boiling require care and some empiric chemical knowledge.

In former days the cane was always crushed in a rude wooden or stone mortar, in which the pestle was slowly revolved by the patient labour of the oxen. This inefficient and wasteful machine has been largely replaced by the more economical iron roller mill, which enables the crop to be crushed as it ripens, reduces the amount of wastage, and supplies the juice in a cleaner state. This is the only modern farming implement which the peasant has up to the present readily adopted. But much still remains to be done to improve the system of manufacture. A great improvement would at once result from the establishment of co-operative factories on the model of an English or Danish creamery, but the suspicious nature of the people and lack of capital at present render this impossible. With better appliances, more technical knowledge of improved methods of manufacture, and greater regard for cleanliness, it is probable that before long Northern India will not only fully supply local wants, but leave a large margin for foreign exportation. As it is, cultivation is largely increasing, and the area under the crop has more than doubled in half a century.

Rice, again, to the east takes the place of wheat to the west, and here alone is it largely used for food. The people to the east eat rice and pulse; those to the west wheat, barley and millets. Rice thrives best under the heavier rainfall of the northern submontane districts. Hence in this part of the Province the Kharîf or rain crop is all important. The farmer to the west pays his rent out of his wheat and cotton, and grows a patch of maize or millets as food for his family and fodder for his cattle; to the east he lives mainly on the earlier crop of broadcast rice, and grows a finer transplanted variety for sale.

To continue the distinction between these two parts of the Province, there is a striking contrast in the village life. The tradition of raid and rapine, when the land was harried by Sikh and Marhatta not a century ago, survives to the west in the form of the homestead. Here the houses are heavy-walled, flat-roofed, crowded within a limited area, generally planted on a mound rising over the surrounding lowlands, and the village from the outside looks like a miniature fort, the entrance narrow and winding, the outer wall circuit obviously arranged with a view to defence against sudden attack. To the east the village site is more open, and the houses less huddled together within a narrow space; the population freely disperses itself in unprotected hamlets spread in convenient positions over the whole village area. This growth of hamlets is a predominant factor in the village economy. Not only is it the direct result of a long period of uninterrupted peace, but it has the special advantage of ensuring the more even distribution of manure over the whole village area, brings labour nearer to its scene of work, and allows the menial castes,—the currier, sweeper, and their kindred, who are an abomination to the orthodox Hindu,—to establish their little independent communities in which they can practise their special industries without offending the feelings of others, and freed from the irksome restraints imposed by their more orthodox neighbours.

The predominant feature, however, distinguishing the east from the west is that in the latter the pressure of population on the resources of the soil is much less. This will be discussed more in detail in another connection. Here it is sufficient to note that while Ballia has 805 souls to the square mile, Sahâranapur at the other end of the Province has but 446. To the west, then, the pressure on the land is much less severe; rents are lower, and the landless village labourer is much less a half-starved serf.

We have noticed in passing the village groves which, though finer and more abundant in the country north and east of the Ganges, are a striking feature in the landscape all over the Province. The planting of a grove is regarded as one of the means of religious advancement, and the destruction of them among orthodox Hindus is opposed by a stringent sanction. This conception of the holiness of the grove is further shown by the rule which prohibits the use of the fruit until one of the trees is married to the adjacent well by a parody of the regular ceremony. Some of these groves are of enormous extent. There are in many places groves known as the Lâkh Pera, because they are supposed to contain 100,000 trees. Others are of great antiquity, the trees as they decay being carefully replaced. That at Mandâwar in the Bijnor district is perhaps the most ancient grove in India, being now situated on the very spot where the Buddhist pilgrim Hiuen Tsiang rested in the seventh century of our era.

The grove holds a prominent part in the social life of the village community. Beneath its shade nestles the common shrine; here the cattle find shelter in the fierce heats of summer; it is the playground of the children, the halting place of strangers, from the Collector with his camp in the cold weather to the wandering trader and the long haired, ash-smeared Jogi or Sannyâsi on his rounds to visit his clients. The fruit is very generally regarded as common property, and when the country mango with its tart, turpentine flavour is ripe, it supports a large number of the poorer village menials until the early autumn crops are fit for food.

Nothing is more picturesque in a quiet way than one of these village groves in the camping season. The pleasant contrasts of light and shade, the brown, gnarled trunks of the trees, the dark green foliage of the mango, the lighter coloured leaf of the pîpal, the feathery branches of the bamboo, the delicate tamarind, always a favourite with the early Muhammadan settlers, reflected in the still water of the neighbouring tank, the graceful spire of the Saiva shrine, by which sits a contemplative Brâhman or ascetic smeared with ashes, his thoughts far from the concerns of this world of sense, make up a charming picture, especially in the morning when a tender haze softens every outline, or at evening when the cattle wander slowly to their sheds from the pasture. Hence the Sanskrit writers, with a keen sense of natural beauty, called the eventide Godhûli, the time when the dust rises as the kine come home.

The ravages of war have often played havoc with these village groves. General Sleeman, writing in 1835,[1] says that there was not a grove or avenue, only a few solitary trees to be seen between Delhi and Meerut, where now the country is covered with splendid plantations. This was the work of Sikh raiders. In the time of Bishop Heber,[2] 1825, the beautiful avenue of trees on the road between Agra and Fatehpur Sikri seems not to have been in existence; at least an observant traveller like him could hardly have failed to mention it. Arboriculture is a matter on which our Government has ever laid much stress. The banks of the Canals and their distributaries have been largely utilised in this way. There are now nearly forty thousand acres of Canal plantations, and in modern years all the more important roads have been provided with the shade which is so welcome to the wearied traveller.

In close connection with the village grove is the village tank. These are most numerous to the east of the Province, where they are largely used for irrigation. In one of these districts, Azamgarh, there are no less than 1500 artificial tanks, and few villages in the country do not possess a foul depression where bricks are made and clay excavated for building purposes. These become brim-full of water in the rains; but as the season advances it is spent on the fields or drunk by the cattle till it becomes almost dry in the cold weather. Some of the larger artificial reservoirs date from prehistoric times, and to the east are attributed to the Suiris or Râjbhars, Dravidian races who probably became lords of the country during the temporary eclipse of Aryan civilisation, after the fall of the Gupta dynasty. Some of these ancient tanks are of much larger area than those of the present day, which are seldom more than an acre in extent. The old tanks are distinguished by a difference of form

[1] *Rambles and Recollections*, ii. 231.
[2] *Journal*, ii. 13.

obviously based on religious considerations. The new tanks have their greatest length from east to west in connection with sun worship; those of older date from north to south. Bathing in some of these tanks is a deed of piety, and acts as a cure of disease; others are holy because they adjoin some sacred shrine. At some of these tanks it is part of the pilgrim's ritual to assist in deepening it by removing a basketful of mud from the bed. But a rich man who proposes to excavate a tank always selects a new site, either because he wishes it to be altogether identified with his name or dreads sharing the ill luck of the old excavator. Hence many tanks are wofully silted up and hold little water. The tank, with its lofty earthen banks covered with fine trees, looks like an ancient fort, and is a conspicuous feature in the landscape of the Plains. But as the water is drunk by men and cattle, used for purposes of ablution, and by the washerman, specialists in sanitation look upon it with well-grounded suspicion, and it is doubtless an agent in the diffusion of epidemic disease.

Of large lakes the Plains are singularly destitute. Marshes there are in plenty, and a day's journey will seldom be passed without meeting with one of these depressions, often the ancient channel of some river, a mass of coarse grass and rushes abounding in all kinds of water-fowl. Such is the Noh Jhîl in Mathura, six miles long, about half the length of Windermere, which is supposed to be an old channel of the Jumna. The Bakhira or Moti Jhîl, the pearl lake, on the border of Gorakhpur and Basti, is rather smaller than this; the Suraha Jhîl in Ballia is about the same size, and practically a back water of the Ganges. More interesting than these are the splendid artificial lakes which Bundelkhand owes to the enlightened Chandel dynasty. These are formed by enormous masonry dams built across the mouth of the valleys. One of them at Mahoba in Hamîrpur has a circumference of five miles. Some enclose craggy islets or peninsulas crowned by the ruins of exquisitely ornamented granite temples.

At Gorakhpur the flooding of the lowlands in the neighbourhood of the Station covers the country with water over a stretch of many miles in the rainy season. This is about the only place where anything in the shape of good yachting can be enjoyed in the Plains.

The Himalayan lake is of a different type. It has often been formed by a landslip, which blocks the outlet of a valley and forms a more or less permanent embankment. Such was the Gohna lake, which was suddenly formed about three years ago by the subsidence of the hill-side on one of the upper tributaries of the Ganges. Behind this the water gradually accumulated till it overtopped and washed away the barrier. This fortunately was slowly scoured away by the torrent; if it had suddenly collapsed a terrible inundation would certainly have devastated the valley below. One of the Kumaun lakes, Naini Tâl, seems to have been formed in the same way, but here the embankment has continued permanent; others, according to the theory of some observers, are the result of glacial agency. These lakes are not of any considerable size. Naini Tâl has a circumference of rather more than two miles; Bhîm Tal is slightly larger, Naukuchiya, as its name implies—"the lake of the nine corners"—is distinguished by its varied outline. These lakes, all in the immediate neighbourhood of the sanatorium occupied by the heads of the Local Government, in the hot and rainy seasons provide the visitors with ample amusement in the way of fishing and boating.

Many of the lakes in the Plains support a large and industrious community of fishermen and bird-catchers, growers of the Singhâra or water-nut, diggers of edible roots, planters of the Boro rice on the slushy banks, as the water recedes. These plantations, patches of the brightest emerald green, are a welcome break in the otherwise dreary landscape of the hot season.

Something has been already said of the hill flora, which is remarkable for its variety and beauty. Among trees we find many which approximate to the Chinese type, such as the Magnolia and the Tea tree; the Abies, Juniper, Yew, Deodâr cedar, and Holm oak, with orchids, ferns, and numerous other varieties. That of the southern hills is more scanty and uninteresting. Poorest of all is the flora of the Plains, where the plants are not only few in kind but singularly unattractive. "Everything in India smells except the flowers," is one of the two feeble epigrams, which, on the authority of Sir Ali Baba, form the only permanent intellectual enjoyment of jaded visitors at Simla. The explanation of the poorness of the flora of the Plains lies in the uniformity of the soil and the rigour of the climate—parching heat and steamy dampness succeeded by sharp cold destroy all but the hardiest plants. Most of the land is under cultivation, and the peasant persistently destroys everything which can be called a weed. Any green stuff which grows in secluded corners is devoured by cattle or goats, or grubbed up as fodder for horses or stall-fed animals. For the abundant vegetation, the bright flowers and luxuriant plant life usually associated with a tropical country, we must look elsewhere than in northern India. It is only in the Tarâi that the coarser grasses and reeds attain a considerable vigour of growth, and it is only in Gorakhpur, to the extreme east, where the plants characteristic of the Gangetic Delta begin to appear, that any variety in the flora can be found.

The fauna, on the contrary, is large and varied and more interesting to the ordinary European resident, where every one is more or less devoted to sport. Practically there is no preservation of game except in the jungles owned by some of the native nobility, who maintain the game for their own amusement or for an occasional battue on the visit of some official magnate, or in the Jât villages to the west, where the peacock is regarded as a sacred bird and the people are quite ready to turn out with their bludgeons and attack Mr Thomas Atkins if he venture to shoot one. In tracts again owned by landholders of the banker class, who have the Jaina prejudice against the destruction of animal life, the sportsman will meet little encouragement, if he do not encounter actual resistance. But ordinary sport is well within the means of the young officer who during his home service cannot afford to rent a grouse moor or deer forest in Scotland. This is one of the chief alleviations of Indian service, and it is devotion to shooting, polo and pig sticking that produces in the subaltern that activity, coolness and self-reliance which have made him such an admirable leader of men on active service. In most places pig sticking, coursing, snipe, partridge, ducks, quail, an occasional antelope, spotted or ravine deer can be found without much trouble and within fairly easy distance of headquarters.

But within the present generation the larger game have been much reduced by the clearance of jungle and the extension of cultivation. The Muhammadan Emperors hunted large game in places where they no longer exist. Thus, Fîroz Shâh hunted the rhinoceros in Sahâranpur in 1379; they are now met with only in Assam and the Nepâl Tarâi, but semi-fossilised remains of the beast have been found in Bânda. There are still a few wild elephants in the Siwâlik range; formerly they were much more common. According to Dr Buchanan Hamilton they were numerous and destructive in Gorakhpur in the early years of this century. Akbar used to hunt them at Narwar near Jhânsi, in Bundelkhand, and at Kantit, close to Mirzapur. In quite recent times the Râjas of Balrâmpur captured herds of them in the Gonda forests of Northern Oudh.[1]

The same is the case with the tiger, which was formerly much more widely spread than is the case at present. Thus, Dr Buchanan Hamilton describes how in 1769, in a year of famine, so many cattle perished that the tigers, deprived of their ordinary food, attacked the town of Bhawapâr in Gorakhpur and killed about four hundred people. The inhabitants fled, and the place remained for some years deserted.[2] In 1803 they were shot on the Ganges below Kanauj. These animals are very unwilling to venture into the open Plain unless there be a continuous belt of jungle, which enables them to reach the hills or the jungles of the

[1] Buchanan Hamilton, *Eastern India*, ii. 502; Blochmann, *Aîn-i-akbari*, i. 122: ii. 158; Blanford, *Mammalia of India*, 464.

[2] *Ibid.*, ii. 500.

Tarâi. Hence, though they were very numerous in Gorakhpur after the Mutiny, their numbers have largely decreased in recent years, and the same process is at work in South Mirzapur, where they abounded in quite recent years. The last haunt of the tiger is now along the sub-Himalayan districts and in the Vindhyan and Kaimûr ranges in Bânda, Allahâbâd and Mirzapur. There seems no immediate danger of their becoming extinct in these parts of the country for the present, but every year they become more wary. There is at least one officer of the Provincial Civil Service still doing duty who has killed with his own rifle more than a hundred tigers; such a feat is not likely to be repeated.

The methods of tiger shooting vary. In the sub-Himalayan districts the usual course adopted is to beat the animal out of the swamps and covers in which he conceals himself and surround him with a line of elephants. This is undoubtedly the finest form of the sport. A considerable number of sportsmen can combine in the hunt, and in the final struggle every one has a chance of a shot. This method is impossible along the Vindhyan hills. The valleys are too precipitous and the jungles too thick and abounding in thorny trees to admit the free passage of the elephant with the howdah. Here, when the presence of a tiger in a particular jungle is proved by his killing the young buffalo tied up as a bait, the hills lining the valley in which he has his lair are guarded by a number of men posted in trees, who act as "stops," in case the animal attempt to slink away, and he is then driven in the directions of the machâns or posts where the sportsmen take their stand. The hunt by means of elephants is certainly the finer form of the sport; but in the other the odds against the tiger are not so great as is commonly supposed. If he is an experienced beast, who has gone through the ordeal of a drive on some former occasion, the chances are that he will either creep past the "stops" who are posted on the crest of the ravine, or he will conceal himself in a clump of grass and break back with a series of growls through the line of beaters; or when he does face the rifles he often charges with a roar, or bounds through the thick underwood or the rocks which cover the bed of the ravine. Under such circumstances it needs a cool hand and steady eye to kill or mortally wound him. If he once escape into the thick jungle behind the machâns the case is almost hopeless.

What makes tiger shooting such a fascinating sport is its infinite variety and unexpectedness. The beast is extraordinarily wary, of enormous activity and resource. No two tigers will behave in the same way. One from the outset assumes the offensive, charges the beaters, springs at the "stops," and if he is in the end forced to face the rifles, does so with magnificent courage and ferocity. Another will slink in the undergrowth, creep through the grass and bamboos, to the colours of which his own stripes are so admirably adapted, and meet as he deserves the fate of a coward. The interest of the business is really intense when the animal is known to be afoot. Any moment he may burst the jungle screen which conceals him from the sportsman, and his footfall is so light, his wariness so extreme, that there is no time for preparation to meet him. One rustle in the grass, one streak of yellow and black flashing through an opening in the jungle, and if the bullet does not strike him truly he is lost for ever.

The lion has entirely disappeared from the Province. The last specimen killed was at Sheorâjpur near Allahâbâd in 1864. Now-a-days it is only in Kâthiâwâr, on the western coast, or in the wilder parts of Râjputâna, that a stray survivor of an almost extinct race is encountered.

In some places, particularly in the rocky hills of Mirzapur, Bânda or Jhânsi, the leopard is often found. He can seldom be shot in a drive, as his cunning is extreme, and he will lie in the grass and break back or slink along a crevice in the rocks as the beaters advance. When cornered he is perhaps more plucky and dangerous than even the tiger. A squealing goat tied up near his haunts in the dusk is often an irresistible bait for this exceedingly cautious beast.

The wolf is seldom shot, though numerous in some parts. In the very early dawn he may sometimes be met with galloping home to the shelter of some patch of dense scrub after his nightly prowl near the pens of the shepherd.

Sometimes he takes to killing children, and will charge in the dusk along a village lane and snap up one of the babies as they play. The Kanjar gipsy tracks him to his den and smokes him out for the sake of the Government reward. But he often passes off jackal cubs as those of the wolf, and it is not easy to detect the fraud. In all probability the number of wolves killed is much smaller than would appear from the statistics. In the three years ending in 1892 the number of persons killed by wild animals was 702. In 1891, 34 persons were killed by tigers; leopards, wolves and hyenas accounted for the rest. In 1895 the ferocity of wolves, more particularly in the Rohilkhand and Meerut Divisions, was remarkable. They killed no less than 246 persons, mostly young children, and it has been found necessary to offer enhanced rewards for the destruction of these brutes. In the same year a man-eating tiger in Kumaun caused 27 deaths before he was shot.

The loss of life by snake-bite among the native population is more serious. The statistics show within the same period 17,565 deaths from this cause, and the accidents reported are probably much less than the actual number. In the year 1895 in these provinces 4536 persons died of snake-bite. At one time the destruction of snakes was actively encouraged by granting rewards to the professional snake-killing tribes; but it was found that speculators took to rearing snakes. This led to the discontinuance of the reward system, and the Government was obliged to be contented with an academic warning to the people to clear away jungle from the neighbourhood of their houses, and to avoid poking into corners and walking about in the dark. Many old ladies still believe that the risk of being bitten by a snake is one of the chief dangers of Indian life. As a matter of fact, many Europeans spend years in the country and never see a venomous snake. The bungalow is a place where snakes do not usually visit, and if they do venture there their presence is easily detected. It is hardly too much to say that the number of authenticated deaths from snake-bite among the European population, for the last generation, might be almost counted on the fingers.

The graceful black buck is an animal which has much decreased since the extension of railways and the introduction of long-range rifles. Dr Buchanan Hamilton, speaking of the eastern part of the Province, says that in 1813 a sportsman might see a thousand of them in a day, and he notices a quaint belief current at the time, that "formerly the whole country being covered with long coarse grass swarming with muskitoes, the antelope bred only once in two years; but since much has been cleared, and the number of muskitoes decreased, it is alleged that they breed every year."[1]

With the clearance of jungle, the finest Indian deer, the Sâmbhar and Chîtal, have also much decreased in numbers. They still abound in the preserves of the Mahârâja of Benares in the Mirzapur district, when he beats his best jungles for the amusement of some favoured visitor. No one who has seen the stream of animals beaten out on such occasions will ever forget the sight.

Passing from the flora and fauna, we may close this chapter with some account of the soils and climate.

The proper classification of Indian soils is based on two distinct factors—the chemical or physical constitution of the soil and its relation in position to the village site. For practical purposes, and in particular for the fixation of rent, the latter is the more important. From this point of view the lands of a village are usually divided into three concentric belts—that close to the homestead, which receives most of the manure, more frequent irrigation and more careful tillage, adapting it to the production of the most valuable crops—the finer cereals, sugar-cane, and cotton, garden vegetables and opium; the middle belt, inferior in quality and less carefully manured, irrigated and tilled; and lastly, the belt on the outskirts, which receives little or no manure, and grows the coarser and poorer crops, which are in some places exposed to damage from pigs, deer, monkeys, and other forms of animal life. To illustrate the respective values of these classes of soil, we may take the case of parts

[1] *Eastern India*, II. 503.

of the Aligarh district, where, for the best irrigated land in the belt close to the homestead, the rent is Rs. 12 per acre; in the intermediate belt, Rs. 8-12-0; in the most distant Rs. 4-12-0.

Viewed, again, from the physical aspect, soils may be roughly divided into loam and those in which clay or sand preponderates. This is the case generally all over the Plains, where, in the geological character of its soils, India exhibits far less variation than England. The loam is probably in a great measure an artificial soil, the result of the application of manure, irrigation, and the careful tillage of centuries to various grades of clayey or sandy soils. The two really distinct types are the clay and the sand. The localisation of clay is due to the fact that the alumina of the neighbouring slopes, being soluble, is conveyed by the agency of water from the higher ground and deposited in the depressions. Hence the slopes, being denuded of their clay, are usually lighter than the higher uplands, and often exceedingly unfertile.

The characteristics of a clay soil are the extreme minuteness and adhesiveness of its particles, which render it compact and tenacious. It is capable of absorbing a large amount of moisture which it assimilates slowly and retains with obstinacy. In seasons of drought it cakes and gives little sustenance to plant life. It has a strong power of retarding the decomposition of animal and vegetable matter. It is difficult to plough except under the most favourable conditions. If the season is too wet it clogs the share, and it is impossible to turn it up; in a dry year it resists the plough like a brick. Owing to its density and obstinacy, those plants thrive best which have the smallest and most fibrous roots, such as rice, wheat, gram, and peas; those with bulbous roots will not thrive in it. There are various grades of clay—some containing hardly any organic matter, others more; others, again, whitish or yellowish grey in colour, and sometimes impregnated with noxious salts or some compounds of iron.

In direct contrast to these are the sandy soils. This is

the detritus of rocks in the water-shed of the chief rivers, worn down and triturated by friction until the particles have become minute in the extreme. We see it at its worst in the sandy deserts of Râjputâna. Much of it has been blown by steady winds from the river beds, and deposited over the adjoining slopes, where the action of the periodical rains soon robs it of any admixture of clay. One has only to experience an Indian dust or sand storm to realise the effect produced by the wind in dispersing it. In the depth of the hot season, a sudden increase in the torrid heat, and a lull in the wind, presage a storm. Presently a dense black cloud rises in the horizon; darkness rapidly spreads over the sky; all nature is hushed in anticipation, and the birds hasten to the nearest thicket for shelter. Often with a burst of thunder the storm breaks; masses of sand and dust are driven across the plain. It penetrates through the most closely-fitted doors and windows, and everything is soon covered with a coating of almost impalpable dust. Then perhaps with a few drops of rain a welcome coolness revives exhausted man and beast, only to be succeeded by a more intense heat a day or two later on.

Hence we often find the sand taking the shape of low, billow-like mounds, as the snowdrifts after a winter storm on the Yorkshire moors. These sand dunes may be traced in the Upper Duâb almost from the banks of the Ganges to those of the Jumna. As is the case on parts of the French coast, these dunes tend to encroach on the more fertile lands; but usually before long they become compacted by the roots of plants, and are in time culturable, growing a niggard crop of starveling millet.

The main distinction between the clay and the sand lies in their power of retaining moisture. The alluvial soil of the Plains is composed of alternating strata of these two classes of soil, and the fertility of any given tract depends on the degree to which they are intermixed. Where clay prevails to excess the soil is dense and intractible; where sand predominates cultivation is straggling and unprofitable. Even where the stimulus of canal irrigation is applied, unless the thirsty sand is dosed with plentiful manure, the sudden luxuriant growth is only temporary, and after a few seasons of fatness the land ceases to respond to the industry of the peasant. And each class of soil feeds its own race of men. The Jât and Kâchhi, the former the type of the general farmer, the latter of the market gardener, cling to the rich loams; the Kurmi and Lodha, growers of rice, prefer the deep clays; the Gûjar and Râjput, whose profession is the tending of cattle, who detest fatigue and the monotonous toil of husbandry, draw a precarious livelihood from the meagre sandy tracts.

In the southern hilly region, besides the barren gravels which Virgil tells us "scarce serve the bees with humble cassia flowers and rosemary"—

> "*Nam ieiuna quidem clivosi glarea ruris*
> *Vix humilis apibus casias roremque ministrat*"—

we find the Regar, or so-called "black cotton" soil, characteristic of Bundelkhand. In some places it is supposed to be derived from basalt by surface decomposition; in others from the impregnation of argillaceous earth with organic matter, often with a considerable amount of carbonate of lime. But the various processes by which it has been created are still imperfectly understood, and some peculiarities in its distribution require further explanation. In some parts this soil prevails to a depth of from 20 to 60 feet; it swells under the moisture of the rains like an Irish bog, and is then quite impassable; in the winter and hot weather it cracks into immense clods, which make riding over it most dangerous. It is commonly believed to need no manure; but Dr Voelcker[1] is inclined to doubt if it be so rich in organic matter and nitrogenous ingredients as to be incapable of exhaustion. It yields with little trouble to the peasant excellent wheat and the finest varieties of Indian cotton.

The climate varies extremely with the diversities of geographical feature. To take, first, the Himalayan tract, which

[1] *Report*, p. 47.

contains the chief health resorts, for half the year the climate is that of the sub-tropical rather than the temperate region. From October to April the weather is admirable; the rainfall on the outer range, which first meets the force of the monsoon, is 80 inches, decreasing to 40 in the inner ranges. The heat, except in the more confined valleys, is never excessive, and every year the winter brings snow on the higher levels, and in some seasons it falls over the whole mountainous tract; while frosts, especially in the valleys, are often severe. A change to the hills acts as a welcome stimulus to constitutions debilitated by the heat and damp of the Plains; but many of the severer forms of fever and hepatic affections yield only to the air of Europe. With a better and more rapid steamer service to England, the attractions of the hill stations have decidedly decreased. The journey home and back can now be performed in little more than a month, and an officer on three months' leave can enjoy two of them at home at little more cost than a trip to the hills.

Beneath the hill tract comes the Tarâi, where the prevalent malaria renders permanent residence impossible; and though much has been done to improve the sanitary conditions, it still remains as dangerous to human life as the jungles of Ashanti or the Campania.

In the central Plain during the summer months the heat is of tropical fierceness. In June the thermometer in the shade has on occasions risen to 115° in Agra, and 119·8° at Allahâbâd. In the latter station the average annual thermometer reading is about 77°. But between the eastern and western districts there is this important difference, that the latter is less exposed to the hot west wind of summer, which blows with much less force as we move east. To those in vigorous health the hot season, though trying, is seldom dangerous. With suitable clothing and a carefully regulated diet the most extreme heat of the sun may be faced with comparative impunity. By the use of screens of dampened grass, a well built house, with every door and window closed in the early morning, may be kept moderately cool. East of Allahâbâd the west wind blows only intermittently, and ceases altogether in the neighbourhood of Benares, for about a month before the beginning of the monsoon. It is then replaced by a flow of heated vapour from the direction of the Bengal Delta, presaging the approach of the monsoon. This dull, damp heat is most relaxing and debilitating. With the arrival of the rains the temperature is considerably reduced; but instead of dry heat, the air is impregnated with vapour, and the malaria rises from the saturated soil. If there is a break in the rain the heat immediately increases. September is, perhaps, the most trying month; when this is over the cold weather rapidly advances, and the European is able to enjoy the camping, shooting, and exercise which this, about for a time the finest climate in the world, renders possible.

But here the conditions of the east and west greatly vary. In the former the cold weather sets in later and ends sooner. In Ghâzipur or Mirzapur it is too hot to march comfortably in tents till November is well advanced, and by the close of February it becomes unpleasantly warm. In Sahâranpur, as compared with Ghâzipur, you gain a fortnight or more at the beginning, and at least a month at the close of camping season. On the other hand, for those liable to attacks of fever or rheumatism, the dry heat of the eastern districts is less trying than the damp of Meerut, where canal irrigation is widely extended. For most people, perhaps the healthiest part of the Province is about the centre, in the neighbourhood of Agra or Mathura. In the summer the heat here is excessive, but the dry west wind, for those in good health, is not injurious, and there is less risk of attacks of malarious fever.

For the new-comer, in the earlier years of residence, the most deadly disease is typhoid or enteric fever. Within the last few years the outbreaks of this malady have been most fatal and mysterious. It has appeared time after time in stations hitherto regarded as about the healthiest in India—Meerut, Allahâbâd, Lucknow. In 1896, at Allahâbâd, in spite of the new supply of filtered water, it caused great mortality. It is said that the pipe water supplied was itself pure, but that the microbe lurked in the vessels in which it was stored in the barrack-rooms. In some cases it has been attributed to milk, in others to soda-water procured by soldiers in the bâzâr. So far it has baffled the resources of the science of sanitation, and is much more fatal than cholera. Its nidus is probably the filthy native slums which surround our cantonments.

We shall elsewhere refer to the epidemic of malarious fever which was so fatal in the central Duâb. This disease is largely affected by the amount of the annual rainfall. The average for the year at Allahâbâd is 41 inches; at Agra, 26; at Bareilly, 40; at Sahâranpur, 34; at Mussoorie, 92 inches. Over a large part of the Scotch Highlands it is more than 80 inches. But it must be remembered that the fall in India is concentrated within about four months, and the rest of the year is practically rainless, except for a shower or two about Christmas time. On occasions the rainfall has been excessive. In August 1885, in some of the western districts, as much as 20 inches fell within twenty-four hours; in Basti, in 1888, over 30 inches fell in the same time; a fall of 34 inches in one day is recorded at Bijnor. With sudden and excessive downpours like this, serious floods are far from uncommon. In recent years the most remarkable floods were that in the Kâlinadi in 1885, which demolished the aqueduct at Nadrâi which carries the Lower Ganges Canal across the valley, and that at Jaunpur in 1871, when the waters of the Gûmti wrecked 4000 houses in the city and 9000 in villages along the banks of the river. The more famous Gohna flood in 1894 was due to a landslip forming a dam in one of the upper tributaries of the Ganges. No one who witnessed the rush of the water at Hardwâr, and the floating relics of towns and villages swept down by it, will ever forget the sight. Were it not for special arrangements made to warn the people, there must have been enormous loss of life.

We have, again, records of storms of great violence. In 1888, in a storm on the Bareilly-Pilibhît railway, eighteen miles of telegraph were demolished, and several waggons were blown off the line and capsized. Not long since, the residences of the officials in the civil station of Morâdâbâd were almost completely wrecked by a hurricane.

Hailstorms are distressingly frequent, just as "the hounds of spring are on winter's traces," and the wheat and barley are nearly ready for the sickle. There was a famous hailstorm in Azamgarh in 1818, which almost caused a general famine. In 1888, 230 people are said to have lost their lives in a hailstorm in the Morâdâbâd district. But, as a rule, these storms are local in their character. The hail will sweep along a tract of country three or four miles long and a mile or two in breadth, demolishing all the standing crops in its course, smashing ear and stalk into chaff, so that it is hardly worth gleaning. Woe to children or cattle who chance to be caught by it unsheltered in the open country.

CHAPTER II

THE PROVINCE UNDER HINDU AND MUSALMÂN RULE

THE earliest history of the Middle Land can only be tentatively pieced together out of a mass of myth and legend. According to the most recent authorities, the original home of the Âryas was somewhere in Central Europe, and, from a comparison of the legendary history of the Assyrian kingdom and the campaigns of Semiramis on the Indus, it has been supposed that the Âryas may have been settled in the neighbourhood of that river in the fifteenth century before Christ. It was there, and perhaps soon after their arrival, that the great collection of lyric poetry, known as the Vedic hymns, may have been composed. At that time it would seem that the new-comers knew little of the Ganges, because in the Rig Veda that river is mentioned only twice, and then without any special note of reverence. Their last settlement west of the Jumna was probably between the two sacred rivers, the Saraswati and Drishadvati, near the modern Thânesar, in what is now the Ambâla district of the Panjâb. Thence they gradually forced their way along the course of the Ganges and Jumna, until in the Epic period, as represented by the Mahâbhârata, we find them settled at Hastinapura, in the present Meerut district.

It is probable that, at the earliest stage of their colonisation, the dense forests which then covered the middle Plains presented almost insurmountable obstacles to their progress. Following the example of all colonists in tropical lands, they would naturally cling to the highlands which flank the valley, and avoid the deep, malarious jungle infested by beasts of prey. The references to an Âryan civilisation of an advanced type on the slopes of the Siwâlik range and

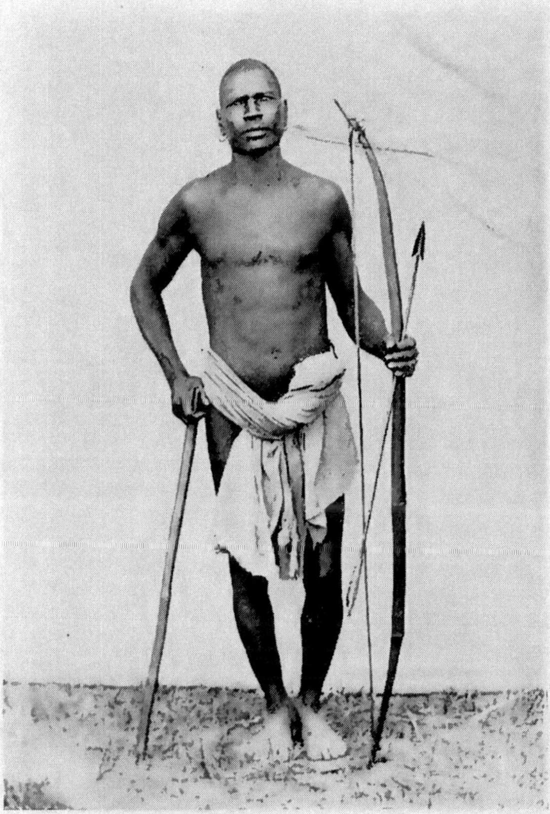

A PURE DRAVIDIAN KORWA. MIRZAPUR.

the lower Himâlaya indicate that this may have been their earliest route to the eastward. Here they encountered the indigenous races. At one time the relations between the new-comers and the old settlers would seem to have been amicable, for we read that, at Hardwâr, Arjuna espoused the daughter of King Vâsuki, of the Nâga or serpent race. Later on we learn that the Âryas destroyed the Nâgas, and burnt them out of the Khândava forest in the valley of the Jumna, near Indraprastha, or old Delhi, which may have been one of the early frontier posts.

The Vedas represent the Âryas as having attained a high grade of civilisation. They had acquired a knowledge of the higher handicrafts, and—though many of them were nomads, living on the produce of their flocks and herds—others had already occupied the land, were engaged in the cultivation of the soil and had founded villages and towns.

As they advanced they came in contact with a race whom they called Dasyu, a word which, if derived from an Âryan root, seems to mean "hostile." These people are represented as autochthonous. The popular theory of the ethnology of Northern India describes this black, jungle-dwelling race as conquered and enslaved by the white invaders. Recent investigations, and particularly anthropometry, make it probable that the absorption of the indigenous races may have been more complete than is indicated by the myths of the invaders. The new-comers were probably, at least in the earlier stages, limited in numbers, and may have freely intermarried with the population which then occupied the land. This absorption may have gone on in the Panjâb at the close of the Vedic period, and was continued as the advance to the eastward progressed. From it arose the present Hindu race, the institution of caste, and the national polity and religion.

This Dasyu race was possibly itself the result of two streams of migration—the Negritic or Dravidian, which occupied the Central Indian hill tract, with its nucleus in Chota Nâgpur; and the Mongoloid or Lohitic, which flowed from north-east Bengal into the centre of the Province, and thence into the valleys of the Gandak and Ghâgra. The former are now represented by the Santâl, Orâon, Kol, and Bhîl of the southern hills; the latter by the Kurmi, Bind, Dusâdh, and other servile tribes of the eastern Plain. That the culture of these races was, on the whole, at a much lower level than that of the Âryas is generally admitted. They, too, seem to have clung to the hills flanking the Plain, in preference to the deeper forest of the valley. This is indicated by the absence, so far as enquiries have progressed, of any remains of the Stone Age in the Ganges-Jumna Duâb; but all along the southern hills, as at Jagner in the hilly tract of Agra and on the Vindhyan plateau of Bundelkhand, Mirzapur, and Chota Nâgpur, we meet the primitive cemeteries, menhirs, and dolmens erected by these races. As far south as the Narbada valley, neolithic stone weapons abound, and in some places, as at Kon in the Mirzapur district, we can examine the workshops of these early craftsmen. If the evidence of rude ochre drawings in some of the caves of the Vindhyan range is to be trusted, these Dravidian tribes, up to comparatively modern times, may have slain the rhinoceros and the sâmbhar stag with their agate-tipped arrows, spears, and axes. Even now the form of the weapons used by the hillmen indicates that they cannot be far removed from the neolithic age. That some of them on the outskirts of the real Dravidian fringe may, as the Âryan legends indicate in speaking of their forts and castles, have reached a higher stage of culture, is perhaps possible.

But what it is really important to grasp is that the fusion between the old and the new peoples must have been more complete than has hitherto been supposed to be the case. To use Mr Nesfield's illustration, the Ârya became absorbed in the Dasyu as the Lombard in the Italian, the Frank in the Gaul, the Roman (of Roumania) in the Slav, the Norman in the Frenchman, the Moor of Spain in the Spaniard, the Indian Portuguese in the Indian. This conclusion rests on the evidence of anthropometry, which establishes the substantial unity of the Hindu race as we now find it in Northern India. It is probable, then, that the Âryan conquest was more moral and intellectual, more a blending of the new-comer with the native, than a substitution of the white man for the dark-skinned people.

What we must also understand is that the Âryan invasion was not a definite conquest carried out once for all as the Norman Conquest of England or the French occupation of Tonquin. From the very earliest times there must have been a constant flow of settlers from the hilly tract of Central Asia into the lower Indian Plain. The completeness of the absorption of or fusion with the indigenous races was certainly at all times not uniform. Thus, one of these waves of invasion from Scythia may have remained more completely isolated from the indigenous races and developed into the Râjputs, Jâts, and Gûjars of the Western Plain. Another party of colonists may have been the forefathers of the Agarwâlas and some of the prouder Vaisya or Banya tribes, which are perhaps more free from local admixture than most of the races existing at present.

Between the fourteenth and fifth centuries before Christ—the period extending from the era of the composition of the Vedas to the construction of the law code which we know as the Institutes of Manu—the present Hindu polity was established. It represents a period about as long as that between the Norman Conquest and the creation of our Colonial Empire. In this time the great institution which we call caste was built up. The Vedas know nothing of caste. In the code of Manu it is fully developed, even if its rules are somewhat less stringent than at the present time.

We are now in a position to conclude with tolerable certainty that the basis of caste was not ethnical but occupational. The Brâhmans, instead of being a body of pure Âryan Levites, we know to be a mixed race, representing on the one hand the body of churchmen who took the place of the Âryan house-father when ritual and the worship of the gods became gradually more and more intricate ; on the other hand they absorbed the Baiga and the Ojha, the devil priest and ghost-finder of the forest races. Even now-a-days we see traces of this intermixture in the Dakaut or beggar Brâhman, and the

Mahâbrâhman who superintends the funeral rites, who have little kinship except in name with the contemplative sages of Mathura and Benares ; and in the local groups, such as those of Gonda or Gaur, those of the trans-Sarju land, the Prayâgwâl and Chaubê who act as cicerones to the pilgrim along the holy rivers. So with the Râjputs, who represented the higher political class of the infant Hindu State. Some of these, like the prouder septs of the western deserts, have maintained a dignified isolation, and boast a pedigree longer than any family of the western aristocracy; others, like many of the Oudh Râjputs, are almost certainly of local origin. Even at the present day many of the Dravidian tribes of the Vindhyan range are being gradually promoted to Râjput rank.

Beneath those the mass of the people has organised itself in endogamous groups of the eponymous, territorial, and more particularly of the occupational type. New castes of this kind are every day becoming separated from the parent stock, with which, on the ground that they accept or prohibit widow marriage, from some dispute connected with precedence, or from the use of or abstinence from special kinds of food, they decline to intermarry. The effect of the break-up of the Hindu polity under the stress of the Musalmân inroads is shown by the number of groups known by Muhammadan names.

Within the same period of about nine centuries the social institutions of Hinduism were founded. These were codified in the compilation known as the Grihya Sûtras, which probably dates from the eighth century before Christ. Some two hundred years later—about two hundred years before the Leges Regiae of Rome were reduced to writing—we find the system of government fully established as it appears in the Institutes of Manu. Here the duties of the Râja and his ministers, the ideal career of the Brâhman recluse, the arts of war and peace, the rules for the collection of the revenue—in short, the whole organisation of the Hindu State—are set forth in detail. The code assumes throughout the supremacy of the Brâhman, the division of the people into four functional groups, of which the lowest or the Sûdras were quite outside the pale of civil law. Much of it is perhaps an ideal picture of how a State might be guided under a benign priestly rule. It inculcates a body of criminal law, in which the high caste man is beyond control and the outcast is cruelly repressed. But comparing it with the codes at that time in force in Europe, that of the Romans, Germans, or English, it contains much to deserve the reverence which the modern Hindu lavishes on this, the greatest of his Shâstras.

It is from legend alone that we learn that this supremacy of the Brâhman Levite was not attained without a struggle. Their ascendancy was fiercely contested by the Kshatriya, or warrior race. One legend, that of Parusarâma, tells how "thrice seven times did he destroy the Kshatriyas." The same contest is represented in the strife of Vasishtha the priest with Visvamitra the warrior. In the end the Kshatriya wins admission to the priesthood.

When the Brâhmans emerged successful from this struggle they used their triumph with discretion. They continued the kingship in the hands of the military order, and preferred to enjoy the pre-eminence in the council of the State. In their priestly guise they controlled the policy of the kingdom, the forerunners in an earlier age of Pandulf or Wolsey.

Meanwhile they devoted their energies to the conversion of the heathen, and the whole country to the east and south was overrun by Brâhman missionaries. They worked on the same lines as the wandering Jogi or Sannyâsi of our day who is ever spreading the knowledge of the faith among the Gond, Bhîl, or Kharwâr of the central highlands. No missionary reports tell the story of these pioneers of Hinduism, the prototypes of Xavier or Las Casas. At a later date the Râmâyana gives a picture of their sufferings, which would be almost pathetic if it were not ludicrous.—"These shapeless and ill-looking monsters testify their abominable character by various cruel and terrific displays. These base-born wretches implicate the hermits in impure practices, and perpetrate the greatest outrages. Changing their shapes and hiding in the thickets adjoining the hermitages, these frightful beings delight in terrifying the devotees. They cast away the sacrificial ladle and vessels, they pollute the cooked oblations, and utterly defile the offerings with blood. These faithless creatures inject frightful sounds into the ears of the faithful and austere eremites. At the time of sacrifice they snatch away the jars, the flowers, the fuel, and the sacred grass of these soberminded men."[1] We can almost picture the precise Brâhman being harried by a pack of shock-headed jungle men. One of the greatest of these saints has come down to us by name—the Muni Agastya, who is said to have converted southern India, and whose grave is to this day shown in the Gonda district in north Oudh, near the banks of the Ghâgra.

This conquest of the older by the new creed followed the general lines of Aryan colonisation. It was by the absorption, rather than by the annihilation, of the local deities that Brâhmanism triumphed. We hear of none of the persecution, none of the iconoclasm which characterised the Musalmân inroad. A fitting home was found in the Brâhmanic pantheon for the popular village deities, the gods of fear and blood of the indigenous faith. Under these changed circumstances and to meet the wants of the new Hindu people the Vedic theology was reconstructed. The vague nature deities of the older faith were gradually and without any sudden dislocation of familiar traditions modified into the supreme triad—Brahma, the Creator; Vishnu, the Preserver; Siva, the Destroyer and Reproducer. The first two were in name at least found in the Veda; the last was assumed to represent Rudra, the Vedic storm god. But the conception of Brahma was too abstract to suit the taste of converts reared in the traditions of a coarsely animistic faith. He has fallen out of popular regard, save so far as he is identified with Parameswar, the Almighty of these later days, or has been revived by some modern, struggling theistic sects. Vishnu, by his successive incarnations, has been made the vehicle for conciliating the tribal gods or totems of tribes now well within the fold of Hinduism. Siva as Mahâdeva—the great god—with his consort Kâli, Devi or Durga, has swept up and

[1] Muir, *Ancient Sanskrit Texts*, II., chap. iii., section iv., 427.

absorbed much of the demonolatry of the indigenous servile races.

This reformed Brâhmanism provided the land not merely with a new faith but with a new philosophy. These sages in their secluded hermitages scattered through the eastern and southern jungles were deep students of the mysteries of life and of the mind of man. Hence came the six schools of Hindu philosophic thought, which endeavoured to solve those problems which will remain the battle-ground of thinkers as long as the world exists—how matter was evolved from chaos, how the soul by a succession of new births is to be freed from the burdens of sensual existence, and finally absorbed in the divine essence of the universe.

The contrast between the militant faith of the Âryas in their early settlement east of the Jumna at Hastinapura, in the Upper Ganges-Jumna Duâb, and the later faith evolved after centuries of peaceful meditation, is marked by the difference of tone of the two great epics. The Mahâbhârata, the Iliad of the Hindus, is one long pæan in commemoration of martial glory. The Râmâyana, their Odyssey, must be later than Manu's Institutes, which were almost certainly compiled before the Aryan missionaries crossed the Vindhyas. In the one the poet sings of "the battle of the warrior with confused noise and garments rolled in blood"; in the later epic we have little of activity and self-assertion, and these are replaced by the calm resignation of the saint, the passionless observance of duty, the reticence, the self-sacrifice of the ascetic. In the one we find the Sturm und Drang of the Iliad, in the other the stiller life and artistic calm of the Odyssey. One is eozoic in its stern intensity: the other neozoic—the scene is lapped in the softer air of peace and meditation. The hero of the later poem emulates the eremite of the woods, who has shaken himself free from the bondage of the flesh and lives to God alone.

Thus Brâhmanism, which had its birth within or on the frontier of the Province, pursued its quiet path, but not for long. It yielded for a time to another faith which, while it now offers salvation to half the world, has hardly a follower in the land of its birth. If the supremacy of Brâhmanism be fixed about 1000 B.C., it lasted till the fifth century B.C., when Gautama Buddha was born at Kapilavastu, which has perhaps erroneously been identified with Bhuila Dih in the Basti district. All we really know about the situation of this place is that it lay on the route between the Buddhist cities of Gorakhpur and Sravasti in Gonda and somewhere between the rivers Ghâgra and Râpti. The well-known tale of his miraculous birth, his marriage, the Great Renunciation, his studies as a recluse in the hermitage at Râjagriha, his enlightenment, his missionary journeys through a large part of the Province, and the pathetic story of his death at Kusinagara, said, probably incorrectly, to be the modern Kasiya in Gorakhpur, need not be told again.

The historical facts of the great reformer's life are shrouded in a mass of legend, and the chronology is most uncertain. Many of the places sacred to his followers through the various incidents of his career have been identified by General Cunningham in the course of the Archæological Survey. We have already mentioned Kapilavastu and Kusinagara, the scenes of his birth and his attainment of Nirvâna, the release attained by the performance of duty from the recurring series of new births in the world of existence. We know with more or less certainty that he visited and expounded the law at Ajudhya in Faizâbâd, at Benares, Mathura, Sravasti (now Sahet Mahet, in Gonda), and at Sankisa in Farrukhâbâd : and that after his cremation his ashes were enshrined in a Stûpa at Moriyanagara, possibly Barhi in Gorakhpur. The piety of his followers adorned these sites and many others supposed to be associated with the events of his life by a series of stately Stûpas or richly ornamented sepulchral mounds, containing relics of the Teacher. There seems no reason to doubt that his begging bowl, the Grail of eastern legend, after being removed to Peshâwar, is now shown to the pilgrim at Kandahâr.

It was not for at least two centuries after the death of the Teacher that his faith under the influence of Asoka, the Constantine of the new revelation, became the established religion of Northern India. The new faith, we must remember, did not at least in its early days involve the overthrow of the existing belief. Buddha would undoubtedly have called himself a Hindu, and admitted that his was only one of the multitudinous sects which Hinduism is always throwing off. It was an immediate consequence of the system of the four Âsramas, or stages in which the life of an orthodox Brâhman was supposed to be passed. "If," he would say, "it is only at the third stage that perfect truth can be attained, why should any one waste time over the preliminary stages and in sacrifices and oblations which profit nothing?" His attitude towards Brâhmanism was not that of St Paul in the face of the paganism of Greece or Rome, but rather that of Isaiah towards the Mosaic law as interpreted by the later priestly schools. Of the causes which led to the establishment of the new faith as the State religion, we can only form conjectures. The movement was possibly as much social as theological. It found, on the one hand, a haughty, bigoted priesthood, on the other an aristocracy ruthless in its coercion of the lower races. According to Manu,[1] the sole duty of the Sûdra was to serve the twice-born classes, "without depreciating their worth." There can be no doubt that their condition was one of galling servitude and oppression. The bonds of the caste system lay heavily upon them. The conquest had been completed and the country was broken up into a number of petty principalities, which waged internecine war upon each other. The childlike joy of life, so marked in the Vedic literature, had been replaced by a dull age of settled government, from the control of which they were excluded; theology had fallen into the hands of a body of pedants. To people like these the personal influence of the Teacher, his sympathy for the oppressed, his life of charity and benevolence, his repudiation of caste, his preaching of a lofty moral code, must have come as a new revelation. As Christianity in its earlier days was the consolation of the fisherman and the slave, Buddhism opened a new world to the village menial serf. That Brâhmanism was thoroughly extirpated from the land is most improbable, that Buddhism

[1] *Institutes*, i. 91.

never called in the aid of persecution against the rival sectaries is certain. The two religions may in many places have existed side by side, as Jainism and Hinduism do at the present time. Probably the peasant continued to worship his fetish, to bow before his holy tree, to bathe in the sacred rivers, as we see him doing to-day.

After the death of the Teacher, the foundations of the new faith were consolidated at the two general councils held at Râjagriha in the Patna district, and Vaisali in Muzaffarpur, both beyond the eastern frontier of the Province. With the accession of Asoka to the throne of Magadha, the modern Bihâr, another stage is reached. During his reign (264-223 B.C.), Buddhism rose to the rank of the State religion. He published the principles of the faith throughout northern India, from Peshâwar to Kâthiâwâr on the western, and Orissa on the eastern ocean. Within this Province copies of his edicts have been found at Khâlsi on the Jumna in Dehra Dûn, on the pillar taken to Delhi from Meerut by Fîroz Shâh, on a third removed at the same time from Paota in Sahâranpur, or Bara Topra in Ambâla, and lastly, on the well-known pillar now shown in the Allahâbâd Fort. All these, with some slight variations, preached a creed, much of which might have been taught at Olney or Little Gidding. He inculcated the duty of obedience to parents, kindness to children and friends, mercy to animals, compassion towards the weak and suffering, reverence to Brâhmans and members of the Order, suppression of anger, passion, cruelty, and extravagance ; generosity, tolerance and charity.

To the historian these edicts are of supreme importance, because they lead to a settled chronology. The Khâlsi pillar names five Greek kings as contemporaries of Asoka—Antiochus Theos of Syria (B.C. 261-46); Ptolemy Philadelphus of Egypt (B.C. 285-47); Antigonus Gonatas of Macedonia (B.C. 276-43); Magas of Cyrene (B.C. 258); and Alexander of Epirus (B.C. 272-54). This brings the date of the pillar to about 253 B.C., about the time of the campaign of Regulus against Carthage. With this begins the series of dated monuments in India.

But about half a century before this, the synchronism of dates in the histories of India and Europe had been established through the travels of the Greek traveller Megasthenes, who came as the ambassador of Seleukos, the ruler of Syria, from 312 to 280 B.C. Megasthenes lived for some time at the court of Sandrokottos, king of the Prasii, as the Greeks called him, but who is known to Indian historians as Chandragupta, king of Magadha, whose capital was at Pataliputra, the modern Patna. Chandragupta seems to have been an adventurer who rose to power after the convulsion caused by the invasion of Alexander, when he (327-6 B.C.) pushed his conquests of the Panjâb as far as the Hyphasis or Biyâs, but never reached this Province. It was Megasthenes who first opened the world of the East to the curious Greeks. His account follows much the same lines as that of the Institutes of Manu. The people were truthful, sober, and industrious; there were Brâhmans and members of the Buddhist orders; there were inspectors and supervisors of morals, who perhaps acted the same part as the news-writers of Mughal times and of modern China. The rural economy was much the same as we found it twenty centuries later.

"It falls to the lot of most nations," says Mommsen, "in the early stages of their development, to be taught and trained by some rival sister nation." The same service which the Greeks performed for Rome, they conferred on India. Their influence on art, as we see from remains recently discovered at Mathura, was no less profound than that exercised on science and religion, philosophy and social life. The school of architecture which arose under their guidance has been styled by Dr Ferguson the Indo-Roman or Indo-Byzantine, and reached India through Gandhâra or Kâbul in the period subsequent to the Christian era. But the theory that any of the legends or doctrines of Buddhism were due to Christian influence is disbelieved by the best authorities.[1]

The next standpoint in history is the invasion of the Indo-

[1] Rhys Davids, *Hibbert Lectures*, 1881, p. 151.

Skythians, which occurred in the first century before Christ. They introduced the northern form of Buddhism, which, for the next six centuries, competed with the earlier form established by Asoka. This new form of the faith was organised by the council of Kanishka, held in 40 A.D., while Caligula reigned in Rome. He appears to have done the same service to Buddhism in Gandhâra, or Afghânistân, as Asoka did in the Indian Plains—that is to say, he made it the State religion. His reign marks the introduction of Buddhism in its corrupt form into Tibet, Burma, and China, a movement which has been compared by Dr Ferguson with the supersession by Gregory the Great of the simpler primitive form by the hierarchical system.

Of three of these Indo-Skythian monarchs—Kanishka, Huvishka, and Vasudeva—inscriptions have been found at Mathura; from Pâdham in Mainpuri comes a record of the satrap Saudâsa, and their coins abound in the piles of ruins scattered all over the Province. Earlier even than these are what are known as the Punch-marked coins, which General Cunningham thinks may be as old as any of the coinages of Greece or Asia Minor. It is on the basis of this fragmentary inscriptional record, and from the evidence of numismatics, that the early history of the Province is now being patiently worked out.

The effects of these Skythic raids on the people are very uncertain. There seems reason to believe that some of the Râjput septs and perhaps the Jâts and Gûjars are descended from these invaders; but they have become so intermixed with the indigenous races that the verdict of anthropometry is uncertain, and the evidence from survivals of custom equally vague.

The final overthrow of the Indo-Skythian kingdom is attributed to the Indian hero Vikramaditya of Ujjain, and he is said to have founded the Sambat era (57 B.C.) in honour of his victory. Of him we practically know nothing, and as the restorer of the ruined shrines of Ajudhya he has perhaps been confounded with Chandragupta II. of the Imperial Gupta dynasty.

This kingdom forms the next landmark in our local history. Our slight knowledge of these monarchs is being gradually worked out from a study of their inscriptions and coins, the latter of which, owing to their rarity and beauty, are a treasure to the numismatist. The most recent authority on the gold coinage of the Guptas[1] fixes their era about 160-170 A.D., and the death of Skandagupta, or at least the downfall of his empire, in 318-19 A.D. All we know about them is that they were most probably Kshatriya princes and reigned at Patna. The Hindu character of their coins is a legible record of a native reaction against the domination of the foreign Skythian power. There were seven princes of the line, of whom Samudragupta has left an inscription at Mathura; Kumâragupta at Bilsar in the Central Duâb; Samudragupta, on the Asoka pillar at Allahâbâd; and Skandagupta, the last of the line, at Bhitari in Ghâzipur. One of them, Srigupta, may have been a Buddhist; all his successors were certainly Hindus. But they could not have been bigoted Brâhmanists, if one of them was the monarch whose gifts made to the Buddhist Stûpa at Sanchi are recorded on that famous monument.

By this time, in fact, Buddhism was on the decline. The degradation of the faith seems to be indicated by the introduction of the Statue worship of the Teacher. Dr Ferguson thinks that none of these images can be dated earlier than the first century of our era. It has been supposed that the fall of the Gupta dynasty was due to fresh incursions of Huns or Tâtars from the west. Buddhism probably decayed because the faith became more and more the religion of priests and monks, and gradually lost its hold on the affections of the people. But of the details of its decline we know practically nothing. It is tolerably certain that the reform of Brâhmanism exercised a powerful influence, and the old religion, warned by the experience of fifteen hundred years of eclipse, again strove to regain the confidence of the nation. At last, about the tenth century, when the Norman was invading England, it finally disappeared from Northern

[1] Mr. V. A. Smith, *Journal Asiatic Society of Bengal*, 1884, pp. 120, *sqq*.

India, leaving scarce a trace of its dominion save the ruins of its noble religious edifices.

For this period of decline, we have the valuable records of three Chinese pilgrims, who visited this part of the country —Shih-Fa-Hian (A.D. 400); Sung Yun (A.D. 518); Hiuen Tsiang (A.D. 629).[1] The information which these travellers give of the country and people only makes us long for more. Thus Hiuen Tsiang, writing of Mathura, tells us that the soil is rich and fertile. "This country produces a fine species of cotton fabric, and also yellow gold. The climate is warm to a degree. The manners of the people are soft and complacent. They seem to prepare secret stores of religious merit. They esteem virtue and honour learning."[2] There the Buddhist ascetics apparently lived in holes scraped in the high mounds which surround the city.

Everywhere we find signs of the Brâhmanical reaction. At Matipura (Mandâwar in Bijnor) "the followers of truth and error are equally divided. The King belongs to the caste of the Sûdras. He is not a believer in the law of Buddha, but reverences and worships the spirits of heaven."[3] In Brahmapura or Garhwâl he found heretics mixed with believers in Buddha. There the country was ruled by women, a story which has been supposed to be a ramification of the widespread fable of the Amazons.[4] At Govisâna, Kâshipur in the Tarâi, "there are many believers in false doctrine who seek present happiness only." At Vîrasâna, which was perhaps Bilsar in the Central Duâb, the people were chiefly heretics. "There are a few who believe in the law of Buddha."[5] Kanyakubja, the modern Kanauj, was ruled by the great king Siladitya, whom the pilgrim calls a Vaisya, perhaps a Râjput of the Bais sect. He wavered between the two rival creeds, but was finally converted to the true faith by a miracle.[6] At Prayâga or Allahâbâd, he finds the people "much given to heresy."[7] At Sravasti in Gonda the city was in ruins, and there were

[1] Beal, *Buddhist Records of the Western World.* [2] *Ibid.*, i. 180.
[3] *Ibid.*, i. 190. [4] *Ibid.*, i. 199; Yule, *Marco Polo*, ii. 339.
[5] *Ibid.*, i. 201. [6] *Ibid.*, i. 207. [7] *Ibid.*, i. 230.

numerous Brâhman temples. Of Kausambi, the modern Kosam near Allahâbâd, he says: "The law of Sakya becoming extinct, this will be the very last country in which it will survive; therefore from the highest to the lowest all who enter the borders of this country are deeply affected, even to tears, ere they return."[1] When he came to Benares and ended his pilgrimage in the Province, he describes the people as mostly unbelievers: a few reverence the law of Buddha. "In the capital there are twenty Deva (Brâhmanical) temples, the towers and halls of which are of sculptured stone and carved wood. The foliage of trees combines to shade the sites, while pure streams of water encircle them. The statue of the Deva Mahesvara is somewhat less than a hundred feet high. Its appearance is grave and majestic, and appears as though really living."[2]

According to current belief the downfall of Buddhism was accompanied by massacre and persecution. The ruins of the Sarnâth monastery near Benares appear to indicate that the building was consumed by fire; and it is possible that in some places the passions of the mob may have been roused against the adherents of an unpopular faith. On the other hand, the travels of the Chinese pilgrims, as we have seen, indicate that the believers in the two rival cults were then living together on fairly amicable terms, and if the growth of Brâhmanism had been aided by persecution they would hardly have failed to notice the fact. Their relations seem to have been much as we find Jainas and orthodox Hindus living side by side at the present day. The decay of Buddhism seems to have been gradual, and it was by degrees replaced by the more liberal form of Brâhmanism, to the growth of which it may have given the original impulse. In many cases the Brâhmans occupied the sacred sites and even the buildings of the Buddhists. Thus we constantly find that images of Mâya the mother of the Teacher, have become the village Devi, or guardian Mother. At Ahichhatra in Rohilkhand images of Buddha robbed from the adjoining Stûpa are to this day worshipped by Hindus;

[1] Beal, *Buddhist Records of the Western World*, i. 257. [2] *Ibid.*, ii. 45.

in Benares many Buddhist edifices have been utilised both by Hindus and Musalmâns, and can now be recognised by the fragments of the characteristic railings of the Buddhist monasteries; the famous temple at Gola Gokarnnâth in the Kheri district of northern Oudh has been built on the ruins of a Stûpa. The same was the case at places like Mathura, Hardwâr and Prayâg (Allahâbâd), held sacred by the followers of both faiths.

With the decay of Buddhism came the first beginnings of the Jaina faith. The earliest images of this religion appear to be those found by General Cunningham at Mathura with dates which are with some probability assigned to the first and second centuries of our era. Though many links in the chain of evidence are still wanting, it seems probable that the architecture of the Jainas was derived from Buddhist models; at any rate, the late Buddhist and early Jaina bas-reliefs and sculptures are practically indistinguishable. That the later faith was the direct descendant of the earlier is proved by a long series of facts. The Jainas worship the Jinas, a line of deified worthies who have gained exemption from the constant changes of transmigration, and their tenets thus discard a personal God and a Ruling Providence. Like the Buddhists, their laity are known as Srâvaka or "hearers"; Buddha himself is often called Jina or "the vanquisher"; the Swâstika is the sacred symbol of both; both call their temples Chaitya, and those who have gained perfection, Arhan; both point to Bihâr as the cradle of the faith, and Buddha is often called Mahâvîra, the name of the last of the Tirthankaras or Jaina saints. In this Province the characteristic Jaina architecture is best represented at Mathura, Ahichhatra, Dinai, Khukhundu, and Sahet Mahet.

While Buddhism thus rose on the ruins of the older form of Brâhmanism, only to be itself in turn discredited and expelled from the land of its birth, the change in religion had been accompanied by a profound change in the political situation. The action of the new religion in discarding the bonds of caste naturally brought it into sympathy with the emancipated inferior races. Not that the mass of the people seem ever to have been ardent votaries; but the humanitarian tendencies of States where Buddhism was the official faith probably influenced them in taking the side of a government which was at least somewhat less intolerable than those to which it succeeded. Thus, in Oudh apparently, after the fall of Sravasti, a State in alliance with or subject to the Imperial Gupta dynasty, the northern districts fell for a time into the hands of a tribe whom tradition calls Bhars, and to whom it attributes many of the old ruined cities, wells and tanks which are found all over the country. The modern Bhars, a widely spread tribe of landless labourers and village drudges, know nothing of the glorious deeds of their ancestors, and there can be little doubt that some at least of these ruins were not their work. We have no evidence from coins or inscriptions to settle the matter. It may be that this widespread local tradition does rest on some basis of fact, and that the hewers of wood and drawers of water of the Aryan colonists did gain a brief lease of power during the internecine struggles of their masters, or on their ruin by some inroad of Huns or Tâtars from the west. This much seems tolerably certain, that when the Râjput colonisation began in the twelfth or thirteenth century, the new colonists found the country occupied by low caste tribes whom they conquered and brought into subjection.

In the seventh century of our era the Province was divided among a number of petty kingdoms. The Upper Ganges—Jumna Duâb was included in the kingdom of Sthânesvara, which included a tract to the west of the Jumna with the holy land of Kurukshetra, the traditional site of the war of the Mahâbhârata. Higher up the Ganges in the neighbourhood of Hardwâr was the kingdom of Srughna, the ruins of whose capital have been traced close to the Western Jumna Canal. Western Rohilkhand was under the rule of a petty State with Mandâwar as its chief town; and further north the present Garhwâl and Kumaun highlands owed allegiance to the Râjas of Brahmapura. The Tarâi was a kingdom of itself, ruled from Govisâna, the modern Kâshipur; and the numerous remains found in the jungles testify to a degree of prosperity which was hardly possible except under climatic conditions much more favourable than they are at present. Southern Rohilkhand and the Central Ganges—Jumna Duâb were included in the kingdom of Panchâla, divided into two regions by the Ganges—that on the right bank governed from Ahichhatra in the modern Bareilly district, and the part west of the Ganges from Kampil in Farrukhâbâd. Further west Mathura was the capital of another Râja who ruled a strip of the Duâb, and what are now the Native States of Bhartpur, Karâoli and Dholpur on the right bank of the Jumna. The Lower Ganges—Jumna Duâb was under the kingdom of Vatsya with its capital at Kausambi near Allahâbâd. North Oudh and the trans-Ghâgra region were included in the kingdom of Kosala, while southern Oudh had two kings—one of Paschhima-râshtra, or the western State, the other of Pûrva-râshtra, the eastern.

This collection of petty States possessed none of the elements of permanence. They were engaged in constant local struggles, and all that remains of them is the shapeless mounds which cover the ruins of their cities. Some of these have been to a certain extent explored; it is only by their excavation that the local history of the country can be recovered.

Many of these kingdoms were tributary to the Gupta Empire; but some of them enjoyed at least the right of issuing a local coinage. At Mathura the series commences with a line of Rajubala and three other Indo-Skythian Satraps, all of which have legends in Greek; these are followed by the coins of eight Hindu princes. So for the kingdom of Panchâla we have the names of twelve kings whose coinage was in copper and the characters later than the time of Asoka and earlier than the Christian era. They contain no Buddhist symbols, and the princes who issued them were almost certainly followers of Brâhmanism. At Ajudhya, again, we find a dynasty ruling not earlier than the second century before Christ. It is impossible to judge from their coins whether they were Buddhists or Brâhmanists; possibly they were indifferent to both religions.

UNDER HINDU AND MUSALMÂN RULE

It was about the middle of the seventh century that the pressure of the Musalmâns of the West began to be felt in India, and this continued up to the accession of Sultân Mahmûd (997-1030 A.D.), by whom the conquest was first undertaken in earnest. This led indirectly to an important modification of the political condition of the Province, due to the inroad of the Râjputs, of which ordinary histories take little account. But it marks the point at which the organisation of the land, as we find it at present, took shape. It was one of those ethnical movements which have been landmarks in the history of the world, and was produced by causes which had their counterpart in the events which pushed the Umbrians on the infant city of Rome, the Gauls into northern Italy, the German tribes into Gaul, and finally the Goths and their kinsfolk over the Roman Empire. This movement continued over a lengthened period. Some of these Râjputs appeared in the Province in the tenth century; others were displaced and emigrated as a result of the campaigns of Muhammad Bin Sâm in the end of the twelfth century; much of the colonisation of Oudh took place under the Mughal Empire in the sixteenth century.

With the opening of the period of Musalmân invasion we meet two powerful Râjput dynasties—that of Delhi and Kanauj. The Tomar Râjput dynasty of Delhi appears to have been founded by Anang Pâl in 736 A.D., and the nineteenth Râja in succession to him was Prithivi Râja or Râê Pithaura, in whose time (1193 A.D.) the capital was besieged and captured by Muiz-ud-dîn Muhammad bin Sâm, or Shihâb-ud-dîn, as he was known in his youth. It has been supposed that the Tomar kingdom originally included Kanauj, and that the rebuilding of Delhi about 1052 A.D. was due to the loss of Kanauj, which was then conquered by Chandra Deva, the founder of the famous dynasty of the Râhtaur Râjputs. Delhi seems to have been captured by the Chauhâns about a century later (1151 A.D.). Visala, the Chauhân Râja, married the daughter of the Tomar Râja, who became his dependent, and adopted as his heir his grandson, known to history as Prithivi Râja.

The Tomar dynasty of Delhi ruled over a great part of the eastern Panjâb, and the Ganges-Jumna Duâb up to the Kalindri or Kâli Nadi, which drains it, and rising in the Muzaffarnagar district, joins the Ganges at Kanauj. A kindred house of the same sept ruled at Gwâlior.

The kingdom of Kanauj seems to have been even more powerful. Hiuen Tsiang, the Chinese pilgrim, found Harsha Vardhana (607-648 A.D.) at the zenith of his power. He tells us that his kingdom extended from the foot of the Kashmîr hills to Assam and from Nepâl to the Narbada river. The dominions of their Râhtaur successors were more limited; still it was a goodly heritage. From the Kâlinadi eastward they occupied most of Oudh, and one of the line, Sri Chandra Deva, conquered the old Buddhist sacred city of Sravasti in Gonda, which at that time was held by a family of Jaina princes—one of the last in Upper India who professed that faith. The son of the great Jaya Chandra himself, Lakhana Deva, erected a pillar of victory in 1196 A.D. in the Mirzapur district. From inscriptions and land grants of Jaya Chandra himself it is clear that his rule extended to the eastern boundary of the province.

Here a third Râjput kingdom appeared upon the scene—the Chandel dynasty of Mahoba, which ruled in the present Bundelkhand, south of the Ganges, and left as their monuments the splendid temples of Khajuraho and the vast irrigation reservoirs along the base of the Vindhyan range. Between the houses of Delhi and Kanauj constant wars occurred. Jaya Chandra, the Râhtaur, chief of Kanauj, celebrated the Asvamedha, or horse sacrifice, and the feud was increased by Prithivi Râja of Delhi carrying off in open day the Râhtaur princess, who threw herself into the arms of her lover. A quarrel between the Râjas of Delhi and Mahoba led to an invasion of Bundelkhand, and to the annihilation of the Chandel monarchy, which was supported in the struggle by a contingent from Kanauj. Thus weakened, the Hindu houses of Upper India were in no position to resist the attacks of the Musalmâns under their king Muhammad bin Sâm. In his first campaign in 1191 A.D. he was defeated by the

Hindu monarch on the plain of Pânipat, where the fortunes of India were so often decided. Two years after he returned, defeated Prithivi Râja, captured Delhi, and next year the tide of battle turned on Kanauj. The decisive battle was fought at Chandwâr in the ravines of the Jumna in the Agra district. Another legend fixes the scene of the death of the Hindu king at Benares. We are told that his corpse was recognised by the gold stopping of his teeth.

Thus the last great Hindu monarchy of northern India ended in ruin. Eighteen years after, the grandsons of their monarch, with a scanty troop of followers, abandoned the land of their birth and journeyed into the western desert to avoid the hated invader. Like Aeneas of old in the Roman story, they founded another kingdom in Mârwâr, which played an important part in the later history of India, and their descendants are its lords to the present day. A princess of the house, Jodh Bâi, became the wife of the Emperor Jahângîr.

Here we may pause to consider the architectural remains which are left of the period of Hindu domination. As has been already said, there is nothing in the way of a stone or brick building which can at present be proved to be older than the time of Asoka, or the latter part of the third century B.C. The explanation of this is probably to be found in the fact that the earlier buildings were constructed of wood, as is the case to this day in Burma.

The buildings of the Buddhist period have been classified by Dr J. Ferguson as—Lâts or pillars; Stûpas or sepulchral mounds; Rails; Chaityas or assembly halls; Vihâras or monasteries. Of all of these numerous interesting remains exist in the Province. We have the pillars of Asoka already enumerated—Stûpas at Sarnâth near Benares; Kasiya in Gorakhpur; Sahet Mahet in Gonda and many other places; the Buddhist cave at Pabhosa near Allahâbâd; the Vihâra at Sarnâth; the Jatavana Vihâra, one of the eight most celebrated Buddhist buildings in India, at Sahet Mahet; the fragments of the Buddhist railing found at Mathura. Putting aside as at present inconclusively proved the identification of the sites of the birth and death of the Teacher in the

Gorakhpur and Basti districts, it is at least quite certain that at Bhuila Dih, Khirnipur, Maghar, Râmpur Deoriya, Barhi, Chetiyâon, Kasiya, Rudrapur and Sohanâg, we have a series of sites connected with the faith and extensive ruins, images and buildings, which, when their secret is finally solved, will throw enormous light upon the origin, development, and final destruction of Buddhism in northern India. The same is the case with Mathura, Benares, Sankisa, Kausambi, Bihâr, and many other places.

In remains of the early Brâhmanical and Jaina periods there are also vast materials which await investigation at places like Benares, Karanbâs, Soron, Chitrakût, Rudrapur, Khukhundu, Ajudhya, Ahichhatra, and many other sites.

But though the Archæological Survey has done much to elucidate the early history of the country, it is needless to say that much still remains to be accomplished. Even in the more famous sites the amount of excavation already done has been quite inadequate. It is true that the Vandalism of past generations, which permitted the sale of the marbles of Agra, the removal of the inlaid pictures of the Delhi palace, the destruction of carvings and statues by railway contractors, has been checked, and something has been done to protect and repair the best surviving examples of the architecture of the Mughals. At the same time it is certain that our Government has never risen to a sense of its Imperial responsibilities in this matter. Its own buildings, in their incongruity and tastelessness, are a standing reproach to the administration. It has doled out insignificant sums for archæological research with a niggard hand, while all over the Province immense stores of priceless material lie hid beneath the surface, awaiting the spade of the explorer.

One point may be noted in connection with the sacred buildings of the Hindus—their comparatively small size. It has been said that the limited size of these temples is the result of Musalmân oppression, which enforced the construction of religious edifices of modest dimensions. This is obviously incorrect. The Hindu so-called temple has no analogy to the stately fanes of the western world. The shrine is intended merely for the accommodation of the idol and its officiant priests, not for the attendance of crowds of worshippers, like St Peter's or Westminster Abbey; nor, as is the case with our churches, are they used for the performance of ceremonies, such as marriage or for the disposal of the dead. In this they resemble the Temple of the Jews, which according to Dr Ferguson was only 150 feet in length, breadth and height. So the Govind Deva temple at Brindaban, erected in an era when the liberal policy of Akbar encouraged the construction of splendid temples, is in the form of a Greek cross, the length and breadth of the nave being only one hundred feet, half the length of the transept of Westminster. But in these Hindu shrines the limitation of the floor area and height, as compared with those of the great Christian churches, is made up for by the wealth of decoration which has been lavished on every inch of the surface.

In winding up the history of these Hindu dynasties we have anticipated the course of events. Under Musalmân rule the history of the Province is more or less that of India; and we can only touch on the main incidents so far as they directly influenced the fortunes of the people.

It was in his ninth raid that Mahmûd of Ghazni (A.D. 1016), fifty years before the Norman Conquest, reached the Province. He passed down the Duâb, where he found Baran, the modern Bulandshahr, ruled by Haradatta, a Râjput of the Dor sept, who submitted—as the chronicler says—"they proclaimed their anxiety for conversion and their rejection of idols." Thence he went on to Kanauj, then a great city, but its splendour, as far as we can judge from existing remains, was much exaggerated. The thirty miles of circuit, of which a Hindu writer talks, were as unreal as the thirty thousand shops for the sale of betel which are said to have existed within its walls. At any rate in the eyes of the rude invader it was not lacking in magnificence. Mahmûd himself in a letter to the Governor of Ghazni speaks of "a thousand edifices firm as the faith of the faithful, most of them of marble, besides innumerable temples. Nor is it likely that the city has attained its present condition but at the expense of many millions of Dinârs. Nor could such another be constructed under a period of two centuries." With such greed and wonder must the Goths of Alaric have gazed on the temples and treasures of Rome. The Râja, Jayapâl, the Tomar, submitted, became a feudatory of the invader, and was spared.

Thence he went to Mathura, which he calls Maharatu-l-Hind. There, also, to quote the annalist, "he saw a building of exquisite structure, which the inhabitants said had been built not by men but by genii, and there he witnessed practices contrary to the nature of man, and which could not be believed but from evidence of actual sight. The wall of the city was constructed of hard stone, and two gates opened upon the river flowing under the city, which were erected upon strong and lofty foundations to protect them against the floods of the river and rains. On both sides of the river there were a thousand houses to which idol temples were attached, all strengthened from top to bottom with rivets of iron, and all made of masonry work; and opposite to them were other buildings supported on broad wooden pillars to give them strength. In the middle of the city was a temple larger and firmer than the rest, which can neither be described nor painted. The Sultân thus wrote concerning it—'If anyone should wish to construct a building equal to this he would not be able to do it without expending a hundred thousand red Dinârs, and it would occupy two hundred years, even though the most experienced and able workmen were employed.' Among the idols there were five made of red gold, each five yards high, fixed in the air without support. In the eyes of one of these idols were two rubies of such value that if anyone were to sell such as are like them, he would obtain fifty thousand Dinârs. On another was a sapphire purer than water and more sparkling than crystal; the weight was four hundred and fifty Miskâls. The two feet of another idol weighed four thousand and four hundred Miskâls, and the entire quantity of gold yielded by the bodies of these idols was ninety-eight thousand three hundred

Miskâls. The idols of silver amounted to two hundred, but they could not be weighed without breaking them to pieces, and putting them into scales. The Sultân gave orders that all the temples should be burned and levelled with the ground."[1]

Thence he went to Mûnj, which is believed to be lower down the Jumna in Etâwah. There he found a fort full of fighting men. "Some rushed through the breaches on the enemy, and met that death which they no longer endeavoured to avoid; others threw themselves headlong from the walls and were dashed to pieces; others burned themselves in their houses with their wives and children, so that not one of the garrison survived."[2]

Mahmûd returned to Ghazni laden with the spoils of conquered cities. On his way home he captured so many prisoners at Sarsâwa in Sahâranpur that captives sold in his camp at from two to ten Dirhams each, and he brought over five thousand slaves in his train to Ghazni. Mahmûd, with all his ferocity, was a scholar, a patron of literature, and his admiration of the Indian architecture was shown by the splendid buildings with which he adorned his northern capital.

For a century and a half the land had peace, the Panjâb remaining an appanage of the Ghazni kingdom. It was not till 1191 A.D., as has been already mentioned, that Muhammad bin Sâm appeared before Delhi, and three years later Kanauj was overthrown. The Hindu kingdoms had doubtless failed to recover from the raids of Mahmûd, and their internal dissensions left them an easy prey to the invader. He carried fire and sword through the Duâb from Meerut to Benares; the Ganges was no longer an obstacle to the Musalmân arms, and he crossed into Rohilkhand and sacked Budaun. Koil (Aligarh), Atranji Khera, a little lower down the Duâb, Kâlpi on the Jumna, afterwards to become a Muhammadan outpost to facilitate the passage into Central India, and Allahâbâd, all fell before him. At Patiyâli on the old course of the Ganges he erected a strong fort to guard the passage into Rohilkhand. He seems to have met with no serious

[1] Elliot, *History of India*, ii. 44. [2] Briggs, *Ferishtah*, i. 59.

opposition. As the chronicler says of the conquest of Koil: "Those who were wise and acute were converted to Islâm, but those who stood by their ancient faith were slain with the sword."

He had two able lieutenants who aided in the conquest. Bakhtiyâr Khilji led an army into Bengal and reduced Bihâr and eastern Oudh. Mahmûd of Ghazni himself introduced the practice of promoting distinguished Turkish slaves. Shihâb-ud-dîn followed his example, and left his Indian dominions in charge of his viceroy, the slave Kutub-ud-dîn Aibak, and another Turkish slave, Altamsh, succeeded him. It is to the former we owe the magnificent pillar at Delhi, called after him the Kutub Minâr—the tower from which the call of prayer summoned the faithful to worship in the stately mosque close by, with colonnades constructed out of the pillars of a Hindu temple. It became the custom of the early Musalmân conquerors to utilise the edifices of the conquered religion in this way. Thus Altamsh built the mosque at Budaun on the ruins of a Saiva shrine. The mosque at Amroha has still the old Hindu chain hanging from its roof, that at Hathgâon in Fatehpur has been built out of the ruins of four Hindu temples, and the same is the case with Mandâwar in Bijnor, Mahâban and Noh Jhîl in Mathura, Etâwah, Ajudhya, and many other places. In fact, when we remember that to the early Musalmâns the destruction of a Hindu shrine furnished the destroyer with a ready means of building a house for himself on earth as well as in heaven, it is wonderful that so many temples should have survived to our day. Of all the places which they permanently occupied, in Mahoba alone did they spare one of the shrines erected by the Chandel princes, and this probably owed its preservation to its isolated position on a rocky island in the deep waters of the Madan Sâgar lake. Everywhere else "Bel boweth down and Nebo stoopeth" before the ruthless troopers of Central Asia.

We have only scattered notices of the ruin which must have accompanied this destruction of a historic civilisation. When Kutub-ud-dîn captured Budaun we are told that nine hundred queens committed sati. When he seized Kalinjar the annalist tells that "the temples were converted into mosques and abodes of goodness, and the ejaculations of the bead-counters and the voices of the summoners to prayer ascended to the highest heaven, and the very name of idolatry was annihilated."[1] Most significant of all, when Bakhtiyâr Khilji took Bihâr, he found a library of Hindu books, but it was impossible to get them read because "all the men had been killed."

Still his attack was merely a raid, not a permanent conquest, and though iconoclasm and massacre raged through the land, after the tempest of war and rapine the people settled down again to till the fertile soil and enjoy the kindly fruits of the earth. But the memories of this crowning disaster to the Hindu polity still live in the recollection of the people. The heroism of Jaya Chandra and the Banâphar heroes, Alha and Udal, who fought in vain for their race in the hills of Bundelkhand, form the subject of an epic still sung round village fires. Even to this day the respect for the brave Chandel princes is so widely felt that no one dares to beat a drum near the ruins of Mahoba, lest their heroic spirits should be roused to vengeance.

It was in the time of Nâsir-ud-dîn Altamsh that the greatest of oriental travellers, Ser Marco Polo, visited India and recorded his impressions of the southern kingdoms ere yet the Musalmân kings of Delhi, occupied at home with Mughal incursions, had been able to devote time to the conquest of the Deccan. It is one of the misfortunes of literature that the shrewd Venetian did not include northern India in his wanderings. What would we not give for his views of the condition of the country in his time? We miss his graphic pictures of social life. In Malabar "there is never a tailor to cut a coat or stitch it, seeing that everybody goes naked." He tells of the animals who to escape execution are allowed to sacrifice themselves to an idol; of the debtor confined in a holy circle till he payeth what he oweth; of the temple dancing-girls who when the god has partaken remove the viands to be eaten by themselves "with great jollity"; "the

[1] Elliot, *History*, ii. 231.

children that are born here are black enough, but the blacker they are the more they are thought of, so that they become as black as devils"; the way the Brâhmans take omens; the Jogis, some of whom live to one hundred and fifty years of age; the chewing of betel; the monkeys of Comorin, "of such peculiar fashion that you would take them for men"; and so on. This was the first real revelation of the East to western men, and one can fancy the gallant wise explorer convincing his relatives of his identity after an absence of half a century by cutting out the piles of diamonds and precious stones sewn up in his garments, and in an honourable old age describing to a wondering audience the marvels he had seen.

During the period which followed these events the eastern movement of the Râjputs continued. Thus in Oudh the Janwâr sept marched eastward after the fall of Kanauj, and a cadet of the clan crossed the Ghâgra and founded the Ikauna Râj, now included in the principality of Balrâmpur. Then followed the Dikhits from Gujarât, who were settled from Kanauj. They were closely followed by a contingent of the blue-blooded Chauhâns from Mainpuri and by the Raikwârs, who left their home in Kashmîr in the beginning of the fifteenth century. It was about the middle of the thirteenth century that the powerful Bais clan, lords of southern Oudh, settled at Dundiya Khera on the lower Ganges. They came from Rajputâna, where they are said to have conquered the powerful Râja Vikramaditya of Ujjain, and they received from the lords of Argal in the lower Ganges-Jumna Duâb the broad fat lands they now hold in southern Oudh in gratitude for their rescue of a princess of their house from the lust of one of the Musalmân governors of Oudh.

Further east as far as Ghâzipur the same tale is told of an emigration of the septs to escape the detested invader, and of the long struggle which gave the Râjputs mastery over the Bhar and the Suiri, the Pâsi and the Arakh, Dravidian races which ruled the land from the time of the overthrow of the early Aryan civilisation. It was possibly the fact that the

Râjput tribes were but new-comers and recent conquerors of the low caste peoples that accounts for the feeble resistance they offered to the Musalmân inroad.

This eastward advance of the Râjputs has continued into quite recent times. The later lords of Agra and Delhi with whom the conciliation of and alliance with the Râjputs became a settled policy in substitution for the older programme of persecution and repression, encouraged bands of western settlers to colonise the rich plains of Oudh and the Duâb, and completed the land settlement of the country which has lasted to our day. Later still the Chandel and Gaharwâr clans gained the mastery over the Dravidian Kols and Mânjhis of the broken hilly tract between the lower course of the Son and Ganges in Bundelkhand and Mirzapur.

To return to the Musalm n conquest, the Slave dynasty reigned at Delhi from about the beginning to near the end of the thirteenth century (1206-1290 A.D.). The greatest king of this line, Altamsh, had by the time of his death, in 1236 A.D., brought the whole Province—Bengal, Rajputâna, and Sindh—under his authority. He it was whose independence was first recognised by the Khalîfa of Bâgdâd, the overlord of Islâm, a dynasty which but a short time before had lost all but the semblance of power under the attack of the Tâtars. The Slave dynasty had to contend with constant internal revolt and the pressure of Mughal raids from the north-west. The last but one of the line, Balban, was obliged practically to reconquer the Duâb. Of his cruelty to the Hindus we have most ghastly narratives. We are told that the gates of his palace were decorated with the skins of captives, who would seem to have been slaughtered for the purpose. As William the Conqueror devastated Yorkshire from the Humber to the Tees, so Balban converted the country for forty miles round Delhi into a preserve for the larger game. His stern measures of repression followed the lines of the instructions of the Roman Emperor Gallienus to his lieutenant in Illyricum.[1] When Katehr or Rohilkhand rebelled, to use the words of the chronicler, "sending forward a force of five

[1] Gibbon, *Decline and Fall*, i. 412.

thousand archers, he gave them orders to burn Katehr and destroy it, to slay every man, and spare none but women and children, nay, not even boys who had reached the age of eight or nine years. The blood of the Hindus ran in streams, heaps of slain were to be seen near every village and jungle, and the stench of the dead reached as far as the Ganges. This severity spread dismay among the rebels, and many submitted. The whole district was ravaged, and so much plunder was made that the royal army was enriched and the people of Budaun were satisfied. Wood-cutters were sent out to cut roads through the jungles, and the army passing along these brought the Hindus to submission. From that time to the end of the glorious reign no rebellion made head in Katehr.[1]

The Slave dynasty of Delhi was succeeded by the house of Khilji (1290-1320 A.D.). The founder of the dynasty, Jalâl-ud-dîn Fîroz Shâh, was treacherously murdered at Karra, near Allahâbâd, in 1295 A.D., by his nephew, Alâ-ud-dîn Muhammad Shâh, the ablest of his line, who, between repelling a Mughal invasion at Delhi and extending the Musalmân Empire in southern India, was too much occupied to find leisure for local politics. His restless career closed in 1315 A.D., and the Khilji house was overcome by the rebellion of another Turki slave, Ghayâs-ud-din Tughlak, who built, perhaps, the most impressive of all Musalmân edifices, the Cyclopean walls of his new capital at Tughlakâbâd, near Delhi. His successor, Muhammad Tughlak, a curious compound of scholar, warrior, and relentless tyrant, a planner of wild schemes of conquest in Persia and China, but who possessed some dim idea of the necessity of a settled revenue system, spent his reign (1324-51 A.D.) in fighting the Mughal invaders and suppressing revolts, the result of his own insane cruelty and maladministration. The cessation of pilgrim records during the Khilji and Tughlak times at shrines like Soron is silent evidence of the character of their rule.

His son, Fîroz Tughlak (1351-88 A.D.) pursued the same policy. The chronicler tells us how he instructed his lieu-

[1] Elliot, *History*, iii. 105.

tenant, Malik Dâûd, an Afghân, to remain at Sambhal in Rohilkhand, and "to invade the country of Katehr every year, to commit every kind of ravage and desolation, and not to allow it to be inhabited till the rebel Kargu was given up. The king himself, also under the pretence of hunting, marched annually in that direction to see that his orders were fulfilled, and to do what Malik Dâûd had left undone; and for six years not an inhabitant was to be seen in the district, nor was a single acre of the land cultivated." [1]

At the same time he was a great builder, and to him was due the beginning of canal irrigation in northern India. The Jumna Canal was his work. He was the builder of Fîrozâbâd, now a pile of ruins on the outskirts of Delhi, which he ornamented with one of the pillars of Asoka; and to him is due the conversion of the Atala Devi temple at Jaunpur into a stately mosque. But he did nothing to strengthen and organise the government, and ten years after his death (1398 A.D.) the terrible raid of Timûr broke over the country.

After defeating Mahmûd Tughlak under the walls of Delhi, Timûr captured and sacked the capital. Then crossing the Jumna he pillaged Meerut, and massacred in the Hardwâr gorge an enormous crowd of Hindus, who had retreated there in the vain hope of saving their lives. His own Memoirs give the most vivid pictures of these terrible events. Of one fight on the Ganges, in Muzaffarnagar, he writes: "I mounted my horse, and taking with me one thousand troops who were at hand, we struck our heels into the flanks of our horses and hastened to the side of the river. As soon as my braves saw the boats, some of them rode their horses into the river and swam to the vessels; then seizing fast hold of the sides, they defeated all the efforts of the Hindus to shake them off. They forced their way into some of the boats, put the infidels to the sword, and threw their bodies into the river, thus sending them through water to the fires of hell. Some of my men dismounted, and proceeding to the ford, assaulted the enemy with arrows. The occupants

[1] Elliot, *History*, vi. 229; Briggs, *Ferishtah*, i. 457.

of the boats returned the arrows, but the vessels were at length wrested from their possession, and were brought with their contents to my presence. The enemy had lashed ten of their boats together with chains and strong ropes, and these vessels maintained the fight. My men plied them with arrows till they slew many of them; they then swam off, and, boarding the boats, put every living soul to the sword, sending them through water to the fires of hell." [1] So we find in the story of the Meerut raid another familiar incident. When he ordered an assault, "many of the Râjputs placed their wives and children in the houses and burned them; then they rushed to the battle and were killed." When, again, he tells of the massacre at Hardwâr, he says: "Spurring their horses, shouting their war-cry, and brandishing their swords, they fell upon the forces of the enemy like hungry lions on a flock of sheep." [2]

It is impossible to exaggerate the misery caused to an unwarlike people by savage raids like those of Shihâb-ud-dîn and Timûr. They rank with the deeds of the Spaniards in Peru or Mexico, or a foray of Kurds or Turkomâns in our day.

The Delhi kingdom never recovered from this supreme disaster. Henceforward the Mughal supremacy was inevitable. But this was not to be till a century and a quarter more had passed in decadence and misrule.

The most noteworthy figure in the interval is that of Sikandar Lodi (1488-1517 A.D.), about the period between the accession of Henry VII. and Luther's break with Rome. He was a soldier and a statesman, and re-established his authority over the province and Bihâr. But he was a bigot of the most extreme type. He has left his name in the towns of Sikandra Râo in Aligarh, and Sikandrâbâd in the Bulandshahr district. Near the latter place, at Shikârpur, he had his hunting lodge, a fertile plain now watered by the Ganges Canal, which must in those days have been an extensive jungle. The mound which covers the ruins of his lodge

[1] Elliot, *History*, ii. 453.

[2] *Ibid.*, iv. 25; iii. 455, 513. The authenticity of these Memoirs has been disputed, but Professor Dowson accepts them.

is suggestively known to the peasant of our days as Anyâi Khera, or "the tyrant's mound." He completed the work of Shihâb-ud-dîn at Mathura by destroying all its temples. He also left his mark at another holy city, Soron, by demolishing its most sacred shrine.

But his most important act was the transfer of the capital from Delhi to Agra, which marks the increasing importance of the Duâb, now that the Panjâb was practically lost.

It was in the time of his son Ibrahîm that the dynasty of Delhi ended, by his defeat and death at the battle of Pânipat, which left northern India at the mercy of Bâbar and his Mughals. Why it fell is stated by the embassage of nobles which came out to meet the conqueror: "Sultân Ibrahîm ill-treats his father's nobles, and has put twenty of them, the supporters of his kingdom, to death, without any cause, and ruined their families. He has suspended some from walls, and has caused others to be burned alive. When many of the nobles saw that they could hope for no safety from him, they sent me to your presence. They are all ready to obey you, and look with anxiety to your coming."[1]

The Mughals are the well-known Mongols of Central Asia. The poet Khusru had the ill luck to fall in with them, and his account represents what the effeminate Indian Musalmâns of his day thought about them. He speaks about them in the tone which Bailie Nicol Jarvie would speak of Rob Roy. "There were more than a thousand Tartars riding on camels, great commanders in war, all with steel-like bodies, clothed in cotton, faces like fire, with caps of sheepskin on shaven heads. Their eyes were so sharp, they might have bored a hole in a brass pot; their smell was more horrible than their colour; their faces were set on their bodies as if they had no necks; their cheeks were like empty leathern bottles, full of knots and wrinkles; their noses extended from cheek to cheek, their mouths from ear to ear; their mustaches were of extravagant length; they had but scanty beards about their chins; their chests were covered with vermin, and their skin rough like shagreen; they ate dogs and pigs."[2]

[1] Elliot, *History*, v. 24.

[2] *Ibid.*, ii., *Appendix*.

Bâbar is the first character in Indian history of whom we can claim any personal knowledge. His Memoirs are nearly as naïve and amusing as those of Mr Pepys. He has been called a mixture of Henri Quatre and the Roi d'Yvetot; but this rather exaggerates the festive side of his character, and his confessions of his love for wine. He was a man of infinite observation; he had a sharp eye for scenery and the world of nature; he was a keen observer of humanity, and made curious ethnological enquiries and suggestions unknown to the men of his time. By Europeans he would have been regarded as distinctly a good fellow, and his personal tastes inclined him rather to the more polished Persians than to his own rude kindred. His life was spent in wandering, in war, in sport, so that he says he never kept the Ramazân fast twice in any one place. Even in his later days, without any particular reason for dispatch, he rode from Kâlpi to Agra, 160 miles, and swam the Ganges twice. He died at Agra three years after his great victory, and his body rests at Kâbul.

Of Hindustân he formed a poor opinion. "It is a country," he says, "that has little to recommend it. The inhabitants are not good looking; they have no ideas of social pleasures or of friendly intercourse; they have no genius or comprehensive ability, no polish of manner, amiability or sympathetic feeling; no ingenuity or mechanical inventiveness; no architectural skill or knowledge; they have no decent houses, ice, or cold water; their markets are not well supplied; they have neither public baths nor colleges; neither candles nor candlesticks. If you want to read or write at night, you must have a filthy fellow standing over you with a flaring torch."

We must turn back to describe another kingdom which arose in the eastern portion of the province after Timûr's raid. In 1388 A.D., Malik Sarwar Khwâja, a eunuch who had become Wazîr at Delhi, was deputed by Muhammad Tughlak to govern the eastern Province, which extended from Kanauj to Bihâr. In 1393-94, this ambitious upstart, taking advantage of the disorder of the country, proclaimed his independence and called himself Sultân-us-shark, or the Eastern Emperor. Six kings in succession occupied the throne of Jaunpur, with the control of the eastern part of the Province and Oudh. The most noted member of the family was Ibrahîm Shâh Sharki, whose reign of thirty-nine years (1401-40 A.D.) was spent in a long struggle with the Delhi kings for the possession of Kanauj and Kâlpi on the Jumna. In these projects he was for the most part unsuccessful; but he ruled over a splendid tract of country from Kanauj to Bihâr, and from Bahraich in North Oudh to Etâwah. The Jaunpur kings, in contrast to their Delhi rivals, were great builders. The only Delhi monuments of this period are tombs at Delhi and Budaun; the Jaunpur kings were simply laid to rest in the open air, but they adorned their capital with a series of splendid mosques and a noble fort. They were equally great iconoclasts, as every mosque is built on the site of a Hindu temple. The grandest of these mosques is the Atala Masjid, erected on the site of a temple of Atala Devi, said to be the work of Jaya Chandra, the last Râhtaur king of Kanauj. This magnificent building was completed in 1408 A.D. Larger, but of less architectural beauty, is the Jâmi Masjid or Cathedral Mosque, which was completed about seventy years later. Of the fort, only the ruins remain, the walls having been needlessly demolished after the Great Mutiny. The fine stone bridge over the Gumti river was the work of the Mughal governor in the time of Akbar.

In 1477-78, Husain Shâh, the sixth monarch of the line, having made ineffectual efforts to resist Bahlol Lodi, the King of Delhi, was defeated in a great battle at Kâlpi on the Jumna. Flying to Kanauj, he was again defeated, lost all his western dominions, and his capital was seized. But Husain was permitted to live there as a dependent and complete his Cathedral Mosque.

If we date, then, the effective establishment of a Musalmân dynasty at Delhi at the very end of the twelfth century, we find that, up to the Mughal conquest in the first quarter of the sixteenth, a period which roughly corresponds to the age from the accession of King John to the fall of Wolsey, the Delhi kingdom had altogether failed to secure complete control over the Province. We read of raids, wars, and insurrections; the kings exhibited at the capital a certain rude magnificence, while viceroys ruled the more distant provinces, and often took occasion from the disasters which overtook their lords to assume temporary independence.

But of the people we hear nothing, and no records exist to show how they lived, what revenue they paid, how order was maintained, how justice was administered. With a much smaller population the pressure on the soil was much less intense than is the case at present. At the same time the repeated famines which devastated the land show that a terrible amount of misery must have existed. The petty local Râjas doubtless continued to hold the country as dependents of the Delhi suzerain, or his lieutenants. The village organisation, with its priest, its watchman, its artizans, and at the top of all, the Râjput headman, under the local Râja, must have gone on much as it does at present. This social life withstood the tyranny and maladministration of the overlord, not so much perhaps because in itself, except in the kinship of the members of the clan, it possessed elements of permanence, but because the wants of the people were so few, and their accumulated capital so small, that, after the tempest of war was overpast, the peasant was able to re-establish his meagre household, though one of his stalwart bread-winners may have fallen before the lance of a Tâtar trooper, or his daughter had been swept away within the walls of a harem at Agra or Delhi.

To illustrate some of the phases of the gradual progress of the Musalmân conquest, we may take the case of Rohilkhand, which was in the days before artillery protected from invasion on the west by the broad stream of the Ganges.

It began with the raid of Shihâb-ud-dîn in 1194 A.D. In 1252 A.D., Nâsir-ud-dîn Mahmûd again invaded it, and directed an attack "such that the inhabitants might not forget for the rest of their lives." In 1266 Balban appeared, and we have already described the vigour of his proceedings.

In 1290 Fîroz II. arrived, and the Musalmâns "made their swords red with the blood of the Hindus; whatever live Hindu fell into the king's hands was pounded into bits under the feet of the elephants. The Musalmâns who were country born had their lives spared, and were distributed among the chiefs as slaves." In 1380 A.D. there was another rebellion. "The Emperor's justice," the chronicler admits, "in this instance degenerated into extreme cruelty. Neither did the misfortunes of these miserable captives satisfy his thirst for revenge. He returned every year under pretence of hunting to that unhappy country; but the people, and not the beasts of the forest, were his prey. He by degrees cut off all the inhabitants, and converted whole provinces into wildernesses." It was not till 1424 A.D., after nearly two centuries of conflict, that the Hindu leaders surrendered, and the country was pacified. When we remember the short distance of Rohilkhand from Delhi, this throws a lurid light on the incapacity of the Delhi kings. Under much more difficult circumstances, the pacification of Upper Burma was concluded by the British in less than a decade.

In Oudh the course of events was very similar. The story begins with the romantic tale of Sâlâr Masaud, which has become so shrouded in the mists of legend that it is difficult to judge where myth ends and sober history begins. He is said to have been nephew of Mahmûd of Ghazni; to have led his forces as far as Ajudhya; then to have sacked Meerut and reduced Kanauj, Mathura, and Benares. He is supposed to have met his death at Bahraich in Northern Oudh, in 1033 A.D. Some of the Musalmân settlements, which were the agency in the spread of the faith, are alleged to date from this time. But even his very existence has been doubted, and according to some authorities he is little more than the hero of a solar myth. He has now been deified under the title of Ghâzi Miyân, the counterpart of Krishna and Narcissus, the divine youth snatched from the joys of earth in the prime of boyish beauty. In this form, he claims the devotion of one and three-quarter millions of people in the Province.

Most of the Oudh colonies, planted on the Roman system to coerce a subject population, date from a later period. Such were the Sayyid colony at Jarwal in Bahraich, the Shaikhs of Bilgrâm and Gopamau in Hardoi in the thirteenth, the Sayyids of Birhar, in Faizâbâd, at the end of the fourteenth, and the Shaikhs of Malânwân, in Hardoi, in the beginning of the fifteenth centuries.

Many of the existing towns throughout the Province, not to mention the Imperial or provincial capitals, like Agra, Lucknow, or Jaunpur, owe their importance to having been early seats of the local Musalmân governors. Such are Sahâranpur, in the Upper Duâb, and lower down, Farrukhâbâd and Ghâzipur; in Rohilkhand, Bareilly, Shâhjahânpur, Budaun, Râmpur, and Morâdâbâd; in Oudh, Bahraich, and Faizâbâd; in Bundelkhand, Bânda. Many of these Musalmân towns, in the good old days, supplied a large proportion of our native officials. But the Hindu, with his aptitude for English education, has proved a dangerous competitor. The lanes become more and more deserted, the fine brick mansions more and more dilapidated; and if ruin is to be avoided, the attitude of the Musalmân towards the new learning must undergo a radical change.

On the death of Bâbar, his son Humayun succeeded to the throne. He was then at the age of twenty-two, and the young, inexperienced monarch soon found himself opposed by a master in statecraft—the Afghân Shîr Shâh. He headed the reaction of the Hindustâni Musalmâns against the Mughals. Humayun led a force eastward and captured Chunâr, the strong fortress on an outlying scarp of the Vindhyan range, which commands the lower course of the Ganges. But he was out-manœuvred by his adversary in the plains of Bengal. By the compromise with his brother Kamrân, he had surrendered Kâbul, and thus lost the advantage of reinforcements of hardy mountaineers. Humayun himself was of voluptuous disposition, an opium eater, and the Indian Plains proved to be the Capua which demoralised his forces. In the ninth year of his reign he was defeated in a decisive battle at Chaunsa, near the Karamnâsa river, just beyond the limits of the Province; and the next campaign ending in another defeat at Kanauj, he was compelled to fly across the western desert, where his son Akbar was born, and thence to Persia.

To the extraordinary man who had driven Humayun from the throne, it can hardly be said that the ordinary histories do sufficient justice. Himself an adventurer from the Afghân hills, he learned the details of administration in Bihâr. He was the first Musalmân ruler who studied the good of his people. He had the genius to see that the government must be popularised, that the king must govern for the benefit of his subjects, that the Hindus must be conciliated by a policy of justice and toleration, that the land revenue must be settled on an equitable basis, that the material development of the country must be encouraged. All this and more Akbar strove to do later on; but Shîr Shâh was the first who attempted to found an Indian empire "broad-based upon the people's will."

He carried a great military road from Bengal to the Indus, and it was he first who established Sarâis or hostelries, which opened up trade throughout the empire. His revenue system was, for the first time, based upon the measurement of the land and calculation of the produce. He relaxed the oppressive Muhammadan law code, and provided for the administration of justice. That he introduced such extensive reforms in his short reign of five years—interrupted as it was by campaigns against Rajputâna, in the course of which he met his death—is a wonderful proof of his executive ability. "No government, not even the British, has shown so much wisdom as this Pathân," is Mr Keene's summary of his career. He was killed by the accidental explosion of a magazine at the siege of Kalinjar, in Bundelkhand, in 1545; and though his son Islâm Shâh carried on to some extent the wise policy of his father, he alienated the nobility by his cruelty, and when he died, in the ninth year of his reign, the road was open for the return of Humayun from exile.

He was only forty-eight years old when he was restored. But he was wearied, and in indifferent health; the vicissitudes of his career had taught him the uncertainty of human greatness; he was unfit for great enterprises. Perhaps he found in religion a solace for his troubles. At any rate, he was killed by a fall on the steps of his palace at Delhi, as he rose to obey the call to prayer. His remains rest in a noble mausoleum, where, by the irony of fate, the last degenerate princes of his line, stained with the innocent blood of helpless Europeans, fell by the sword of Hodson.

The life of his successor, Akbar, is the history of India during his long reign of forty-nine years (1556-1605 A.D.), and his personality stands high, even when compared with his great contemporaries—Elizabeth of England and Philip II. of Spain. In his courage and strength, his love of sport, and knightly exercises, he was curiously like another notable prince of the same age—Henri IV. of Navarre. He was only thirteen when, with the aid of the gallant Bairâm Khân, he crumpled up the Afghân host, on the historic field of Pânipat. It is a curious sign of the degeneracy of the Hindustâni Musalmâns that they had to accept as their leader Hemu, who, brave as he was, was a Banya or corn-chandler, a caste rarely endowed with military prowess.

When his rule was thus established, the later life of Akbar falls, as Mr Keene has shown, into three periods.—"During the first, which lasted about fifteen years, he was much occupied with war, field sports, and building; and the men by whom he was ultimately influenced were still at that time young, like himself. Opinions were forming; territorial and administrative operations were in hand. About 1576 began a second period, marked by the arrival of certain Shiahs and other persons of heretical opinions from Persia, and the growth of their influence over Akbar. At the same time the emperor, now in the maturity of his intellect, turned his attention to the Hindus, and to the amelioration and establishing of the revenue system, by which they were so much affected. This period lasted for about fifteen years, and was followed by that sadder period when, as must happen, except under exceptional circumstances, men in power grow old without having found competent successors. In such conditions originality drivels into cant and caution withers into decay. One by one the reformers, a few years since so full of hope and vigour, drop into senility, or, more fortunate, into the tomb. No one is left but some lover of letters who, wiser than the rest, retires betimes into the shade to prepare the record of departed greatness."

Let us endeavour to sketch the state of the country in his time. That, in spite of the prevailing disorder, there was a considerable amount of prosperity is certain. Bâbar, though he writes with a backward glance at the bleak hill country of his birth, speaks of Hindustân as a rich and noble country, abounding in gold and silver; and he expresses astonishment at the swarming population, and the innumerable workmen in every trade and industry. That there was much waste and jungle where we now see smiling fields is clear. The chronicler writes: "It had become manifest to Akbar that much of the culturable land of Hindustân was lying uncultivated; and, to encourage cultivation, some rule for dividing the profit of the first year between Government and the proprietor seemed to be required."[1] Bernier, writing in 1664, in the reign of Aurangzeb, says that in the neighbourhood of Agra and Delhi, along the course of the Jumna reaching to the mountains, and even on both sides of the road leading to Lahore, there was a large quantity of uncultivated land, covered either with copse wood or with grasses six feet high.[2]

We know that, for instance, in Bulandshahr and Shâhjahânpur, the plains, now green with wheat and sugar-cane, were occupied by extensive jungles. According to the Aîn-i-Akbari, the cultivation in Azamgarh amounted to 106,005 acres, and the revenue was R.x. 25,264. The present cultivated area is 587,797 acres, and the revenue R.x. 165,810. We really know too little of the purchasing power of money in those days to make any trustworthy comparison. As the Settlement Officer, Mr J. R. Reid, writes: "What trust is to be placed in the figures of the Aîn-i-Akbari it is difficult to say. Probably they understate the areas rather than

[1] Elliot, *History*, v. 383.   [2] Constable's Edition, p. 375.

exaggerate them. . . . In respect to the revenue recorded in the Aîn-i-Akbari, it may be questioned whether it was not an ideal assessment, and whether it was ever collected for the State. We have also to bear in mind that Akbar professedly took one-third of the average value of the land. In our day the Azamgarh cultivator cannot pay that and live. Moreover, we profess to take half the rent that the landlord or middleman realises, or ought to realise, from the actual cultivator. To judge by our figures, our present revenue arrangements are, with reference to the fall in the value of silver, less favourable to the State than were those of Akbar. But we scarcely know enough of the domestic history of the population in the latter's time to draw a comparison between its condition and that of the population at the present day."[1]

We may with advantage leave Akbar's revenue system to be discussed in another place. It is easy to see on what grounds the fame of Akbar as a statesman is based. He was the first of the Indian rulers, with perhaps the exception of Shîr Shâh, who accepted the responsibilities of government as we understand it. Before his time nothing that can be called a civilised administration existed. This he found time to establish, though much of his life was spent in war. He was the first ruler who displayed a spirit of tolerance and a desire to improve the condition of his Hindu subjects. How his predecessors treated them is graphically described by the annalist of Fîroz Shâh. "When the Collector of the Dîwân asks the Hindus to pay the tax, they should pay it with all humility and submission; and if the Collector wishes to spit in their mouths, they should open their mouths without the slightest fear of contamination, so that the Collector may do so. In this state, with their mouths open, they should stand before the Collector. The object of such humiliation and spitting into their mouths is to prove the obedience of the infidel subjects under protection, and to promote the glory of the Islâm, the true religion, and to show contempt to false religions."[2]

[1] *Azamgarh Settlement Report*, p. 176.

[2] Blochmann, *Aîn-i-Akbari*, i. 237.

In direct contrast to this, which it may be hoped was only a counsel of perfection, Akbar showed extreme consideration for Hindus. For instance, one result of his visit to Brindaban in Mathura, accompanied by a train of Hindu princes, was his permission or advice for the erection of the group of splendid temples, the finest examples of Hindu architecture in the Province. He interdicted on certain occasions the use of beef, which the modern British Government dares not propose. He made careful rules to prohibit injury to the peasants' crops by the horde of followers which thronged his camps. He married at least one Hindu princess, the daughter of Râja Bihâri Mal, the Kachhwâha Râjput, who was the mother of his successor Jahângîr. He employed a host of Hindu officers both in the army and the Civil Service. Bernier, writing at a later date, describes in detail the objects of this policy—to utilise the large Râjput contingents as auxiliaries; to keep in check other Râjas not in the Emperor's pay; to foment jealousy between those whom he favoured and their brethren; to coerce the Pathâns or rebellious governors; to oppose the Persians who were of the Shiah sect and opposed to the Mughals, who were Sunnis.[1] Râja Todar Mal, a Khatri of Laharpur in Oudh, was his chief revenue officer; Râja Bîrbal, a needy Bhât or genealogist of Etâwah, became his Wazîr, and round him and his learned daughter a large cycle of modern folk-lore has collected.

But granting all this, and fully admitting the enormous advance in the principles of Government which he effected, no one who reads the Aîn-i-Akbari, the cyclopædic annals of his rule, can fail to be conscious of a certain lack of departmental perspective. Akbar, it is needless to say, was a master of detail: but here detail is pushed to the extreme. We find careful accounts of the organisation of the camp and household, the stable and wardrobe, the armoury and the hunting establishment. For all these rules are prescribed with the greatest minuteness; but it is everywhere assumed that the control of business depends on the compilation of appropriate registers, which is one of the besetting delusions

[1] *Travels*, p. 210.

of the native official of our days. On the other hand, we learn little of the essentials of administration as we understand it—about the police and judicial services, the development of the national resources, the relief of famine, education and medical aid. We would give much of the Aîn-i-Akbari, valuable and amusing as it is, for one Census or Settlement Report, with its elaborate statistics and full information regarding the social condition of the people. But no contemporary government thought it part of its duty to put its proceedings on record for the instruction of posterity.

What Gibbon says of the Antonines may be said of Akbar —"The labours of these monarchs were overpaid by the immense reward that inseparably waited on their success, by the honest pride of virtue, and by the exquisite delight of beholding the general happiness of which they were the authors. A just but melancholy reflection embittered, however, the noblest of human enjoyments. They must often have recollected the instability of a happiness which depended on the happiness of a single man. The fatal moment was perhaps approaching when some licentious youth or some jealous tyrant would abuse to the destruction that absolute power which they had exerted for the benefit of the people."[1]

So it was with the Mughals. Their system of education and training entirely failed to maintain a line of promising heirs-apparent. Humayun was an opium eater; Akbar's son Dâniyâl died of delirium tremens; his nephew Kaikobâd was addicted to drugs; Salîm, the heir-apparent, was the slave of wine and opium. Akbar himself, it is said, could neither read nor write, and his immediate descendants, when they were educated at all, were trained in the old Musalmân style—the recitation of the Korân, quibbles of theology, the dull verbiage of legal subtleties were their mental food. In early boyhood they lived amidst the vain gossip and squalid intrigues of vicious women who filled the harem. As they grew up, the jealousy of rival queens forbade their taking a leading part in the politics of the capital. The herd of

[1] *Decline and Fall*, i. 217.

knavish flatterers and adventurers, the palace gang, were averse to their acquiring a competent knowledge of administration. A prince who took his proper part in the council of the State was suspected of intriguing against the monarch; so he was often packed off to a distant province, where the same influences opposed his training. The local viceroy acted as his bear-leader, and took care to hoodwink him and prevent him from meddling in the conduct of affairs. He was better pleased to see him waste his time in dissipation than to educate him in statecraft. The case has ever been the same among societies organised on the polygamous plan —in Imperial Rome, Teheran, or at the Yildiz Kiosk in our time. Hereditary succession, in short, is only tolerable under a system where the responsibility falls on a Ministry, which screens the viciousness or incompetence of the occupant of the throne.

Such a Ministry the Mughals were never able to organise. Deprived of the assistance of the princes of the blood royal, the monarch was obliged to fall back on the mob of adventurers who crowded round his Darbâr. Even the best of these, men like Abul Fazl or Faizi at the court of Akbar, were of the dilettante type, literateurs, minor poets, dabblers in religion and philosophy, destitute of any defined principle, whose function was more to amuse their master than to act as a modern Cabinet or Council of State. Bernier, a very shrewd observer, says: "The Omrahs, therefore, mostly consist of adventurers from distant nations, who entice one another to the Court, and are generally persons of low descent, some having been originally slaves, and the majority being destitute of education. The Mogol raises them to dignities or degrades them to obscurity, according to his own pleasure and caprice."[1] Again he tells us that situations of trust were filled indifferently by Mughals and strangers from all countries, "the greater part by Persians, some by Arabs, and others by Turks. To be considered a Mogol, it is enough if a foreigner have a white face, and profess Mohametanism."[2] Even adventurers from Europe crowded round the

[1] *Travels*, p. 212. [2] *Ibid.*, p. 3.

Court of Akbar. Such was the sordid palace gang which led the last French Empire to destruction.

It was never the Mughal policy to foster the growth of a hereditary aristocracy, or to encourage anything to be compared to an established Church. Islâm in India has always remained politically weak because she has never dreamed of an Episcopate or even of a Convocation. To quote Bernier again: "The Omrahs of Hindustân cannot be proprietors of land or enjoy an independent revenue, like the nobility of France and the other States of Christendom. Their income consists exclusively of pensions, which the King grants or takes away according to his own will or pleasure. When deprived of this pension they sink at once into utter insignificance, and find it impossible to borrow the smallest sum."[1] Hence the main object of every rising man was to obtain a lucrative provincial government, where he could feather his nest, as Verres did in Sicily, or a Turkish or Persian Pasha does to-day in Anatolia or Khorasân.

There was thus a constant tendency, as for instance in the case of Jaunpur or Oudh, for the provincial viceroy to become independent. This was the result of the centralisation of the power and expenditure of the Empire at the capitals, Delhi or Agra. The surplus revenue was spent there in paying the army or carrying on splendid public works, while the Provinces were starved. It is only a bureaucracy of the highest class, like the Roman Senate or the modern Indian government, that can maintain a vigilant control over its outlying provinces. Akbar was, it is true, for a time successful in curbing his Pashas, but it was only because his activity was incessant and his industry unwearied. The example of Philip II. of Spain proved once for all that such a task is beyond the powers of any single man, however clear-sighted and laborious. The results of the same arrangement in weaker hands is seen in the case of Aurangzeb and his successors and in the Turkish and Persian Empires of our own time.

Gibbon fixes the era of the decline of the Roman Empire

[1] *Travels*, p. 65.

in the age of Commodus. When it is asked when the Mughal Empire showed signs of decadence, it may be answered that even in the time of Akbar it could have been saved only by a radical change in the methods of government, by a closer tightening of the bonds which united the provinces, by a wise development of the resources of the country, by the establishment of a competent police and judiciary. That this task was beyond the powers of a genius such as that of Akbar is a lesson which every Englishman in India would do well to remember.

It was the consciousness of this failure and the prescience of trouble in the future which clouded the last years of the great statesman, as the scandals of his family broke the spirit of Augustus. With Akbar the work of practical government gave place to a vain seeking after a creed which he could believe, in disputations about theology with Hindu Pandits, Parsi fire-worshippers, or European Jesuits. Out of these he hoped to work out a new faith, a State religion of which, like Henry VIII., he was to be himself the head, a faith based on natural religion which was to draw both Hindu and Muhammadan within its fold. Such a scheme was from the outset hopeless. Thus the end came at last; the friends of his early days were taken from him one by one; from his own family he could derive no consolation. The gloom of his spirit speaks in the inscription which he, the master builder, graved on the great portal of the mosque at Fatehpur Sikri—"Said Jesus, on whom be peace! The world is a bridge: pass over it, but build no house there; he who hopeth for an hour may hope for an eternity; the world is but an hour, spend it in devotion; the rest is unseen."

The reign of his successor, Jahângîr (1605-27), a period covering a little more than that of our James I., need not detain us long. He spent most of his time beyond the Province, at Ajmîr, Lahore, Delhi, or Kashmîr, and did little in the way of local administration. He was, as we have seen, the son of a Hindu mother. Badly educated and uncontrolled in his youth, with no sage counsellor to guide his early manhood, he fell into indulgence in wine and drugs. Sometimes, as in the case of his eldest son Khusru's revolt, he gave way to horrible cruelty. He thus writes himself of the punishments inflicted on the associates of his unhappy son: "I gave Khusru into custody, and I ordered these two villains to be enclosed in the skins of a cow and an ass, and to be placed on asses, face to the tail, and so to be paraded round the city. As the skin of a cow dries quicker than the skin of an ass, Husain Beg lived only to the fourth watch, and then died. Abdul Azîz, who was in the ass's skin, and had moisture conveyed to him, survived."[1]

The best account of him is that by the English ambassador, Sir Thomas Roe: "The king hath no man but eunuchs that comes within the lodging or retyring room of his house; his women watch within and guard him with manly weapons. He comes every day to the window called the Jaruco (Jharokha) looking into a plain before his gate, and shewes himself to the common people. At noone he returns thither and sits some houres to see the fights of elephants and wilde beasts. Under him within the raile attend the men of ranke; from whence he retyres to sleep among his women. At afternoone he returnes to the Durbar before mentioned. At eight after supper he comes down to the Guzlecan (Ghuslkhâna), a faire court, wherein in the middest is a throne erected of freestone, whereon he sits, but sometimes below in a chaire, to which none are admitted but of first quality, and few without leave, where he discourses of all matters with much affabilitie. There is no business done with him concerning the State, Government, disposition of war and peace, but at one of these two last places, where it is publickly propounded and resolved and so registered; which, if it were worthe the curiositie, might be seene for two shillings; but the common, base people know as much as the Council, and the newes every day or the King's new resolutions, tossed and censured by every rascal. This course is unchangeable, except sicknesse or death prevent it; which must be knowne, for as all his subjects are slaves, so he is in a kinde of reciprocall bondage; for he is tyed to observe these houres and customs

[1] Elliot, *History*, vi. 301.

so precisely that if he were unseene one day and no sufficient reason rendered, the people would mutinie; two days no reason can excuse, but that he must consent to open his doores, and be seene by some to satisfie others. On Tuesday at the Jaruco he sits in judgment, never refusing the poorest man's complaint, where he hearcs with patience both parts and sometimes sees with much delight in blood the execution done by his elephants."

The same writer describes the end of a party given in honour of Muhammad Roza Beg, who had recently arrived as ambassador from Shâh Abbâs, the King of Persia. "The King returned at evening, having been overnight farre gone in wine; some by chance in malice spoke of the merry night past, and that many of the Nobilitie dranke wine, which none may doe but by leave. The King, forgetting his order, demanded who gave it; it was answered, 'The Buxie' (Bakhshi), (for no man dares say it was the King, when he would onely doubt it). The custom is that when the King drinkes (which is alone), sometimes he will command that the Nobilitie shall drink after, which if they do not, it is an offence too, and so that every man who takes the cup of the wine of the officers his name is written, and he makes Teselim (Taslîm), though perhaps the King's eyes are mistie. The King, not remembering his own command, called the Buxie, and demanded if he gave the order. He replyed 'No' (falsely, for he received it and called such by name as did drinke with the Embassadour); whereat the King called for the list and the persons and fined some one, some two, some three thousand rupias, some lesse; and some that were neerer his person he caused to be whipped before him, receiving one hundred and thirty stripes with a most terrible instrument, having at eache end of foure cords irons like spur rowels, so that every stroke made foure wounds. When they lay for dead on the ground, he commanded the standers-by to foot them, and after the Porters to breake their staves upon them. Thus most cruelly mangled and bruised they were carried out, of which one dyed in the place. Some would have excused it on the Embassadour; but the King replyed he only had given him a cup or two. Though drunkennesse be a common and a glorious vice, and an exercise of the King's, yet it is so strictly forbidden, that no man can enter into the Guzelchan where the King sits, but the Porters smell his breath; and if he have but tasted wine is not suffered to come in; and if the reason be known of his absence, he shall with difficulty escape the whip; for if the King once take offence, the father will not speake for the sonne. So the King made the company pay the Persian Embassadour's reward."

In reading the account of this terrible scene, almost as bad as any of the acts of the insane Roman Emperor in his seclusion at Capreæ, we remember what Mr Pepys says of Charles II.: "Sir H. Cholmley tells me that the King hath this good luck, that the next day he hates to have any one mention what he had done the day before, nor will he suffer any one to gain upon him that way."[1]

Yet with all this wild, wilful cruelty, there is something very human about Jahângîr. His Memoirs show the struggles of a weak nature to resist temptation. He has been much blamed for his dealings with Shîr Afgan and his wife, the future Empress Nûr Jahân, a tale which, as commonly told, is one of the mad lust of a tyrant, a story of the type of David and Bathsheba, or Nero and Poppoea Sabina. But, as Mr Keene has shown, the fact that she did not marry Jahângîr till she had been four years a widow puts quite a different complexion upon the case. One of the best points in his character is the love and confidence he lavished upon this lady, who seems to have fully deserved the honour to which she was raised. Her affection for him was some consolation to him for the undutiful conduct of his sons, Khusru and Shâh Jahân, both of whom rebelled against him. Khusru died of cholic in the Deccan; his remains rest under a fine tomb in the Khusru Bâgh at Allahâbâd, where the Anglo-Indian society occasionally meets to dine and dance.

Jahângîr was a mighty hunter. He kept up his game-book carefully, and he tells us that from the age of twelve to

[1] Wheatley, *Pepys' Diary*, vii. 122.

fifty he killed 28,532 animals and birds. This curious bag includes 86 tigers, 889 nîlgâê, 1372 deer, 36 wild buffaloes, and 3276 crows! He must have had considerable taste, as he is said to have remodelled the design of his father's tomb at Sikandra, which shows decided traces of Hindu or Buddhist influence. The beautiful tomb at Agra of Itimâd-ud-daula, father of his queen Nûr Jahân, was apparently completed in the year after the Emperor's death.

Jahângîr died in 1627 A.D., and he and Nûr Jahân, who survived him for many years, are buried at Lahore.

The reign of his successor, Shâh Jahân, familiar to the Europe of his day as The Great Mogul (1628-58 A.D.), includes nearly the period from the commencement of the struggle between Charles I. and his Parliament to the Restoration. He had little influence on local history, save in the erection of his splendid buildings at Agra—the Tâj Mahal, raised as a memorial to his queen, known as Mumtâz-i-Mahal, "the exalted one of the palace," who was niece of Nûr Jahân, bore Shâh Jahân eight sons and six daughters, and died in childbirth at Burhânpur, in the Deccan, in 1631; the Moti Masjid, or Pearl Mosque, and the Zanâna of the Agra Fort and Shâhjahânâbâd, or modern Delhi, with its splendid palace, the last home of his degenerate successors, until this Alsatia was cleared out after the Mutiny.

The wealth and magnificence of this famous monarch are part of the world's history. In his early days he was a keen soldier; but he was three parts a Hindu, and to this was due the support of the Râjputs in the early part of his career. In his time that persecution of the Hindus, which was fated to cause the ruin of the dynasty, recommenced. Jahângîr seems to have treated their religion with contemptuous toleration. His own belief was too vague to encourage iconoclasm. But in 1632, the year after the death of Mumtâz-i-Mahal, Shâh Jahân embarked in active persecution. The chronicler writes: "It had been brought to the notice of His Majesty that during the late reign many idol temples had been begun, but remained unfinished, at Benares, the great stronghold of infidelity. The infidels were now desirous of completing them. His Majesty gave orders that at Benares, and throughout his dominions in every place, all temples that had been begun should be cast down. It was now reported from the province of Allahâbâd, that seventy-six temples had been destroyed in the district of Benares."[1] This evil example was followed with disastrous results by his bigoted successor.

The popular idea is that Shâh Jahân was always absorbed in the pleasures of the harem, and neglected the duties of administration; this is certainly incorrect. In his early years he followed the example of his famous grandfather, in a laborious attention to the affairs of the empire. It was the opinion of Mr Elphinstone, himself a trained statesman, that, as was the case of Rome in the days of Severus, the Empire as a whole never enjoyed such good government and prosperity as in the time of Shâh Jahân. The native chronicler says that, in his days, "the Pargana, the income of which was three lakhs in the days of Akbar (whose seat is in the highest Heaven!), yielded in this happy reign a revenue of ten lakhs."[2]

But later on in his career the sensuous side of his nature, the natural result of his birth, developed a taste for splendour and display. He devoted himself to the erection of those splendid buildings which are the glory of his reign, and he more and more entrusted the active work of government to his son Dâra. How his latter days were clouded by the war between his sons and intrigues in his family; how Aurangzeb, by ceaseless machinations, finally succeeded in supplanting his elder brother Dâra, whom, with the aid of his brother Murâd, he defeated on the field of Samogarh, near Agra, in 1658; how the luckless Emperor was confined as a State prisoner in the Agra Fort, where he died after seven years of imprisonment, has been often told.

Nor can we linger over the long reign of Aurangzeb (1658-1707 A.D.), which extended from the death of Cromwell to the campaign of Blenheim. As has been already shown, the decadence of the Empire commenced at least from the

[1] Elliot, *History*, vii. 36.

[2] *Ibid.*, vii. 171.

later years of Akbar's life. That it lasted so long was due to the fact that, up to the closing years of Shâh Jahân's government, the Râjput power, linked by ties of blood to the reigning dynasty, was always ready to fight its battles. The original causes of weakness—the centralisation of the government at the capital where the revenues were lavishly expended on public works; the failure to control the governors of the more distant provinces; the want of attention to the development of agriculture, industries, trade, and communications; the unsuitability of the law of Islâm to the wants of the people, and the lack of a well-organised police and a competent judiciary; the degradation of the nobility and Church; the cabals of the adventurers who crowded in the Imperial Darbâr—all these are found intensified when Aurangzeb ascended the throne.

Of his character and policy it is not easy to form a fair estimate. In popular parlance he was called Namâzi—"the man of prayer." He was honest and conscientious, as James II. was when he lost his throne in the attempt to force a hated faith on his people; as Philip II. was when he let Alva loose on the Netherlands. Figures like these, men good enough in their way, but led aside by some cruel flaw in their nature to desert the ways of tolerance, and think that in killing the votary of another faith they do God service, are among the most pathetic in history.

His foreign policy failed because it was based on wrong principles. It seems now obvious enough that the destruction of the Musalmân kingdoms of the Deccan was calculated to remove the last barrier between the Marhattas and northern India; that any objects which kept the Emperor engaged for a quarter of a century in a remote part of his dominions, cut off from his capital and the main sources of his power, could not be worth pursuing; that his Empire, as it stood, with its obvious administrative needs, would tax the powers of any ruler, however industrious and energetic. It is at the same time quite possible that he felt that without war the spirit of the nation would decay, and that the vast accumulation of wealth in the treasury of his father had led him to form a too sanguine view of the resources of the country; or, that once embarked in a campaign like this, it had to be fought out to the bitter end.

Aurangzeb has gained the name of being the archiconoclast of India. It has been suggested that much of his alleged destruction of temples is mythical, because, were it true, he would be held in much more general abhorrence by Hindus; and that many of these legends were invented to enhance the reputation of some shrine which he failed to destroy, because the deity himself intervened by a miracle to prevent the sacrilege—letting loose a swarm of hornets to repel the enemy, or causing blood to flow from an image when struck by the sword of the Musalmân. That many such tales are current may be readily admitted. But there is good evidence that he destroyed several famous temples, and built mosques on the sites which they occupied. Thus, there seems little doubt that the Alamgîri mosque at Benares was built on the site and out of the materials of the temple of Kirtti Visvesvara, at that time quite a modern shrine of Akbar's period; that at Mathura he replaced the desecrated shrine of Kesava Deva; that he partially destroyed the Sîtârâmji temple at Soron; that one of his officers slew the priests, broke the image, and defiled the sanctuary at Devi Pâtan in Gonda. At the same time it seems probable that the scarcity of early Hindu remains at places like Benares is to be attributed more to the lack of temple-building instincts among the Brahmanical Aryans than to Musalmân iconoclasm.

But it would almost seem as if the institution of the Jizya or poll-tax on Hindus gave greater offence. A protest against it forms the chief part of the famous letter of remonstrance from Râna Râj Sinh of Mewâr.[1] This impost was avowedly based on a religious motive. The chronicler writes: "With the object of curbing the infidels, and of distinguishing the land of the faithful from an infidel land, the Jizya or poll-tax was imposed upon the Hindus all through the provinces."[2] As in the days of Wat Tyler, it led to serious rioting and disaffection.

[1] Tod, *Annals* (Calcutta reprint), i. 403.

[2] Elliot, *History*, vii. 296.

But there is much to be said against this indictment of Aurangzeb. He never sanctioned direct persecution, torture, the devastation of the country, of which we have many instances in the time of his predecessors. His zeal against the Hindus shows itself in a constant suspicion and distrust, deprivation of civil employment, prohibition of fairs and religious ceremonies, with the occasional destruction of a shrine, or the erection of a mosque on one of their most sacred sites, to remind them that they were a conquered race, and to mark the triumph of the true faith. All this is bad enough, as was the case of James II. coercing an Oxford College, or prosecuting the Seven Bishops; but, after all, there is a great difference between acts like these and the sterner methods which led Hooper to the stake.

We have seen already what an importance in public opinion was assigned to the appearance of the Emperor at the daily Darbâr. We are told that many Hindus were known as Darshani, because they would not eat till they had enjoyed their daily view of the Emperor. "His religious Majesty," says the annalist,[1] "looked on this as among the forbidden and unlawful practices; so he left off sitting in the window and forbade the assembling of the crowd beneath it." It was marked as the introduction of the detested customs of the East when Diocletian secluded himself from the sight of the people.[2]

As in the case of Akbar, the last years of Aurangzeb, whose methods of government differed so widely from those of the founder of the Empire, passed on clouded with the sense of failure. In his old age he wrote: "The instant which has passed in power has left only sorrow behind it. I have not been the guardian and protector of the Empire."

It is unnecessary to attempt a detailed account of the age of anarchy which followed the death of Aurangzeb in 1707 A.D. Just a century of chaos was to be endured to prove that no tolerable native government was possible.

"The history of the successors of Theodosius," writes Lord

[1] Elliot, *History*, vii. 284. [2] Gibbon, *Decline and Fall*, ii. 94.

Macaulay,[1] "bears no small analogy to that of the successors of Aurangzeb. But perhaps the fall of the Carlovingians furnishes the nearest parallel to the fall of the Moguls. Charlemagne was hardly interred when the imbecility and disputes of his descendants began to bring contempt on themselves and destruction on their subjects." The story of their fate best enables us to realise the horrors of the years which followed. Out of twenty princes, fourteen were murdered or died violent deaths: four were blinded; two died in prison. We are reminded of the later Roman Empire, when from Commodus to Decius, a period of fifty-nine years, eleven princes wore the purple; in one hundred and seventy years, seventy Emperors sat on the throne.

We now come to the rise of the kingdom of Oudh. It was not till the time of Akbar that this part of the Province came completely under Mughal influence. The revenue settlement was introduced and the country was ruled by a viceroy; but the Hindu Râjas remained practically undisturbed because the new government was too weak to dream of exterminating them. Some of them were supported by grants out of the revenue; others were allowed to hold estates revenue free. Many of them were conciliated by posts in the public service and by high-sounding titles of honour. The Râjput chief of Hasanpur Bandhua adopted the faith of the conqueror, and was placed as a sort of superintendent over the Râjas to the south of the Province.

On the fall of the Empire, before the attacks of the Marhattas, these chiefs became practically independent, and the more powerful houses aggrandised themselves at the expense of their poorer neighbours. This was the period of the creation of the Talukas or principalities, which so deeply affected the later history, of the Kânhpuriya Râjputs of Râê Bareli, the Bais of Dundiya Khera in Unâo, and the Bisens of Gonda.

It was in 1732 that Saadat Ali Khân, a Persian merchant, was appointed Mughal governor of Oudh, and founded the dynasty which ruled till 1856. He became hereditary Wazîr

[1] *Essay on Clive.*

of the Empire, and before his death in 1743 he had brought the country into subjection, and converted it into an independent State. He was succeeded by his son, Safdar Jang, who reigned from 1743 to 1753. He was a soldier and a statesman, and was engaged in wars with the Marhattas and Rohillas. He lived little in Oudh, and was buried at Delhi in a stately monument.

His son Shuja-ud-daula (1753-75) made Faizâbâd his capital. He it was who first came in contact with the British. He was tempted to interfere in Bengal politics, but his army was crushed in the battle of Baxar (1764), and he lost the provinces of Kora and Allahâbâd in the peace concluded in the following year. His son, Asaf-ud-daula (1775-98) was obliged to surrender on his accession the districts of Benares, Jaunpur and Ghâzipur, with the dominions of Chait Sinh of Benares, while he was confirmed in the possession of Kora and Allahâbâd, which were recovered from the Emperor. It was he who removed the seat of government to Lucknow, and to him are due some of the finest buildings in the city—the Rûmi Darwâza or fine gate leading out of the Machhi Bhawan Fort, and the great Imâmbâra in which his ashes rest. It was he who negotiated the Chunâr treaty of 1781 with Warren Hastings, and the proceedings in connection with the Begams, widow and mother of Shuja-ud-daula, formed one of the counts in the indictment tried at Westminster Hall. Asaf-ud-daula gained a reputation for liberality; but from his time dates the decline of the kingdom.

His half-brother, Saadat Ali Khân, succeeded in 1798, but the pressure of Sindhia on the advance of Zamân Shâh to the Indus led to a new treaty in 1801, by which he lost half his dominions, and Rohilkhand passed under British rule. To him are due the group of tawdry palaces in Lucknow—the Farhat Bakhsh, the Dilârâm, the Dilkusha, and the Sikandar Bâgh—names familiar to English readers of the story of the Mutiny campaign.

His son, Ghâzi-ud-din Haidar, the first king of Oudh, was followed by three princes—Nâsir-ud-dîn Haidar (1827), Muhammad Ali Shâh (1837), and Amjad Ali Shâh (1841), who followed that career of reckless extravagance, maladministration, and sensuous luxury which made the Court of Oudh a byword in the last generation. Of the demoralisation and ruin of the country under the last king, Wâjid Ali Shâh (1847), we have a graphic account in General Sleeman's famous report which formed the justification of the annexation by Lord Dalhousie in 1856.

Meanwhile, except in the later days of the kingdom, Oudh enjoyed perhaps a happier destiny than the western part of the Province and the Ganges-Jumna Duâb. The Delhi Empire in the earlier years of the eighteenth century was menaced by Marhattas from the south and Sikhs from the north-west. Bundelkhand, south of the Jumna, had been lost even during the lifetime of Aurangzeb, when a Bundela chief Chhattar Sâl raised the standard of revolt. Later on (1732) he was so hard pressed by the Pathân chiefs of Farrukhâbâd that he was forced to call in the aid of the Marhattas, and at his death two years later one-third of his dominions fell into the hands of the Peshwa.

In the same way in Rohilkhand the Rohillas, themselves newcomers into the country and not the ancient lords, as it pleased the accusers of Warren Hastings later on to assert, rose in rebellion. Their first leader, Ali Muhammad Khân, after conquering the hill tract of Kumaun as far as Almora, was finally defeated by the Emperor Muhammad Shâh. His successor, the notorious Hâfiz Rahmat Khân, was engaged in war with the Wazîr of Oudh, allied with the Marhattas. The end came when the Oudh Government called in the aid of a British contingent, and the stormy career of the Rohilla chief ended in his death in 1774 at the battle of Mîranpur Katra. It is needless to say that these events led to protracted controversy. A consideration of fresh evidence tends to acquit Warren Hastings of blame in the transaction.

Further west the last blow fell on the feeble Delhi Empire in the invasion of Nâdir Shâh of Persia, who captured and plundered the capital in 1738, and perpetrated a horrible massacre of the inhabitants. After his departure the Marhattas became paramount over Delhi and the greater part

A JÂT.

of the Duâb, until their power was shattered and their last hopes of founding an Empire in northern India defeated on the fatal field of Pânipat, when the Marhatta chivalry went down before the onset of the Persian chief Ahmad Shâh Durrâni.

During this general chaos another race, the Jâts, made a bid for power in the Central Ganges-Jumna Duâb. They had always been more or less independent. Both Timûr and Bâbar were obliged to turn aside to repress these sturdy freebooters. In the latter half of the eighteenth century they, too, joined in the general scramble for the Duâb carried on by the Wazîr of Oudh, Marhattas, and Rohillas. After the rout of the Marhattas at Pânipat they managed to seize Agra. The guides still show the crack in the black marble throne of Jahângîr which occurred, they say, when the impious Jât of Bhartpur placed his foot upon the seat of the Emperor. Another story is more probable, that they tore off and melted down the silver ceiling of the Dîwân-i-Âm or private audience chamber of Shâh Jahân. The Jâts were wise enough to ally themselves with the stronger power when at last the British, under Lord Lake, invaded the Duâb in 1803. But their allegiance was short-lived, and in 1805 Lake made an ill-judged attack on Bhartpur. The means at his disposal for conducting the siege were insufficient, and the fortress was more capable of defence than he supposed. The attack was defeated, and Bhartpur remained the virgin fortress which had foiled the conquering power till 1827, when it fell before the assault of the British forces under Lord Combermere.

Here on the fall of the Muhammadan Empire we may pause to consider the main features of the splendid buildings which remain their monument.

The style begins with the Pathân, as it has been inaccurately called, because the only true Pathân dynasty was that of the Lodis. This lasted from the conquest of Shihâb-ud-dîn to the time of Akbar—about three centuries and a half—(1193-1554 A.D.). The finest examples of this style are found outside the province at Delhi and Ajmir. At Delhi we have the Kutab Minâr and the adjoining mosque constructed out of the materials of one or more Jaina temples, and the great mosque at Ajmîr. The notable improvement which marks the buildings of this style is the arch of the pointed form; it was only the horizontal arch without radiating voussoirs with which the Hindus were acquainted. Thus writing of the great mosque of the Kutub, near Delhi, Dr Ferguson says: "It seems that the Afghân conquerors had a tolerably distinct idea that pointed arches were the true form for architectural openings, but being without science sufficient to construct them, they left the Hindu architects and builders whom they employed to follow their own devices as to the mode of carrying out the form. The Hindus, up to this time, had never built an arch, nor, indeed, did they for centuries afterwards. Accordingly, they proceeded to make the pointed openings on the same principle on which they built their domes. They carried them up in horizontal courses as far as they could, and then closed them by long slabs meeting at the top."[1]

The chief beauty of this style is the elegance with which the Cufic and Tughra inscriptions are adapted to serve the purpose of surface decoration. This elaborate style gave way in the later buildings to one of almost puritanical simplicity. It was at a later period that the minaret was associated with the bulbous dome; with the earlier architects it was used more as an emblem of victory than as a necessary adjunct to a house of worship, from whence the Muezzin could raise the call to prayer. The power of the earlier kings was too limited to encourage the erection of buildings in this style. Within the Province, all that remains of the time of Shihâb-ud-dîn is the tomb of Makhdûm Shâh Wilâyat at Meerut; another Meerut tomb, that of Sayyid Sâlâr Masaud, is attributed to his viceroy, Kutub-ud-dîn Aibak. Of Shams-ud-dîn Altamsh, we have three tombs at Budaun, and one in the Râê Bareli district. Alâ-ud-dîn Khilji left no remains; Muhammad bin Tughlak erected no original building, he repaired the Jâmi Masjid mosque at Budaun.

[1] *Indian and Eastern Architecture*, p. 504.

Fîroz Shâh Tughlak (1351-1388 A.D.) was one of the chief builders of the Delhi kings, but his main work is at his capital. He is perhaps best known further east as removing the pillar of Asoka to Allahâbâd, and by at least commencing the conversion of the Atala Devi temple at Jaunpur into a mosque.

We have already noticed the fine series of buildings erected by the dynasty of Jaunpur. Dr Ferguson shows that these buildings illustrate the transition between the Hindu and the Musalmân styles, the main building displaying the arch work of the newcomers, and the corridors the flat roofs formed of slabs of stone, characteristic of Hindu construction. The reason of this was that most of the workmen were Hindus, and clung to their traditional methods.

To attempt any review of the grand series of works executed at Agra and its neighbourhood by Akbar, and particularly by Shâh Jahân, would be beyond the scope of a sketch like this. We have only to mention the magnificent palace in the Agra Fort; the pile of buildings at Fatehpur Sikri, a grand mosque and archway, and the palace, which, more than any building of the Mughal period, enables us to realise in some degree what the Court and home life of the Emperors may have been. One characteristic feature of Agra is the splendid garden tombs—the Tâj, Akbar's mausoleum at Sikandra, which is supposed to have been planned on a Buddhist model, thus illustrating the Catholic views of the early Emperors, and that of Itimâd-ud-daula, father of the queen of Jahângîr, Nûr Jahân, which, marvellously beautiful as the inlaid decoration is, Dr Ferguson thinks to be one of the least successful of its class: "The patterns do not quite fit the place where they are put, and the spaces are not always those best suited to this style of decoration."

Of the great Agra buildings, the Tâj, perhaps, would be to some extent disappointing, were it not for its noble surroundings—the mighty river flowing at its base; the delicious greenery of the foliage; the grace of the flanking minarets; the grandeur of the gateway through which the first view of it is caught; the artistic design of the mosques beside it. But it is a poem in stone, and worthily commemorates the love story of which it is the subject. A lady said to General Sleeman: "I would die to-morrow to have such another over me!" As Bishop Heber wrote in words which have become proverbial: "These Pathâns built like giants and finished like jewellers." For sheer delicate beauty, nothing is more lovely than the cool marble court, graceful Saracenic arches and domes of the Moti Masjid, which, from a distance, look like bubbles above the dark red masses of the Fort.

Nothing is more eloquent of the decay of the Empire than the sudden failure in taste which set in with the accession of Aurangzeb. Not a single building of the latter days deserves notice, and the style finally degenerated into the crude stucco palaces with which the kings of Oudh endeavoured to decorate their capital. Only one of their buildings, the grand Imâmbâra, embodies any survival of the genius of the older architects.

In the period immediately preceding our occupation, the European adventurers are the most notable figures.

Samru, or Sombre, was a butcher from Luxemburg, whose real name was Walter Reinard or Reinhard. He deserted from the French to the British service, and back again to the French. He then joined Mîr Kâsim in Bengal, and was the leading actor in the brutal massacre of the English prisoners at Patna in 1763. After a series of adventures, serving at one time the Jâts, at another the Marhattas, he settled as a free-lance at Sardhana, in Meerut, where he occupied an extensive tract of country. He died in 1778, leaving a widow, the famous, or infamous, Begam Samru, a Musalmân of Arab descent. Of her early career the less said the better. A few years after she joined the Roman Catholic Church, and appointed as her lieutenant George Thomas, a native of Tipperary. He remained in her service till 1792, when the Begam married a young French adventurer, M. le Vaisseau. In 1798, Thomas formed the design of carving out an independent principality for himself in the country west of the Jumna. If gallantry and genius, the power of forming extensive political combinations, the faculty of influencing lawless confederates could have ensured success against enormous odds, this remarkable man might have made a great name in Indian history. But the Marhattas, under their French commander, General Perron, were too powerful. His forces were surrounded and routed, and he himself escaped across the British frontier, only to die soon after in Bengal.

Meanwhile the Begam Samru and her husband, Le Vaisseau, carried on desultory warfare, at one time against Ghulâm Kâdir, the ruffian who had blinded the Emperor, Shâh Âlam, now against Thomas, her former confederate. She seems to have found Le Vaisseau incompetent to control the disorderly elements of which her force was composed; she may have had grounds for jealousy. At any rate, husband and wife seem to have made a vow to commit suicide together. A sound of a pistol from his wife's palanquin, the wails of her attendants, and the sight of her garments stained with blood, convinced him that she had taken her life, and he shot himself in a fit of remorse and despair. By another and perhaps a more probable story, she did really wish to die, but the dagger failed to do its work, and she had not resolution to repeat the blow. She lived to make terms with the British after the capture of Delhi in 1802. Her career did not close till 1836. Henceforward she lived as a semi-independent potentate at Sardhana. Dark tales are told of her private life. She is said to have buried alive a slave girl who offended her, and, to make her deadly purpose sure, to have had her buried beneath her tent, and her bed arranged over the wretch's grave. She was a devoted believer of the Roman Catholic Church, built a Cathedral and an Orphanage at Sardhana, distributed large sums in charity, and died in the odour of sanctity. Her grandson, Dyce Sombre, visited England, where his eccentricity and extravagance led to a *cause celebre* in the English Courts. The estates are now held by the Forester family.

Two other large estates to the west of the Province have had a less happy fate—one founded by Colonel James

Skinner, an officer in the Marhatta service, who afterwards joined Lord Lake, and received a large assignment of lands in Bulandshahr; the other by Colonel William Gardner in the Central Ganges-Jumna Duâb. Both these properties have fallen on evil days through the mismanagement and extravagance of the descendants of the original grantees. Part of the Skinner estate has been saved by the protection of the Court of Wards; that of the Gardners was wasted in profuse extravagance, and an English peerage granted to a gallant naval officer in the wars with the French is now claimed by the head of the Indian branch of the family, who is destitute of funds to pursue his claim.

The fate of these great properties, which, if retained intact, would now be a worthy endowment of an English dukedom, is a melancholy example of the result of the surrender of the European to the fascinations of a sensuous Oriental life.

We have now reached the point at which British rule became paramount over the province; and it may be well to summarise the stages by which it came under our authority.

In 1775, Asaf-ud-daula, Nawâb of Oudh, ceded to us the eastern portion, including the present districts of Ghâzipur, Benares, Jaunpur, and part of Mirzapur, which, for the time being, were left in charge of Chait Sinh, Râja of Benares.

In 1801 the Nawâb again ceded to us, in lieu of a subsidy, the present districts of Gorakhpur, Basti, and Azamgarh, as well as his dominions in the Duâb, comprising our districts of Allahâbâd, Fatehpur, Cawnpur, Etâwah, Mainpuri, Etah, Farrukhâbâd, and the greater part of Rohilkhand. In the same year the Nawâb of Farrukhâbâd, who had then become our tributary, ceded his dominions to the Company in consideration of a pension.

In the next year (1802), as the result of General Lake's campaign against the Marhattas, we obtained, by the treaty of Surji Anjangâon, the country included in the present Meerut division, and the greater part of the present districts of Mathura and Agra, besides considerable territory west of the Jumna.

In the next year (1803), by a new treaty with the Peshwa, we obtained the present Bundelkhand province, south of the Jumna, in exchange for other territories ceded to us under the treaty of Bassein.

By the treaty of Sigauli, which closed the Nepâl war in 1815, we gained the hill tract, comprising the present Garhwâl, Kumaun, and Dehra Dûn districts.

In 1840 we obtained, by lapse on the death of the Râja of Jalaun, who died without an heir, a tract in western Bundelkhand, to which were added, in 1853, the dominions of the Râja of Jhânsi.

Except a recent readjustment of the frontier with Sindhia in Jhânsi, the boundaries of the Province, as they now stand, were finally settled by the annexation of Oudh in 1856, and in 1858 the Delhi and Hissâr divisions, west of the Jumna, were transferred to the Panjâb, and in 1861 the outlying tract to the south, known as the Sâgar and Narbada territories, were included in the Central Provinces.

We have thus endeavoured to sketch the tangled and romantic history of this Province. We have seen how the Hindu religion and polity were established to the west under the earlier settlers from the north; how this faith became the heritage of a tribe of Levites, and failed to retain its hold upon the people: how a polity based on the depressing restrictions of caste and priestly domination possessed no elements of permanence; how Hinduism succumbed before Buddhism, and how, many centuries after, it reasserted its authority over a religion which became gradually inert; how the Hindu kingdoms sank into decrepitude, and were unable to offer any successful resistance to another swarm of invaders from the north; how the eastward movement of the Râjputs saved the Hindu faith in the hour of its direst need; how the Mughal Empire rose to the zenith of its glory, and—in spite of the wise revenue policy initiated by Shîr Shâh, and the tireless devotion to details which characterised Akbar—was itself worm-eaten at the core, and sure to fail when the first pedant or bigot became its master. Then came the weary century of chaos, when Marhatta, Sikh, and Jât, and European free-lance growled and squabbled like so many jackals round a carcase.

Perhaps the best parallel to this wonderful story is that of Spain, with its ancient Phœnician colonies; its conquest by Roman and Goth; its absorption into Islâm, which gave it master-pieces of Moorish architecture, as Shâh Jahân did at Agra and Delhi; the establishment of a national government; its splendid empire, followed by political degeneration, saved from foreign domination only by English aid. And, as we have seen was the case with Hinduism, there was all through the course of Spanish history a power of resistance and a capacity for recuperation which ensured its existence, even after much affliction, and secured it an honourable position among the nations of the world.

CHAPTER III

THE PROVINCE UNDER BRITISH RULE

IN the opening years of the nineteenth century the British Government had thus brought the most valuable portion of the Province under its control. But we did not enter the country as the heirs of a civilised administration in the ordinary sense of the term. Even in the best days of the Mughal rule no effective measures had been taken to develop its resources, to secure internal peace, to protect the people from outrageous oppression. The resources of the State had been lavished on warlike preparations, or on the construction of splendid edifices at the capital. The case was indescribably worse in the century of misrule, which followed on the decay of the Empire.

The only law administered by the Courts was the code of Islâm. "The penal code of the Moslems," writes Mr Keene,[1] "has the incurable evil of being derived from revelation. Imagine the Central Criminal Court administering Leviticus, and sentencing a coster-monger to death for selling oranges on Saturday. Even then but an imperfect idea would be formed of the interfering nature of the legal system of Islâm, or of the terrible, though uncertain, severity of its punitive sanctions. And this on the supposition, probably not always justifiable, that the stern casuists of these tribunals were as honest and impartial as they were indifferent to human suffering." And he goes on to say: "Besides regarding all law as a direct emanation from the Deity, the law of Islâm regards some crimes as penal, because of their being offences against the Divine Majesty. It also classifies offences according to whether they are punishable by (1) retaliation; (2) statutory penalties; (3) discretion of the Magistrate.

[1] *Turks in India*, 150 sq.

Under the first come offences against the human body, including murder, where the prosecutor was *dominus litis*, and might accept or remit the price of blood. Under the second were ranged offences against property, drinking wine and committing adultery; these latter, being offences against God, could not be compounded. The third included punishments, extending from riding backward on a donkey to death or mutilation—for offences as to which there was a doubt regarding the class to which they might belong; and murder was not only regarded practically as less heinous than drinking, but its definition depended, not on the intention to cause death, but on the instrument employed. As to procedure, the like eccentricity prevailed. Approvers were not recognised, nor was the evidence of one witness, under any circumstances, sufficient. In the testimony of witnesses the most absurd technicalities existed, as on that question on which the Sheikhs so much differ, as to whether or not it is a condition of testimony that the witness should say: 'It is incumbent on this defendant that he should shorten his hand.' The trial opened with the praise of God; the judge was bound to invoke the guidance of the Almighty in a set form before pronouncing sentence. No wonder that Lord Cornwallis spoke of the 'gross defects' of a law under which such hairs were pivots."

Of the method of trial we have an instance in Tavernier's account of the proceedings of the Nawâb Mîr Jumla.[1]—"While we were with the Nawâb, he was informed that four prisoners, who were then at the door of the tent, had arrived. He remained more than half an hour without replying, writing continually, and making his secretaries write; but at length he suddenly ordered the criminals to be brought in; and, having questioned them and made them confess with their own mouths the crime of which they were accused, he remained nearly an hour without saying anything, continuing to write and making his secretaries write. Among these four prisoners who were brought into his presence there was one who had slain a mother and her three infants. He

[1] Ball, *Tavernier*, i. 292 sq.

was condemned forthwith to have his feet and hands cut off, and to be thrown into a field near the high road to end his days. Another had stolen on the high-road, and the Nawâb ordered him to have his stomach slit open and to be flung in a drain. I could not ascertain what the others had done, but both their heads were cut off. While all this passed the dinner was served, for the Nawâb generally eats at ten o'clock, and he made us dine with him."

The civil law, again, was used as a direct means of advancing Islâm at the expense of other religions; and the law of inheritance, based on regulations suitable enough for the partition of the cattle and camels of a pastoral Arab tribe, was quite inadequate for the distribution of landed property.

Bernier, writing to Colbert, thus sums up his experience of the Courts:[1] "In Asia, if justice be ever administered, it is among the lower classes, among persons, who being equally poor, have no means of corrupting the judges and of bringing false witnesses—witnesses always to be had in great numbers, at a cheap rate, and never punished. I am speaking the language of several years' experience: my information was obtained from various quarters, and it is the result of many years' careful enquiries among the natives, European merchants long settled in the country, ambassadors, consuls and interpreters."

It has sometimes been asserted that during the Mughal Empire there were less peculation and dishonesty among the native official class than in our time. It would be difficult to produce any evidence in support of this statement; there are many facts which suggest that the reverse was the case. The elaborate rules contained in the Aîn-i-Akbari for the periodical parades of the troops, for the management of the horses, elephants and so on, imply the necessity in those times of a most minute scrutiny of the War Department and Commissariat. This has always been the case under an oriental despotism. We know on the authority of Mr Curzon and other travellers that the Persian army is to a great measure a paper force. On the general tone of official morality he

[1] *Travels*, 237.

writes:[1] "Under its political aspects, the practice of gift-making, though consecrated in the adamantine traditions of the East, is synonymous with the system elsewhere described by less agreeable names. This is the system on which the government of Persia has been conducted for centuries, and the maintenance of which opposes a solid barrier to any real reform. From the Shâh downwards, there is scarcely an official who is not open to gifts, scarcely a post which is not conferred in gifts, scarcely an income which has not been amassed by the receipt of gifts. Every individual, with hardly an exception, in the official hierarchy above-mentioned, has only purchased his post by a money present either to the Shâh, or to a minister, or to the superior governor by whom he has been appointed. If there are several candidates for a post, in all probability the one who makes the best offer will win."

So we read in the time of Akbar of Abdun-nabi, the Sadr or officer in charge of the land grants, who was guilty of gross corruption. "When His Majesty," we are told,[2] "discovered that the Qâzis were in the habit of taking bribes from the grant-holders, he resolved with a view of obtaining God's favour, to place no further reliance on these Qâzis, who wear a turban as a sign of respectability, but are bad at heart, and who wear long sleeves, but fall short in sense." The result of his enquiries was the dismissal of a number of these officers. In the middle of the seventeenth century, Tavernier, a shrewd man of business, found it necessary, before he could dispose of his goods, to give bribes to the Court officials to the value of £1739, an enormous sum in those days.

Except the canals constructed by Ali Mardan Khân in the time of Shâh Jahân, which, owing to faults of alignment and absence of subsidiary channels, could at no time have been a very effective source of irrigation, it would be difficult to point to any considerable work intended to promote the prosperity of the country. Shîr Shâh and his successors drove a great military highway through the land. Part of

[1] *Persia*, i. 438.

[2] Blochmann, *Aîn-i-Akbari*, i. 269 sq.

this must have been, occasionally at any rate, doubtless with a lavish use of the *corvée*, kept in tolerable order. We know that Jahângîr was able to travel from Ajmîr to Agra in a coach-and-four and urged his nobility to provide similar equipages for themselves.[1] In the time of Tavernier the journey from Agra to Surat occupied between thirty-five and forty days. He travelled in a bullock cart, and tells us that some oxen could trot twelve or fifteen leagues a day. He also used to ride on an ox, a mode of conveyance which would astonish a modern Anglo-Indian. He adds the sage advice—"But you should take care when you buy or hire an ox for riding that he has not horns longer than a foot; because, if they are longer, when the flies sting him, he chafes and tosses back the head, and may plant a horn in your stomach, as has happened several times."[2] Most people performed their journeys on horseback, as was the case in England till stage coaches were introduced in the latter half of the seventeenth century.

Worse than the want of good roads was the danger of robbers. Tavernier tells us that he who desires to travel with honour in India ought to take with him twenty or thirty armed men, some with bows and arrows and others with muskets.[3] On one occasion in the reign of Jahângîr a caravan on its way from Mathura to Delhi was delayed for six weeks at the former place until a suitable escort could be collected. In fact, short of holding the wretched villagers in the neighbourhood of the main lines of communication responsible for loss of life and property, there was no efficient police and no means of repressing disorder except by occasional expeditions against some specially notorious tribe or village.

The periodical progresses, again, of the Emperor with his enormous camps must have been a terrible source of oppression. Now-a-days the people have learned to grumble at the loss inflicted by the modest camps of our officers on tour. We have seen that Akbar made some attempts to remedy this evil, but in the time of Aurangzeb the camp followers

[1] Elliot, *Historians*, vi. 347. [2] Ball, *Tavernier*, i. 42. [3] *Ibid.*, ii. 46.

seem to have been uncontrolled. Bernier[1] says that he was accompanied by at least one hundred thousand horsemen, one hundred and fifty thousand animals, including horses, mules, and elephants, fifty thousand camels, and nearly as many oxen and ponies of the grain-sellers and camp-followers. Many guessed that the camp contained between three and four hundred thousand persons. "Accurately to determine the question the people should be numbered. All I can confidently assert is that the multitude is prodigious and almost incredible. The whole population of Delhi is in fact collected in the camp, because deriving its employment and maintenance from the Court and army, it has no alternative but to follow them in their march or to perish from want during their absence."

When this was the condition of things under the only settled government which the country ever enjoyed until the advent of the British power, we may easily imagine the state of affairs during the anarchy which followed the break-up of the Mughal Empire.

There was perhaps most disturbance in the western part of the Province, where Sikh and Marhatta, Rohilla and European adventurers struggled for the mastery. We see signs of this even in the present day in the appearance of the villages. The western village is like a miniature fort, the houses huddled together by preference on some ancient mound, from whence the approach of an enemy can be observed. The entrance is narrow and commanded by the heavy mud houses of the landlord. The eastern village is of a much less militant type, the houses less strongly built, the lanes and spaces wider, while the population is more dispersed in hamlets, which are to the west all of quite modern growth—the creation of a period of tranquillity.

For the Sikh raids in the Upper Duâb we have the evidence of Dr Guthrie in Sahâranpur.[2] The villages were sunk in poverty owing to the extortions of these freebooters. They often reduced the landlords to total ruin by burning their houses and driving off their cattle. The appearance of the

[1] *Travels*, 380 sq.

[2] *North-West Provinces Gazetteer*, ii. 211.

villages showed the general state of insecurity; almost every one was surrounded by a wall or ditch, or both, as a means of defence against invasion. "Though the Musalmâns were the first objects of their attack, the Sikhs were not restrained by any considerations of religion or any mercy for age or sex. Whole communities were massacred with wanton barbarity, and it is said that even the bodies of the dead were dug up and thrown out to the birds and beasts of prey."

Across the Ganges in Rohilkhand the state of affairs was hardly better. Mr Tennent, who passed through it in 1799, describes the country as a vast desert.[1] "Extensive wastes everywhere meet the eye which were lately in cultivation, but which are now covered with long grass." "The wild animals are in danger of devouring the people and their sustenance." "Few manufactures are vended in a country where the inhabitants are scanty, and where even these are so poor as not to aspire to any of the luxuries of life."

So from Cawnpur one of the first Collectors writes[2]—"The subjects in this part of the country are in the most abject state of poverty. Let the face of the country be examined and there will hardly be a manufacture found, or an individual in such circumstances as to afford the payment of a tax. The whole is one desolate waste, in which tyranny and oppression have hitherto universally prevailed."

It was such a country, with a people depressed by misgovernment, a Province lacking in all the essentials of civilised government, without roads or bridges, public buildings, courts, jails, police stations, schools, and hospitals, that the first generation of British officers set themselves to organise. We shall see that they made mistakes; in particular, the demands of the central government enforced an assessment of the land revenue which an exhausted tenantry were unable to meet. But we must consider the extreme difficulties under which they laboured, the magnitude of the task which was imposed upon them. As one half-despairing officer in the early days writes from Cawnpur[3]:—"I found

[1] *Settlement Report*, 40 sq. [2] *North-West Provinces Gazetteer*, vi. 91

[3] *Ibid.*, vi. 82

an ignorant and incapable establishment, an inefficient and corrupt police, unacquainted with or disregarding the most common rules prescribed for their guidance, a community in which honest men were at a discount, and rascality, fraud, and insubordination were the only means of protection; extensive combinations between individuals who had profited by the old system; and finally, a want of co-operation on the part of the subordinate officers, both covenanted and uncovenanted."

It was, in short, much the same condition of things which was exposed to a later generation by General Sleeman's merciless disclosures of the condition of Oudh a short time before annexation. We have an exact parallel in the Persia of our own time; the Austrian officers who took charge of Bosnia could tell a similar story.

It was not possible to remedy this condition of things by a stroke of the pen. The people were, even up to the time of the Mutiny, armed to the teeth with swords and matchlocks—the latter more than a match for the musket of the British soldier of those times. The country swarmed with petty forts, which it was necessary to reduce and demolish. The Central Duâb, Aligarh and its neighbourhood, was notorious for the lawless character of its people, for the abundance of Thags and Dacoits. The Farrukhâbâd landlords are described as a bold, uncivilised race, preferring the chase and fighting to labour, much of their income being derived from the protection they afforded to refugees from Oudh, who flocked in when the Amil or Prefect, with a small army, made his annual tour to collect the revenue.

The western districts were thus hemmed in by a circle of Alsatias. Central India was then practically in the hands of the free-booters, known as the Pindâris. One of these, Amîr Khân, raided into the province in 1805, plundered the holy city of Gokul in Mathura, crossed into Rohilkhand, looted the town of Kâshipur, and, after an active pursuit and defeat by General Smith and his dragoons, was forced to recross the Ganges. Even after our control of the country was well assured, the elements of disorder still existed.

Bishop Heber, writing of Bareilly in 1824,[1] describes the disaffection of the people, the large amount of crime, "the crowd of lazy, profligate, self-called Sowârs (troopers), who, though many of them are not worth a rupee, conceive it derogatory to their gentility and Pathân blood to apply themselves to any honest industry, and obtain for the most part a precarious livelihood by spunging on the industrious tradesmen and farmers, on whom they levy a sort of blackmail, or as hangers-on to the few noble and wealthy families yet remaining in the province." Of such ruffians, "who had no visible occupation except lounging up and down with their swords and shields, like the ancient Highlanders," it was estimated that there were no less than one hundred thousand.

It was out of such disorderly elements that the industrious and fairly well-conducted people of the present day have been disciplined by the force of British law. Save for the brief carnival of loot and massacre in 1857, and some religious riots, directed more against the followers of rival sects than against the Government, the Queen's peace has not been seriously disturbed for nearly a century.

The police have always been the weakest point in the administration. There is a certain danger of exaggeration in general charges of corruption and misconduct brought against a body of men who work in isolated places, beyond the control of their superior officers, opposed by the whole criminal population and their partisans, and encouraged to make some one or other responsible for an offence because the efficiency of their work must be, to a large extent, judged by statistics. But here it is necessary to distinguish. There is a minor form of misconduct which shows itself in petty bribery, in the exaction of supplies of food, forage, and the like. From such acts it is very improbable that a low-paid service, with Oriental traditions of morality, and drawn from a class much inferior to that which supplies candidates for other branches of the public service, would habitually abstain. On the other hand, there is misconduct of a much more serious kind—the fabrication of false charges, the procuring

[1] *Diary*, i. 243 sq.

of information or confessions by coercion or actual torture. Charges of this kind are readily made, and with difficulty disproved; and it is not easy to imagine that a high-spirited peasantry, like that of northern India, would endure oppression of this kind, which we know was at one time rife among the more submissive Madrasis.

Many causes have contributed to obstruct the efficiency of the native police. Such are the absence of a healthy public opinion, of respect for law, of a courageous spirit of independence, particularly among the upper classes. False accusations are, again, promoted by the feeling of caste partisanship which so widely prevails. The cowardly Oriental sees that his best chance of ruining his enemy lies in bringing him within the grasp of the law; when his kinsman is in trouble the tie of blood prevails above the claims of justice, and he holds it no sin to forswear himself in his defence. This low conception of moral duty is shown in Manu's rule,[1] lacking though it be in the sense of perspective:—"To women in order to win their love, or on a proposal of marriage, in the case of grass or fruit eaten by a cow, of wood taken for sacrifice, or of a promise made for the preservation of a Brahman, it is no deadly sin to take a light oath."

The reorganisation of the police has lately engaged the serious attention of the Local Government. What is chiefly wanted is to raise the general tone of the service, and encourage recruits of a better class. This will hardly be secured by a small increase in the rates of pay. The evils which exist would be much abated if the higher classes of the community exhibited a larger measure of public spirit, and showed a greater readiness to co-operate with the authorities in the repression of abuses.

While few people have a good word for the police, we may select two instances in which their work has been successful —Thagi and Infanticide.

Though the peculiar form of strangling practised by the Thags prevailed from very early times, and was known to our officers soon after we occupied the country, it did not

[1] *Institutes*, viii. 112.

attract much general attention till the revelations of Captain (afterwards General) Sleeman were published about 1830, when it became apparent that this brotherhood of crime had its agents all over India. Traders and pilgrims, dancing girls, and soldiers returning from leave, were all victims of these fiends in human shape. Many of these ghastly tragedies, played at these lonely halting places, or even in frequented camps, where the tent of the European officer was sometimes pitched over the very grave of the victim, will never be told on this earth. But enough was soon known to put the detectives, aided by the statements of informers, on the track of the strangler. In the ten years between 1826 and 1835, 1562 persons were tried in India for this crime, of whom 1404 were convicted, and sent to the gallows or transported for life. Many who escaped the hangman were interned for the rest of their days in a special prison at Jabalpur. By 1860, after a steady campaign prosecuted for thirty years, these gangs had been completely destroyed, and Thagi, in its original form, was completely stamped out.

But, as too often happens, one form of crime disappears only to be succeeded by another of a similar type. In this case the poisoner followed on the tracks of the strangler. A little powdered datûra or stramonium deftly mixed in the food of some traveller at a native inn was sufficient to produce insensibility or even death, and afford the criminal an opportunity of appropriating the valuables of his victim. The increase of travelling consequent on the extension of railways in the latter half of this century gave a temporary stimulus to this class of crime; but by a patient system of investigation the chief offenders were hunted down, and the crime is now comparatively infrequent.

At the same time, there is reason to suspect that secret poisoning is not so uncommon as it is generally believed to be. The secrets of Zanâna life are seldom disclosed, and the existence of polygamy and concubinage supplies an obvious motive. To this may be added the occasional outbreaks of deadly epidemics which supply favourable chances of evading detection. Proposals for the control of the sale of poisons have often been suggested, but they have always failed, on the ground that even if the sale of mineral poisons were supervised, this would do nothing to check the use of those of vegetable origin, which grow almost in every hedge.

Infanticide, though first attacked by our Government, has prevailed among certain tribes, the Gakkars of the Panjâb, for instance, from time immemorial. In this Province attention was first directed to it by Mr Jonathan Duncan, one of the ablest officers of the Civil Service, who, in 1789, found it prevalent among the Râjkumâr Râjputs of the eastern districts. For many years the Government endeavoured to counteract it by the personal influence of its officials, by tribal conferences, and engagements for the reduction of marriage expenses. It was soon realised that the practice rested on social influences of great stringency. Râjputs, one of the tribes chiefly addicted to the practice, follow in their marriage arrangements what has been called hypergamy; in other words, the rule is that the honour of the family depends on the alliance of girls with youths of a sept superior in rank to their own. This involves, if not the actual payment of a bridegroom price, such inordinate expenditure in marriage entertainments and dowry as seriously cripples the resources of a man whose quiver is full of daughters.

The result of this feeling among Râjputs, Jâts, Gûjars, and Ahîrs, the castes among whom it most widely prevailed, was the wholesale destruction of new-born girls. In 1843, among the Chauhâns of Mainpuri, one of the proudest of the local Râjput septs, there was not a single female child to be found. Under pressure enforced by the district officers, notably by Messrs Unwin and Raikes, the number rose to 299 in 1847, and 1079 in 1854. At the same time, Mr Raikes recognised the futility of all attempts to enforce a sumptuary law. "The real motive for extravagance, and, therefore, the hidden cause of infanticide," he wrote,[1] "lay entirely beyond the reach of any such law. A Thâkur's ambition to make an illustrious alliance could only be gratified by purchasing a son-in-law of

[1] *North-West Provinces Gazetteer*, iv. 574 sqq.

nobler blood than his own; the nobler the alliance the larger the sum. So long as this costly ambition remained rooted in the Thâkur's soul, the scale of expenditure could not be controlled. The habit of contracting equal marriages must be naturalised to him directly by advice and encouragement, and indirectly by the enactment of heavy penalties to follow the destruction of daughters."

The Government was still loath to adopt direct measures of repression; but later enquiries showed that determined action could no longer be delayed. In 1868, a special census of the suspected clans showed only 22 per cent. of girls in the whole minor population. It was found, also, that the wise councils of the local officers had done little to check marriage expenses. In 1869, the Râja of Mainpuri, the head of the Chauhâns, married his daughter to the son of the Râja of Bhadâwar; and though there was no actual dowry paid, the relations of the bridegroom appropriated whatever took their fancy, and the total cost was not less than a lâkh and a half of rupees (R.x. 15,000).

All this led to the enactment of the law of 1870, which has remained in force since that time. The main provisions of the statute prescribed special registration of births and periodical parades of the infant population, registration of the movements of women of the child-bearing age, special inquests in the case of the death of girls, and control over the village midwives. The result of these measures, according to the latest available statistics, those of 1893-94, may be thus summarised:—The proclaimed population included 92,135 persons, spread over 608 villages in 21 districts. In 100 children under the age of six, there were 40 girls to 60 boys, the provincial average of girls under five years of age being 1020 to 1000 boys. The statistics are to some degree affected by the fact that among the tribes known still to practise infanticide, there is a natural tendency at each decennial census to conceal the existence of girls, whose presence unmarried in a family is a mark of dishonour. Thus, in the Central Ganges-Jumna Duâb the last census showed in 10,000 of the population 4581 females to 5419 males. Here the figures point to a concealment of females at all the age periods.

The general result is that infanticide is decreasing everywhere except in the block of districts represented by Etah, Etâwah, Mainpuri and Budaun, where it was always most prevalent, and even in those districts the improvement since the first introduction of repressive measures has been marked. There seems also to be an increasing tendency to the exaction of a bride-price, one of the most efficient checks on the practice; and, among some of the more intelligent castes, the movement for the reduction of marriage expenses has met with a certain degree of success. The actual murder of little girls has in a great measure ceased, but it has been replaced in some of the tribes by a degree of carelessness hardly less criminal. It is found in some districts that, when fever is prevalent, the girl deaths, and more especially in the first three years of life, so largely exceed those of males that it is impossible not to believe that but small efforts are made to save the girls, and in many places deaths caused by disease of the lungs or malnutrition suggest the same conclusion.

The only effective remedy for this is to utilise the provision of the Act which empowers the Magistrates to take charge of sickly infants and rear them at the expense of the parents. This rule of the law has been enforced in some places with marked success. There is little chance of securing the conviction of the parents where deaths occur through neglect, and it seems clear that the only chance of repressing this crime is to make the supervision so effective and irksome that the people will find it to their interest to protect their girls until they reach a percentage which will entitle them to exemption from the control of the law.

The lack of brides among Râjputs, in that part of the country where infanticide was most rife, seems also to be one of the causes which have contributed to that outbreak of violent crime which has been a distinguishing feature of the returns in recent years. Young men, deprived of the chance of enjoying married life, have been forced into connections with women of the vagrant tribes—Hâbûras, Beriyas, and the like, who are nothing short of a pest to the country. It is the children of such unions who have been foremost in the outbreak of dacoity in the Central Duâb and Rohilkhand.

Dacoity or gang robbery usually appears in one of two well-recognised forms. There is, first, that of the bread-riot type, which occurs in seasons of scarcity and high prices. Here the outbreaks are generally isolated and fortuitous, and easily repressed. The other and more serious form is more fitful in its occurence, and the first essential to success is an efficient leader. It is aided by the neighbourhood of Native States, whence recruits can be obtained, and where the gang can take refuge when pursuit by the police becomes really serious.

In the four years ending with 1893, 736 of these gang robberies occurred. These bands of ruffians were fairly well armed; they were organised under regular leaders, and in some cases they risked open conflict with our police. The loss of life and property, chiefly among the trading classes, who are always the victims, was most serious. In some cases, the gangs were led or reinforced by wild spirits from Gwalior and other Native States south of the Jumna, but they consisted mostly of Râjputs and other local tribes, among whom restlessness, the effect of the increasing pressure of population on the soil, and sales of landed property in execution of Civil Court decrees, formed an incentive to crime of the highwayman or bushranger type. To these were sometimes added the nomads of the gipsy class, among whom the Sânsiyas of the upper Ganges-Jumna valley had been for years most notorious. These dacoit gangs were gradually hunted down and dispersed, not without some loss of life, and then the Government directed special attention to their nomad allies.

The North Indian gipsy in many ways resembles his European brethren. The latter probably had their origin in Indian soil, but in the course of their wanderings the race has been largely modified in its new surroundings, and in particular, they learnt the new arts of the tinker and the horse-coper. The eastern gipsy is a nomad pure and simple;

a wanderer on the face of the earth; he lives in a miserable state of squalor under a wretched tent or shelter made of reeds; he steals corn at harvest time, or a lamb from the shepherd's flock, and he is tolerated merely because of his women, who dance, perform on the tight-rope, or earn their living in less reputable ways. He is a pilferer of any small article that comes in his way, and he is ever ready to engage in violent crime.

Of these pests, the most notorious tribes are the Sânsiyas of the western districts, the Barwârs of Oudh, and the Sanaurhiyas of Bundelkhand. When the Barwârs were brought under the provisions of the Criminal Tribes Act in 1884 they were about 4000 in number, and sixty per cent. of their adult males had undergone imprisonment. The law attempted to deal with these people on somewhat the same method which the English police apply to the ticket-of-leave man. They are subject to periodical registration and inspection; wandering beyond the boundaries of the settlement is forbidden without a pass. But in recent years the Sânsiyas had passed the limits of forbearance, and in 1890, by an executive order of the Provincial Government, the more stringent provisions of the law were applied to them. In a single night their camps throughout the western districts were surrounded by a cordon of police, and 1236 men, women, and children suddenly found themselves under arrest. The adult males, who were practically all incorrigible criminals, were swept off and interned in the jail at Sultânpur, where it was intended that they should remain for the rest of their lives, treated with as much indulgence as was compatible with their safe custody, and allowed to practise any of their petty handicrafts for their own advantage. Similarly the women and children were removed to a settlement at Farrukhâbâd, where they were brought under discipline and educated. Some were apprenticed in the factories at Cawnpur; others were assisted to emigrate to one of the Colonies, with a chance of gaining a respectable livelihood. The young ladies of the tribe were a more embarrassing charge, and grave Magistrates have found themselves saddled with the delicate duty of negotiating suitable matches for these blushing maidens. The English tramp, as he enjoys the comforts of the doss-house or casual ward, might, if he only knew the fate of his eastern brethren, thank Heaven that he does not enjoy the blessings of a paternal government.

Recently, on a change in the head of the Local Government, this policy has been reversed. The present view seems to be that the Sânsiya is more a loafer than a criminal; that the stringent measures enforced against him in recent years were unnecessary and unjustifiable, and that he must be at once released. It is not possible at present to estimate the force of the considerations which may be held to justify this sudden *volte face*. It may be that the present system is too indiscriminate; but with all the Sânsiyas again at large it is certain that the gangs will re-establish themselves, and the old condition of habitual pilfering and occasional outbreaks of violent crime will recommence.

Though there is perhaps no class in Europe so completely abandoned to a criminal life as some of the Indian nomad tribes, and though chiefly owing to the absence of means for isolation, jail discipline has little deterrent effect, and the average of reconvicted prisoners is very high in proportion to their total number, the general amount of crime is satisfactorily low. It is out of the question to draw any useful analogy from the crime statistics of two countries so different as England and Wales and the North-Western Provinces. One main cause of the difference is the temperate habits of the people. Drunkenness is a crime hardly known to the Indian magistrate; in 1894 in England and Wales 595 in every 100,000 of the population were tried for this offence. The number of persons brought to trial in 1892-93, out of a population of forty-seven millions, was a quarter of a million, of whom half were convicted—about the number prosecuted in the home country for drunkenness and under the Licensing Acts. The admissions to jail were 86,000, of whom about a quarter were convicted of petty theft. The incidence of this crime is closely connected with the character of the season—

a bad season like 1880 raised the average jail population to 27,000, to fall to 18,000 in 1885. The popular proverb that crime is due to woman, money, and land is amply illustrated by the returns. The latest returns indicate that the scarcity which now prevails is producing its usual effect by increasing crime.

One of the greatest boons which any Government has ever conferred on the people is the system of canals. We have seen that artificial irrigation commenced with the canals constructed from the Jumna by Ali Mardan Khân in the time of the Emperor Shâh Jahân. They were of comparatively small dimensions, lacked a chain of distributaries, and being built without sufficient experience of the complex problems which such a work involves, could even at their best have been but of little practical value. For the great modern series of irrigation works, the country is indebted to the genius of a distinguished Engineer officer, Sir Proby Cautley.

Classifying the canals of the province into productive, ordinary and protective, the first class includes the Upper Ganges, the Lower Ganges, the Eastern Jumna and the Agra Canals; the second, the canals of Rohilkhand, Dehra Dûn and Bijnor; the third, the Betwa Canal in Bundelkhand, south of the Jumna.

The Upper Ganges Canal, the first constructed from the designs of Sir Proby Cautley, owes its origin to the severe famine of 1837-38, which first directed the attention of Government to the protection of the crops by means of irrigation. Commenced in 1842, it was opened in its earliest form in 1854. It starts from the Ganges at Hardwâr, where by a series of embankments the water is diverted into the old channel of the river flowing under the town, and thence to the head-works proper of the canal, where by means of a magnificent series of sluices the supply is finally regulated. In the early part of its course the engineering difficulties were enormous. It crosses four torrents, which in the rainy season are subject to dangerous floods from the Siwâlik hills, along the base of which the canal is constructed. Two of these torrents are carried over the canal; the third is passed on a level crossing provided with drop gates; over the fourth, the Solâni, the canal is carried by a fine aqueduct with fifteen spans of 50 feet each. It is thus brought to the Bângar or central plateau of the Ganges-Jumna Duâb. At the twenty-second mile the Canal throws off the Deoband branch to the west, 52 miles long; at mile 50 the Anupshahr branch, 107 miles long, and at mile 181 it bifurcates into what were called, before the construction of the Lower Ganges Canal, the Cawnpur and Etâwah branches, the former 172 and the latter 179 miles in length. Since the construction of the Lower Ganges Canal its irrigation has been combined with that of the older work, and crossing both these branches, they are supplied with water from it, and are considered below this point to belong to the Lower system. The total length of the main course of the Upper Ganges Canal is 213 miles; the original main line is navigable to the junction with the Lower Canal. When fully developed the Upper Ganges Canal will be capable of irrigating a million and a half acres, an area as great as that of the County of Galway.

The Lower Ganges Canal is taken from the Ganges at Nadrâi in the Aligarh district, 140 miles below Hardwâr. It is now, as we have seen, combined with the Upper Canal. Its area of possible irrigation is 1,100,000 acres.

The Eastern Jumna Canal starts from the river just at the foot of the Siwâlik hills and thence waters the Panjâb districts west of the river Jumna to a point opposite Delhi. Its irrigating capacity is 300,000 acres.

The Agra Canal is taken from the Jumna close to the point where the Eastern Jumna Canal ends. It waters the trans-Jumna portion of the Province country towards Mathura and Agra, and will ultimately irrigate 240,000 acres.

When fully developed these four canals in the western portion of the Province will ultimately water nearly three and a quarter million acres, an area nearly as great as that of the counties of Aberdeen and Argyllshire joined together.

The other canals in the northern tract are petty works,

which utilise, to the great advantage of the country, the smaller streams which flow from the lower hills. The Betwa Canal is a more important undertaking. It is intended to protect the tract in the neighbourhood of Jhânsi, the poorest and most famine-stricken part of the Province, from the periodical droughts which may always be expected. In a season like the present, when drought again prevails in Bundelkhand, the value of this Canal will be decisively proved. Its total length with its branches is 167 miles, and its irrigating capacity 150,000 acres.

The Canals of the Province have thus a main line length of 1464 miles, 6706 miles of distributaries, and 2003 miles of drainage channels—in all, 10,173 miles, or about half the length of all the railways in the United Kingdom, more than twice the distance from London to Calcutta *viâ* the Suez Canal. The financial results of the irrigation system, according to the figures of 1895-96, may be thus summarised. In all, 11,437 villages and over 2 million acres were under irrigation; the value of the crops irrigated was estimated at R.x. 6,410,000; the total income in 1893-94 was R.x. 716,658; the net income R.x. 428,540; the total capital spent up to date, R.x. 8,286,659, on which the interest realised was at the rate of 5-17 per cent. The undertaking has thus been a great financial success.

Besides the works already completed, another enormous scheme has been prepared for the irrigation of parts of Oudh and Rohilkhand. This is known as the Sârda Canal, and it is intended to utilise the surplus water of the Sârda, a snow-fed Himâlayan river, called further down its course the Chauka or Ghâgra. According to one version of this scheme, the Canal was to start in the Tarâi of the Pilibhît district, and lower down, to divide into three branches—one running south into the district of Shâhjahânpur; the second to be navigable throughout and tail into the Ganges, near Benares; the third, before ending in the Ghâgra at Faizâbâd, was to throw off branches to Azamgarh and Jaunpur. The estimated cost of one scheme was about four millions sterling, and the income was expected to realise 8 per cent. on the outlay; by another version the cost was to be over six millions, and the protected area over two and a quarter million acres.

This undertaking has been for the present suspended, and the proposals have given rise to much controversy. It was opposed by the Oudh Talukdârs, who appear not to desire the interference with their methods of estate management, which would result from the invasion of their villages by a troop of canal officers. Much of the land also which would come under the influence of the new canal is already fully supplied with wells.

Oudh has been on the whole much less exposed to famine than the sister Province, and the dread of subsoil saturation which has produced such disastrous results in parts of the Central Duâb will probably, for the present at least, cause this project to be deferred; but another drought such as that now prevailing in this part of the country is sure to revive the scheme. With the prospect of famine now hanging over the Province, the most reasonable forecast of the situation seems to be that the divisions of Meerut and Agra, with an area of 21,465 square miles and a population of about ten millions, are tolerably safe. The strain will probably be most severe in the divisions of Allahâbâd which includes Bundelkhand, Benares, and Gorahkpur, with an area of 37,169 square miles and a population of nearly eighteen millions. The condition of Oudh and parts of Rohilkhand, which are unprotected by canals, is also dangerous. In the former, with an area of 24,217 square miles and a population of twelve and a half millions, there has been a succession of indifferent harvests, and the poorer tenantry and day labourers will suffer acutely. Much, however, depends on the weather during the present cold weather (1896-97). The latest accounts report welcome rain during the winter which will do much to improve the prospects of the spring harvest and promote the growth of fodder. This was followed by ample showers about Christmas, by which the tension will be much reduced. But in any case the high prices of food grains which must prevail until the crops ripen next spring are certain to cause widespread suffering, which can only be alleviated by the opening of relief works and poorhouses on an extensive scale, and by liberal private benevolence.

In fact it would seem that for a time, unless in the event of the occurrence of famine, the policy of construction of great irrigation works will remain in abeyance, and the opportunity will be taken to develop the existing canals to their highest capacity, and to supplement them by drainage operations, which must do something to check the more crying evils which critics, imperfectly acquainted with the facts and ignoring the special climatic influences to which the country is habitually exposed, have attributed to them alone.

And here a word may be said of the staff of officers under whom this vast system of irrigation is controlled. Partly drawn from the Royal Engineers, partly from the Civil Engineering College at Cooper's Hill, and partly from the Thomason College at Rurki, the Government possesses no more able or devoted body of officials. The exigencies of his work compel the Canal Officer to be always on the move among the people. In the more busy agricultural seasons he is occupied with the distribution of the water-supply over a network of minor channels. He has to see that each village receives its due share of water; that the distributaries are kept in perfect order; that no favour shall be shown to any special class of the peasantry; that wanton waste of the precious fluid is checked. In the slack season, during the hot weather and rains, he is employed in works of repair and construction. He sees little of the amusements and hospitality of the headquarters station; his time is spent in solitude, marching day by day from one rest-house on the Canal bank to another. Hence he sees much more of the villager and his social life than other officers do whose tours are confined to the cold weather. He thus accumulates an immense store of experience regarding agriculture and the conditions under which the peasant lives: and he is usually a benevolent Hâkim, who directs the issues of prosperity. As he has little to say to imposing taxation or realising revenue, he can hardly fail to acquire popularity, sympathy, and insight; if he uses his unique opportunities aright he must gain wide influence over the rural classes. For a young man of active habits, with an observant eye and unfailing good temper, no career can be more attractive. On the other hand, it is a life with no amusements except those of sport and healthy exercise; to the man who longs for the flesh-pots of civilisation, who has no rural tastes and no idea of relaxation except in the ball-room or on the tennis-lawn, it must be insufferably tedious. But here Government has been well served by its officers, and there is no more striking instance of the unselfish devotion to duty, often irksome, always tedious and monotonous, than is seen in this branch of the public service. From its ranks has been drawn a select staff which has applied the fruits of experience gained in India to the reconstruction and development of Egyptian irrigation.

The extent to which the country can be protected from famine must always depend on the intensity of drought and on the amount to which the water supply provided by the canals can be supplemented by irrigation from wells and tanks. Assuming the necessary amount of food grains per unit of the population to be five maunds, or four hundred pounds, it was calculated in 1878 that in the Ganges-Jumna Duâb districts, working on the food-irrigated area, the protection afforded by the canals varies from one-tenth in Etah and Farrukhâbâd to three-fifths in Muzaffarnagar, and, working on the total irrigated areas, the protection is a minimum of one-ninth in Etah to a maximum of two-thirds in Muzaffarnagar. It was assumed that on the completion of the Lower Ganges and Agra Canals the protection would be to the extent of rather more than one-third of the area under food grains. But since the time when these estimates were framed the situation, as far as the food supply is concerned, has been largely modified by railway and canal extensions.

The case for and against canal irrigation may perhaps be briefly stated, as follows:—In the event of protracted drought the protection afforded by it is of the highest value. The main canal supply, being drawn from rivers fed by the Himâlayan snows, is practically beyond the reach of the causes which from time to time affect the periodical rains. It releases a large amount of labour usually employed on wells, which can be devoted to better and wider tillage. By the security it confers it has largely increased the area sown with the more valuable food crops, replacing the poorer millets by wheat and sugar-cane, and thus improving the land revenue. Lastly, it has exercised a most civilising effect on the wilder and more intractable races, such as the Râjputs and Gûjars, who since its introduction have turned their swords into plough-shares, and have adopted a life of prosperous industry, while their brethren beyond its influence have quite maintained their ancient evil reputation.

On the other hand, the abundant water supply has promoted the cultivation of inferior lands, which for a time respond to the stimulus, but owing to the limited manure supply rapidly decrease in fertility, and thus confirm the impression current among the peasantry that the soil is steadily becoming less productive. Another complaint is that the canal water has been introduced into villages where the supply from wells was already abundant. That this has occurred in some places cannot be denied, but on the other hand there are instances where the canal, by raising the water level, has made the supply from wells more accessible. Such a competent authority as Dr Voelcker makes light of this objection.[1]

What is more to the point is the allegation that the canal by raising the water level in the tracts under its influence has seriously affected the health of the population, and is accountable for the terrible epidemics of malarious fever which have devastated the Duâb in recent years.

This increase in the mortality from fever is one of the most severe disasters which have attacked the people since the Mutiny. People who are unaware of the facts speak as if the main dangers to human life in Northern India arose

[1] *Report*, 69.

from cholera and snake-bite. As a matter of fact, owing to improved sanitation and in particular to the precautions enforced at religious fairs, cholera has been in no sense serious in recent years. During the decade 1881-91 cholera accounted for only 4·22 per cent. of the total deaths, but has had a large share in determining the variation from year to year in individual districts. Smallpox, always endemic, is not accountable for any serious mortality. The number of deaths from snake-bite is quite inappreciable.

The case with fever is quite different. The annual death-rate from all classes of disease in the period 1881-91 was thirty-two per thousand, of which twenty-four was due to fever. Admitting that ignorant natives class all kinds of inflammatory disease under "fever," the result is sufficiently startling. Fever in the rainy season attacking the majority of the people is followed naturally with the first chills of winter by pneumonia, which, spreading among a community ignorant of the most elementary principles of hygiene, poorly fed, insufficiently clothed, destitute of medical aid or appliances for nursing the sick, is often attended with fatal results. To quote a graphic account by a writer on the spot [1]—"In Bulandshahr in the autumn of 1879 an unusually heavy rainfall, following upon several years of drought, developed a terrible epidemic, which literally more than decimated the population of the district. The crops stood uncut in the fields: the shops remained closed in the bâzârs: there was no traffic along the high roads, and no hum of business in the market-places; the receding flood of the great rivers showed their sands piled with corpses, while scarcely a water-course or wayside ditch but contained some ghastly relic of humanity hastily dropped by hireling bearers or even by friends too fearful for themselves or too enfeebled by disease to observe the funeral rites which are ordinarily held so sacred. In most of the towns and villages there was not a single house in which there was not one dead; in many entire families had perished—parents, grand-parents and children, and whole streets became deserted. Probably not a thousand

[1] Mr F. S. Growse, *Calcutta Review*, lxxvii. 352.

people in all from one end of the district to the other escaped without some touch of the disease." The result was that in a flourishing agricultural tract the population between 1871 and 1881 fell from 937,427 to 924,882.

Again in 1885 there was a mortality of 1,124,150 persons from fever, or 25 per mile of the population, chiefly in the Duâb and Rohilkhand. Commenting on this fact the Local Government writes[1]—"So much for the scientific facts, as far as they are reliable, and these bear out our former contention, that while in an undrained country abnormal rainfall increases the normal death-rate, and defect of rainfall decreases it, precisely the same law holds good in irrigated districts, with this important difference, however, that as irrigated districts suffer from what may be called a higher fever tension than exists in non-irrigated districts in the same country, increase of rain which in these Provinces generally might raise the fever rate, might at any time cause an explosion of fever in the irrigated districts. For this result the only available remedy is to keep the subsoil water moving at a lower level."

It may be freely admitted that much of the water-logging of the soil is due to the wasteful method in which the peasant uses the Canal water. Many attempts have been made to construct a workable water module, something like our household gas meter, which would register the actual amount of water supplied to each peasant and afford a means of levying the water rate according to the quantity consumed. The appliances hitherto proposed to meet this want have failed, either because they were too delicate or complicated, or because they became gradually clogged by the mass of silt which the water carries with it. Possibly at the present time there is no machine which would confer a greater advantage both on the Government and on an enormous population whose health is seriously affected by the over-saturation of the soil than a simple and effective appliance for registering the water supply to each holding. In default of such an appliance, the only method of controlling supply is by regulating the number and

[1] *Administration Report, North-Western Provinces*, 1885-86, p. 170.

capacity of the inlet pipes through which the water flows to each village, and by insisting as far as possible on a limitation of the size of the beds into which for irrigation purposes each field is divided. These checks on wasteful use of water are admittedly rude and inefficient.

While extravagance in the use of water among an extremely ignorant and jealous people, destitute of regard for the public weal and too suspicious of each other to combine to secure what is of primary importance to their welfare, must eventually lead to subsoil saturation and induce epidemics of fever, there is some ground for believing that this outbreak of disease may depend on wider causes. During the last twenty years parts of Bengal have suffered from what is known as Bardwân fever, from the district where its effects were most conspicuous. In twelve years before 1881 the fever which prevailed in Bardwân is said to have carried off not less than three-quarters of a million of people. In the next decade its effects in western Bengal were hardly less destructive. It was more of the choleraic than of the malarial type, and it would almost seem that the wave of infection can be traced through the North-West Provinces and into the Panjâb between 1887 and 1892. It appears, in fact, to have been one of those terrible remedies which, in spite of all that human sanitary science can do, Nature from time to time applies to check the over-fecundity of her children. All the great epidemics which have devastated the world, such as the Black Death of the fourteenth century, have been accompanied by violent climatic changes, even by earthquakes and other geological disturbances.[1] Influenza, which in some of its forms closely resembles the Dengue fever, which has from time to time been epidemic in India, has been connected by some authorities with inundations in China, by others with the eruption of the volcano of Krakatoa. It is possible that other than local causes may have contributed to produce the fever epidemics of Northern India.

It is only quite recently that the Province has been aroused from its attitude of complacency on the question of education.

[1] Creighton, *History of Epidemics in Britain*, i. 143.

It has always been regarded as an axiom that if we were surpassed by the Bengali in the matter of English education, we were, thanks to Mr Thomason, the founder of the system of village schools, and Sir W. Muir, the patron of the higher studies, well ahead of other parts of the country in elementary instruction. And while it was admitted that Muhammadans were somewhat behindhand in taking advantage of the new learning, it was naturally supposed that a steady taste for the higher culture spread from centres of the Hindu faith like Mathura and Benares.

But the chill evidence of statistics has proved that this feeling of self-satisfaction was ill-founded. We are now assured on the best authority that these Provinces enjoy the distinction of being the most illiterate tract in India, except the Central Provinces, where educational facilities are few, and where the jungle dweller has naturally no desire to learn.

The figures on which these results are based are in themselves surprising. It may be true that, owing to a misunderstanding of the Census schedule, only those "learners" were recorded as such who were attending a Government School. But even granting this, the so-called private school is a negligeable quantity so far as culture is concerned. If the school be devoted to the sciences of Islâm, the pupils squat in a row and sway their bodies backwards and forwards, all shouting in different keys the passages from the Korân which they are occupied in committing to memory. If the teacher be a Pandit, and his pupils young Brâhmans, he is teaching them the science of constructing a horoscope or the mysteries of astrology. Nor is it surprising that the number of "learners" recorded at the Census does not correspond with those entered in the departmental records. In every school there is a lowest class of tyros, who scrabble in the dust and chatter a letter or two of the alphabet to each other, and would certainly not pass the entrance examination of an English Kindergarten.

What is really important is to know the extent of the literate class, and even here the definition is wide enough to include learning of the meanest order. But still in every

10,000 males only 615 are "literate" or "learning," and only 21 females out of 10,000 fall in either category; or to put the case in another way, out of 1000 of each sex, 937 males and 997 females are illiterate. In the most backward of European countries, Portugal, the corresponding figures for males and females are 750 and 892. In Scotland there are only 46 illiterate males and 82 females in 1000 of each sex.

Again, comparing the results of the last two decennial enumerations, the rate of progress is far from satisfactory. It is true that in the case of males there is an increase of 12 per cent. of "literates" and boys under instruction, as contrasted with an increase of 6 per cent. in the total population; but with the vague standard for children under instruction this information is of little value. There is also the fact that the number of women educated or being educated has about doubled in ten years; but the numbers of such females—46,872, or 21 in 10,000 of the population, are exceedingly small.

The degree of literacy among the main religions and castes is worth considering. In the case of Hindus, out of 10,000 of each sex, there are 8103 males and 8553 females illiterate. The proportion for Musalmâns is slightly higher, but though this part of the country was the centre of their power, the seat of their courts and capitals, and the amount of land held by them in proprietary right higher than in other places, education has progressed less rapidly among them than in other parts of India. The best educated class in the whole community is that of the Christians; then follows the small body of Âryas and Jaina trading classes, whose occupation makes some education a necessity. About 50,000 people, half of whom are Christians, are recorded as knowing English.

Among castes, the best educated are naturally the Kâyasth or writing class, with 61 per cent. of literates; next come the Banyas or trading caste, while among Brâhmans only 18 per cent. of males and 6 per cent. of females are educated. As a matter of fact, the great mass of the Brâhmans are agriculturists, and the amount of learning which suffices for the village priest is the power of mumbling a few texts in a language of which he does not understand a word.

We are thus in this Province face to face with a standard of ignorance, which, when compared with that of civilised countries, is simply appalling. It is no wonder that every foolish rumour is believed; that any factious agitator finds an audience. According to the returns of 1893-94, the number of primary and secondary schools amounted to 4814, each school thus serving 22 square miles of area. But this does not quite represent the actual facts, as the total area includes the vast hilly tracts to the north and south of the valley, where the population is exceedingly sparse. And it would hardly be just to assert that there is a demand among the people for a considerable extension of State schools which the Government has been unable or unwilling to meet. If the policy has been mistaken, the error lies in diverting the labours and expenditure of the Educational Department towards the provision of higher class teaching instead of instructing the mass of the people.

But, in the present condition of things, it is impossible that the State can at once change its policy and withdraw its aid from higher education. This would immediately lead to the closing of a large proportion of the existing schools. If there were no other reason against adopting such a course, it is obviously necessary to maintain a supply of qualified clerks for our offices and candidates for the subordinate Civil Service. The progress of the country absolutely depends on the creation of a body of educated men for the Bar and Bench, the medical and engineering professions, business and the higher handicrafts. If the efforts of the Local Government were checked in this direction, it is certain that the want would be supplied by the immigration of the Bengâli Bâbu, the *Groeculus esuriens* of modern India, who would exclude the youths of the Province from every post of dignity and emolument. On the other hand, candidates for such employment are drawn, as a rule, from the wealthier classes, and it is only reasonable that they should bear a much larger proportion of the cost of that class of school which is now maintained for their personal advantage and advancement.

It also seems obvious that it would be to the advantage

of the State to dissociate itself as far as possible from the direct control of the higher education, instead of centralising it, as is the case at present, under the Education Department. It has been more than once suggested that these schools should be, as far as possible, made over to any respectable local bodies, who could give reasonable security that the cause of education would not suffer from a transfer of management, the Committee agreeing to adopt the prescribed text books and submit the pupils to periodical inspection, a grant in aid on the principle of payment by results being sanctioned. At present the youth, who has been trained in the higher learning mainly at the public cost, looks to the local authorities for an appointment, in fact, almost claims as a right that due provision should be made for his support in after life. This tends to give undue prominence to the public service as a career in preference to trade or other industrial pursuits. It imposes a serious burden on the official class which they should not be forced to assume, and it tends to create a class of discontented semi-educated men, who are a standing reproach and almost a menace to the administration.

It is this class which supplies the writers to the vernacular press of the country, a body of journalists who, to use the words of Oliver Wendell Holmes, are "full of the flippant loquacity of half-knowledge." It is easy to say that the circulation of these papers is small, and their influence slight among the illiterate masses; but it cannot tend to the well-being of the country that the acts of its rulers should be habitually misrepresented, and its officers constantly vilified with practical impunity. On this point it may be well to quote the deliberate opinion of the head of the Government, whose calm review of the situation is impressive from its extreme moderation:—[1]

"The native press of these Provinces is to a considerable extent free from the charge of excess which characterises the press of many other parts of India. A more temperate tone and habit of thought exists here; but there is a tendency, probably a growing tendency, to imitate the violent style and the unreasoning methods of the native press elsewhere.

[1] *Administration Report, North-West Provinces*, 1888-89, p. xxxv. sq.

The adoption of the tone which characterises most of the native press is the more to be regretted, as it robs it of value as a guide and assistance to the Government, its attacks being without qualification and discernment. All that emanates from Government being found by this section to be equally bad, it is too often useless to turn to its pages for intelligent, discerning criticism of its measures, or for any useful statement of the views and wishes of the people. There exist, happily, in these Provinces certain native papers which no way expose themselves to these strictures. Nevertheless, the native press is in too great measure in the hands of needy men, who use it to blackmail their respectable fellow-citizens; and apart from its uselessness, for the reasons above stated, as a guide to general native opinion, the licence which at present characterises it is in the highest degree odious to the large and important class who are thus laid under contribution. The Lieutenant-Governor does not at present see any ground for supposing that the intemperate language of the native press, and its indiscriminating attacks on officials in India, have in any degree corrupted the general tone of thought among the people or led them to adopt its point of view. It is in no sense of the word a representative press, need and greed being its main features. It is difficult, however, to believe that the uninterrupted and increasing circulation of newspapers, habitually imputing to the Government of India the basest designs, and to its officers the most unscrupulous conduct, can fail in course of time among a very ignorant people, such as are the masses here, to create a strong feeling of hostility to a Government which is confidently, and as far as they can see, without contradiction, stated to be animated by such motives and served by such subordinates. All that can be said upon the subject at present is that the ignorant classes seem so far to have formed and retained juster conceptions on the subject than those who have assumed the mission of instructing them."

Another want seriously felt is the provision of a wholesome popular literature. Many of the cheap books on sale are either gross or stupid drivel, without any elevating influence. Many of the current publications are extracts from or commentaries on religious books, so-called "science" of the Oriental type—treatises on magic, astrology, and the like—or cheap cram books for native students. On the other hand, the class trained in English is too limited, and their knowledge of the language insufficient to popularise the study of our literature. Translations, again, of the best foreign books fail to suit the Oriental mind. A society for encouraging the production and dissemination of books suited to the comprehension of the student class would find a most extensive field of operations.

So far the youths trained in our schools and colleges have shown little aptitude for the pursuit of literature. The acquisition of a degree is considered only a qualification for official employment, or for entrance into professions such as the Bar. When once this object is attained, the student has no ambition to continue his search for knowledge, and he lacks that mental discipline which the habit of reading through middle and later life secures to the cultured European. Hence we too often find among the native educated classes the sublime self-confidence of the half-educated man, the lack of power to concentrate the mind on a special subject, of the taste for minute, laborious investigation; these are replaced by a love of frothy declamation, of hastily formed theories of life and conduct which do not rest on the solid basis of reflection. The mental powers are overstimulated in early youth, and in after years become weakened from disuse. In particular, the present system of education seems to develop little taste for practical science. Though the field for new inventions or adaptations of western discoveries to agriculture, irrigation, and the mechanical arts is immense, little has been done. The same is the case with sociology and ethnology, the study of the classical languages, local history and folk-lore, to which the contributions of the natives of the country have been inconsiderable.[1]

In considering the results of our higher education we have passed by the really important subject of the gross illiteracy of the masses. Europe can, at least for the present, find all the scientific knowledge which the nation can assimilate. But were it only to protect the peasant from the money-lending shark or the knaveries of the village accountant, the

[1] At the same time the experiments recently carried out by Professor J. C. Bose, in connection with the polarisation of the electric ray, give promise of greater success in the field of scientific enquiry. But he is a Bengâli, not a native of Upper India, and in Calcutta and Bombay the standard of culture among the educated classes is much higher than in the interior of the Peninsula.

encouragement of elementary education is an obvious public duty. The people are illiterate, because no less than 75 per cent. of them depend for their livelihood on agriculture—an occupation which in all countries is divorced from literature. The wearied peasant in the short hour of dusk before bed-time finds sufficient mental exercise in the gossip over village politics, by the smoky fire or under the pîpal tree. If he sends his boy to school at all, his attendance is irregular, because his services are needed to pasture the goat, cut forage for the cow, or scare the green parrots from the millet. Besides this, why does he support the Brâhman Levite or the Kâyasth writer, if it be not that they have the monopoly of learning? And the Brâhman himself finds that the keen-witted school-boy is apt to laugh at his old-fashioned learning, and to lower his repute as the sole depositary of culture by wild talk of sciences beyond his ken. "We can thus see that the field in which the seeds of literacy have to be sown consists of a few square yards of what we may call relatively good soil, prepared to receive all the seed it can get, and thirsting for the whole of the attention of the husbandman. Then comes the vast stony waste of labour and menial offices, without sufficient depth of soil to allow the seed to strike root, and, lastly, the many miles of arable mark, so taken up with the production of the food and clothing of the whole community, that whatever else is sown in it is inevitably choked before it can ripen."[1]

With female education the case is even stronger, for here the influence of Mrs Grundy comes into play. The learned lady has ever been an object of suspicion to her less advanced sisters, and in India book-learning has always been deemed to suggest in the woman who possesses it some analogy to the free-living Hetaira. The duties of the housewife are prescribed by immemorial custom to be—to bear a son, to cook the savoury dishes which her lord loveth, to distribute charity to the religious mendicant. Thus saith Manu, the sage[2]:—"Let the husband keep his wife employed in the collection and expenditure of wealth, in purification and female duty

[1] Baines' *Indian Census Report*, 1891, p. 212. [2] *Institutes*, ix. 11, 17, 18.

in the preparation of daily food, and the superintendence of household utensils. Prone are they to love of their bed, of their seat, and of ornament, impure appetites, wrath, weak flexibility, desire of mischief and bad conduct. They have no business with the texts of the Vedas." Within an horizon thus bounded by cooking and spring cleaning there is no room for the intellectual companionship of man and wife, the ideal of wedlock in the West. The wife is ever in tutelage, married when a child, a mother when European girls are at school; monotonous household work, the tending of the cattle, the weeding of the field, the scaring of the birds, are her portion from maidenhood to old age. Petted in the beauty of youth, when this is gone she is a drudge in her later years. All through her life education is not to be thought of, even if it were not choked out by meaner cares.

One thing is quite clear—the provision of education for these illiterate millions is entirely beyond the resources of the State. All that can be done is to save in the expenditure for the higher education, and work up the hedge schools to some degree of efficiency.

In another department the results are more encouraging. It would really seem that we have now succeeded in convincing the peasant of the superiority of our medical, or rather surgical, treatment over his familiar methods. The last few years have shown an enormous increase in the hospital attendance. In 1893-94, this amounted to no less than 3¾ millions of patients. In particular, the confidence of the people in the ophthalmic skill of our surgeons is obviously increasing year by year. The conditions of village life—the close smoky air of the huts, the fierce glare of the summer sun, the dust, the flies—are all causes of eye affections. Added to these, the inferior quality of the food, especially in fatty and saline principles, the prevalence of malarial fever and the leprosy taint are all favourable to the development of cataract and other forms of eye disease. The native oculist, with his rough methods, coarse instruments, and lack of scientific knowledge or sanitary precautions, is now pretty generally discredited. The average number of blind people in 100,000 of the population for the whole of India is 164 men and 171 females; the corresponding figures for these Provinces are respectively 216 and 224 —more than double the English average. Blindness is thus exceedingly prevalent, and the only parts of India where it is more common are Berâr, the Panjâb, and Upper Burma. There seems no doubt that there has been a decrease of no less than 15 per cent. in the number of the blind since the last decennial Census. Probably the main reason of this is the diminution of smallpox, which, before vaccination was introduced into England, accounted for 35 per cent. of the cases of blindness. But much of the decrease is certainly due to the skill of our surgeons, who, in the same period, dealt with 54,535 cases of eye disease, of which 47,081, or 86 per cent., were cured or relieved—a record which would do credit to any country, but particularly laudable considering the adverse circumstances under which the work was done as compared with the well-equipped ophthalmic hospitals of Europe.

The same is the case with the use of quinine as a remedy for malarial fever. A generation ago its high price was prohibitive; now-a-days, with improved methods of manufacture and increased culture of the cinchona tree, it is within the reach of all. In Bengal it is now sold in penny packets at every Post Office, and it is quite time that this boon was extended to other parts of the country. Anything which would reduce the terrible loss of life, and, even when the patient recovers, the weakness which accompanies convalescence, would be an inestimable blessing. No more painful sight is to be seen in rural India than a line of pallid wretches warming their chilled bodies in the morning sun, while the cattle stand idle in the shed, and the broad fields lie unploughed, because the husbandman's energies have been sapped by the foul malaria fiend.

The progress made in sanitation during the last thirty years serves only to emphasise the fact that the task is of stupendous difficulty, that much of it is beyond the power of any Government to undertake unless it throws to the winds all considerations of finance, and all regard for the prejudices of the people. The striking fact in this connection is that with a very liberal definition of a "town," only 11 per cent. of the people are urban, occupying 484 sites. To put this in another way—of the total population nearly 5½ millions live in the towns; about 42½ millions occupy 105,716 villages. This distinction is vital from the point of view of sanitation. In the towns we may do something: who will dare to apply sanitary regulations to the villages?

To take the city and town population first—out of these 103 cities or towns with a population of 3¼ millions are managed by Municipal Boards, which realise an annual income of nearly R.x. 300,000 mostly by means of an octroi tax, and spend about 45 per cent. of their income on sanitation. The remaining towns are under the direct management of the district Magistrate, and a small income is realised by means of a house tax assessed by a body of members, of which part is spent on the town Watch and Ward, and part on roads and sanitation.

The cities under Municipal control are as a rule fairly well provided with surface drainage, latrines and a conservancy establishment. During the last decade the larger cities have at considerable cost provided a good supply of filtered water. In some cases these works are a serious burden on the Municipal finances.

In the smaller towns which are not managed by a Municipal Board the income, much of which is levied from very poor people, suffices only to maintain a small conservancy staff and to carry out sanitary works of the simplest kind. Where the town is the headquarters of a Tahsîldâr or Sub-Collector the control is fairly efficient; in the more isolated towns a general spring cleaning goes on when the visit of an official may be expected. At other times many of these places revert to their primitive state of filth. The death returns for the ten years prior to the last Census show 119 deaths in towns for each 100 in villages for equal numbers living. In England there are 111 town deaths for every 100 country deaths, and though in India the record of deaths in the urban is more accurate than in the rural circles, the existing figures, when allowance is made for the inevitable overcrowding in the towns, probably closely represent actual facts.

The constant crusade carried on to enforce some degree of cleanliness among the town population has undoubtedly been to some extent effective. The Hindu in regard to the preparation of his food, the purification of his person and raiment, professes to be under the influence of religious sanctions which are ostensibly of a most stringent nature. From these the Musalmân holds himself in a large measure relieved. But while all classes of the people profess an academic acquiescence in rules enforcing cleanliness, practice always tends to lag behind theory. While, for instance, the cooking place of the Hindu is carefully guarded against pollution, and the touch, or even in some cases the shadow of a low caste person, will be held to defile the food; in the purity of the water which he drinks, in the disposal of his house refuse, in the minor decencies of civilised life he is absolutely careless. And it is also very noticeable that the habit of cleanliness does not improve as we compare the richer and higher classes with the poor and those of low degree. The narrow hut of the leather-worker or scavenger will be usually found purer than the mansion of the banker; and the English-speaking clerk or lawyer will as consistently neglect the commonest rules of cleanliness as his most ignorant neighbour. This is particularly the case among those classes which enforce the seclusion of their women, and resent with the most passionate insistence any attempt to explore the mysteries of the Zanâna.

It is this fact which makes the cleansing of the Augean stables in our towns a task of such difficulty and delicacy. The roads may be regularly swept, the street drains periodically flushed; but it is only, after all, the cleansing of the outside of the cup and platter, while behind these jealously-guarded walls lies a region where sanitation cannot be enforced without offending the most deeply-seated prejudices of the people.

The problem of village sanitation has been debated *ad nauseam.* Something has been done by means of extensive drainage works to remedy the water-logging of the Central Ganges-Jumna Duâb, where the outbreaks of fever have been most destructive. Vaccination has been pressed forward, and the main prejudice against it on the assumed ground of interference with caste is gradually being overcome by the object-lesson of the protection afforded by it against the ravages of small-pox. But the problem of applying sanitary regulations to the vast village population distributed over an enormous area remains pretty much where it was. All are agreed as to the advantage of some reform, but the practical difficulties are overwhelming. Officials in their periodical tours can and do something to help in the struggle against dirt; but steady, effective control involves the appointment of a great special staff, which, unless paid at rates which are at present prohibitive, would involve far-reaching evils. A sanitary inspector must be a man of tact, common sense, and honesty. He must contend with the patent difficulty of reconciling the requirements of the law with the needs of established industries, such as the muck-heap of the Jât cultivator or the tan-pit of the Chamâr. To hustle or worry either of these pillars of the State would be as intolerable as to prosecute every old lady who scours her cooking pots outside her narrow hut, and drag her before a Magistrate who holds his Court perhaps fifty miles away. Village cleanliness is an ideal not to be lost sight of; not to be secured by ill-judged, fussy interference with people whose ways of life are prescribed by immemorial custom, and who measure the efficiency of a Government by the degree to which they are carefully let alone. On the other hand, much good may be done by regulating the village well and protecting it from the worst forms of pollution. But as for a general crusade against filth in rural India the people will not endure it, and no Government in its senses would seriously propose to wage it. Like many other reforms in lands more advanced than India, it must await the growth of a healthy public feeling in its favour.

The sphere in which our work has been most beneficial to the people is undoubtedly in the matter of communications. What the condition of things was at the commencement of our rule may be gathered from the accounts of contemporary writers. We have seen that the Mughal Government, beyond the construction of a great highway for military purposes, did little in this direction. After we took over the country we introduced the *corvée* system, and from Dr Buchanan's account of Gorakhpur in the first decade of the century the result was, as might have been expected, unsatisfactory. He suspected, not perhaps without good reason, that many of the roads had been made for the convenience of gentlemen going on shooting parties.[1] Writing in 1824, Bishop Heber says[2]—"Nothing could be more unfounded than the assurance which I have heard in Calcutta that an open carriage is an eligible method of travelling in the Duâb on any other ground than cheapness. I have been told that the road as far as Meerut would answer perfectly for a gig. The fact is there are no roads at all, and the tracks which we follow are often such as to require care even on horseback. By driving slowly no doubt a gig may go almost anywhere, but it is anything but an agreeable pastime to drive along tracks which, when beaten, are so poached by the feet of horses and cattle and so hardened by the sun as to resemble a frozen farmyard; while if the traveller forsakes those roads he encounters cracks deep and wide enough to break his wheels. Here and there is a tolerably level mile or two, but with a few exceptions there is no fast or pleasant driving in this part of India." And when he came into Oudh things were even worse. We can now hardly realise that he devoted anxious enquiries to ascertain whether there was any practicable route between Lucknow and Bareilly. Even about 1840 things were not much better. An officer on service writes[3]—"The road between Allahâbâd and Cawnpur passeth all understanding. The head of our column got on pretty well, not sinking much above their knees in the impalpable soil;

[1] *Eastern India*, ii. 579.

[2] *Diary*, 192, 227.

[3] *Military Service and Adventures in the Far East*, ii. 20.

but the centre and rear staggered blindly onward, and not unfrequently downward, through the clouds raised by their predecessors till they reached more substantial ground; others jostled against mud walls and trees, trod on their neighbours' toes, or wandering from their comrades, groped their way out of the dense atmosphere and only discovered the locality of the column by the glimpse of a few miller-like objects preceding the column."

In those days the journey from Calcutta to Benares cost R.x. 76 in a palanquin; the first-class fare is now about one-fourth of this. In 1851 the post took four days to travel from Calcutta to Patna[1]; the mail train now conveys it in little more than a quarter of this time. It was not till 1833 that the great highway known as the Grand Trunk road from Calcutta to the Panjâb was commenced; it was not till 1852 that it was extended to Ambâla. In 1841 mail carts were first brought into use, and about the same time the modern Dâk Gâri or travelling carriage was evolved out of an invention by which the palanquin was laid on a truck and dragged from stage to stage by coolies. It was in the year 1856, just before the Mutiny, that railways were introduced. The last returns show 2734 miles of railway open in the Province, and this will soon be largely increased by the lines of Light Railways which are now being started as famine relief works. The increase in travelling has been enormous. The number of passengers conveyed by the Oudh and Rohilkhand line rose between 1881 and 1891 from 2,632,000 to 5,254,000, on the East Indian railway from 2,437,000 to just under 4,000,000. The whole country has been covered with a network of roads, of which those that are bridged and metalled are excellent.

The effect of this extension of communications has been most remarkable. The theory that the high-caste native, through dread of contamination from his meaner fellow-passengers, would not use the railway, has been quite discredited. Considerations of obvious convenience have in this case, as in the use of pipe water in the larger cities,

[1] *Good Old Days of John Company*, ii. 89.

caused a modification of the rules of social life and traditional custom. From the point of view of the railway official the native is an admirable passenger. Possessed of little sense of the value of time, he does not care for a high rate of speed, and he will wait for half a day with sublime patience till his train chances to draw up at the platform. He does not mind overcrowding, and will pack his carriage with malodorous bundles of luggage which he is much too canny to make over to the guard. He will gladly accept a seat in a cattle truck if no better conveyance be forthcoming, and once he has secured his seat his power of enduring fatigue makes him quite callous to minor inconveniences against which a less stolid race would fret and fume.

Though the facility of travelling has increased the attendance at the great bathing fairs, the rush of pilgrims shows as yet no signs of becoming unmanageable. The pilgrim is beginning shrewdly to understand that at these enormous gatherings he and his womenkind are liable to be hustled and overcharged; he chafes under the sanitary restrictions which a crowded fair necessitates. So he finds it to his interest to defer his visit until times are quieter, and then he receives better terms and more attention from his Brâhman cicerone. This personage does not entirely approve of the new regime. If more pilgrims visit his shrine, they stay for a shorter time, pack in visits to more than one sacred place on the journey, and have less to spend at each. Railway travelling is making the Hindu more of a man of the world, more self-reliant, less easily fleeced, more disposed to depart at once if he finds himself ill-treated. But life has become sensibly brighter to the village yokel and the blushing, giggling maidens since a bath in the holy water of Mother Ganges has been brought more within the reach of their narrow purses.

Trade under the changed conditions has been simply revolutionised. The telegraph now flashes the hourly fluctuations of the market from Calcutta to Peshâwar; "time bargains" and "corners" in wheat or cotton gratify the native merchant's innate love of a gamble. The great

MALLÂH BOATMEN WITH "DUG-OUT."

ancient merchant houses with their wide storehouses, their fleets of boats, their convoys of merchandise, have disappeared, and the middleman is rapidly sharing their fate. The petty village cloth merchant or corn chandler deals direct with the agent of some firm in Bombay and Calcutta. Prices have become practically the same all along the line. The old-fashioned days in which grain or other produce lay stored in the warehouses till the river rose, or the chance of turning a large profit appeared, have passed away, and have been replaced by the new system of rapid sales and quick, if smaller, returns on investments. Many historic marts, like Mirzapur, which once commanded the trade with the Deccan or Fatehgarh, which was the business entrepot between Oudh and the west, have found themselves stranded in a commercial backwater. Their warehouses are empty, their once busy bâzârs deserted, and business has sought more convenient centres, like Cawnpur, Agra or Hâthras.

Far the most famous of the old commercial firms was that of the Seths of Mathura, who in former days ranked as the Rothschilds or Barings of Northern India. Founded in the commencement of the century, this banking house acquired enormous wealth, and became well known by their distinguished loyalty to the Crown and their widespread beneficence. Between 1845 and 1851 they erected on the Madras model the splendid temple of Vishnu in his manifestation as Rangji, at Brindaban, at a cost of nearly half a million, and their expenditure on works of charity and celebrations of worship has been always on a princely scale. No more striking spectacle can be witnessed than the annual procession of the god on a car like that of Jaggannâth. But under changed conditions this great commercial house has failed to maintain the pre-eminence which it once enjoyed in trading circles.

With this shaking up of the dry bones of Indian commercial life has been born the new organisation of trade which has brought the wheat of the Upper Duâb on English breakfast tables, and has made the merchant of Mark Lane anxiously watch the progress of the monsoon or the failure of the winter rain. One condition precedent to a more extensive exportation is the maintenance of a low silver exchange. Should the course of events tend to re-establish the value of the rupee it will act as a check to trade. In any case the widespread native opinion that it is this increase of exports which has led to the great rise in prices is obviously incorrect. The fear that the amount of these exports would intensify scarcity is no less ill-founded. The rise of internal prices caused by drought would at once operate as a check on foreign exportation, and the amount of wheat exported at present is only one per cent. of the total food grains produced in Northern India, and only one-tenth of the total crop of wheat.[1]

This leads to the subject of Famine—one of the most notable chapters in the history of our rule. Lying, as we have seen, at the meeting-point of the two chief rain currents, the Province has been from time immemorial liable to scarcity of rain. Of the famines which occurred before we assumed charge of the country we have no clear accounts, and some of them were perhaps due as much to the ravages of war as to actual drought.

One of the earliest famines of which we have any record occurred in 1291 A.D., in the reign of Fîroz Shâh Khilji. "The Hindus of that country," says the chronicler, "came into Delhi with their families, twenty and thirty of them together, and in the extremity of hunger drowned themselves in the Jumna. The Sultân and his nobles did all they could to help them."[2]

The next famine we hear of was caused mainly by the oppression of the Sultân, Muhammad bin Tughlak (1327-35 A.D.). The traveller Ibn Batuta was a witness of this. He says he saw women eating the skin of a horse which had been dead some months, and others fighting for blood at the slaughter-houses. The Government is said to have distributed food for six months.[3]

[1] Voelcker, *Report*, 295.
[2] Elliot, *Historians*, iii. 146; *Gazetteer, North-West Provinces*, ii. 35.
[3] Elliot, *ibid.*, iii. 238.

The invasion of Timûr was followed by another terrible scarcity. Many died of hunger, and for two months Delhi was desolate.[1]

We have an account of an outbreak of cholera in 1616 A.D., caused by a famine which prevailed for two years in succession. "Life was offered for a loaf," says the annalist,[2] "but no one would deal." The Emperor Shâh Jahân opened kitchens and remitted revenue. Again in 1660 many districts lay entirely waste, and crowds of people made their way to the capital.

The century of misrule which preceded our occupation witnessed at least one severe famine. Scarcity, as might have been expected, followed in the train of Nâdir Shâh's raid on Delhi in 1739 and on the Sikh inroads in the western districts which occurred soon after. The terrible famine which ravaged Bengal and Bihâr in 1770 had little influence further west, except that excessive exports raised the local prices.

But in 1783-84 occurred the great famine, of which vivid stories still live in the memories of the people. This was in popular parlance the Châlîsa or "fortieth," so called because it occurred in the year 1840 of the Sambat or Hindu era. A complete failure of the autumn rains followed two years of partial drought. Its ravages seem to have been most serious in the Central Duâb. Mr Girdlestone tells us[3] that in the emigration of the famine-stricken wretches to Oudh, where the scarcity was supposed to be less severe, "death left its mark freely along the road. Such was the general apathy that the bodies were not removed from the place where they lay, even in towns and villages. No relief was held out to the sick and dying. Every man's hand was against his neighbour, and the strong ruthlessly seized the portion of the weak, for the struggle to maintain life overcame all scruples." Warren Hastings was at the time in Benares, and was a personal witness of the misery of the people. Many a deserted village mound is in the popular tradition attributed to the ravages of the dreaded Châlîsa.

The first years of our administration were clouded by

[1] Elliot, *Historians*, iv. 38. [2] *Ibid.*, vi. 346. [3] *Famine Report*, 8.

famine, a calamity which the people were not slow to associate with our conquest. Famine in their view of the case, like disease or any other calamity, is not a misfortune due to natural causes, but to the sins or ill-luck of their rulers. At one time it has been attributed to the operations of the Survey, a sacrilegious interference with the benign Mother Earth, who is sure to resent the insult of meting her out with chain and compass and confining her with boundaries by withholding her kindly fruits in their season. At another it is the profane slaughter of sacred kine which aroused the wrath of the gods, as it did when the ill-fated companions of Odysseus slew the holy cattle of Helios Hyperion. In this case the scarcity which followed the footsteps of Lord Lake was due in 1803-4 partly to a natural drought, partly to the interruption of husbandry by the contending armies. The Duâb, again, was the chief seat of the scarcity. The Government met the emergency by a remission of revenue to the amount of R.x. 300,000.

In fact, these early years of our rule seem to have been marked by an unusual amount of scarcity, to which excessive revenue assessments, the disorganisation of the district establishments, and the ignorance of the Civil officers of the resources of the country and the needs of the people doubtless contributed. In one of these scarcities parts of Bundelkhand, already harassed by the Central Indian marauders, suffered severely.

But all these minor disasters pale before the horrors of the famine of 1837-38, which, on the analogy of the Châlîsa, is known as the Chaurânavê, or "ninety-four," because it occurred in the year 1894 of the Hindu era. It affected the whole country between Allahâbâd and Delhi, but was most severe in the Central Duâb, in the neighbourhood of Agra and Cawnpur. Including Râjputâna, the population exposed to it was about 28 millions. In 1836 the rains failed, and the distress was intensified by poor harvests in the preceding years. Grain merchants closed their shops, the peasantry took to plunder; cattle starved and died; in the part of the Mathura district west of the Jumna, the village thatches were torn down to feed the starving beasts. There was a general move of the people in the direction of Mâlwa, that Cathay or land of plenty, where, in the imagination of the North Indian rustic, the fields always smile with golden grain and poverty is unknown.

We have graphic accounts from eye-witnesses of the sufferings of the people. In Farrukhâbâd.[1] "Brâhmans, who had before rejected their cooked food if the defiled Christian came too near, were now seen by us stealing the scraps from our dogs. Mothers sold their infants to the despised foreigners, or left them a prey to the wolves; society was entirely disorganised, and horrors of every kind pervaded the land." Prices rose to three times the ordinary rates, but common grain seldom sold at less than 20 lbs. to the rupee—a rate which would not now-a-days indicate extreme tension.

This famine for two reasons marks an important change in the attitude of the State to calamities such as these. Now, for the first time, the obligation of the Government to provide for the relief of the starving masses was recognised. Lord Auckland, the Governor-General, personally assumed charge of the operations. Nearly half the land revenue of the affected tract was remitted; public works were opened for the able-bodied; while charitable organisations assisted the helpless and infirm. But our officers did not then possess that grasp of the country which they afterwards secured, and the agricultural statistics of the time were very incomplete. In spite of all exertions there was a lamentable loss of life. It was long after calculated by Colonel Baird Smith at 800,000, but this is probably much below the mark.

The second important result of this famine was the plan for the construction of the Ganges Canal, to which reference has been already made.

After this for about twenty years the land had rest. The disturbances of 1857-58 seriously interrupted agriculture, much property was destroyed, and the land remained untilled. Two scanty years were followed by failure of the rains in 1860, and though the injury to the crops was sup-

[1] *Gazetteer, North-West Provinces*, viii. 53.

posed to be not less than in 1837, the area of suffering was much smaller. This time it again severely attacked the country between Delhi and Agra, inhabited by about 5½ millions of people. The Government actively interfered on the lines laid down in 1837-38. But, on the initiative of Sir John Strachey, then Collector of Morâdâbâd, the system of supplying cooked food to persons who consented to be temporarily confined in an enclosed workhouse was for the first time introduced, and secured an admirable check on the class of professional mendicants. This arrangement has been embodied in the standard Code regulating the principles on which famine relief is administered. The general result is that the able-bodied labourer is provided with work at a living wage, either on extensive public works managed by a trained engineering staff, or on smaller local undertakings supervised by the district officials; while the sick and weak, old people and young children, are relieved in a poorhouse or famine camp, where medical attendance is supplied and sanitary rules enforced. A further extension of artificial irrigation, and in particular the construction of the Lower Ganges Canal, followed this famine.

There was another drought of less intensity in 1868. In 1873-74 Government was again called upon to start relief works in the Benares division, which, however, was less seriously affected than the neighbouring districts in Bengal and Bihâr. By this time, as a result of the drought of 1868, the principle had now become established that it was the object of Government to save every life, and that its officers would be held responsible for any preventible mortality. The experience in Gorakhpur showed that it was absolutely necessary, by the reduction of wages to the limits which provided a mere subsistence, to put a check on the masses who, at certain times of the year when agricultural work is slack, will always crowd on relief works. With stricter supervision and the enforcement of the rule that labourers should remain continuously on the works, and not occasionally return home, as soon as the rains set in the vast masses of paupers melted away. The same policy was pursued in the drought which occurred in the western parts of the Province in 1877-78, and though the Government did not escape criticism for the rigidity of its methods, the suffering was nowhere of a really serious type. Since that period, except for the drought which in 1896 prevailed in parts of Bundelkhand, there has been no exceptionally severe distress. But the failure of this year's monsoon, following on, at least in Oudh, a couple of lean seasons, has again brought the question of famine relief to the front.

It will be shown later on that the increase of the population does not progress at such a rapid rate as is commonly supposed, and that natural causes and prudential considerations do exercise some check upon the fertility of the people. At the same time, there is in some parts of the Province a dangerous degree of congestion which creates a depressed residuum, exposed to want on the occurrence of even a minor check to agriculture, their only means of support. Putting aside the earlier enumerations, which were to some extent imperfect and affected by changes of area, we have the definite fact that in twenty years (1872-91) the population of the North-West Provinces rose from 30¾ to 34¼ millions, and that of Oudh from 11¼ to nearly 12¾ millions. Parts of the country offer instances of a density of population which can be compared only with that of exceptional tracts in Europe, where industrial and commercial life is most highly organised. This people, again, definitely refuses to avail itself of that relief by emigration to less congested areas which led the surplus population of Ireland to the American Continent, and is now driving Italians to Brazil or Argentina, and the Chinaman to the Malay Peninsula and the islands of the Southern Sea.

The State is thus here confronted with a problem which would tax the resources of the greatest Governments. There is, perhaps, no more pathetic situation in the whole range of human history than to watch these dull, patient masses stumbling in their traditional way along a path which can lead only to suffering, most of them careless of the future, marrying and giving in marriage, fresh generations ever encroaching on the narrow margin which separates them from destitution. Anxious statesmen peer into the mists which shroud the future, and wonder what the end of all this may be. Will some grand agricultural discovery, some invention in the way of a new system of culture, some secret of chemistry which the world as yet knows not, some idea which will flash through the land, simple and cheap enough for any rustic to employ, and yet such as will not give a shock to his habitual methods, expel for a time the demon of poverty, and give them another start? Or will Nature in one of her relentless moods intervene, as she has often done before, and sweep away the useless mouths by pestilence or famine? Or will some sudden impulse, the trumpet voice of some teacher, drive them, as it drove Goth or Vandal or Tatar, to seek new homes under another sky in Burma, the jungles of Central India, or Uganda?

Meanwhile, all that can be done is being done; the resources of the Province are being steadily developed by the construction of railways and canals; the conditions of the more depressed tracts, such as Bundelkhand, have been carefully investigated; in the pigeon-holes of each district officer are to be found a number of well-considered estimates for public works, which can be put in hand when necessity arises; and the principles which should regulate the action of the Government have been formulated.

The expense of meeting an emergency of this kind is a serious financial difficulty; but economy is secured by the enforcement of the principle that famine relief is a Provincial, not an Imperial charge. And it must be remembered that the annual charge for poor relief in England and Wales is nearly ten millions per annum, from which, so far, India has escaped. Nowhere has the practice of charity been more generally raised to the level of a religious duty. Much of it, it is true, such as the food and gifts lavished on Brâhmans and religious mendicants, is sheer waste; much of the marriage alms and daily doles distributed to all-comers by rich traders are merely a form of ostentation, and do harm by pauperising the recipients. On the other hand, there is a vast amount of quiet, simple benevolence in rural life. The widow is ever bringing her gift to the treasury, and the very poor can always find a handful of grain for the destitute. With a large indigent population the temptations to start some form of permanent relief is largely felt; but the risk of pauperisation is fully recognised, and it is very doubtful if sufficient voluntary contributions could be secured. All native benevolence takes the personal form, and regular subscriptions to permanent charities, like hospitals, are not readily given. In any general scheme of relief, the burden thus undertaken would ultimately fall on the State, which has no sufficient funds to meet it.

Nor is much to be expected from the local organisations known as District Boards. At present the incidence of Municipal taxation is only three-quarters of a rupee per head of the urban population per annum. Nor is it probable that this amount can at present be exceeded. The town residents have lost heavily in recent years through the rise in food grains, and the class of unskilled town labourer suffers from the danger of being swamped by the hungry emigrants from the villages round him. City industries, particularly that of weaving, are depressed. The hand-loom has given way to competition with machinery, both English and local, and it is very doubtful how far recent fiscal legislation will improve it. In any case, the village weaver is more and more abandoning the use of hand-made yarn for the cheaper article turned out by the mills.

It is not easy to estimate exactly the effect of this devolution of the business of government upon local bodies. When these measures were first brought into force, the Government admitted that it was prepared for a certain amount of failure, which would be, it was hoped, compensated for by the educational value of the training in practical administration. In most cases the Magistrate continued to act as Chairman of the Local Board; he was to dry-nurse the administrative bantling, and gradually train it to walk by itself; at the same time, he was to work more by advice and persuasion than by active personal interference. This was obviously a task requiring the utmost tact and discretion. He had to waste valuable time listening to turgid harangues over petty details, which an official trained in business could dispose of summarily; he had to close his eyes to some amount of jobbery and partisanship. In some few places the control of the Board has been fairly efficient. But as the Lieutenant-Governor himself remarks [1]—"Public spirit is little known in these Provinces, and must not be confounded with public agitation. The co-operation of individuals and classes for the common good, as distinguished from the co-operation of individuals and classes for religious or race aims, is extremely rare. The Lieutenant-Governor has usually found that those who are most conspicuous in the latter direction are the last to assert or exhibit the smallest sympathy or interest in schemes having for their aim the general well-being."

The membership of these boards is a post of some distinction, inasmuch as it confers the much-coveted honour of a seat in the district Dârbar, and the parvenu values this privilege in direct proportion to the repugnance with which the local Râja or Nawâb deigns to associate with the *novus homo* on such occasions. But it is one thing to put in the minimum amount of attendance at the municipal meetings and another to devote time and trouble to the practical duties of administration—to check the collection of octroi, to supervise the conservancy establishment, to encourage vaccination, to visit schools and dispensaries. Sanitary work in particular always involves some amount of odium, and to preach the gospel of cleanliness—of which the would-be preacher is himself only an indifferent disciple—stirs up local ill-will, which the class out of which municipal members are drawn is naturally unwilling to provoke. With the official it is another matter; he is only discharging his ordinary duty, and people who violate sanitary rules will tolerate interference from him which they will resent at the hands of their neighbour, the corn chandler or attorney. The influence of caste and religion is also potent in such matters, and the amateur apostle of hygiene has one way of looking at short-

[1] *Administrative Report, North-West Provinces*, 1888-89, pp. iv. sqq.

comings when the offender is a Brâhman or a kinsman, and another if he be a stranger or a scavenger.

What is a worse point in the existing system is that the controlling body is perhaps inevitably drawn from classes which are not in complete sympathy with the mass of the people. The banker who has sufficient business in his own counting-house, and the pushing pettifogger, who, but for the honour of the thing, prefers to spend his morning hours in coaching witnesses for the court in the afternoon, have little community of interest with the Ishmaelite of the slums, an ignorant fanatic who would loot the Banya's storeroom or explore the attorney's harem if he got the chance. And behind them all are the wild shock-headed Jogi and the gloomy Mulla, both of whom loathe what we call civilisation, and are by policy and tradition steadily opposed to progress. Recent events in Benares showed that while the sleek city counsellors were calmly debating on what they thought a petty dispute about a ruined shrine, the rough of the slums was being preached at till he broke out in a wild passion of riot, and would have massacred and plundered to his heart's content had he dared to look down the muzzles of the rifles of English troops.

The sphere of the District Board is, on the other hand, much more limited. It has practically no income under its own control. It prepares an annual budget, to meet which funds are doled out by the Government, but it has no power of raising its income by taxation, and even the income from local rates is not spent in each district but credited to a general fund, from which grants are made by the central authority. This policy has enabled the Government to carry out various works of general utility, such as provincial light railways and the like; on the other hand, it deprives the Board of all power of initiative. It may and does advise expenditure, but the control of the purse lies in other and stronger hands. There is, again, in the case of public works and education a division of control which hardly tends to efficiency. The more important buildings and roads are in direct charge of the Public Works Department and with these the Board has no concern. Similarly the higher schools and colleges are beyond its control, being managed by the Educational Department. The primary schools are inspected by the Department, but the appointment of and discipline over the masters lies with the Board. The Board has its own overseer to manage the repair of the village roads, mere cart tracks mostly impassable in the rainy season, and roughly repaired when traffic recommences with the opening of the cold weather. With these the trained district engineer, who must use them as he visits works in progress throughout his charge, has no concern. The evils of this system of divided control are chiefly seen in the neglect of primary education, to which reference has been already made. In the case of the minor roads the exclusion of the expert from all supervision is a clear waste of power.

This is not the place to suggest remedies for all this. It will possibly be found that the only radical cure is a policy of decentralisation, when the district will become a self-supporting unit, with a definite income for local purposes, and relieved from the bondage of the Departments.

But far more important to the people at large than these rather humdrum duties of daily administration is the fact that whatever our Government may have done or failed to do in the matter of local administration, it can at least claim the credit of having given the Province for nearly a century almost uninterrupted peace.

The only great convulsion which has disturbed the general tranquillity for about a hundred years was the Mutiny of 1857, which, though its more important events took place within the Province, is more a part of the national than local history. The causes of this outbreak have hardly as yet passed beyond the range of controversy. As regards the military side of the revolt, the circumstances which led up to it seem fairly clear. The native army had been for a long time in a condition which, in the eyes of many far-seeing officers, was fraught with all the elements of danger in the future. It was largely drawn from a single class—the Brâhmans and Râjputs of Oudh and the immediate neighbourhood, or from the turbulent, faithless, restless Pathâns of Rohilkhand. This force had been for a long time so ill-controlled that a spirit of insubordination had become almost normal; breaches of discipline had been either ignored or explained away, and the problem of adapting what was originally a force raised for local purposes to the needs of a rapidly increasing empire, and the provision of armies and garrisons for service on distant expeditions, still awaited solution. The officers were in many cases too old—too wedded to tradition, their energies sapped by long periods of service in a debilitating climate. With them a complacent reliance in the fidelity of their men had become habitual, until they looked upon the sepoys as their children, and shut their ears to warning till it was too late.

Hence resulted a feeling among the native soldiery that they were essential to the State, and that the toleration with which their vagaries were treated was due to the fears of their masters. This feeling was increased by the weakening of the European garrison during the Crimean war, and exaggerated accounts of the inefficiency of our army before Sebastopol. To this was added a fatal ignorance of the resources and warlike spirit of the mother country, and in particular of the influence which was secured to her from the command of the sea. That the Oudh Brâhman should ignore this, the potent fact of modern politics, is not wonderful when we remember that it was left to an American naval strategist to bring the lesson home to our generation. In those days the sepoy in the long, quiet days spent in his secluded lines continued to dream that freedom, as he imagined it, could be won if he could only sweep away in one common massacre the little party of wearied, listless men, pale-faced ladies and children, the feeble contingent which was all the petty island beyond the seas could spare to keep him in thrall. Fortunately for us there were at least two Indian statesmen, Jang Bahâdur in Nepâl and Sâlâr Jang in Haidarâbâd, who knew better.

Further, irrespective of the weakness of the British garrison, the country was much more powerful to resist us than is the case at present. To begin with, every man was armed, and the rude blunderbuss or musket which he carried was a weapon rather more efficient than that with which the European was armed. It was not till the sepoy understood the effect of the Menai rifle later on in the struggle that he realised how circumstances had changed. The artillery, again, since the time of the Mughals, had been a dominant factor in Oriental warfare, and at this time our guns were largely in the hands of native artillerymen, while every petty Râja had a park of ordnance nearly as good as our own. All this has been changed by the introduction of rifled guns, all in the charge of British troops, and of breech-loading rifles, for which the native cannot improvise ammunition. Still more dangerous at the time was the lack of railways and telegraphs, which prevented concentration, and allowed mobs of rabble to sweep away our outlying stations. Lastly, the people themselves, with the traditions of war still fresh in their minds, were much more formidable than they are now. It was not till later days that the half-savage cattle-raiding Gûjar or the predatory Râjput of the western districts was tamed and induced by the spread of Canal irrigation to turn his sword into a ploughshare, or the little Oudh Râja learned that his ill-manned guns and ragged regiment of matchlock-men were unfit to face regular troops.

"The matter of seditions," says Bacon, "is of two kinds—much poverty and much discontent. The causes and motives of seditions are—innovation in religion, taxes, alteration of laws, breaking of privileges, general oppression, advancement of unworthy persons, strangers, dearths, disbanded soldiers, factions grown desperate, and whatever in offending people joineth and knitteth them in a common cause." It is worth while considering how far this summary represented the state of things at the time.

There was a general suspicion that the progress of our government involved interference with religion. The matter of the greased cartridges shows that this was the case. There was undoubtedly a feeling of restlessness and suspicion among the religious classes, who believed that we seriously meant to limit their privileges and undermine their authority. The cartridge question may have been only a pretext for disaffection, but it certainly was the outcome of a widespread feeling, quite baseless of course, but all the same vividly held by a people most conservative in their instincts and just then ready to believe any story, however wild and improbable.

The annexation policy of Lord Dalhousie had sent a thrill of alarm among the ruling families, and it awoke the sympathy of a people always tolerant of maladministration provided it were of the familiar Oriental type; prone to acquiesce in vices of their rulers if only they would lavish their revenue on those Court pageants so dear to the native mind, inasmuch as they cause money to flow in the cities, the centres of social life. No one dreamed of questioning the acts of the King of Oudh, who wasted the public funds on tawdry shows or tasteless buildings and lavished them on pandars and dancers. It was enough that the bâzârs were crowded, that he was devoted to almsgiving, that he supported a host of riffraff, the recipients of *panem atque Circenses*, which the mob of Lucknow valued as much as did the mob of Rome. That he never made a road beyond the boundaries of his capital, that he never opened a school, that he sent his Amils round to collect his revenue with a battery of guns—all this was only the old Eastern way of government, which half the world still complacently accepts, and which no one dreams of resisting.

It may be seriously doubted if with our methodical Puritanism we have not erred in the opposite direction. Even now the yokels of an English provincial town reverence the Judge at the Assizes because he has the Mayor to meet him and an escort of cavalry and trumpeters. Our Anglo-Indian Judge strolls into Court dressed in a shooting-coat; our Magistrates administer justice in hovels. But one has only to watch how the people delight in an unaccustomed show, how they scramble for places to see the Râja go past with his scarecrow troopers mounted on broken-kneed screws, the Banya's son with his ragamuffin rout starting to fetch his bride, the air thick with dust, the whole neighbourhood resounding with discordant music and the crash of a few fire-works—and the thought comes into our minds that we are perhaps mistaken in our contemptuous disregard of pomp and pageant in our every-day dealings with the people.

As social influences which affected popular feeling, we may notice the rigid action of our Civil Courts and the constant sales of landed property. Like the Ofellus of Horace, the man who had to plough the land he no longer owned could not be a loyal citizen. Our revenue system, again, was too hard, and though remissions of revenue, as in the famine of 1837-38, were sometimes granted, there was little consideration for the tax-payer in less serious calamities.

The weighty words in which Mr Hume, than whom no man had better knowledge of the facts, summed up the matter should be graven on the heart of every officer in India:—"Give the Râjputs and fighting men more reasonable means and happy homes, free from those instruments of torture, the Civil Courts and the native usurer, and they will fight for order and the Government under whom they are well off. Make it easier for your Gûjar, Ahîr, and thief classes to grow richer by agriculture than by crime, and besides making criminal administration cheaper, most of them will side with the Government. Tax the Banyas, Kâyasths, Mahâjans, and such like, who, while growing rich by the pen, oust their betters from their ancestral holdings, and then are too great cowards to wield a sword either to protect their own acquisitions or to aid the Government which has fostered their success."

But allusion to these causes of rural discontent assumes that the revolt was in a large degree agrarian. This was probably not the case. That the Gûjars of Meerut, the yeomanry of Oudh joined in it, murdered Europeans, plundered Government buildings and Civil Stations, is certain. But in most places the attitude of the villagers seems to have been apathetic; they had no particular feeling of loyalty, but the advent of native rule was welcomed with little enthusiasm. They troubled themselves as little about the Nâna as about the Faringi, and were as careless as the English squire during the Great Rebellion, who, as Horace Walpole was so fond of telling, was seen calmly riding out with his hounds to look for a hare as the armies were mustering for the battle of Edgehill.

So Mr Sherer writes[1]:—"I followed but the other day close upon the retreating footsteps of Fîroz Shâh (in Cawnpur), but I found the ploughman in the field; the boy singing at the well as he urged the bullocks down the slope; the old woman sitting at her door, twisting her little cotton gin, and her daughter grinding the millet—all supremely unconscious of the descendant of Timûr, who, with somewhat unseemly haste, had made but yesterday a royal progress through their fields and villages. The taste for misrule has clearly for the time departed. The people have seen that neither Râja nor Nawâb can construct a practicable administration, and the old rule seems better than none."

Again, it seems doubtful, though possibly discontent and vague hopes of the advantage to be gained from an outbreak may have been widespread, whether there was any definite conspiracy for anything like a simultaneous revolt. It may be that the occurrences at Meerut and Delhi precipitated matters; but a study of the Mutiny narratives does not reveal any general intention of this kind. Many regiments and detachments waited for weeks before declaring themselves. Some appear to have been driven into mutiny by the sudden attack of some ruffians on their officers by which their comrades were involved.

That the rebellion centred round the miserable, degraded survivors of the Mughal royal family, who, with a degree of folly which now seems almost incredible, had been allowed to continue their sordid regime in the Delhi palace, seems clear. Observers at the time, who were in the best position to ascertain the facts, like Mr Fleetwood Williams at Meerut, were agreed, in spite of cases of individual loyalty, in considering that the rebellion was planned by Musalmâns.[2]

[1] *Gazetteer, North-West Provinces*, vi. 195. [2] *Ibid.*, ii. 116.

This is not the place to attempt a review of the military operations which resulted in the suppression of the revolt. It is possible that an immediate advance of the Meerut brigade to Delhi would have prevented massacre, saved the city, and paralysed the forces of disorder by the occupation of the Fort and the capture of the king and his followers. But it seems clear that the Bengal army was rotten at the core, and sooner or later the time must have come when mutiny in some form or other would have broken out. Had the revolt been summarily suppressed, it would have deprived the British race of the splendid object lessons which the men who fought and died left as a legacy to their successors. We should never have known the real dangers which accompany a native mercenary army; the magnificent courage which the imperial race can display, fighting against overwhelming odds in the fierce heat of an Indian summer and the stifling damp of the rains. What the English soldier could do had been proved on a hundred battle fields. What the Mutiny taught us was that their brother officials who had never worn the red coat could display valour not less admirable, self-reliance in the face of danger as heroic as that of men trained in the art of war. Above all, the world learned how nobly the traditional courage of English womanhood had been sustained in the stress of trial more terrible than it had ever been forced to share.

"These are they," says the inscription on the well at Cawnpur, "which came out of great tribulation." A proud race like ours cannot secure an empire such as that of India without grievous sacrifices. What these have been is shown by the thickly clustering monuments of the dead, brave men, patient women, little children which fill the God's acre of our Indian stations. But losses like these, grievous as they are, to a people which entrusts year by year the best of its youth to the dangers of a tropical climate, do not impress the imagination of the nation as the Aceldama of Cawnpur or Lucknow does. These will ever remain a memorial how English men and women, splendidly isolated as none of their kin ever were before, are prepared to dare in the face of death. Well will it be for the Empire if it is always so served in the hour of its direst need. It is over the memories of some of these half-forgotten heroes that the Englishman in India loves to linger—John Mackillop, the young Cawnpur civilian, appointed captain of the well, and when wounded to the death, begging that the lady to whom he had promised a drink of water might not be disappointed: Captain D'Oyley at Agra, who with his last breath prayed that it might be recorded on his grave-stone that he died fighting his guns: Alan Hume and Claremont Daniel, in the face of tremendous odds attacking the temple at Jaswantnagar; Brand Sapte, Turnbull, Melville, and Alfred Lyall, charging the guns at Bulandshahr; John Power at Mainpuri fortifying his Court-house, and gaily reporting to the Sadar Court that the file of a riot case "prepared after the last and most approved fashion, and thickened with false evidence, is an excellent article of defence and has by experience been found to be bullet-proof."

There were, again, the men who nobly stood to their posts when all the world was against them, and maintained the Queen's authority in the midst of a host of enemies—Spankie and Robertson at Sahâranpur; Dunlop with his Khâki Risâla and Cracroft Wilson at Meerut; Watson and Cocks at Aligarh; Colvin at Agra; and many others whose very names are almost unknown to this generation. And we must not forget the natives who stood firm against those of their own race and creed, saved the lives of Europeans or fought beside them—Sayyid Ahmad Khân at Bijnor; Lachhman Sinh at Etâwah; Khushi Râm, the Jât at Bulandshahr; Sayyid Mîr Khân at Meerut.

Another fact which the Mutiny narrative brings out clearly is the absence of any man with even a pretence to be regarded as a statesman on the losing side. The Nâna Sâhib, even with the traditions of Marhatta supremacy, failed to do anything but murder women and children; the blood-stained dastard only saved his miserable life to die like a dog in the jungles of the Tarâi. Three men at least had a chance of proving that they could organise a new government on the ruins of the old—Khân Bahâdur, the grandson of Hâfiz Khân, the brave Rohilla, at Bareilly; Tafazzal Husain, the Bangash Nawâb of Farrukhâbâd; Muhammad Hasan at Gorakhpur. They were all for a time in more or less undisputed mastery of these districts. But the result was in every case the same—internal dissensions and internecine quarrels, the plunder of the helpless by the strong, murder and anarchy, utter failure to establish an efficient government, inability to organise the forces of resistance to oppose the avenging armies which soon gathered round them. The monuments of all these bear the inscription—*Mene, Tekel, Upharsin*—"God hath numbered thy kingdom and finished it; thou art weighed in the balances and are found wanting. Thy kingdom is divided and given to the Medes and Persians." The only really heroic figure is that of a woman—Lachhmi Bâi, Râni of Jhânsi, who though stained with innocent European blood, had the courage, like Cleopatra, to die in the hour of disaster rather than grace an English triumph.

Since the Mutiny the Province has been spared the horrors of war and civil tumults. The only casual interruptions to the reign of tranquillity have occurred through religious quarrels directed rather by the partisans of one faith against those of the other than in opposition to the Government. Disputes of this kind are not the creation of our rule, and were common under the native administration. They were, in fact, the natural legacy of the intolerance of the later Muhammadan rulers, and it was inevitable that when the Hindus awoke to a sense of their power and came under a Government which showed an ostentatious tolerance of both religions, the chance of reprisal would be utilised. Even under the Oudh administration, which was in no sense fanatical, on at least two occasions in modern times such outbreaks occurred. In 1850 General Sleeman describes how a Muhammadan mob at the Muharram nearly killed a respectable merchant at Shâhâbâd in Hardoi and looted his goods. In 1855 at Ajudhya a fight over a temple resulted in the slaughter of seventy-five Musalmâns and eleven Hindus.

In our own days Rohilkhand has gained an unenviable reputation for such outbreaks, as at Bareilly and Pilibhit in 1871, and in Bijnor at a later date.

Since then, in various parts of the Province, though there have been few actually serious riots, the coincidence of the Musalmân Muharram and the Hindu Dasahra, the dates of which being regulated by the lunar calendar come together at the end of recurring cycles, has caused much trouble and anxiety to district officers. Only three years ago, the weavers of Benares, always a turbulent, fanatical class, took advantage of a quarrel over an almost deserted Hindu shrine, with which they had no possible concern, to spread rapine and outrage through the city. Unless some *modus vivendi* can be established between these fanatical sectaries, it may be necessary in the interests of law and order to prohibit all processions of a religious nature in the crowded streets of our Indian cities. Perhaps one of the most amusing instances of this religious tension is that recorded at the last Census in Bengal, where a Hindu clerk deliberately recorded a large number of the followers of the Prophet as lepers.

But more serious than this friction between the followers of rival creeds is the crusade against cow-killing, which was started a short time ago in Bihâr and the eastern districts of this Province. Here the people had been always regarded as about the most law-abiding subjects of the Crown. Ballia, a little sleepy hollow, supposed to be one of the easiest of district charges, was the seat of the worst trouble. Here it was suddenly discovered that a really serious movement had been started; the country was marked out into circles, each under a local committee; considerable funds were raised in support of the agitation; boycotting and intimidation were freely resorted to against the eaters of beef; disorderly mobs assembled and committed serious acts of violence; in some cases they even risked an encounter with our local officials and police.

The agitation was promptly suppressed and the ringleaders brought to justice. But of the causes which led to the disturbance no satisfactory explanation was ever given.

By one account it was connected with the agitation against the Revenue Survey in Bihâr; by another with the protest of the Bengâlis against the prohibition of infant marriage. It is very doubtful how far it was influenced by such causes. More probably it was an outcome of the general restlessness of Hinduism in the face of the progress encouraged by our Government. Brâhmanism is subject to these periodical revivals, as its ignorant leaders think they feel the world slipping from beneath them, and to put off the evil day encourage their half-hearted disciples to raise the trumpet call of danger to the faith.

The policy of our Government in the face of movements like these is prescribed by well-defined considerations. The ignorant masses must be, on the one hand, reassured once more that the State has no concern with religious belief, and has, and never had, any desire to interfere with their faith and worship; on the other hand, they must be taught that the tolerance they enjoy is conditional on its being shared equally with the Musalmân and the Christian. The missionary of any creed must be protected so long as he carries on his propaganda in an orderly way, without giving wanton offence to people who disagree with his teaching, so long as he refrains from that intolerant vituperation which the best creeds carefully discourage.

Besides this there is another side to the question of the protection of the cow. The wealthy European seldom uses beef, except perhaps for a short time in the cold weather; but it is a necessity to the European garrison, and is the only animal food within the reach of the poor Musalmân of the towns. To check its use in any way, as Akbar seems to have done, is out of the question. All that can and should be done is to secure by municipal regulations that the slaughter of cattle and the sale of beef shall be rendered as little offensive as possible.

We have now to consider the general result of the system of Government which we have been describing. Contrasting the condition of things now as compared with the time of the Mutiny, we remark among the upper classes a wider diffusion of intelligence, due largely to better communications, more travelling, and education. But this has not been accompanied by a corresponding improvement in culture. Among the classes brought more in contact with Europeans there is a noticeable increase in the knowledge of English, in the adoption of English titles of courtesy and the foreign habit of dress. Among some of the more advanced Musalmâns there has been a movement to associate more freely with Europeans at entertainments and social meetings of various kinds. But these influences have not extended to the mass of the people, and have little affected the traditional customs of the race—such as infant marriage, the seclusion and enforced ignorance of women, the rules of caste particularly as regards exogamy, and the precautions against the contamination of food by mere contact with an unbeliever. In religious matters there has been little weakening of old prejudices; the tension between Hindu, Musalmân and Christian is as strong as ever, the priestly classes as nervous and suspicious. The Brâhman and the Sâdhu are as opposed as they ever were to the new learning, the orthodox Musalmân as bigoted as at any period of his history.

The practical work of administration has largely fallen into native hands. Nearly all the subordinate Civil Courts are manned by native Judges, assisted by a native Bar. It is only what we in England call the Courts of Assize and the High Court of Justice, which are largely held by European judges and Barristers. At the close of 1895, out of six judges of the High Court, one was a native; seven natives out of thirty-one held the post of District and Sessions Judge; all the twenty-two posts of Subordinate and Small Cause Court judges were held by natives of the country.

On the other hand the executive magisterial-revenue charge of districts is almost entirely held by members of the Civil Service. With the existing tension between Hindus and Musalmâns this arrangement must continue for some time to come.

Another leading influence in the spread of intelligence is the Post Office. In 1893-94, throughout the Empire, 8978 post offices conveyed 370 millions of letters, newspapers, &c. In the time of the Mutiny there were only 810 offices open. The business is, it is true, small as compared with our British department, which disposed of 1771 millions of letters in 1894-95, and distributed seven newspapers for every one in India. But considering the illiteracy of the people the work done is very large; and besides, all that the British Post Office does in the way of selling stamps, receiving deposits, insurances and the like, the Indian Post Office transmits a large amount of revenue, and does a considerable business in collecting tradesmen's bills by what is known as the Value Payable system.

To this and similar causes are due the largely extended use of European fabrics, and foreign articles like matches, kerosine oil, and umbrellas, which are seen even in the most remote corners of the land. Quite recently a movement, said to be started by the oilman caste to boycott kerosine oil, has largely spread in Bihâr. It is as difficult to put new wine in old bottles in India as anywhere else.

Our record is thus on the whole creditable. We have kept the peace; we have settled the land; we have relieved the miseries of famine; we have spread artificial irrigation; we have made railways, roads, and telegraphs, established the education and postal systems, codified the law with a due regard to local custom and social wants, organised medical relief and sanitation. We have made corruption and oppression an unwelcome incident instead of an element of the civil administration. We have freely admitted natives to public office; we have given them municipal and local government. Lastly, we have striven to secure toleration of all religious beliefs; we have shown a desire to treat all classes fairly, without tyranny or prejudice, without regard to caste or creed. To compare this with the condition of things which we found at the beginning of our rule is usually considered a sufficient answer to any one who asks if our rule commands the love and admiration of the people.

Besides all this, we have not encountered the same difficulties which met us in other lands. There is no really patriotic feeling in the country, no yearning for the return of a dynasty of exiled kings such as influenced the Scotch Jacobites; no craving for the revival of a constitution such as that exhibited by the Irish Celt. The Musalmâns, even with their recent memories of empire, have no place of national pilgrimage. No one dreams under an impulse of patriotism of visiting the tomb of Akbar or the Council Chamber of Shâh Jahân. There is no sacred site which stirs the blood of the race like Westminster, the Chapel in the Tower, Runymede, or Stratford-on-Avon. Still less are the affections of the Hindus associated with the heroes of their race. There is nothing which leads them to revere Buddha or Asoka, Jay Chand or Todar Mall. All their reverence takes a religious shape as in the cultus of Krishna or Râma.

And yet in spite of all we have done in advancing civilisation, and though we have no rivals in the historical past, we have not succeeded in exciting any ardent feelings of devotion to our rule. Many individual officers have, it is true, gained the affection or respect of large masses of the people. But these were rather men of the old type—strong-handed and autocratic, prompt to punish crime, and at the same time conciliatory and polite, ready to respect traditional prejudices, not prone to innovation, never wearied by complaints, however petty or prolix. Most sensible people probably believe that ours is for the present the only possible government, that a constitution on a popular basis is out of the question, and that our withdrawal from the country would be the signal for internecine war and terrible misery.

The Englishman in India is what he is in most parts of the world—strong and energetic, with a thorough belief in himself, and a way of looking down on people who do not think exactly as he does. He makes on the whole an excellent ruler of weaker races, but he is wanting in imagination, insight, and sympathy, inclined to be brusque in manner, and to despise those little convenances which the Oriental values so much.

Each class of the community has its special grievance. The nobility feel themselves excluded from the only occupation which they feel they can accept without loss of dignity—military service. They disapprove of the cold impartiality of our law, which has abolished the traditional distinction between the gentleman and the menial, and makes it possible for the serf to drag the Râja before one of our courts. This is shown in the ardent desire of the higher classes to secure exemption from personal attendance before our judges. They dislike the democratic policy which gives them a seat on our Boards, but only on condition that they tolerate the banker or educated parvenu as a colleague. They know well that they must lose influence under any system of representative government. They prefer the rule of a gentleman who is usually polite and sympathetic to the control of a committee filled with the parvenus whom they loathe. They miss the chances of amusement which a native court provided; they have no real desire for public improvement, and they would like fewer roads and schools and more Darbârs and ceremonial functions, where they would be received with dignity and have a chance of gaining a higher seat than some detested rival. They think our rule is deficient in colour and stateliness. They despise our orders, which they have to share with the rich trader who builds a school or endows an hospital. What they really love is to hear the artillery thunder when they arrive at a cantonment, and more diplomacy is exerted to add a gun to the salute than to win the jewel of the Indian Empire.

The middle classes are perhaps those who most approve of our Government, but they do not like the restrictions, ineffective as they are, which we try to enforce in order to prevent them increasing their hold on the land, and they find the Courts slow to enforce their decrees with adequate rigour. They, too, dread being dragged before a judge when some menial dares to sue them. They agree with the Râja in detesting the educated interloper. Business has, it is true, increased, but it is spread over a wider area, and the popularisation of trade is ruining the middleman. It is less easy to make a great coup, to start a "corner" in grain or cotton. With the railway and telegraph the margin of profit has been reduced. The European merchant meets them everywhere. It is less easy to make a large fortune in a short time. They dread the police, and their timidity and want of independence expose them specially to extortion, which is always possible with an under-paid menial establishment. At the same time they are equally afraid of the town rough and bully—those whom De Quincey calls "the ferocious but cowardly Ishmaels of imperfect civilisation." The Banya dreads that these gentry may blackmail him, loot his warehouse, or explore his harem. He thinks our laws weak because such persons are not summarily strung up, and because the Courts are indisposed to take action against them in the absence of a prosecutor—a role which he has no desire to play. Above all, he objects to direct taxation, and the income tax is his nightmare.

The town labourer finds his handicraft less remunerative because he has to compete with machine-made goods, and he has suffered from the rise in the price of food for which he has no other explanation than that it is somehow the result of our action. Of the economic causes which have brought about this result, the pressure of an increasing population on the resources of the soil, he has not the dimmest conception.

The people who like us best are undoubtedly the village yeoman class. As long as they are let alone, not too much bothered over new-fangled measures, such as sanitation and the like, as long as the revenue demand is kept within moderate limits and they are granted reasonable protection for life and property, they will remain fairly content. If it were possible to relieve them from the incubus of the money-lender, and restrict the sale and mortgage of ancestral holdings, we would certainly secure, if not ardent loyalty, which is hardly to be expected from a stolid race immersed in a sordid life, at least their contented acquiescence in the stability of our rule.

Another boon we can and should confer upon them is cheaper and more certain law. The costs of petty civil, and revenue suits are far too high; the opportunity of appeal is recklessly abused; the crowd of pettifoggers which surrounds our Courts encourages purposeless litigation, much of which would be better disposed of by the village council of greybeards. Our Codes, as they stand, are models of legislation, but we have allowed them to become overlaid by immense masses of judge-made law, decisions many of which are conflicting, dangerous traps for a native judiciary, whose minds are naturally inclined to quibbling and a taste for the mint, anise and cummin, rather than the weightier matters of the law.

To quote Bacon again :—"Contentious suits ought to be spewed out as the surfeit of Courts. A judge ought to prepare his way to a just sentence, as God useth to prepare his way, by raising valleys and taking down hills; so when there appeareth on either side a high hand, violent prosecutions, cunning advantages taken, combination, power, great counsel; then is the virtue of a judge seen to make inequality equal; that he may plant his judgment upon an even ground."

CHAPTER IV

THE PEOPLE: THEIR ETHNOLOGY AND SOCIOLOGY

THE course of the ethnological history of northern India has ever been prescribed by the physical features of the country. To the north and north-west the mountain barrier of the Himâlaya and Hindu Kush, while it prevented wholesale movements of the people, such as that described in De Quincey's classical account of one of the Tartar migrations, has been constantly passed by armies of invaders or small bodies of colonists, influenced by that tendency of all northern races to reach the southern lands of the continent. When they emerged from the hilly region, they found before them the fertile lands of the Panjâb, which were first occupied and where the beginnings of the Hindu social polity took shape. As they advanced, their progress to the south-west was barred by the deserts of Râjputâna. They were thus directed into the region watered by the upper courses of the Ganges and Jumna. The lowlands, now the seat of a crowded agricultural people, were then probably covered with jungle, and the migration followed the route along the lower slopes of the northern hills, whence the new-comers gradually spread into the plains below, cleared the forest, and adopted an agricultural and pastoral life. To the south, again, their movements were checked by the Vindhyan range, the backbone of the peninsula, then occupied by fierce forest tribes whose conquest was not seriously undertaken till a much later date. The course of conquest or colonisation was thus directed along the basins of the two great rivers. It was not till many years had passed in conflict and the absorption of the indigenous peoples that the new civilisation spread into the delta of Bengal.

The advancing bands of colonists, at the earlier stages of

their progress, seem to have thrown out offshoots which occupied Kashmir and the other more fertile valleys on the fringe of the northern range. As they pushed eastward they appear to have found the land which we now call the western Panjâb occupied by a yellow race, who were perhaps like themselves of foreign origin. These people may have in very early times moved to the east and south under pressure from the Mongol or Tartar races of the central Asian plateau. This race, which has been supposed to be Skythian, appears to have worshipped the snake, and the early legends record the contests of the whiter-skinned people who called themselves Ârya, or "noble," with these yellow races, one of whose titles seems to have been Nâga, "the kindred of the dragon," which they may have deified as the tribal totem. One famous tale tells how the great Khândava forest in the valley of the Jumna was occupied by these Nâgas under their king Takshaka, and how they were expelled by fire and forced to take refuge in the hills. But in some cases the two races amalgamated, and we read that Arjuna, one of the Pândavas, visited Hardwâr and there married Ulûpî, the daughter of the Nâga king Vâsuki. Of his city we are told that it contained two thousand krores of serpent inhabitants, "and the wives of all those serpents were of consummate beauty; and the city contained more jewels than any person in the world has ever seen, and there was a lake there which contained the waters of life and in which all the serpents used to bathe." Thence led by Agni, the fire god, the Âryas continued their conquest as far as the banks of the Gandak, which divides the Province from Bengal.

It was in the course of this later migration that they encountered the second race which had occupied the country prior to their arrival. These are collectively known as Dasyu, and between them and the Âryas we are told that there raged continual war. No terms are too vile to describe these people as we know them from Aryan literature. They were dark of skin, low-statured, treacherous, foul in manners, eaters of raw flesh, an abomination to the new-comers, and this was probably the basis of much of the early stories of

A GROUP OF KOLS. MIRZAPUR

cannibalism. At the same time there are indications that they had acquired a certain degree of culture. The common theory represents these Dasyus as finally reduced to the position of helots or serfs of the new-comers. But later evidence, mainly based on anthropometry, indicates that they must have been gradually absorbed among their foreign conquerors; that the numbers of the Âryan colonists were never large, and that from the union of the white, the yellow, and the black men, arose the modern people of northern India.

Much speculation has been devoted to working out the ethnical affinities of these black people[1]—whether they were autochthonous or immigrants, and if immigrants from what direction they reached Indian soil, and whether they were one or a combination of several distinct races.

By one, and the current theory, they consisted at least of two stocks—the Drâvidians and the Kolarians, the latter entering Bengal by the north-eastern passes and thence pushing on to the north and north-eastern portion of the Central Indian plateau; while the Drâvidians found their way into the Panjâb by the north-western valleys, the route afterwards followed by the Âryas. The two streams are supposed to have converged and crossed in the Central Indian Tract; the Drâvidians being the stronger, crushed and pushed aside the Kolarians, and advancing occupied the southern portion of the peninsula.

That these Drâvidians were of the Negritic type seems fairly certain, but the theory that this African migration took place through Suez, Arabia, Palestine, and Persia is opposed to all our knowledge of these ancient lands, where their way was barred by the Semites in Egypt and Coelo-Syria by the Turanian Hittites and by the empires of Babylon, Nineveh, and Persia. The rise of the Hittite empire may have originated the southern movement of the white or yellow races, but it must have been an insurmountable obstacle to the Negritic movement eastwards.

[1] Baines, *Indian Census Report*, 1891, p. 121 sqq.; O'Donnell, *Bengal Census Report*, 1891, p. 250 sqq.

Another and perhaps more plausible theory would account for the arrival of these Negritic people on Indian soil by the existence of an ancient continent now submerged. "A chain of islands," says Mr O'Donnell, "is known to still feebly connect Madagascar and Southern India, but they are only the remnants or relics of lands of much greater magnitude. Many of them are atolls or are surrounded by encircling coral reefs, which Darwin and Huxley have proved to be the most certain sign of sinking land. Deep sea soundings have also proved the existence of a vast shoal or submerged island, nearly as large as Madagascar, extending from a point only 250 miles north-east of Madagascar to the Admirante and Seychelles group of islands. Midway between the latter and India a similar expanse of shoal, which lifts itself above the water as the Chagos Islands, marks the third great halting-place between Africa and Southern India, of which Madagascar is the first. The Lacadive and Maldive Islands, the summits of a long narrow island on the south-west coast of India, form the last link in the chain."

But whether these black people arrived in India from the north-west, north-east, or south-west, one fact is tolerably certain—the distinction between the Drâvidian and Kolarian races, which depends mainly on the evidence of language, is disproved by anthropometry and must now be definitely abandoned.

The invasion popularly known as the Âryan was followed by that of other races of cognate origin, classed under the great head of Skythian. In fact the Âryan invasion and the subsequent inroad of the Muhammadans were only incidents in the southward march of the northern peoples which has continued since prehistoric times. The chief seat of power of these Skythians was in the Panjâb, and thence they threw out colonies down the valley of the Indus. Attempts have been made to identify this race with certain tribes occupying the western part of this Province and the eastern Panjâb, such as the Jâts and Gûjars. It has been suggested that there are survivals of custom among these tribes which closely link them to the Central Asian type, but these customs, if they ever existed, have become so modified by their new environment as to afford no safe basis for argument, and the philological conclusions, though plausible, are not quite convincing. At any rate this race seems to have only slightly influenced the people of this Province, and the Ganges, like all rivers in ancient times, was a most effective ethnical barrier. Thus the Panjâb type has been less affected by Negritic or Drâvidian influence, and this becomes more potent as we pass eastward along the great river valleys.

All that the evidence at present available warrants us in concluding is then that from very early times Upper India was occupied by a dark race who lived in the Age of Stone and occupied the slopes of the northern valleys where their remains in the shape of flint weapons, kistvaens, and other primitive forms of sepulture are to be found in abundance; that these people were of the Negritic type and possibly crossed into the south of the peninsula either from Africa or Melanesia and pushed their way northward across the plateau of the Deccan; that they were conquered or absorbed by successive waves of invaders of the Âryan or Skythian race; that this process of colonisation and absorption was not, as the Hindu legends lead us to infer, the work of a single age or of one body of invaders, but was gradual and spread over an enormous period of time—the result being the population of the present day.

What it is really important to grasp is that the Drâvidian element was prepotent and that the so-called Âryan conquest was more social than ethnical, more the gradual enlightenment of the indigenous peoples by scattered bands of missionaries and teachers whose civilisation was of the peaceful, unwarlike, and intellectual form rather than the upheaval and wreck of the existing polity by an army of conquerors who forced their law and civil institutions on the necks of their slaves. The hymns of the Rig Veda and the earlier Âryan literature would in this view not be an historical record of the conquest as the hymns of Moses and Deborah commemorate the conquest of Canaan. They are probably of an age far subsequent to this ethnical movement. They more probably represent the desire of the Court bards to provide a respectable pedigree for the ruling classes of the people when the various elements of which it was composed had been finally absorbed. It pleased the fancy of these writers to cast their thoughts back to the times when the forefathers of their patrons were supposed to have lived beyond or on the lower slopes of the northern mountain barrier, and to imagine that their superiority in the arts of peace and war was the result not of a slow evolutionary process but of racial supremacy.

To the theory that the existing population represents at the top a white-skinned race and beneath it a mass of black helots, anthropometry, the final test, lends no support. Still less does it provide any proof that the Brâhman and Râjput, as we see them before us, are in any sense the kinsfolk of the modern Englishmen who have reduced them as well as the dark non-Âryan to subjection.

On the contrary, the evidence, so far as it has been collected, tends to prove the essential unity of the existing races. As Mr O'Donnell puts the case—"On the evidence of anthropometry, in Bengal the Brâhman is at one end of the scale and the cultivated Kâyasth at the other, whilst at the top of the Bihâr list the fisherman, priest, farm labourer, landlord and cowherd are in close proximity. In the North-Western Provinces the Kshatriya, the Râjput soldier, and the Khatri, the Râjput trader, stand at opposite extremes, rat-catchers, carpenters, dancing women, cultivators, toddy-drawers and priests coming in between. No evidence could be more convincing, if anthropometery has any meaning. The Indian races and tribes in the valley of the Ganges from the Afghân frontier to the Bay of Bengal are so absolutely intermingled in blood, that it is impossible to discriminate between the skull characteristics of the castes or functional guilds which have grown up under later Brâhmanical usage."

The existing type of man in northern India is thus probably the result of the combination of at least three strains of blood—Aryan, Skythian and Drâvidian : but of these the last is distinctly predominant. The new-comers, in fact, imposed their religion, their culture, their social polity upon the old races; but they have been themselves absorbed, as the Portuguese in India have been; as Normans into Frenchmen, Alexandrian Greeks into Egyptians, and as Irishmen, Germans, Italians and half-a-dozen other European races are being combined in the Yankee.

The truth seems to be that, as Mr Pearson has shown, the emigrant from Northern lands has no chance against the more vigorous tropical races. Unless the stock is maintained by constant streams of emigrants, the higher race inevitably succumbs to the rigour of the climate; if supplies of fresh blood from the old country fail its only chance of survival lies in amalgamation with the indigenous peoples.

There is ample evidence to show that even the higher so-called Aryan tribes—the Râjputs and Brâhmans, for instance—have largely drawn recruits from the native races. It is perhaps possible that some of the highest septs, such as the Sisodiyas of Mewâr, the pedigree of whose ruling house goes back to Râma and can certainly be traced to the second century of our era, may have maintained their lineage almost uncontaminated. But this is certainly not the case with many of the septs of lower rank. Even the names of many of these indicate that they were of meaner descent. There is fairly good evidence to show that many of the Oudh septs were promoted from the lower castes within historical times. It is only quite recently that many of the Gond tribes of Central India have been elevated to the rank of Râjputs, a general term which with them merely implies that they are the descendants of men holding the rank of princes. Undoubtedly, as the amalgamation of the races progressed, many of these local Râjas were dignified with the rank of Râjput and established the right of connubium with those who possessed or claimed to possess genuine Râjput blood.

This is still more the case with the aggregate known as the Brâhmans. The early legends abound in stories of Kshatriyas being promoted to be Brâhmans. In later times whole sections of the lower races were elevated to priestly rank. Thus the Baiga, or devil-hunting priest of the jungle tribes, was converted into a Brâhman Ojha or exorcisor of evil spirits. There are sections of Brâhmans, such as the Dakaut or sturdy beggar class and the Mahâbrâhman who discharges the functions of funeral priest who are also without doubt drawn from the lower races and are an object of abhorrence to the higher ranks of the tribe, the keen-faced, intellectual Pandits of Mathura and Benares.

We must, in short, discard the theory which professes to identify distinct races in the existing castes. The native of our day, so far as he has any definite views of the matter, regards caste as based on religion : as eternal and immutable : as peculiar to his own people. The modern view refuses to admit any of these assumptions. It regards the endogamous groups which we call castes as more social aggregates than based on any religious principle. We see them changing before our own eyes. We know that the same system prevailed among other nations. The legend tells us that in the beginning of things the Brâhman was produced from the head of the primal male. But, as has been already pointed out, there are historical evidences of the creation of Brâhmans in modern times. Even in the time of Manu the rule of endogamy was only in the making, and it was not till the revival of Hinduism after the decay of Buddhism that the modern rule requiring a Brâhman to marry in his tribe was enforced.

Caste, in short, is in the main based on function, as was the case among the Egyptians and the Perso-Aryans. At the outset there were in all probability two main divisions of the people, the Vaisyas, or "settlers," and the Sûdras or helot serfs. It was not till a much later period that the privilege of connubium between these two classes was lost. Out of them two great functional groups, the Brâhman or Levite and the Râjput or landholder, were evolved. The distinction between the Patres and the Populus Romanus grew up in the same way.

It was soon discovered by the Brâhman guild that it was an essential condition of their existence that the privilege of intermarriage with the lower tribes should cease. The primitive Aryan priest was the house-father, who performed the simple family rites at the household hearth. But by and by, as ritual became elaborated, a special class of officiants was required, and these gradually asserted novel claims. They pretended to possess authority over all in earth, beneath the earth, and in the heaven above. They held the secret of this world and the next; they were equal to, in some respects superior to, the gods themselves; by them alone could meet sacrifice be offered; they alone could bless the marriage rite; they alone could safely pass the disembodied soul to heaven. Hence the obvious advantage of forming a close Levite guild which maintained the monopoly of all religious functions, prohibited all connection with outsiders, and has ended by making this group of priests an iron-bound caste of inter-related families.

It was probably in imitation of the rule of endogamy thus established that the practice was adopted by the other occupational groups.

This stage of Brâhman supremacy in the religious world was not, however, reached without a struggle. The early legends are full of the contest between the Brâhman and the Kshatriya, and even between one Brâhman group and another. Parasurâma, "Râma with the axe," is said to have cleared the earth twenty-one times of the race of the Kshatriyas, and to have given the land to the Brâhmans. The contest between the rival sages, Vasishtha and Visvamitra, regarding the right to be family priest to Râja Sudâs, marks the struggle within the Brâhmanical body itself.

To disguise this development of caste on the basis of occupation, the fiction was invented, which we find in the Code of Manu, that all the minor castes were derived from an intermixture between the four so-called original castes—Brâhmans, Vaisyas, Kshatriyas, Sûdras. Thus, we are told, that the Ambastha or physician is the offspring of a Vaisya woman by a Brâhman father. But here a distinction was made, and a special stain was attached to the connection of a Brâhman woman with a Sûdra. Their child was the Nishâda, the degraded race from which the forest tribes of the Central Indian hills are by the Brâhmanical fiction supposed to have sprung.

It is perhaps needless to say that the early grouping of the castes into a fourfold division no longer exists for practical purposes. The present Brâhman group contains elements very different from that of the ancient, contemplative Rishis, who, in their hermitages, meditated on the problems of life and death. The Râjputs are, as we have seen, much debased by intermixture with meaner tribes. The Vaisyas practically no longer exist, unless they have been perpetuated in some of the higher Banya castes, such as the Agarwâla. The aggregate of Sûdras, also, contains the most diverse elements and hardly survives, except as a convenient term of abuse for tribes which are supposed to be in a low grade of purity.

But though the basis of caste is probably in the main occupational, any grouping of the existing castes, according to occupation, is out of the question. Only quite a minority of Brâhmans devote themselves exclusively to the study of the law and the Scriptures, or to other religious duties. Many are agriculturists, domestics or clerks, serve in the army or in the police, or engage in trade. The vast majority of the Râjputs are not landowners. There is no identity of occupation characteristic of the Vaisya or Sûdra groups.

It is, however, possible in a rough way to arrange the castes according to their traditional occupation, though, as has been observed, this does not even approximately represent the actual state of affairs.

In the first great group we have a population of about 17 millions, or 36 per cent. of the whole, who are more or less devoted to agriculture or kindred occupations. Among these we have—first, about 4½ millions who are either owners of land or yeomen, the most notable of these being the Bhuînhârs and Tagas, who claim to be Brâhmans, but have now completely abandoned sacerdotal functions, and the higher class of yeomen, such as the Jâts and Râjputs. Next come 6½ millions of the middle class cultivators, of whom the most important is the great Kurmi race. This has thrown off numerous endogamous groups, such as the Kâchhis, Koeris, Kisâns and Mâlis, mostly employed as market-gardeners and growers of the more valuable crops—opium, spices, flowers, and so on. These are followed by about 5½ millions of people, whose traditionary business is the management of cattle and the sale of milk and other products. Of these the leading castes are the Ahîrs, Ghosis and Gûjars, who tend milch cattle, and the Gadariyas, who breed sheep, sell wool or blankets. This division is completed by about 200,000 from the Drâvidian fringe, who inhabit the southern hills or the malaria-haunted Tarâi. The latter shows only the Thârus, who number about 25,000 souls; most of these people come from the Vindhyan range—the Kharwârs, Kols, Cheros, and their brethren, who link the Bhîls and Gonds of the western part of the range to the Santâls of Bengal.

Next come about 6¼ millions of people traditionally devoted to a religious life and the service of the gods, or who act as writers, genealogists, dancers, singers and actors—rather a miscellaneous culture group. Of these the great majority, 4¾ millions, are Brâhmans. Next come over half a million of Fakîrs, who include both the devotee class and the common beggars. Next in importance are the Kâyasths or writers, a most intelligent and pushing people, about whose origin and social rank there has been much controversy. The Code of Manu classes them as the children of twice-born men begotten on women of the class immediately below them. That the Brâhmans, their rivals in the State council, should tell scandalous stories about them is only natural. But the evidence of anthropometry tends to show that they have little intermixture of Drâvidian blood. Under our rule their aptitude for Western learning has greatly improved their social position, and, like all people on their promotion, they are extremely sensitive to any imputation on the purity of their descent. The group is completed by a mixed body of Bhâts or genealogists, who represent in function the panegyrists or Court ballad-singers of the earlier era, and by a mass of singers, dancers, actors and mimes, many of whom are really drawn from the distinctively gipsy or nomadic tribes.

The third group is that of the trading classes, who number a million and a half. Nearly all of them are Banyas, who are also a very mixed class. Some of them, like the Agarwâlas, are perhaps that part of the present population which has remained most unaffected by local influences; others are drawn from lower races and hardly claim to be the successors of the ancient Vaisyas.

Below these comes the great collection of artisans and village menials, numbering in all 19 millions and 40 per cent. of the whole population. Most of these are distinctly of Drâvidian blood. Nearly 6 millions, or 12½ per cent. of the whole population, are ranked as workers in leather—the Chamâr and his kinsman the Mochi, who makes shoes, and the Dabgar and Dhâlgar, who makes shields or leathern jars. As most of them eat beef and some work up the hides of the sacred cow, they are looked upon with detestation by orthodox Hindus. Where the tanning business is carried on local prejudices insist that it shall be conducted in an isolated hamlet, apart from the dwellings of people who claim a higher rank of purity. But the majority of Chamârs do not work in leather: they till the soil, act as labourers and village drudges, as grooms, messengers and the like. In the chief centres of the leather trade, like Cawnpur, many of them have amassed considerable wealth, and have even begun to seclude their women, which is the first object of a man who has attained a fairly respectable social standing.

The only other members of this artisan class who labour under special social discredit are the butchers and breeders of fowls—an unclean bird in the opinion of orthodox Hindus. But here there is a sharp line of distinction drawn between the cow butcher, who is loathed by his Hindu neighbours, and was in the recent disturbances arising out of the cow question often boycotted, bullied and ill-used: and the man who deals in mutton and goat's flesh, which is eaten by many of the higher classes and involves no social discredit. Lower still are the 400,000 sweepers, closely allied to the Dom, who is regarded as the very dregs of impurity—a scavenger and remover or burner of corpses, the descendant of the Chandâla of Manu, who is ranked by the law-giver with the town boar, the cock, the dog, and a woman in a state of impurity, none of whom are allowed to see a Brâhman lest they may defile his food. They must live outside the town, eat out of potsherds, have as their sole wealth dogs and asses, wear the cerecloths of the dead, have as their ornaments rusty iron, and roam continually from place to place. "Let no man who regards his duty, religious or civil, hold any intercourse with them,"[1] says the old-world sage.

We have next the great mass of other artisans and handicraftsmen, of which the largest group is that of fishermen, boatmen and bearers of palanquins—the Mallâh, Kewat, Kahâr and their brethren, who number 2¼ millions. After these come the weaving classes—Koris and Julâhas, numbering 1¾ millions, much of whose business has been ruined by competition with Manchester, and they have been forced to adopt other forms of labour. The Telis or oil manufacturers have, again, suffered by the increasing importation of kerosine oil. At the bottom of this class are a million and a half of so-called village watchmen — Pâsis, Arakhs and the like, many of whom are thieves themselves.

To illustrate briefly how little this traditional classification of castes represents actual facts, it is sufficient to note that while, as we have seen, the traditional agricultural castes number about 17 millions, nearly 35 millions are wholly or partly dependent on agriculture; there are 4¾ millions of Brâhmans, but only 156,000 ministers of religion; 466,000 people live by making pottery, while there are 713,000 Kumhârs. Similar differences are found throughout the caste lists.

The regular village menials constitute almost a distinct class of the community. The constitution of the old village body provided for a regular staff of these workmen—the barber, who performed the ceremonial shaving at the initiation of youths, shaved the corpse and acted an important part in marriage; the carpenter-smith, the two functions being often combined, who makes and repairs agricultural implements, and assists in building the hut; the potter, who prepares the earthen vessels so essential to village house-

[1] Manu, *Institutes*, iii. 239; x. 51 sqq.

wifery; the goldsmith who makes jewellery; the washerman who cleans the foul raiment, and hence ranks very low in the social scale. These functionaries have each their body of constituents whose families they serve, and they are remunerated, not by a daily wage, but sometimes by the use of a plot of rent-free land, or more usually by a donation of grain at each harvest per family, or on each plough or cane-press which the peasant owns.

There is no class of the people on whom British rule has worked a more radical change. In the old times they were little better than serfs, *ascripti glebae*, at the mercy of the leader of the village body. But the extension of railways, the needs of modern city life, have attracted many of them to the towns, where they obtain ample remunerative employment. This has been accompanied by a notable increase in their sense of dignity and self-importance; and nothing is more regretted by the conservative yeoman than the fact that the craftsman, who a generation ago was at his beck and call, and was satisfied with the most meagre wage, is now more exacting in his demands, and not alone resents ill-usage, but is quite prepared to drag his betters before our democratic tribunals.

On the other hand, our rule has wrecked the industries of some of these craftsmen. The native courts at places like Delhi, Agra, and Lucknow attracted large numbers of workmen who prospered under the protection of the ruling power, and provided articles of luxury for the King and his nobles who attended his Darbâr with a host of followers in their train. Under our practical and, from this point of view, rather dreary and shabby rule much of this has ceased. The Râja is no longer a permanent courtier in attendance on his sovereign. If he is seen in a city he has come to do business, to pay a visit of ceremony to the chief European officers, to appear at an infrequent Darbâr, to attend a race meeting. And he is now-a-days contented with a much smaller suite. The city is no longer the haunt of the rich roysterer, the cadets of princely houses, and is given over to the merchant and petty trader and craftsman. Many occupations have from this cause permanently disappeared. Thus, the maker of fireworks does not supply one rocket now for a hundred in the good old times. When every one went armed, the trade of the armourer, the gunsmith, the shield maker, was an important industry. Now-a-days hardly any one wears a sword, and if a sportsman uses a gun or rifle it is usually of European make.

In the same way the artistic handicrafts have suffered grievous decline. The fine work in gold, silver, brass, or ivory has almost disappeared. The native demand for the more delicate fabrics, the muslins of Dacca, the lovely embroideries of Benares or Delhi, has been much reduced. English stuffs are much cheaper and have taken their place. The beautiful productions of the jeweller, the engraver, the enameller, the inlayer, have been replaced by foreign productions. Every little town has its "Europe shop," where glassware and crockery, German cutlery, lamps, and a myriad of similar articles are sold at rates with which the native handicraftsman cannot possibly compete. Even in the matter of dress there has been a great revolution. The young lawyer, surgeon, or schoolmaster prefers, to the graceful turban and flowing robes of his forefathers, a caricature of the frock coat and trousers of the Englishman, and he wears shoes or boots of western pattern, because he is thus enabled to escape the necessity of removing them at the threshold of his European host, to which the old-fashioned person with his slippers has to submit.

The same change has come over the occupations of other craftsmen. The national ox cart in which the village landowner or the portly merchant still sometimes rides is being replaced by the dogcart or barouche. The general use of watches has opened out quite a new trade In fact, what support is given to the more delicate native art industries is largely due to European patronage. The English lady uses the embroidered shawls of the Jât woman as hangings or curtains; she invests her surplus cash in Lucknow silver work or Delhi embroideries; she orders carved tables from Sahâranpur, native chintzes from Bulandshahr, brass trays and bowls from Benares. Large quantities of such work of coarser and less artistic make are prepared for the home market. Here fashion is ever changing. The native patterns have been modified to suit the vile taste of the globe-trotter, and when some new local production becomes popular the best specimens are bought up by some one on the spot who has an eye for colour or delicacy of pattern. When the demand develops it is met by coarser replicas of the old work, which gradually lose all its refinement.

It is this development of the original crafts which accounts in a great measure for the constant change which is ever going on in these occupational groups. They are continually by a process of fission giving birth to fresh combinations. We can watch this process going on from one decennial census to another. Thus the old occupation of the Kunjra or greengrocer breaks up into that of the Mewafarosh or fruitseller and the Sabzfarosh or dealer in green stuff; that of the carpenter-smith into those of the farrier, joiner, cabinet-maker, coachbuilder, carver, and gilder. It throws new light on the confounding of all things which resulted from the Muhammadan conquest to notice the change in nomenclature of these occupations. The boatman calls himself by the Arabic title of Mallâh; the old Sûji or tailor has become the Persian Darzi; the painter is Rangsâz, the dyer Rangrez, the firework maker Âtishbâz—all names derived from the language of the conqueror. English titles are, too, becoming more common. The maker of biscuits calls himself Biskutwâla, the meat purveyor Bûchar, or he modifies native titles to suit the new condition of things. The telegraph clerk calls himself Târwâla or "wireman," the watchmaker Gharisâz, from the old-fashioned Clepsydra.

In short, a study of the 419 classes of occupations as analysed at the last census discloses the most curious admixture as the new civilisation develops fresh wants and hustles aside the time-worn duties of primitive oriental life. We meet ear-pickers, tattooers, makers of caste marks, twisters of the sacred thread, tooth-stick sellers, makers of henna and carmine, exorcists, hail averters, astrologers, casters of horoscopes, genealogists, side by side with watchmakers, photographers, journalists, missionaries, astronomers, meteorologists, firemen and shunters, electro-platers, and ice manufacturers. Our old friend "the flatterer for gain," who used so to record himself in former enumerations, has unhappily disappeared.

The rise of this artisan or craftsman class in social respectability has also had an influence on the endogamous groups which we call castes. There are certain usages which naturally disable a group from rising in popular estimation. Such are the marriage of widows or of adult girls, the levirate, the non-seclusion of females. These all savour of vulgarity and mean extraction. So these occupational groups as they rise in the world find it advantageous to follow the usages of their orthodox neighbours in such matters. It is on widow marriage that the most stress is laid. But here common sense or the innate conservatism of the native mind often tends to make a section of the group lag behind their more ambitious brethren. Thus we often find a group split up into two sections over this question. Those who favour the new views announce that they will wed none but virgin brides, and promptly refuse to eat, smoke, or intermarry with their vulgar kindred who prefer the old ways. So a group often divides over some question of food or drink or similar social usage. The curious point is that these disputes generally centre round a social, not a religious controversy. An Englishman who becomes a teetotaller or vegetarian will hardly boycott all his kindred who adhere to the moderate use of beer or beef, while an Anglican household will give short shrift to a member who joins the Church of Rome or the Salvation Army. But it is quite different in India. It is adequate reason for boycotting a person if he eats beef, marries his sister-in-law, or messes with a menial. But many a Hindu Banya has one wife a Brâhmanist and the other a Jaina. The ladies live in perfect amity, but each practises her own religious rites.

The last great division of the people (excluding those of foreign nationality, comprising Muhammadans and Europeans, Eurasians and Armenians, and occasional strange visitors, such as the Bhotiyas of Tibet and emigrants from southern India, in all numbering about 2½ millions) are the vagrant or gipsy tribes, of whom the last census enumerated about 600,000 souls. These are in many ways the most unconventional and interesting of the races of the plains, but their propensity to petty thievery and even to the more serious forms of violent crime has made their control a difficult problem.

But there is much difference in the various elements of which this group is composed. Some of them—like the Khumra, who chips grindstones; the Saikalgar, who is a wandering cutler and knife-grinder; the Dusâdh, a village menial, a swineherd and petty cultivator; the Kharot, a matmaker; and some members of the great Dom race, like the Bânsphor or Basor, who settle in the outskirts of towns, work in bamboos or act as scavengers, while their women practise as midwives—are fairly respectable people. All of them live in poverty and social contempt; but, as it is at present constituted, they are a necessary element in Hindu society. It will be one of the problems of the future to find substitutes for these menial and scavenger tribes, should they, as is not impossible, come under the rule of some teacher, and the word be suddenly passed among them that to touch filth is impious. Even now among the lower menials there are few bodies more touchy and sensitive than the sweepers, and the special trade of scavenging is likely to become more and more odious.

Again, grouped with these scavengers and menial workmen there are others, who, though they lead a partially nomadic life, seldom offend against the law. Typical among these are the Baheliya or hunter, and the Chiryamâr or fowler. The former, whenever he can secure a gun licence, wanders in the jungle and shoots game for sale in towns. To the east he is a fine, bold, athletic fellow, but notoriously untrustworthy. From this caste are drawn many of the best Shikâris, who track down game and arrange shooting parties for European sportsmen. It is he who ties up the young

BAHELIYA SHIKĀRIS.

buffalo as a bait for a tiger, and at the first blush of dawn steals through the jungle and often watches the brute sleeping the sleep of repletion beside his victim. Some of them are exceedingly plucky in such dangerous work, and their knowledge of woodcraft, the habits of game, the marking down of footsteps in the sand of a dry watercourse, are often admirable. But, like their brethren in other lands, they are gifted with a playful imagination, and will beguile the confiding "grif" with tales of legendary tigers of gigantic size and terrible ferocity, from whose clutches they have only by a miracle escaped. Or they will enlist a real jungle man, a Kol or Kharwâr, to do all the really dangerous part of the tracking and claim the credit themselves. But to the sportsman they are indispensable from their marvellous knowledge of the jungle, and if he treats them well and believes a tithe of what he is told they will show him game.

The Nats are another group, more of the real gipsy type. Their peculiar appearance, the dark flashing eye, the black skin, mark them down as essentially non-Aryan. The Nat and his kinsfolk wander all over the country, carrying their paltry goods on the backs of oxen or donkeys, sheltering themselves under a screen of grass. The men are acrobats, perform feats on a long bamboo and dance on the tight-rope. Their women loaf about villages, selling herbs and various simples, love-philtres and charms which extract "the worm" from carious teeth. Like the gipsies of Europe, they practise many uncanny arts, and are supposed to be adepts in sorcery. Many gangs live on the unchastity of their girls, and though they are not exactly of criminal habits, the Nats are a degraded, dissolute race. Much lower than these are the criminal nomads, like the Sânsiya, Beriya, or Hâbûra, to whom some reference has been made in another connection. These people wander about in gangs, commit all kinds of petty pilfering, or even gang-robbery with violence. They are one of the pests of our time, and would receive short shrift from the peasants whom they persecute were it not for the restraining influence of British law, and the countenance and protection they receive from men of higher castes who intrigue with their women. Riding through one of the western districts, you will often come across a camp of these vagrants, which is usually pitched on one of the sand dunes, which are a characteristic feature of the landscape. In the selection of such sites, they seem to be influenced partly by sanitary considerations; partly because from such a coign of vantage they can espy dangerous visitors; partly because the sand is a safe hiding-place for stolen property. The cattle of the gang graze down the neighbouring fields, and the peaceful rustic cares little to interfere with such sturdy marauders. The men, tired after their night-prowl, sleep in the shade; the women cook whatever their husbands have been able to pilfer. They are a wild, fierce-looking people, and their manners and customs when search or arrest is inevitable daunt the rural policeman, who will not interfere with them if he can possibly avoid the necessity. He follows the sage advice of Dogberry in dealing with "vagrom men": "Take no note of him, but let him go; and presently call the rest of the watch together and thank God you are rid of a knave."

Another and perhaps less criminal branch of the same race is the vagrant known as the Bengâli, who has nothing to say to the sleek clerk with his meagre calves and flowing loin cloth, who may be seen at the railway stations. The speciality of this loathsome vagrant is rural surgery, and his "pocket-case" of instruments, a set of rude spikes which he uses as lancets, and a foul bamboo tube with which he empties abscesses, would send a thrill of horror through one of our surgeons trained to the antiseptic method. Much disease and suffering must be due to practitioners such as these.

The Kanjar is another kinsman of these people. He is half tamed from a savage life: traps wild ducks or quail for his European employers: kills wolves or makes up young jackals to resemble them and claims the Government reward. He is a fellow of great interest to a naturalist, for he is a born hunter and trapper, and deeply learned in the ways of beasts and birds. The latter he catches with a series of thin

DOMS.

canes which he fixes together like the joints of a fishing rod. The top he smears with birdlime, and pushes it through a tree; then with infinite deftness and patience he adds joint to joint till it reaches the highest branches where he ensnares some incautious bird. If it is edible he sells or eats it; some he takes to a city where tender-hearted Jaina ladies, reared from childhood to believe that killing an animal is the deadliest of sins, bribe him to let it go.

Lowest of all is the Dom, who is the true survival of the loathsome Chandâla of Manu. Of these there is a settled and a vagrant branch. Those who are settled live in cities, where they work as scavengers or provide a light for the funeral pyres at the burning Ghât. Hence he is detested and despised; but he pays back this contempt by insolence and rapacity when he can practise such arts with impunity. He lords it among the mourners at a funeral, and when the corpse of a rich banker comes to the Ganges bank he acts the bully and extortioner, and will not give the necessary fire except for an exorbitant fee.

The nomadic Dom who infests the eastern districts and Bihâr is a shameless vagrant, an eater of leavings and carrion, a beggar, a thief. Curiously enough he has none of the instincts of woodcraft in which the Kanjar is so expert. Though he frequents the jungle he cannot trap wild game or birds or even catch fish. He will eat almost any carrion and the leavings of any tribe except that of the Dhobi or washerman, between whom and the Dom, other than the hatred which the latter has for cold water, there is hereditary feud.

Not that he is quite irreclaimable. When he once sheds off his nomadic habits he settles down as a scavenger or as a worker in bamboo, and attempts to civilise him have, in recent years in Gorakhpur, the main hunting ground of the Dom, met with some measure of success.

To the ethnologist the Dom is a most interesting subject. Among them he finds some most curious survivals of primitive practice. His reverence for iron marks him down as having only in comparatively recent times emerged from the Age of Stone. He employs his sister's son as his family priest, which leads us back to the time before the growth of the family, when what anthropologists call the matriarchate prevailed, when kinship was reckoned only through the mother, and no account was taken of the father.

He is still more interesting as being almost certainly a close relation of the Gipsies of Europe. One popular legend of their origin describes how about 420 A.D. Bahrâm Gûr imported 12,000 Jât musicians from India to Persia; and it is supposed that their descendants may have entered Europe about the eleventh century. One and perhaps the most plausible explanation of the term Rom and Romani is that it is variant of the Hindi Domra or Dom; and an attempt has been made by Mr Grierson to identify the modern Gipsy tongue with that peculiar dialect of Hindi spoken by the Doms of Bihâr. That Romani contains a number of Hindi words which have survived in almost their original forms is admitted on all sides. The curious fact remains that while the Gipsy term for "a horse" is Hindi those of farriery are Greek. It is probable that the Gipsies learned the arts of the horse-coper and tinker after they left Indian soil. It is needless to say that even if some of the first Gypsies came from India the racial type and language have been largely modified since their residence in Europe. It is thus mainly on linguistic arguments that the Indian origin of these wanderers has been asserted. One element among them may be derived from the Doms, Nats, or wandering blacksmith tribes of India. We find occasional references in English newspapers to a custom common among Gipsies of burning the van and other property of a dead man. This seems to be a survival of the custom common among the menial Indian races, and for that matter among many other savages, of providing for the wants of the spirit in the other world by sending with him food or other necessaries burnt at the grave or left with him in the tomb.

Another most interesting race is that of the Thârus of the sub-Himâlayan Tarâi. They are the pioneers of civilisation, forcing their way into the malarious jungles at the foot of the hills and converting the swamps into rich stretches of rice. They are a curiously shy, retiring race : but they make almost a speciality of tending the elephant, and some of the best drivers employed in capturing the wild herds along the Siwâlik range are drawn from them. As has already been said, the assertion that they are malaria-proof is contradicted by statistics. They have undoubtedly some affinity with the Mongoloid tribes of Central Asia through Nepâl.

A Thâru village in the Tarâi is very different from that of the menials of the Plains. He often raises his huts well above the damp ground to avoid malaria ; he surrounds them with the dense green foliage of the plantain, the fruit of which forms an important article of his diet. Like those of many secluded races, his women folk are supposed to be adepts in witchcraft, and Thâruhat, "the Thâru land," has an evil repute which makes the emigrant from the Plains carefully avoid it. The Thârus themselves are about the most ghost-ridden people in northern India. Once the sun sinks below the horizon they believe that the jungle is full of evil spirits. They sit cowering under their meagre huts in a state of abject terror, and the whistling of the wind in the trees or a rotten branch falling to the ground reduces them to an agony of fear.

But to find survivals of prehistoric custom in the greatest abundance we must go to the pure Drâvidian fringe of jungle-dwellers who live along the Central Indian hills. They are found only in the Mirzapur district and in parts of Bundelkhand, their main habitat being in the present Central Provinces and Berâr, where they form the connecting link between the Bhîls in Râjputâna to the west and the Santâls and other cognate races of the Bengal hills. In this Province the jungle tribes are mainly represented by the Kols, Kharwârs, Manjhis, and Cheros. Many of these have been brought largely under Brâhmanic influence ; in fact, before the expiry of another generation they will have lost much of the primitive customs which make them so interesting to the ethnologist. It is tolerably certain that many of them have only quite recently adopted the use of metals, and are little removed from the Age of Stone.

Of these races the most interesting are the Korwas, a few of whom inhabit the low scrub jungle of south Mirzapur. They have attained only the most elementary social stage; they have no stable exogamous groups and practically no prohibited degrees in marriage; their houses are of the most primitive type—merely a booth of branches arranged in a circle and fastened roughly together at the apex. The true Korwa neither sows nor reaps; he lives in the forest, and with his sharp spud digs up the edible roots which, with the fruit of jungle trees, constitute his food. He uses the bow and arrow, but he kills little game now that wild animals have become much more shy and less numerous. But in the lordly fashion of the jungle-dweller he claims the woodland as his own, and when he makes over his daughter to the youth of her choice her dowry consists of a mountain side, on which she has the monopoly of foraging for food.

In his social arrangements he is a regular troglodyte; he lives apart from his kinsfolk, and has not even reached the stage at which he would refer the disputes of his tribe to the arbitration of a council of elders. Like Homer's Cyclops, "he is not conversant with others, but dwells apart in lawlessness of mind." "These have neither gatherings for council nor oracles of law, but they dwell in hollow caves on the crests of the high hills, and each one utters the law to his children and his wives, and they reck not one of another."

Short of stature, black of skin, with his coarse hair floating unkempt over his shoulders, possessing only a modicum of clothing, the Korwa is of the pure, unmixed Drâvidian type, and is the nearest approach to an absolute savage which northern India can show. His mental culture is on a par with his surroundings. He worships a collection of rude fetishes which his animistic beliefs teach him are the abode of the spirits or ghosts which he dreads. Of a benign Providence he has no conception; he is witch-ridden and demon-haunted. Every hill and forest, every mighty tree and prominent rock holds a divinity active in mischief, which will slay him or visit him with the cholera, the fever, the rheumatism, unless he conciliates the creature in some uncanny way.

KORWAS.

It is one of the sad but inevitable results of the progress of civilisation that these simple, law-abiding jungle races who, in their straightforward independence and manliness are in striking contrast to the degraded serf of the Plains, must exchange the free life of the hillside for the restraints of an ordered existence. As they are now they are certainly much happier than the menials of the lowlands condemned to servitude, cribbed and confined within their narrow holdings, toiling without hope on the most niggard wage. But year by year the road and railway are opening up the secret places of these secluded hills, and with the first settlers comes the money-lender, who jingles rupees before them, suggests new wants and gradually draws them more and more within his clutches. For such people our precise British law brings no message of salvation. They are not like the dweller in the Plains, who has at any rate heard from his forefathers that we have saved the land from war and rapine. These are the veriest children in their recklessness and simplicity, and the State which fails to stand towards them *in loco parentis* is only shirking an obvious duty which it will soon be too late to discharge.

The student of sociology will thus find within the limits of a single Indian Province a complete series of the stages through which civilisation must everywhere progress. We start in the lowest grade with the Korwa, a mere savage, living on the roots or fruits which he can collect in the jungle or the animals which he can slay for food. Little higher is the Dom, whose only industry is a little rude work in bamboo, a loafer, a thief, a beggar, an eater of carrion, a collector of filth. Then we meet the Kanjar or Sânsiya, a pure nomad who lives by hunting birds and animals, and will eat the lizard which has its home in the salt plains. A little higher is the Baheliya and Chiryamâr, who catches birds for food and sale. Then comes the Pâsi, who collects palm juice as an intoxicant; the Bâri, who makes leaf platters for use at fêtes; the Khairaha, who distils catechu from the acacia; the Bânsphor, who makes baskets out of canes or twigs. Then we have the wandering juggler and acrobat like the Nat; the nomad

Lohâr blacksmith; the Bengâli, an itinerant surgeon; the Saikalgar, or peripatetic cutler. Another stage leads us to the Mallâh and Kahâr, who are boatmen, water-carriers, bearers of palanquins, fishermen, and collectors of tank produce. With the Gûjar and Ahîr we come upon the semi-nomad grazier and rearer of cattle, and the Gadariya who breeds sheep and practises agriculture merely as a secondary occupation.

Above these are the peasant cultivators and yeomen, and from these we come to those who supply the spiritual, moral, and luxurious needs of the people—the Levite, the scribe, the genealogist, the jeweller, the perfumer, the coppersmith and so on; while at the top of the industrial ladder stands the Banya capitalist.

It would be easy to press this analysis much further. But even without any attempt at greater precision, it is manifest that in the study of the evolution of these groups there is ample scope for the labours of the sociologist. Though there is no absolute severance of occupation, the barber sometimes holding land and the currier working as a day labourer, still these endogamous groups are fairly distinct, much more precisely defined than in western lands, where the guild system has more or less completely disappeared.

But though labour is the lot of the majority of the people, there is in India no sense of the dignity of labour. A familiar proverb ever on the lips of the people tells us that farming is the best occupation; trade is middling; service is bad; begging worst of all. Here the artisan is significantly left out and agriculture elevated to the highest rank. Yet it is noticeable that Manu depreciated agriculture as a means of livelihood: "Some are of opinion that agriculture is excellent; but it is a mode of occupation which the benevolent greatly blame:" and for this he gives the characteristic explanation: "for the iron-mouthed pieces of wood not only wound the earth, but the creatures dwelling in it."[1] He prescribes as the most commendable occupations of the three higher tribes, respectively, teaching the Veda, defending the

[1] Manu, *Institutes*, x. 84.

people, or keeping herds and flocks.[1] But he permits the Brâhman, if he be unable to subsist by his special duties, to serve as a soldier or even trade like a merchant, or become a tiller of the ground or a tender of cattle.[2]

As for the Sûdra or menial, his proper business is to wait on the twice-born, and it is only if his family be starving that he may adopt a handicraft, but then it should be one of a mechanical nature, such as joinery and masonry, or a practical art, such as painting or writing, by following which he may serve his betters.[3] Any attempt on the part of the menial to rise in the social scale was carefully prohibited. "A man of the lowest class who through covetousness lives by the acts of the highest, let the King strip of all his wealth and instantly banish."[4]

Though the overthrow of the Brâhmanical constitution has given the Sûdra much more chance of rising in the world, still even now the craftsman is held in discredit, and many of them are included in the class from whose hands the Brâhman is forbidden to drink water. Various explanations have been given to account for this. There is not much difficulty in understanding why a butcher, a tanner, a scavenger should be objects of social contempt. But we are told that the washerman is impure because he has to deal with foul raiment; the potter because he is a sort of butcher and cuts the throats of his pots; the oilman, because he is filthy. Even the blacksmith and the carpenter, the weaver, goldsmith, and coppersmith remain menials, though there is nothing defiling in their occupations.

On the process by which these various occupations were evolved the Indian myth of civilisation throws little light. In other countries many tribes endeavour to account for their social progress by the advent of some wise man from the East who taught them the arts of civilised life. By the Indian theory, however, this diversity of occupations is not only of home growth, but the idea of social evolution is barred out by the assertion that in the beginning the Deity

[1] Manu, *Institutes*, x. 80.
[2] *Ibid.*, x. 81 sq.
[3] *Ibid.*, x. 99 sq.
[4] *Ibid.*, x. 96.

prescribed distinct occupations for his creatures, "as they had been revealed in the pre-existing Veda."[1] And here the legends display a curious inconsistency. Brihaspati is the prototype of the priestly body; he is even called the father of the gods, and a widely extended creative power is ascribed to him. By another story this was the special work of Daksha. By a third legend Prithi makes Swayambhuva Manu the calf, milks the earth and receives the milk in his hands for the benefit of mankind. Thence proceeded all kinds of corn and vegetables upon which the people now and for ever subsist. It was Viswakarma who succeeded to the functions of Twashtri, the divine architect of the Vedas, and from him, like Tubal Cain, the forger of every cutting instrument of brass and iron, sprang the race of handicraftsmen.

We have already said something about the divergence of rural and urban life; but as this is one of the most vital points in the sociology of the Province, it may be worth while to attempt to push the analysis a little further.

The first point to be observed is that in Oudh, as compared with the sister province, the average village population is much larger and the settlements are much more closely packed. While in Oudh the average number of souls in each village is 519, and each is one-third of a mile distant from the other, in the larger Province there are 418 souls per village, and between every two there is a distance ot rather more than a mile. The averages, of course, here are kept down by the large and sparsely-peopled mountainous tract. In the hill tract there are only 106 people per village, while in the Upper Duâb, where the villages are much larger, the average rises to 565, and falls to 425 in the east of the province, where, as we have already seen, a long period of peace has encouraged the formation of hamlets. In the Panjâb and Bombay, where the population is more sparse and the amount of waste greater, the villages are much larger—the Bombay village has double the average population of those in this Province; that of the Panjâb is greater by nearly one-third. In Sindh each village has attached to

[1] Manu, *Institutes*, i. 21.

it about 12 square miles of territory; in Oudh the villages are 2⅜ furlongs, and in the North-Western Provinces rather more than a mile apart, which is a little over the Bengal average.

But there is another cause which has contributed to make the villages in Oudh and the eastern part of the Province smaller than those to the west. The land to the west is largely occupied by village communities of the peasant proprietary type, where a large proportion of the residents possess rights of ownership in the soil. Here the communal organisation has tended to knit the coparceners so closely together that there is little encouragement for the surplus population to overflow into new settlements. As the people increase the shares only become more and more minutely sub-divided; any one who has ever attempted to partition a Jât or Râjput village in the Upper Duâb will understand what that means. So, as a man's household increases, he adds a new hut and a new cattle-steading for his married son, and makes over to him part of his farm; but they all use the same general courtyard, very often mess together, and share in the common stock. These sturdy yeomen cling closely to the soil, as the Celts do, and are very unwilling to part with an inch of it. Hence they seldom settle day-labourers on a patch of the ancestral holding. They prefer to do the farming work themselves, and if they employ extra labour at harvest time it is paid for then and there in a cash wage or in kind. Lastly, the canny western man is not much Brâhman-ridden. He will pay his annual dues with a grumble, or he will fee the priest at Hardwâr or Mathura when he visits these shrines on his annual holiday; but, as for settling a Brâhman on part of his land, he is much too calculating, too unemotional in his religious views, to dream of hampering himself in such a way.

On the other hand, in Oudh and to the east, almost all tenures are the result of the conquest of the soil from some ancient race—Bhars, Pâsis, or the like. The traditional way of providing for the cadets of the dominant families was by grants of patches of land, known as Birt or maintenance.

This class was much more under the influence of the priestly body than the hard-fisted western yeoman. It is a point of honour with any one who pretends to princely blood to have a Levite in his employment, and he must also support a Bhât or genealogist, who preserves the tradition of the past glories of the family, and maintains the pedigree which is of primary importance when the inevitable question of settling the girls comes to be considered. Hence the priest or marriage-broker is often supplied out of the estate with a snug little village, where he sleeps away his time under the pleasant shade of the trees, and rouses himself to activity only when an approaching marriage or funeral feast is announced. The Levite and his employer both consider it inconsistent with their dignity to handle the plough. So, a plot must be found for the colony of menial serfs, who cluster round the dilapidated homestead of their master, and do the farming work in consideration for the grant of a rent-free holding.

Thus, contrasting the two types of village, we have to the west a class of hard-handed petty farmers, who work their ancestral fields, and whose love of the soil is as passionate as that of an Irishman; to the east we find more of the middle class, indolent proprietors and their hangers-on. Not that this relief from manual labour promotes any desire for the higher culture which ease renders possible for them. They are perhaps more acute, because they have more leisure for moving about, possess more of that knowledge of the world which intercourse with men and cities produces. Hence they are wont to laugh at the western peasant as a dolt and a drudge; but the appearance of their villages and the character of their farming indicate clearly which type of rural life is the more industrially valuable.

The question of the degree to which the people are crowded within the inhabited area is one of primary importance from the sanitary point of view. To take the case of the towns first, there is a marked distinction between those towns which are the site of a European cantonment and those occupied only by natives. The European finds air and space an absolute necessity for the enjoyment of a fairly healthy life;

and where land is comparatively cheap he is wont to plant his house in the centre of a spacious "compound," part occupied by his garden and the miniature village which accommodates his servants and his horses, and a wide extent of rough, ill-kept land, providing scanty grazing for the cow or two he must keep, if he is not to fall a victim to cholera or enteric fever. The adulterated milk and butter of the bâzâr are one of the main causes of such diseases. The native town, on the contrary, is a maze of squalid, pestilential lanes, and the cultivated area presses up to the very skirts of the settlement, and few open spaces are left. The native rather prefers his house to be closely huddled against that of his neighbour. He believes that he is thus protected against thieves; he has no desire for privacy, and he is quite inured to what we consider the chief nuisances of city life. He will sleep soundly though pariah dogs bark round him from dusk to dawn. To the annoyance of dust, smoke, and smells he is absolutely callous. There is, again, a vast difference in this respect between the old Imperial cities, like Agra, where population has much decreased since Mughal times, and the present outskirts have wide open spaces, the ruins of old mansions, gardens surrounding stately tombs, like the Tâj Mahal, as compared with a religious town like Benares. In the latter sites are much more valuable, and there are no stretches of waste land in the vicinity occupied by the mouldering remains of the tombs, garden houses and mansions of a nobility, the very names of whom have been forgotten.

Thus to take the cities with a population of more than fifty thousand—the most crowded native sites are Cawnpur and Meerut, with a density of 187 and 167 per acre of area. The nearest analogy to these cities, both of which are largely industrial, is Liverpool, with 113 souls to the acre. On the other hand, Lucknow, with 46 persons to the acre, about the density of Brighton or Bolton, owes its open spaces to the palaces and gardens of the King and his nobility; and in Bahraich, a typical country town, there are only 19 people to the acre, about the average of Bradford. As a rule, the small country towns, which were never the seat of a large resident aristocracy, are more closely crowded than the cities. In Oudh, however, where many of the towns are of recent creation, care was taken by our officers to restrict building and provide open spaces to a much larger extent than in the older settlements of the sister Province. To the west, again, the town density, as is the case with villages, ranges much higher than to the east.

But it does not follow that open spaces are an unmixed benefit to a town unless sanitation be efficient. An ill-kept expanse devoted to the accumulation of rubbish and dedicated, as so many places of the kind are, to the worship of Cloacina is, to say the least of it, a very doubtful blessing, and the resident of a closely-packed but well-swept slum probably leads a healthier life.

It is unfortunate that, from the straggling character of such settlements, it has been found impossible to procure statistics illustrating the conditions of village life in the same way. The best authorities suppose that the village density cannot be much below 50 per acre (a little less than that of Birmingham), which is about the lowest urban average. This would suggest a greater chance of health and longevity in rural life, and this is to some extent supported by the figures which have been already given. But the villages lose much of the advantage which they should possess in this respect from the absence of all sanitary precautions and the want of medical relief.

The question of house accommodation, so pressing in Western lands, loses much of its importance in the East. The Englishman always sleeps in his house, and occupies it for a large part of his time; the Oriental only occasionally shuts himself up within four walls. His house is a store for his property, and a place where he secludes his wife and her grown-up daughters, if he has reached that grade of social respectability, of which the leading indication is the seclusion of his women folk. The peasant, with his family, spends most of his time in the field; the artisan, such as the weaver, the potter, the carpenter, almost habitually works out of doors. It is only in the drenching rain of autumn that the family crowds under the narrow thatch. In the sultry summer nights, most of the male population drag their light cots out of doors and sleep there, or roll themselves in a sheet and rest anywhere out of the glare of the moonlight. The streets of a country town present a weird sight in the small hours of the morning when the sleepers crowd the roadway, each wrapped in his white covering, like so many corpses on the slabs of the Morgue.

In England, one of the best tests of a man's means is the rent of the house he occupies. In India, the reverse is the case. You will see a merchant, whose business transactions are immense, balancing his books in a corner of a squalid verandah, by the light of a glimmering oil lamp. To such a man the plate-glass doors and mahogany desks of a European counting-house represent so much frivolous extravagance. Or the broken-down Pathân, who has fallen in the world and owes more than he is worth, occupies the stately brick mansion built by some prosperous ancestor, which his bankrupt successor has no means to maintain or repair. It has, again, been one of the chief problems which our census officials have attempted to solve, how to suggest a definition of a house which will include the sweeper's hovel and the case of the nest of families who, more or less detached, cluster within the enclosure of the so-called joint family.

The result is that there is not much of interest to be gathered from the house statistics. There are, it appears, about 5·7 persons per house, as compared with 5·3 in England, and the average number of occupants is slightly in excess to the East as compared with the Western districts.

But the most important sociological facts are those in connection with marriage, the dominant factor in all Oriental life. First as to the marriage age.—At the last census, 1971 children were found to be married in the first year of life. After that the numbers gradually rise, until we find 13,076 boys and 20,517 girls married under the age of four. The important marriage age is between five and nine, when 433 per 10,000 of the male population of that age period and 999 of the female population are married. "Between ten and fourteen nearly nine-tenths of the female population pass into the marriage state; but considerably more than half of the males remain unmarried. Between fifteen and nineteen there are fifteen married females for one unmarried, whilst at the end of the period only 60 per cent. of the males have been married. By twenty-four practically the whole of the female population have been married, almost the whole of those unmarried at this and later ages being women whose avocations preclude marriage, or whose physical or mental health forbids it. Of men, considerably more than a fourth are unmarried up to twenty-four, whilst an appreciable but diminishing number remain unmarried through all the subsequent age periods."[1]

The significance of these figures will become more apparent from a comparison with English statistics. In 10,000 of the whole population over the age of fifteen, there are 1702 males and 150 girls single as compared with 3918 and 3674 in England. Similarly with the proportion of married and widowed of both sexes above the age of fifteen. In 10,000 of the people, there are in the Indian Province 7292 married men and 1006 widowers; in England, the corresponding figures are 5532 and 550. So of women above fifteen there are 7224 married in India against 5164 in England, and the widows are as 2626 to 1163.

These figures may seem to give some countenance to the agitation against infant marriage. But these early marriages are really nothing more than betrothals, and the cases in which an immature girl cohabits with her husband are happily most infrequent. When the pair are grown up, there is always a Gauna or second marriage, after which married life begins.

Again, the prevailing belief that nearly all Hindu widows remain celibate for the rest of their days is utterly opposed to the facts. Recent enquiries show that out of a population of 40,000,000 of Hindus, 9,000,000, or 24 per cent., prohibit

[1] *Census Report, North-West Provinces*, 1891, p. 246 sq.

widow marriage, while 30,000,000, or 76 per cent., both permit and even encourage the practice. It need hardly be said that widow marriage is freely permitted by Muhammadans. As a matter of fact, among all but the very highest castes, every young widow finds another mate, and the levirate, or custom by which the younger brother-in-law takes over the widow of his elder brother, widely prevails. This rule of widow marriage is a most important factor in the development of the country. It would seem, for instance, that in very unhealthy tracts, such as Eastern Bengal, the offspring of virgin brides is barely sufficient to make up for the wastage by disease and maintain the population. In such parts of the country, only those areas in which widow marriage prevails show a rapidly increasing population.

In connection with the pressure of the population on the soil, the question of the fecundity of the people is most important. Statistics do not bear out the conclusion that the rate of increase is excessive, or even up to the European standard. Assuming the reproductive period to lie for women between the ages of fifteen and forty, we find an average of 251 births per annum for each thousand wives, as compared with the English average of 292. The rate of increase is naturally lowest among those castes of which, like the Banyas, the males lead a sedentary life and the women are secluded. The highest fecundity is among the forest tribes, and here the Bengal figures are most instructive. Thus, the Orâons, a Drâvidian race occupying the southern hills, show among 20,000 people of both sexes 7704 children, while Brâhmans have only 5288.[1]

We have hitherto said nothing about the occupations of women and children. Among a large section of the cultivating tribes the women freely assist the men in field labour; in fact, the effectiveness of husbandry may be to a large extent measured by the degree to which this is the case. You will constantly see the wife of the Kurmi or Jât sowing the seed grain as her husband ploughs, weeding or assisting in irrigation by distributing the water from one little patch

[1] *Bengal Census Report*, 1891, p. 175.

to another, if she does not take a more active share in the work by helping to empty the well-bucket or raising the water-lift. This the Brâhman or Râjput woman is not allowed to do, and her husband has to depend on expensive and inefficient hired labour. Recent enquiries in Bihâr show that here the pressure of population has resulted in driving the males to emigrate, and leaving the women to till the fields at home, as is the case in some of those countries of Europe where the pressure of the conscription is most severe. On the contrary, the growth in wealth in Eastern Bengal, and the extension of the influence of caste ideas, are causing the women of Bengal Proper to withdraw more and more from an active share in the employments of peasant life.[1]

On the whole, the peasant woman of Upper India has her time fully occupied. She is obliged to let her children sprawl in the sun and play at making mud pies while she milks the cow, feeds the calves, picks pottage herbs in the field, collects firewood, or makes the cow-dung into cakes for fuel. She has to grind the wheat and barley, which is the chief food of the household, husk the rice and millet, and do all the cooking, besides taking her share in field work, and scaring the parrots and monkeys from the ripening crops. If she has any leisure, she can devote it profitably to ginning cotton or spinning thread. If her husband be an artisan, she is able to give him material assistance. In a weaver family she cleans the thread or arranges the web; for the potter she collects and mixes the clay; in all cases she does much of the labour of carrying the manufactured goods for sale at the nearest village fair or market. It is this hard monotonous labour which, with the absence of medical aid in child-bearing, converts in a few years the buxom village girl into a wrinkled hag.

But it would be a mistake to suppose the wife of the peasant to be nothing more than a drudge. On the contrary, she is an influential personage in the household, and little is done without her knowledge and advice, whether it is the selection of a husband for a girl, or the purchase of an

[1] *Bengal Census Report*, 1891, p. 272.

ox, or a deal with the village banker. If she misconducts herself, she has to endure hard language and sometimes blows; but if she is badly wronged the tribal council will protect her, and on the whole her position is, perhaps, not worse than that of her sisters in a similar grade of life in other parts of the world. Polygamy, which seems so intolerable to the woman of the west, she looks on much more calmly. It often happens that as she advances in years, and finds the burden of household work beyond her strength, she will encourage her husband to introduce a young widow into the house who will share her burdens.

Children, as soon as they begin to grow up, can all be usefully employed, and it is this which to a great degree keeps down primary education. It is the children who do most of the work of pasturing the cattle, collecting fuel and manure, cutting grass for the buffalo. The begging castes keep them constantly at work, and it is one cause of the dexterity of the artisan that the boys are trained to labour at a very early age. Some kinds of agriculture cannot be carried on without them. It is a pleasant sight on a fine morning in the cold weather to see a whole Kurmi or Kâchhi household at work in the opium field—men, women, and children weeding, watering, puncturing the capsule and collecting the drug. This is a much healthier life than that of the city woman, who has much less liberty and enjoyment of the open air. Her children, if more regularly educated, are more exposed to the demoralising influence of the open profligacy which is tolerated by native opinion.

This survey of rural life from its industrial side tends to correct some current misconceptions. There is here little of the calm of the mild-eyed, melancholy lotos eaters; none of that sensuous abandonment to the delights of a tranquil life which we are wont to associate with the Oriental world. The life of the peasant is one of ceaseless, monotonous toil, among the lower ranks squalid and hopeless, a constant struggle to win from adverse fate the very scantiest means of keeping body and soul together. It is an existence which has no room for the higher aims and ambitions, for the culture of patriotism, for speculation on the problems of the future. But, on the other hand, it enforces an unwearied industry and temperance of life, and it is compatible with a good deal of simple charity and kindliness, and a ready cheeriness which can find amusement in the veriest trifles.

Last of all he has the benign influence of Nature round him. Here one can do nothing but quote once more the words of Sir Ali Baba, which have become almost classical.[1] "God is ever with the cultivator in all the manifold sights and sounds of this marvellous world of His. In that mysterious temple of the Dawn, in which we of noisy mess-rooms, heated Courts and dusty offices are infrequent worshippers, there he offers up his hopes and fears for rain and sunshine; there he listens to the anthems of birds we rarely hear, and interprets auguries that for us have little meaning. The beast of prey skulking back to his lair, the stag quenching his thirst ere retiring to the depths of the forest, the wedge of wild fowl flying with trumpet notes to some distant lake, the vulture hastening in heavy flight to the carrion that night has provided, the crane flapping to the shallows, and the jackal shuffling along to his shelter in the nullah, have each and all their portent to the initiated eye. Day with its fierce glories brings the throbbing silence of intense life, and under flickering shade, amid the soft pulsations of Nature, the cultivator lives his day-dream. What there is of squalor and of drudgery and carking care in his life melts into a brief oblivion, and he is a man in the presence of his God, with the holy stillness of Nature brooding over him. With lengthening shadows comes labour and a reawakening. The air is once more full of all sweet sounds, from the fine whistle of the kite, sailing with supreme dominion through the azure depths of air, to the stir and buzzing of little birds and crickets among the leaves and grass. The egret has resumed his fishing in the tank where the rain is stored for the poppy and sugar-cane fields, the sandpipers bustle along the margin, or wheel in little silvery clouds over the bright water, the gloomy cormorant sits alert on the stump of the dead date

[1] Aberigh Mackay, *Twenty-one days in India*, p. 131.

tree, the little black divers hurry in and out of the weeds, and ever and anon shoot under the water in hot quest of some tiny fish; the whole machinery of life and death is in full play, and our villager shouts to the patient oxen and lives his life. Then gradual darkness and food with homely joys, a little talk, a little tobacco, a few sad songs and kindly sleep."

CHAPTER V

THE RELIGIOUS AND SOCIAL LIFE OF THE PEOPLE

THE materials for a survey of the religious and social life of the people are so ample that it is extremely difficult to bring them in an intelligible way within the limits of a sketch like the present. In dealing with religion it must also be understood that in working our way through the intricate jungle of existing beliefs various difficulties must be encountered. It is all but impossible to frame a working definition of a Hindu: Musalmâns of the lower class cling to many of the beliefs of the faith from which they were originally drawn; everywhere in the lower strata the forms of faith known as Brâhmanical or animistic constantly overlap. On the social side there is the equal absence of a standpoint from which a general survey can be made.

To estimate roughly the prevalence of the two great religions—Brâhmanism and Islâm in northern India—we find that comparing the North-West Provinces with the Panjâb, for 10,000 of the people, there are in the former 8579 Brâhmanists and 1380 Musalmâns; in the Panjâb 3771 of the former and 5575 of the latter. The most Hindu Provinces are in rotation—Oudh, the North-West Provinces, Bengal, and the Panjâb; in the proportion of Musalmâns the series runs—Panjâb, Bengal, North-West Provinces, and Oudh.

Taking these Provinces alone, we find that out of a population of about 47 millions, rather over 40 millions are so-called Hindus: nearly 6½ millions, or 13 per cent., are Musalmâns. This leaves only 178,000 followers of other creeds, of whom nearly half are Jainas; next come 58,000 Christians, 22,000 modern Theistic Âryas, and 11,000 Sikhs.

The other creeds may be dismissed in a few words. Buddhism has absolutely disappeared from the Plains, leaving as the sole representatives of what was once the dominant faith only about 1400 believers, nearly all of whom are residents of the upper Himâlayan valleys and have joined the impure worship of Devi according to the Tantric form to the purer doctrines of the Mahâyana school of Buddhism. Besides these there are some 350 Pârsi shopkeepers and sixty Jews.

Before discussing the two main religions which make up the faith of the people, it may be convenient to dispose first of those which are of less numerical importance.

Jainism, the religion of about 85,000 people, has its main seats in Western India. It is believed to be to a large extent an offshoot of Buddhism; its votaries are chiefly found among the trading classes; its main principles are the reverence paid to a body of holy men, who by long and rigorous devotion have raised themselves to a state of perfection, and are known as Jina or "conqueror" or Tîrathankara—"those who have passed through the pilgrimage of life and attained Nirvâna, or absorption into the divine essence." Besides an elaborate temple ritual, their religious duties are for the most part confined to a strict regard for the sanctity of animal life: and a simple code of morality which inculcates the speaking of the truth, honesty, chastity, temperance, and the repression of immoderate desire.

The high average of wealth among its members has encouraged the erection of splendid temples and a most ornate ritual. To the west of India they appear to show a desire, not as is the case in these Provinces, to emphasise the distinction of their religion from Brâhmanism, with which they have in some places come into conflict by their custom of parading the images of their deities through the towns at certain festivals. But, as has been elsewhere observed, the demarcation between the two faiths does not constitute a bar to intermarriage.

They are divided into two main sects—the Swetambara and Digambara, between whom, irrespective of minor distinctions, the main difference lies in the former wearing white garments and clothing their idols, while the latter worship "sky-clad" or naked gods, and now conform to the laws of decency by insisting on their ascetics wearing ochre-coloured robes and abandoning the ancient habit of nudity. These last are practically the only branch found in this part of the country.

Sikhism is found only as the religion of immigrants from the Panjâb, most of whom serve in our army and police.

The Jews are numerically insignificant. It is only in Bombay and Cochin that they attain to any importance. Possibly the fact that the place of merchants and traders is already occupied by most astute indigenous races has prevented the migration of Russian and Polish Jews to India.

The same is the case with the Zoroastrians or Pârsis, who increase slowly. "The community," writes Mr Baines,[1] "is a small one, and in spite of its general prosperity and the probable infusion of fresh blood from time to time from local sources, the marriage field is a restricted one, and domestic ceremonial, which is very strictly observed, weighs with undue severity on the weaker sex. Hence, especially among the wealthier families, who all belong to the professional and higher commercial classes, there seems to be a tendency towards deterioration in both prolificity and physique, which is not counteracted, as in the case of the middle and rural classes, by outdoor life and the relaxation of caste rule among the latter, or by the energy and success with which the former have of late betaken themselves to athletic sports and exercises."

The Âryas, though numbering only 25,000, are important from the high standard of intelligence of the majority of the adherents and the active propaganda which they have adopted. The principles of their great teacher, Dâyanand, who died in 1883, inculcate a reversion to the primitive Vedic faith, the adoration of one God, abstracted from all ideas of shape and form. "Socially," writes Mr Baillie,[2] "they condemn infant marriage and endeavour to promote

[1] *Indian Census Report*, p. 177.

[2] *Census Report, North-West Provinces*, i. 189.

education, and in particular, female education. They acknowledge the existence of caste and the social relations dependent upon it, but deny the superiority of one caste to another in religious matters. They are strict vegetarians in theory and practice, and condemn the taking of the life of any animal for the purpose of food. Cow-killing is condemned in particular, not on account of any special reverence due to the cow, but on account of its usefulness being more than ordinary. Theoretically, the Samâj keeps itself apart from all religious movements, but it is doubtful whether individual preachers have adhered to the spirit of the rules of the society on the subject." Except through its advocacy of the cow cultus, "which it seems incredible should affect the beliefs of reasoning and educated men," it is doubtful if the religion has much prospect of permanence or extension.

Passing on to Christianity—the number of the European branch varies according to the movements of European residents and troops, and the increasing tendency of Eurasians to record themselves as Europeans. Of 35,000 European Christians, three-fifths are recorded as members of the Church of England, nearly one-fourth are Roman Catholics, and rather more than one-tenth belong to the various Nonconformist bodies.

The statistics of the Native Christian body are more remarkable. They have, according to the last census, increased in ten years from 13 to 23,000—a rise of 76 per cent. The increase is almost entirely confined to the members of the Episcopal Methodist Church in Rohilkhand. It is claimed that the increase has been even greater, and that, owing to the prejudices of enumerators, the statistics do not adequately represent the actual progress which has been made. But, according to the records of the Missionary body, out of 25,000 persons shown as members of the Church no less than 16,000 persons were probationers. "It is certain," writes Mr Baillie,[1] "that the Christian community is in a transition stage, and more than probable that the Missionaries have got ahead of their enquirers in including

[1] *Census Report, North-West Provinces*, i. 187.

them amongst the Christian community." On the other hand the Collector of Budaun seems to have no doubts in the matter. He ascribes the large increase mainly to "a keener appreciation on the part of low caste people of the social and material advantages to be obtained by professing Christianity: and to greater energy on the part of the Missionaries, whose exertions will probably bring Government face to face with a very serious social problem before many years are over." It will be interesting to test how far this exceptional rate of progress can be maintained.

Before discussing the two great religions of the people, it may be well to follow Mr Ibbetson[1] in his review of their external characteristics. The Hindu and Jaina believe in their respective Shâstras or Scriptures; the Buddhist in the Tripitika or "triple basket"; the Sikh in the Adi Granth; the Musalmân in the Korân. Hindu, Sikh, and Jaina usually pray facing the east, never the south; the Musalmân turns towards Mecca. The first three worship in temples, the last in a mosque. The Hindu, Sikh, and Jaina have Brâhman Levite priests; the Buddhist celibate monks; the Musalmân a ministrant drawn from his own congregation. The Hindu venerates the cow, and will not as a rule kill animals, and sometimes abstains from meat; the Sikh is even more faithful to the cow, but kills and eats most other animals; the Musalmân loathes the pig and dog, but here his prejudice connected with animals ends; the Buddhist and Jaina scrupulously protect animal life. All except the vagrant, outcast tribes reject carrion and vermin as food. The Sikh refuses tobacco, but uses other narcotics and ardent spirits; the Hindu may use all; the Musalmân rejects intoxicants. The Hindu and Jaina shave their heads, leaving a scalp-lock; the Sikh allows the hair of his head and face to remain untrimmed; the Musalmân never shaves his beard; he often shaves his head, but keeps no scalp-lock. The Hindu, Sikh, and Jaina button their coats to the right, the Musalmân to the left. The male Hindu or Jaina wears a loin-cloth, the Sikh short drawers reaching to the knee, the

[1] *Panjâb Census Report*, 1881, p. 102.

Musalmân long drawers or a loin-cloth arranged like a kilt. The Hindu and Buddhist special colours are red and saffron, and the former abominates indigo blue; the Sikh wears blue or white and detests saffron; the Musalmân's colour is indigo blue, and he will not wear red. The Hindu or Jaina may cook in, but may not eat out of, an earthen vessel which has been already used for that purpose; his earthen vessels may be ornamented with stripes, and those of metal will be of brass or bell metal; a Musalmân may use an earthen vessel over and over again to eat from, but it must not be striped, and his metal vessel is usually of copper; the Sikh follows the Hindu in the main, but is not so particular. The Hindu and Sikh practise daily ablutions; the Musalmân and Buddhist do not bathe of necessity.

As regards other social observances, the Hindu, Jaina, and Sikh marry by circumambulation of the sacred fire; the Musalmân by formal consent of the parties asked and given before witnesses. The Musalmân practises circumcision, while the Sikh has a baptism of initiation and a ceremony of communion. The Hindu, Jaina, and Sikh as a rule burn, the Musalmân buries, the Buddhist buries or exposes his dead. While, subject to caste rules, a Musalmân will eat and drink without scruple from the hands of a Hindu, no Hindu will either take food or water from a Musalmân, nor will he smoke with a member of a strange caste. This is, of course, only a general sketch, and the variance of social usage among different castes is infinite. There is no communion of custom between the Brâhman on the one hand and the sweeper or nomad gipsy on the other; the meaner Musalmân tribes, comparatively recent converts from Hinduism, retain many of the customs and prejudices of the castes from which they sprang.

How to frame a working definition of a Hindu has long been a vexed problem to Indian sociologists. The term embraces in popular acceptance the most punctilious disciple of pure Vedantism, the agnostic youth of our Universities, the rude hillman who is quite catholic in his diet, the Brâhman whose food is defiled if the shadow of an unbeliever passes over it, the Dom who will eat carrion and the leavings of almost any other caste. Some bury the corpse, some cremate, some fling it into running water. Some worship Siva, Vishnu, Devi, and a host of other deities, some dëified worthies, some bow before a fetish, deities of mountain or river, the god of cholera or small-pox, the snake or the tiger, the cow or the tree. To attempt to frame a definite creed from the Shâstras is out of the question, nor can any clear line be drawn between the Brâhmanic and the Animistic faiths. We know clearly enough who is a Musalmân and who is a Christian, but the faith of the low class Musalmân is largely made up of Hindu beliefs, and the low class Hindu has what is almost a special creed of his own. The practical result is that for the purposes of religious statistics we are obliged to strike out first the members of fairly recognisable religions, and we call every one else a Hindu.

It would be difficult to suggest an analogy for such a state of things as this. The Church of England, to take a common example, is notorious for its toleration of minor differences of belief, and the Anglican or Ritualist, the Broad Church and the Evangelical sections all find shelter within her fold ; but Hinduism is even more comprehensive, and the contrast between the beliefs and practices of the more extreme parties of the English Church is a trifle compared with the gulf which is fixed between the orthodox Pandit and the hillman, gipsy or sweeper. It is this receptivity, this toleration, which has made Brâhmanism what it is, the faith of over two hundred millions of the Indian people.

It is, then, all but impossible to analyse in any intelligible way the beliefs of the forty millions of so-called Hindus. The natural cleavage line is between Brâhmanism and Animism, and it has been found possible on this basis to define the religious beliefs of eastern and southern India, but in northern India this distinction is unworkable. Most of the menial and hill tribes profess theoretically a belief in the Brâhmanical pantheon ; at the same time even the higher classes are more or less influenced by the Animistic beliefs of the lower races.

But here it is necessary to define the terms which have been used. Brâhmanism, to use the words of Sir Monier-Williams,[1] "is a reflection of the composite character of the Hindus, who are not one people but many. It is based on the idea of universal receptivity. It has ever aimed at accommodating itself to circumstances, and has carried on the process of adaptation through more than three thousand years. It has first borne with, and then, so to speak, swallowed, digested, and assimilated something from all creeds; or, like a vast, hospitable mansion, it has opened its doors to all comers: it has not refused a welcome to applicants of every grade from the highest to the lowest, if only willing to acknowledge the spiritual headship of the Brâhmans and adopt caste rules."

As for Animism it may be well to adopt the last recognised definition—that of Dr Tiele[2]—"Animism is the belief in the existence of souls or spirits, of which only the powerful—those on which man feels himself dependent and before which he stands in awe—acquire the rank of divine beings and become objects of worship. These spirits are conceived as moving freely through earth and air, and, either of their own accord, or because conjured by some spell, and thus under compulsion, appearing to men (Spiritism). But they may also take up their abode, either permanently or temporarily, in some object, whether lifeless or living it matters not: and this object, as endowed with higher power, is then worshipped or employed to protect individuals or communities (Fetishism). Spiritism, essentially the same as what is now called Spiritualism, must be carefully distinguished from Fetishism, but can only rarely be separated from it."

The classification of these beliefs adopted by Mr Baillie is far from satisfactory; but nothing better is available at present. There are, to begin with, about a million and a half people who were unable to record which deity they worshipped. This category should certainly be much larger. Next come nearly four millions classed as Monotheistic be-

[1] *Brâhmanism and Hinduism*, 57.

[2] Quoted by Baines, *Indian Census Report*, 157.

cause they profess to believe in a single god—Îswar or Brahma. Following these we find about half a million who describe themselves as followers of the earlier Vedic faith, worshippers of the Sun and other powers of Nature. We then come to rather more definite beliefs—seven and a quarter millions worship Vishnu or one of his many forms; nearly eight and a half millions adore Siva; ten millions the Sâktis or female energies. The seventh class, with over six and a half millions, is a very mob. Over a third of them worship Muhammadan saints; about a fourth special deities of the menial races: the remainder pay reverence to the godlings of disease, the snake, the ghosts of persons who have died a violent death, special caste or ancestral deities, demons, godlings of village, wood or river. The eighth class includes worshippers of sacred places, deified devotees and miscellaneous deities of the Purânas, the Scriptures of the neo-Brâhmanism. These number about a third of a million, and last come nearly two millions of professed devotees, of whom the great majority reverence Vishnu in some form or other.

The brain aches in exploring such a maze as this. The best parallel to it is perhaps the history of Mediæval Italy. "Can any man living," asks Dr Freeman,[1] "repeat—we do not say all the tyrants of Rimini or Faenza, but all the Popes, all the Doges, all the Lords, Dukes and Marquesses of Milan and Ferrara? It would need a faculty savouring as much of Jedediah Buxton as of Niebuhr, to say without book how many times Genoa became subject to Milan and how many times to France." This is pretty much the position of the student of Popular Religion in northern India.

But, in truth, all this pretence at elaboration is misplaced in dealing with such a vague entity as the popular faith. Even in the higher strata there is no more certainty. It is little use defining a man as a Vaishnava if we know that on occasion he will worship other gods as well—will reverence the cow or the pîpal tree, Mother Ganges or the goddess of smallpox. All that it is possible to do is to attempt to describe briefly what the villager on the one hand and the

[1] *Essays, Second Series*, p. 4.

more or less educated man of higher caste on the other believes.

To begin with the peasant. Of transmigration, that most elaborate theory which endeavours to account for the apparent inconsistence of Providence in allowing the righteous to be afflicted in this world while the sinner flourishes as a green bay tree, he does not know much. He may have perchance heard that if he does some impious act he may be reborn hereafter as a flea or a frog, while if he feeds Brâhmans and behaves as a respectable Hindu ought to do, he may become a Râja by and by. But this theory of the future hardly influences his life in this world. So too he has a vague idea that there is a Heaven, or rather several of them, a place of enjoyment somewhere beyond the burning Ghât, and a Hell where the wicked, in other words those who are not Hindus and in particular eaters of beef, are punished. But he knows that if he be a good Hindu, in his sense of the word, he will surely gain the one and avoid the other; and he has the comforting belief that practically all his race join the sainted dead in the other world: that minor lapses from morality, among which he counts the violation of most of the Ten Commandments, do not matter much. Parameswar would never dream of sending such a respectable person as himself to a place of torment.

So too he thinks that prayer and worship do not much affect a man's prospects in this way. They are of use to ward off the dangers from evil-minded gods, ghosts, demons and their kindred, who are always besetting him in this life and need constant propitiation and, in particular, the friendly influence of the higher gods to keep them from doing active mischief. Prayer and worship are useful too because they may bring him some temporal blessing at the expense of his neighbour.

Hence the service of the gods tends to turn into a sort of bargaining, in which the worshipper expects full value for his devotion. A benevolent deity may sometimes be overreached; but on the other hand the worshipper must do nothing which would give the god an excuse for evading his part of the contract. Above all, there must be an intercessor between the man and the god, a pious Brâhman priest who is held responsible that the poor human creature gets his rights.

Hence his moral horizon is decidedly limited. It is good to be charitable and feed a Brâhman ; it is right to be kindly to a clansman ; other people can take care of themselves. It is wrong to tell a lie unless to benefit yourself or to avoid punishment or to help a relation or friend ; to cheat another unless you gain a good deal by doing so, or because your friend would certainly cheat you if he got the chance ; to receive a bribe without giving the promised consideration for it. To take life is bad, particularly when the British Government is looking ; it is excusable if your enemy have taken your land or your wife, or kills a cow. A woman is a very inferior creature, and you may wrong her with impunity ; with a man you must be more careful. Nothing is worse than to lose your caste, to eat with a sweeper or to touch an impure person. Adultery is a comparatively venial matter unless the woman be of low caste, when it is really serious. If your enemy wrongs you the safest mode of revenge is to get up a false case against him and let the Sirkâr do the rest. The Penal Code is a useful summary of things which it is dangerous to do. On social matters and questions of pure morality the final tribunal is the caste council.

He has some sort of undefined belief in a single Providence whose benevolence is mainly shown in restricting malignant heavenly powers from doing mischief. This belief is perhaps most general among Brâhmans on the one hand and Chamârs on the other, who have come under the influence of a curiously powerful monotheistic propaganda. It is in the main the result of the preaching of teachers like Râê Dâs or Kabîr Dâs ; but there can be little doubt that this form of teaching has been largely stimulated by Christian influence.

The peasant knows little or nothing of the greater gods of the faith. He will, it is true, bow at their shrines, and he has their names sometimes on his lips. But he trusts more in the host of godlings who inhabit the pile of stones under the sacred tree which forms the village shrine. And besides this the village godling is a more complacent divinity. As Sir A. Lyall says, you can hardly ask an incarnation of Vishnu or Siva to help you to recover a lost Lota or to smite your neighbour's cow with the murrain ; but these are services which the godling will perform if he be suitably approached.

In the belief of the rustic nothing is the result of natural laws. He would live for ever were it not that some devil or witch plots against his life. It is they who send the cholera, the fever, the rheumatism. No miracle is beyond his belief; in fact, the controlling power normally works through miracle. In omens, in the power of the astrologer to ensure the success of his enterprises by fixing a lucky date for the first move, he has complete confidence. The "cunning man," as he calls him, can charm away a fever; he can counteract the enemy who casts the Evil Eye upon his children and oxen. Most cranky old women are more or less adepts in witchcraft. To avert these and similar troubles the village devil-priest is always prepared with a suitable remedy. Not that he professes himself infallible; this he must indeed admit not to be so from sad experience. But he is a poor man, he tells his patient; he does his best, and if a really powerful devil whose influence is beyond his powers takes the field, he is not to blame.

Above all the means of religious advancement the peasant values a periodical visit to some sacred shrine or bathing place. From the very soil of such a seat of the gods a divine influence exudes and sheds its blessings upon him. The purification of his body in the cleansing waters is represented by an allegory as the purification of his soul from sin, and by this he accumulates a store of religious merit which lasts till his next pilgrimage. It is also the only holiday of the village woman, the only release from the drudgery and self-repression in which her life is summed up. So they may be seen marching on for days, packed in a rumbling cart which crawls for a week at a time from stage to stage in the glare and dust, or hustled into a truck on the railway where the train creeps slowly to its destination. But this is no hardship to people whose sense of the value of time is only partially developed. At last when he sees the golden domes of Benares glittering on the horizon or when he plunges into the healing water his soul is filled with a belief no less steadfast, an enthusiasm quite as exalted as that which draws the European pilgrim to the shrine at Lourdes, or elevates his spirit as he catches the first glimpse of St Peter's across the wide Campagna.

And when the bath is over and the circuit of the holy places finished, there is the sight of the dawdling crowds of happy visitors, and the expenditure of a few pence in glass bangles or an earring, or the haggling over the purchase of a new Lota and a few yards of coarse calico give the women folk as complete satisfaction as a day's shopping does to the English lady.

Among the higher classes there are, as we have seen, only a few who believe in the form of worship derived from the Vedas or from Hinduism prior to its modern revival in the Purânas. The vast majority are divided in the threefold cultus of Siva, Vishnu, and the Sâktis. It would, however, be a mistake to suppose that there is a distinct line of cleavage between these beliefs; on the contrary they are complements of each other.

Saivism, as Sir Monier Williams has explained it, is a faith based on "the awe felt by human beings in the presence of the two mutually complementary forces of disintegration and reintegration; while the worship of the personal god Vishnu, in his descents upon earth in human form, is nothing but the expression of the very natural interest felt by man in his own preservation, and in the working of the physical forces which resist dissolution."

The Saivas, then, who by the returns comprise nearly one-fifth of the whole Hindu population, worship Siva, or, as he is often called, Mahâdeva, "the great god" under the form of the Linga, or conical stone, which in its primary form represents the regenerative power of Nature, but to the vast

A HARIVYÂSA VAISHNAVA FAKÎR.

mass of the people has no meaning except that of a fetish which is occupied by and represents the deity. His attributes have never been better described than in the powerful lines of Sir A. Lyall—

> "The god of the sensuous fire
> That moulds all Nature in forms divine,
> The symbols of death and of man's desire,
> The springs of change in the world are mine,
> The organs of birth and the circlet of bones,
> And the light loves carved on the temple stones.
>
> I am the lord of delights and pain,
> Of the pest that killeth, of fruitful joys:
> I rule the currents of heart and vein:
> A touch gives passion, a look destroys:
> In the heat and cold of my lightest breath,
> In the might incarnate of Lust and Death."

He has many forms—that of the primeval Creator, the chief of ascetics, who has won lordship over the gods by the rigour of his austerities, the king of life, the source of the vivifying influence of Nature. As embodying the functions of the Vedic Rudra, he is lord of death and the active agent in dissolution; as Siva, "the auspicious," he constructs after destruction. He is the chief Brâhman deity, and paramount in places like Benares, where the Hindu Levite class are most influential.

There is another consideration which commends his worship to the economical peasant. His cultus demands none of the sensuous splendour of ritual which that of Vishnu requires. There is none of the elaborate adornment, dressing, and feeding of the image which are practised in the shrines dedicated to Vishnu in his forms of Krishna or Râma. A few flowers, a little water poured over his fetish, are all that he needs.

On the contrary, the Vaishnava cultus, partly from the opportunities which it offers for magnificent display, partly from the absence of blood-offerings, which commends it to a class deeply influenced by the Buddhistic reverence for the sanctity of life, is more popular among the rich merchants of the towns. Here the form which the worship usually takes is that of the adoration of the godhead in one of his many Avatâras or incarnations—as Râma, the hero of the Ramâyana, with his spouse, Sîta, the type of wifely virtue; as Narasinha, the man lion who delivered the world from a demon Hiranya-kasipu, the persecutor of his pious son Prahlâda, because he faithfully worshipped Vishnu; as Parasurâma, "Râma with the axe," who freed the Brâhmans from the arrogant rule of the Kshatriyas; as Krishna, who was possibly the tribal deity of the confederation of Râjput septs in the neighbourhood of Mathura, the chief seat of his worship. Krishna is the Hindu form of that veneration of youth and manly beauty which is so common in the history of the world's religions. He and his consort Râdha, with the Gopis or cowherd maids, with whom the deity sported in the green woods of the land of Braj, represent Hinduism in its most sensuous form.

The recorded worshippers of Vishnu number about three and three-quarter millions, among whom the believers in Râma, Krishna, and the deified monkey Hanumân are most numerous.

In quite a different plane is the Sâkta worship of Devi-Durga, the consort of Siva. This worship is based on that form of the Purânas known as the Tantras, by which every kind of supernatural faculty and mystic craft is associated with her. She delights in blood sacrifice, and her shrines, which, unlike those of Siva or Vishnu, are not found in the main centres of Hinduism or at its most holy places, but are hidden away in remote jungles, or associated with the mountain worship special to her, reek with the blood of victims. Such are those in honour of the Vindhya-vâsini Devi, the patron goddess of the Vindhyan range at Bindhâchal, near Mirzapur, and Devi Pâtan in the Gonda forests. Most of her priests are not Brâhmans, but drawn from the lower castes, and it is in this branch of the faith that Hinduism seems to be most largely indebted to the indigenous idolatries.

But this form of worship has even a darker side than this. It is associated with horrid traditions of human sacrifice, which even now is occasionally reported to occur in the wilder and more secluded corners of the land, and with the foul abominations of what is known as the Bâmmârgi or left-hand worship of the goddess. This is the most loathsome side of the popular belief, and so far from showing signs of disappearance under the influence of enlightenment, it is to Bengâli influence that much of its popularity in northern India must be attributed. And here the weighty words of M. Constant, in his work on Roman Polytheism, represent the exact state of the case:[1] "Des rites indécens peuvent être pratiqués par un peuple religieux avec une grande pureté de cœur. Mais quand l'incrédulité atteint ces peuples, ces rites sont pour lui la cause et la prétexte de la plus révoltante corruption."

We can thus in a manner trace the evolution of the popular faith through all its successive stages. We begin with the sacred grove of the Drâvidians, the trees of which are reserved as an abode for the wood spirits dispossessed as the jungle is cut down. Next comes the cult of the sacred tree—the banyan, the pîpal, and other varieties of the fig tribe. This tree shrine is next supplemented by a pile of stones laid at the base of the tree, which become the abode of the vague collection of the village guardian deities. In a further stage this is replaced by a mud platform, on which the deity sometimes sits and receives the offerings of his worshippers. Here the platform replaces the stone pile, but the thatch is erected under or close to the sacred tree. A higher stage is marked by the village shrine of the Plains—a small masonry building with a platform. When a Lingam is placed on this platform, it becomes a shrine of Mahâdeva or Siva, or another rude stone represents Devi. The final point is attained when the stone is carved into an image, dressed in elaborate robes, and laid to rest according to a sensuous ritual, as in the cult of Krishna or Râma.

This prepares us to understand how all religion in India, so far from being in a condition of stable permanence, is ever undergoing some new form of development. This process

[1] Quoted by Buckle, *History of Civilisation*, ii. 303, note.

follows much the same course in the east as in the west. In Europe the revival of letters and the study of ancient systems of philosophy stimulated enquiry into the validity of theological conclusions, which had been hitherto accepted without question. So, in India, the upheaval of society, resulting from Musalmân invasions and contact with foreign races, brought home to the higher minds of Hinduism that the foundations of their faith were laid on too narrow a basis; and that its only chance of permanence lay in widening its limits, in giving a hope of salvation to the outcasts hitherto beyond its limits, in checking the predominance of sacerdotalism and purifying its ritual.

This was specially shown in the growth of sects, which opened their doors to men of all castes, except the most defiled. Of these we have prominent examples in the Bishnois and Kabîrpanthis. Kabîr was a weaver by caste, and, as Mr Maclagan notes, the connection between weaving and religion in northern India is as interesting as that of cobbling and irreligion in England. With Vaishnavism the reform took a course analogous to the spread of evangelical theology in the West, which recognises as its main tenet the theory of salvation by faith. But in India this belief had a tendency to develop on sensuous lines. This is most clearly shown in the case of the modern Vallabhachâryas, who preach spiritual union with the lord Krishna, with the implication that life and body, soul and substance, wife and children must be dedicated to his service. Thus, the leaders of this sect have become the Epicureans of the Eastern world, and claim the most absolute control over their female votaries, with the natural result that serious scandals have occurred.

It may be true that in the official creeds of many of these sectaries there is nothing objectionable; that, on the contrary, they encourage charity and purity, kindliness and simplicity of life; but the basis of the belief is sensuous, and in the hands of disciples, imperfectly acquainted with the inner mysteries of the cult, it tends to develop in the sensuous direction.

While, then, in the Plains, the primitive animistic beliefs

have, among the upper classes, partially given way to this neo-Brâhmanism; among the lower classes, and especially the jungle tribes, the old religion still flourishes. While these people have assumed the title of Hindus, many of them accept the mediation of Brâhmans, some have reached the stage when cow-killing is regarded as a sin, they still retain much of their primitive beliefs. But a rapid proselytism of these forest races is now in progress, and in a generation or two there will remain little to distinguish them from the menial village population of the more highly-cultivated tracts. We can see before our own eyes the method in which this conversion is being effected. There is nothing startling or sudden about it, no persecution of the old faith, no immediate displacement of it by the new form of belief. The revolution is more in the social than in the religious direction. The hillman, as he rises in the world, is told by the Brâhman or ascetic, who occasionally visits his hamlet, that it is not consistent with his respectability that he should rely solely on the Baiga or devil-priest when he is in trouble; he ought rather, if he values his position, to appoint a decent orthodox chaplain, who will give him no trouble, will not be unpleasantly inquisitive about his domestic worship, and will be quite satisfied if he be allowed to start the cultus of the higher gods side by side with those of lower rank.

It is an essential part of this theory that if you keep a domestic chaplain, you need not take any further trouble; it is quite sufficient to ensure the prosperity of your household and to satisfy the demands of public opinion if you have the prayers said for you and the offerings made by a qualified officiant. So, the old village shrine, with its mossy stones, which shelter Mother Earth or the Snake gods or some deified ancestor of the hamlet, is not disestablished. Here the Baiga, as he always did, continues to offer a goat or fowl when cholera or drought menace the prosperity of the community; here the women bring their simple offerings after a baby is born or when small-pox prevails. The householder sits contented at home, conscious that his Brâhman priest will see that the great gods are restrained from active mischief. But it is to the old gods that he flies when any really serious trouble impends over him.

By and by the village shrine loses its popularity, except to the women folk and the menial classes of the community, about whose religious welfare the Brâhman priest displays no concern; and even the Baiga himself blossoms out into an orthodox mystery man and becomes the Hindu Ojha or wizard; but he clings to the old paths, and takes with him his familiar methods of repelling evil spirits and restraining dangerous ghosts.

A remarkable instance of the receptivity of the popular faith is shown in the worship by Hindus of Muhammadan Saints and Martyrs, a form of religion which has, of course, sprung up in quite historical times. It also shows the curious feeling of resignation in the native mind. These men were heroes of the early Musalmân inroads; they slaughtered Brâhmans and desecrated shrines; but that this was permitted by the gods shows that these persecutors of the faith were semi-divine. The leader of the quintette of these Saints is Ghâzi Miyân, who, if he be really historical, lived in the early part of the eleventh century. If we could realise Englishmen now-a-days worshipping Taillefer, the minstrel, and Odo of Bayeux, with Woden, Thor, and King Arthur thrown in, we may partially understand the matter. Only here there was no such fusion between the races as made Normans and English one nation in a century or so. The worship of these and other deified Muhammadan Saints constitutes the faith of nearly two and a half millions of Hindus.

These are followed by a very miscellaneous crowd. We have, to begin with, a small congregation, who worship various caste, tribal or ancestral godlings, one of the chief of whom is Nathu Kahâr, the patron of the litter-bearers, who is revered because he is said to have been sacrificed by some tyrant of the olden days under the foundations of a fort which he was building. Next comes a collection of deified ghosts, demons, forest or village godlings, and deities of sacred rivers and holy places. These worshippers of godlings of disease

FAKÎRS' HERMITAGE. HARDWÂR.

of hill and forest, Saints, ghosts and demons, amount to no less than seven millions, or nearly one-sixth of the whole population.

But the mode which was employed to elicit the details of religious belief at the last census, the only possible method, tends to lower the numbers of the votaries of animistic beliefs in their varied forms. There is a natural tendency, when a man is asked what god he worships, to name some respectable deity of the recognised pantheon, in preference to some hedge godling whose worship stamps the believer as a person of mean social position. Hence, if we find nearly a sixth of the people admitting that they practise this form of belief, we may be quite certain that those who follow it are more numerous. This at once disposes of the too commonly received fallacy, that the great mass of the population worships the orthodox gods, and, as a matter of fact, these old gods of the Nature type have passed almost completely out of the minds of the people.

Brahma, for instance, owns only 21,000 believers. Indra, who once ruled the sky and gave the kindly rains, is now-a-days only a petty *roi fainéant*, who has a heaven of his own, where he spends his time listening to the songs and watching the dances of the fairies who form his court. Varuna, the great god of the firmament, is only a minor local godling, who is invoked in seasons of drought. The worship of Vishnu, Siva, the female energies, and Animism in their myriad forms, now make up the faith of the vast bulk of the people.

Before leaving modern Hinduism, a few words may be said about the mendicant or ascetic classes, commonly grouped together under the Musalmân name Fakîr, or beggar, who number nearly 2,000,000, or about one-twentieth of the population. This body comprises a most heterogeneous mass of people. There are, first, the religious orders pure and simple, many of whom are of the highest respectability, live the lives of celibates in monasteries, and though few of them are learned Sanskrit scholars, many have devoted their lives to the study of theology. Out of this class is drawn the Guru, or religious guide, whose functions must be carefully distinguished from those of the Purohit, or family priest. While the latter is always a Brâhman, and presides over the domestic ceremonies of his clients, he seldom supplies that religious guidance which is the task of the Guru. By the Guru the Hindu, if inclined to a pious life, is initiated into one or other of the great religious systems—as a Vaishnava, Saiva, or Sâkta. To his Guru he resorts for advice and sympathy in the graver crises of life. The influence of these Gurus is almost wholly for good; it is exerted in the cause of temperance and morality; it is the one tendency working in the direction of holiness which raises the Hindu above the dead level of indifferentism or degradation of thought and action which the low standard of polytheism permits, if it does not encourage.

On the other hand, asceticism always has a tendency to degrade the saint into the mountebank, and many of these wandering ascetics are little more than lusty beggars who traverse the country, extorting alms from the peasantry and trading on their ignorant credulity, acting as exorcisors or charmers of disease, often leading about a deformed cow in whose name they demand charity. The morality of many of them is of the lowest type, and some hardly make a pretence of exercising any religious function whatever. Some act as priests in village shrines, and those who form a recognised part of the village communal body are much more respected than their dissolute, rapacious, nomadic brethren. Our knowledge of the beliefs of the ascetic orders is as yet far from complete. According to the statistics, only about one in fifty out of 2,000,000 follows the Saiva cultus; the great mass of them are Vaishnavas.

Among the greater classes there is an immense number of minor sub-divisions, distinguished either by some minute differences of ritual, or by their special veneration for the god in one of his myriad forms. Among the Saivas, the distinction seems to lie more in matters of outward observance than of belief. They are no more distinct sects than the Franciscans or Dominican friars are in the Christian

A RÂMANDI FAKÎR

world. Among the Vaishnava sects the predominant belief, at least among the modern reformers, is salvation by faith and the recognition of a single benevolent Providence. Here the line of cleavage is found rather in the special worship of one form of the godhead—as Krishna, Râmachandra, and so on, or of the female manifestation as Râdha or Sîta. Many sects again follow the guidance of the teachers from whom they take their name; and the democratic influence is shown by the fact that some of these leaders were drawn from the inferior castes—Kabîr, the teacher of the Kabîrpanthis, was a weaver; Sena was a barber; Nâmdeo, a cotton-printer; Nabhaji, a Dom.

The reformation in Hindu belief, which was accomplished under the guidance of these teachers, took place when the Hindu world first came under foreign influence—the result of the movement of the Musalmâns into the Peninsula. It may fairly be compared with the great religious reformation which took place almost simultaneously in the Western world. But the analogy is far from complete. The Indian religious reformers were in no sense militant theologians like Luther; they were neither enthusiasts nor fanatics, but, as a rule, quiet devotees, with no mission to overturn existing religious institutions, no desire to free the Church from superstitious accretions and re-establish the purer faith of an earlier age. They studiously avoided all idea of resisting the established political government; their followers were merely pupils, and not bound together by any rigid organisation. When the Saint died he seldom left a successor to carry on his work.

Of these sects, that which includes the largest number of followers is the Râmanandi, which takes its name from the teacher Râmanand. They venerate Râma and his consort Sîta, reject the bondage of ceremonial observances and caste so far that many of the heads of the minor sections are drawn from the class of menials. Their leader Râmanand flourished at the end of the fourteenth or beginning of the fifteenth century, and their gospel is the vernacular translation of the epic of the Râmâyana by the poet Tulasi Dâs. This is really the Bible of the Hindus of northern India, and to its poetical beauty and freedom from licentiousness they owe their moral superiority over the more sensuous devotees of Râdha and Krishna, not to speak of the Sâkta worship of Devi.

Next in numerical influence are the Nânakshâhis, the Sikh order founded by Nânak, who was born in the latter half of the fifteenth century, a few years before Martin Luther. By that time the Panjâb, the birthplace of the teacher, had come completely under the Musalmân government, and the influence of Islâm over the teaching of Nânak was momentous. His aim was to free the Váishnavism of northern India from the incubus of caste superstition and idolatry. But a reform which had as its object the reconciliation of Hinduism with Islâm resulted in exciting the most bitter animosity between the two religions. By the time of the fourth Guru, Râm Dâs, the movement assumed so much political importance and was considered so dangerous to the ruling power that Aurangzeb was roused to attempt to extirpate it by persecution, and thus created that undying animosity of the Sikhs towards Muhammadanism which was one of the main causes of the downfall of the Empire.

The last of the more important Vaishnava sects is that of the Râêdâsis, who take their name from their teacher Râê Dâs, who was a tanner. This sect has a large number of adherents among the Chamârs or curriers of Upper India. It is an interesting example of the reformed Vaishnavism, extending to the despised menial races. They follow the theistic form of belief venerating one omnipotent all-seeing god to whom alone worship is due.

It is then of little practical use to speculate on the increase or decrease of Hinduism because it is made up of such diverse elements. The creed, for instance, of the reformed Vaishnava sects, which inculcate the belief in a single Providence, a respect for animal life, and an utter abhorrence of blood sacrifice, has little or nothing in common with the Sâkta worship of Devi or the coarse animistic beliefs of the hillman or village menial. All these people style themselves Hindus but, except the fairly general reverence for the cow, there is no link of connection. Hinduism may on paper, by the inclusion of the animistic beliefs, show an overwhelming superiority: but it is in no sense a creed like those of Europe, which have a permanent constitution. It possesses no functionary like a Pope who can prescribe a rule of faith and thunder forth his anathemas over the Christian world. It has no Bishops, no centre of union like Rome or Canterbury. It holds no Convocation and has never dreamed of convening a General Council. Nor is it at all likely that any powerful teacher will ever arise to reconcile differences of faith and ritual, to sweep away abuses and superstition and form a Church with a well-defined creed and social or political aims. On the contrary, the tendency seems to be rather towards the multiplication of minor sects distinguished each from the other by some quite trivial distinction which the uninitiated outsider finds it very difficult to understand.

Looked at from the outside, it presents the character of a mass of discordant sects: not animated by any desire for propagandism or missionary effort within its own body; quite satisfied to permit each form of belief to develop on its own lines, and absolutely free from any tendency of fanaticism towards nonconformists. It is true that it actively converts the heathen, bringing them within the pale of Brâhmanism by inducing them to accept the ministrations of a Levite. But here the effort stops and the convert is free to follow his ancestral beliefs without any interference from his new priest. Nor is this missionary effort regularly organised in any sense of the word. There is no Missionary Society which collects contributions from the orthodox and supports a staff of teachers. This work it leaves to the solitary wandering ascetic who wins converts to the faith not so much by any actual preaching as by enforcing the social advantages which result from acceptance of his message.

But though Hinduism shows no particular missionary energy it has great powers of self-defence. It is most tenacious of its rights and privileges; it insists on a policy of non-interference on the part of the State; it is prompt to resist any assault from without. An institution which has weathered such storms as the rise of Buddhism and the early Musalmân raids must be treated with respect. And this power of resistance has been greatly aided by the changed condition of things since the British occupation. We have preached, and what is more practised, toleration, and we have ever protected its priests and temples from outrage. The rise of this feeling of safety and the spread of education has made Hinduism not a faith shrinking in a corner and happy if it can escape violence, but a body of worshippers which knows its rights and is determined to assert them. But like a fussy old lady, it thinks that it must always be doing something to make its presence felt and to show everybody that it can hold its own in the face of this new learning and this ridiculous new civilisation: as if indeed the old faith in which their fathers lived and flourished was not good enough for them. So any interference with a petty shrine will set a whole city like Benares or Mathura in a blaze, when all sects and creeds are swept along in a fervour of fanaticism which shrinks from no sacrifice, not even of life itself, and turns for the moment the calm reflective pietist into a desperate bigot. But it is only for a time that this semblance of union prevails. It needs the war cry of religious enthusiasm to rouse it to action. As to combining for any general object—to build a common temple, to relieve the sick and needy, to train the orphan—such union is never dreamed of.

In direct contrast to this is the militant faith of Islâm, which for nine centuries has been more or less in contact and in conflict with Hinduism. At the present time it counts nearly six and a half millions of believers, or rather less than 14 per cent. of the whole population—a little less than that of Egypt, a little more than that of Belgium.

The history of Islâm in India has yet to be written, and when it is written it will be one of the most interesting chapters in the religious annals of the world. It appeared, as we have seen, the faith of a body of savage marauders and conquerors, who swept over the land at intervals in the course of a couple of centuries in a series of cruel raids, bringing rapine and destruction in their train. What we know of the history of the time between the first Musalmân invasion and the final establishment of a fairly settled foreign government in the country is mainly derived from Muhammadan sources. It is a strange sign of the lack of solidarity and patriotic feeling among Hindus, that they never seem to have troubled themselves to place on record their view of one of the most terrible disasters which ever overtook a people and their national faith. There is enough to show that the conquest was not completed without desperate conflict, and that in parts of the country, as for instance in Rohilkhand, the resistance was little short of heroic.

Next followed the earlier Mughal rule, in which the wise, conciliatory policy of Akbar was in general maintained by his successors for about a century, till the accession of Aurangzeb initiated the regime of iconoclasm and persecution of the Hindus. During this period, and particularly in the western part of the Province, the influence of the ruling power and of the Imperial Court at Delhi and Agra was exercised in favour of the State religion and largely promoted conversion: while the same effect resulted from the powerful outposts or colonies established in Oudh and along the Gangetic valley. It is true that the earlier Mughals raised many Hindus to posts of trust and emolument: but at the same time all the witchery of social impulses must have been exerted in opposition to the indigenous religion. It was at a later date that these influences were aided by the sword of persecution. The main force in favour of Hinduism must have been the Imperial Zanâna, which was filled with Hindu ladies and, as we have shown, the successors of Akbar were largely of Hindu blood. And yet the love of Kaula Devi, the wife of Alâ-ud-dîn Khilji, was unable to restrain the cruel tyranny of her husband.

In modern times the tendency to a rapid increase of Musalmâns as compared with Hindus has continued: in the period between the two last decennial enumerations the rate of increase in the former has been 7·15 per cent.: in the latter 6·17.

The causes of this are various. In the first place, Islâm in India has to a large extent shed off those militant, Puritan principles which now survive only among the sect known as the Wahhâbi, or Ahl-i-hadîs, who are purists and reject as idolatrous accretions on the original faith the worship of Saints and their tombs, call ordinary Musalmâns Mushrik, or those who associate another with God, and condemn the smoking of tobacco and the use of rosaries. Islâm has thus become much more tolerant of Hindu beliefs than it was under wild raiders like Shihâb-ud-dîn or the iconoclastic Aurangzeb. This was due no doubt in part to its downfall as an Imperial power, but partly to its lack of organisation. Like Hinduism, Islâm in India has never established a Church or a Synod; it has no well-defined religious centre, and the small isolated colonies which it founded gradually fell under the influence of their environment in the midst of a numerically superior infidel population. As a missionary religion working amid the lower indigenous races, it was in active competition with the reformed Vaishnavism which adopted the most conciliatory methods, and spared no pains to make the burden of belief fall lightly on its converts.

Yet Islâm in India has undoubtedly its strong points. Its creed is definite and well-ascertained; it encourages a lively faith in and resignation to one great controlling Power, which though not by any means a Fatherly Providence, is in direct contrast to the jungle of deities in whom a Hindu believes. In the words "God is great" it shows itself in its highest form—the absolute submission to one Heavenly Master. No cloud of scepticism even temporarily overshadows its placid surface: and yet in tolerating the reverence for Martyrs and Saints, in recognising that a divine breath rises from their graves and relics it provides for the aspirations of votaries raised in an animistic atmosphere.

The current explanation of Musalmân progress is that it is mainly due to the attraction which the freedom from the bondage of caste offers to converts; to the acceptance by Hindu widows of the role of the Musalmân dancing-girl; to the adoption of Hindu orphans into high-class Muhammadan families. To these may be added the democratic character of Musalmân society which makes the householder the priest, and discourages the dominance of the official Levite. In some places, as in western Bengal, much of its progress is due to the active preaching of the ubiquitous Pîr and Mulla. But, as has been shown by Mr O'Donnell in Bengal, the growth of Islâm is due perhaps more to physical than doctrinal forces. The Musalmân, an eater of meat, is naturally of more vigorous constitution than the vegetarian Hindu; his acceptance of widow marriage makes the race more fertile; he and his wife more usually marry at a mature age, and there are fewer senile husbands and child wives. Polygamy is more common, and he more often takes a widow as his second wife, who acts as a convenient, unpaid household drudge and bears children to her master. At present in northern India there seems to be little active proselytism; had this been common the tension between the creeds in recent years on the subject of cow-killing would certainly have brought it to notice. The statistical facts collected at the last census bear out these conclusions. In 10,000 of the population, Musalmâns have 1726 women of the child-bearing age as compared with 1708 Hindus; Musalmâns have 2708 children under ten years of age to 2677 Hindus; there are among 10,000 Musalmâns, 1294 persons over fifty as compared with 1207 Hindus. These differences, though not large, all act in the direction of promoting greater fertility among the followers of the Prophet.

While the distribution of Hindus through the Province is fairly uniform, the proportions of Musalmâns vary largely. This might have been anticipated from the conditions under which their settlements were established, and from the circumstances of their environment. In the northern hill tract Hinduism is preponderant, and as much as 99 per cent. of the people follow that faith. The next most important seats of Hinduism are backward Bundelkhand, and the central and eastern districts, which contain the most sacred shrines—Mathura, Prayâg, Bindhâchal, and Benares. On the other hand, Musalmâns are in excess in the Upper Duâb, where the vicinity of Delhi promoted conversion, and in Rohilkhand and northern Oudh, where their settlements were largely founded in newly cleared country occupied by less stubborn septs of Râjputs than those along the lower Ganges valley.

It is only in the larger towns, like Agra, Aligarh, Bareilly, or Lucknow that Musalmâns of the older type are largely found. For more than half a century after the British occupation, the Muhammadans lagged behind in the educational race. They were less pliant in accepting the new order of things—they preferred to busy themselves among the dry bones of theology and antiquated science to the exclusion of western learning. The result was that, in the competition for public employment, they were for a time outpaced by the more subtle and adaptative Hindu. In recent years this reproach has been to some degree removed by the efforts of some energetic teachers, notably by Sir Sayyid Ahmad Khân, who, in the Anglo-Muhammadan College at Aligarh, has won a considerable measure of success in introducing education of the English University type among his co-religionists. The result of these measures is now shown by the fact that Musalmâns are rather better educated than Hindus. Among 10,000 males, 8049 are illiterate against 8103 Hindus; 13 know English as compared with 8. The figures show the vast room which remains for improvement; but the increase of education among Musalmâns is notable and satisfactory.

In the higher grades of the public service Musalmâns enjoy a well-marked superiority. Their nutritious and varied diet makes them more vigorous and active than the Hindu, and their traditions of Empire promote the power of ruling men. Among deputy collectors or native magistrates the last returns show 94 Musalmâns to 116 Hindus; 8 out of 22 of the chief civil judges are Musalmâns—in both cases their numbers much exceed their numerical proportions.

The record of Musalmân sects cannot fail to be inaccurate. The low caste convert lives under an easy religious rule. He so far follows the rule of his faith as to circumcise his sons, and to abstain from the use of pork; but he retains his old fetishes and animistic beliefs. Even if he occasionally attends a mosque, he still clings to the worship of Devi or some village godling. His marriage ceremonies are performed not by the Kâzi, the orthodox officiant, but by some Dafâli hedge priest, and he takes his omens from a Brâhman astrologer. If he be a Râjput he keeps his Hindu name, simply replacing his title Sinh by Khân; he shaves his beard, which the real Musalmân preserves; he keeps the Hindu top-knot, and bathes and cooks in the old fashion. The lower caste convert calls himself Shaikh, though he has no more kinship with the nomad of the Arabian desert than the *nouveau riche* of our time has with the followers of the Conqueror, in spite of the pedigree which an accomdating herald provides for him.

The two important sects of Islâm are the Sunni and the Shiah. The former are in great numerical preponderance—about thirty Sunni to one Shiah, the latter found as an important body only in Lucknow, where they flourished under the protection of the Court of Oudh. The difference between the two sects is vital, as great as that which divides the Eastern from the Western Church. The Sunni, or traditionalist, differs from the Shiah as to what tradition is to be accepted. The latter lay stress on the knowledge of the true Imâm, a point which the Sunni considers unimportant, and follow Ali, the husband of Fâtima, the daughter of the Prophet. Hence they reject as impostors the first three Sunni Imâms—Abû Bakr, Umar, and Usmân, and detest the memory of the Ummeyid Khalîfas who usurped the lordship of the faith, and in particular that of Yazîd, who slew the martyrs Hasan and Husain.

In memory of these holy men they observe the feast of the Muharram as a season of mourning and humiliation, and carry in procession Tâzias, or paper and tinsel representations of their tombs, a ritual which orthodox Sunnis abhor, though village Muhammadans, almost without distinction of sect, join in its observance. One of the most impressive religious spectacles in India is to watch the long procession of Tâzias and flags which streams along the streets, with a vast crowd of mourners, who scream out their lamentations and beat their breasts till the blood flows, or they sink fainting in an ecstasy of sorrow. One of the most difficult duties of the Indian Magistrate is to regulate these processions and decide the precedence of its members. The air rings with the cries of these ardent fanatics, and their zeal often urges them to violence directed against Hindus or rival sectaries. But the English Gallio is no judge of such matters, and his anxieties do not end until he has steered without conflict or disturbance the howling crowd of devotees through the stifling city lanes into the open fields beyond, where the mimic sepulchres of the martyrs are supposed to be flung into a tank or buried. But the more canny worshipper, when his short-lived frenzy is spent, brings his Tâzia quietly home to grace next year's celebration.

Such are the prominent features of religious life in northern India, and no land on the surface of the earth presents a more interesting field of observation or more startling diversities of belief. In a single morning the student of the popular faiths may watch them in nearly all their chief stages. He can observe it, first, in the Animistic or fetish phase—the worshipper bowing before the stone which enshrines the deity; the respect for the sacred bathing places; the women bowing reverently to the pîpal tree; the holy cow which nibbles unrestrained at the corn-seller's stall; the monkeys gambolling over the temple carvings. He will see the Sannyâsi dreaming away life under the thraldom of intoxicants; the Brâhman poring over the Shâstras; the Mulla counting his beads, as he drones out a passage of the Korân; the white-robed worshippers kneeling reverently in the courtyard of the mosque, as they face in the direction of Mecca; the pious Hindu saluting the Sun as he starts for his day's labour; the Christian missionary preaching the Gospel to a listless crowd of spectators.

Everywhere he will observe a fervour of belief, an intensity of conviction in the power of the Unseen God to rule the destinies of humanity, which is in startling contrast to the calm indifferentism of the religious world of the West. The prevailing note is that of extreme formalism, a confidence in the minutiæ of ritual, in the intercessory influence of the priesthood. And with all this there is an intense belief in the malevolent power of the demon, the ghost, and the witch, which can only be checked by the incantations of the sorcerer and of the exorcisor.

We now pass on to a brief sketch of the social condition of the people.

To begin with the Zamîndâr or better-class yeoman: the house of such a man in the western districts is generally an oblong structure, the walls formed either of small bricks laid in mud, or of masses of indurated clay, which are piled in layers one above the other and allowed to harden in the sun. The roof of the living and store room is supported by cross-beams, over which is placed a covering of brushwood, and this is surmounted by a thick layer of tenacious clay laid in a moist state, pounded down and consolidated by ramming. Such a roof, if properly constructed, affords a good protection from the heat of the sun, and though it often cracks from heat and leaks in the autumn rains, answers fairly well for people who spend most of their time in the open air. Access to the interior is usually through a sort of portico, which is often used as a cart-house or cattle-shed. Inside is a court-yard in which the family live, and in which produce or agricultural implements are stored. If the owner be a Musalmân or high-caste Hindu, there is often an inner courtyard, which is reserved for the women. In the outer part the males of the family live, guests are entertained, and the unmarried youths sleep.

You will find the owner resting, smoking on a wooden platform, where he sees visitors, carries on his business, and dispenses a rude hospitality; and the unexpected visitor will catch, perhaps, on his arrival, a glimpse of a bright-coloured petticoat or mantle, and hear the tinkle of a bangle, or the giggling of the girls, which announce the presence of the women-folk close at hand. Here the pretty naked babies wander about, and are petted by their male relations. In a lower class household the women will be found hard at work in the courtyard, grinding barley, husking rice, cooking, spinning, and chattering all the time to each other.

Further to the east, where there is less danger of damage from hail, the roof of the principal rooms is usually made of tiles, which admit a much freer passage of air, and render the dwelling rooms much less stuffy than in the western districts. To these the chief danger is from the ubiquitous, mischievous monkeys, who scamper in every direction; and though they are an emphatic nuisance, are protected by a most efficient sanction. It is only by spreading a layer of thorns over the tiles or thatch that they can be prevented from bounding over the roof and groping for the grain which has been dropped by the ever-present, vigilant, restless crow.

The prevailing atmosphere, especially in one of the western houses, is one of stuffy frowsiness. Here masses of foul bedding are stored, the air is full of acrid smoke from the fire of cow-dung fuel, the cattle are stabled close at hand, litter is scarce, dry earth conservancy unknown; the result is that the subsoil becomes saturated with filth, and the contempt for sanitary precautions shows itself in a foul drain for the removal of the kitchen refuse, often in dangerous proximity to the well from which the water supply of the family is drawn. The native has a rooted objection to the destruction of rubbish; this and the refuse of his house are stored all round his dwelling-rooms; it is only the house ashes and sweepings which are periodically carried off to the midden, and thence conveyed to the fields. It is only because the habit of living *al fresco* is so common, and the weaker subjects are swept off by epidemic disease at an early age, that these conditions do not more prejudicially affect the general health of the people.

The house of the smaller cultivator or artisan is of a simpler type. Here the walls are of clay and the roof of thatch, which leaks freely in the rains, and when the fierce summer hot wind blows, a fire once started in such a village spreads with dangerous rapidity and often leads to loss of life as the inmates struggle to save their meagre property. Or in the rains the water beats against the fragile walls and the whole structure collapses, often crushing the weak or infirm in the ruin. The wooden seat of the better class yeoman is here usually replaced by a mud platform beside the outer door, on which the master sits in his leisure hour and receives his visitors.

It is only in houses of the better class that there is a courtyard; the ordinary dwelling is a single sleeping hut, and outside the hut the housewife does her cooking, perhaps under a smaller thatch, near which the oxen stand, and the cow, buffalo, or goat is tethered and milked.

Towards the hilly tract as in parts of Agra, the hut has its walls often built of stones piled one over the other without mortar. In Mirzapur and Bundelkhand again, where the soil has too little tenacity to admit of the erection of mud walls, the sides of the dwellings are built of wattle and dab, in the shape of hurdles made of bamboos and brushwood smeared with clay or cow-dung, and instead of being crowded within a narrow site, they are scattered about, each in the corner of the owner's field, and the roofs covered with a thick growth of melons or pumpkins, each a little bower of greenery, present from a distance a pretty enough picture. The dispersion of the huts constituting the village has the additional advantage of promoting cleanliness, reducing the danger of fire, and distributing the labour and manure over a larger area.

On the whole, the dwelling of the poorer tenant or artisan is cleaner and less exposed to insanitary conditions than that of his richer neighbour. The floor and outer cooking-place are carefully plastered; the cattle are less disagreeably prominent, and the unsubstantial materials of which the hut consists allow better ventilation.

In the Plains the best dwelling in the village is that of the Mahâjan or money-lender. It is usually built of brick, periodically whitewashed, with an outer verandah in which the owner sits over his books, meets his clients, and doles out loans to cover the expenses of a marriage or to satisfy the landlord on rent day. Behind this he has a series of storerooms in which he collects grain or other produce, or hides away the jewelry or brass pots which he receives in pawn. Here is a box for his bonds and stamped papers, which he is careful to keep, of various dates in case he has occasion to fabricate a mortgage document. Much of his time is spent in drawing up two sets of accounts, one for his private information, the other for the inspection of the Collector at the next revision of the Income Tax assessment.

The prevailing tone of all the domestic arrangements is squalid in the extreme. The small peasant's furniture consists of a few foul rickety cots, some brass cooking utensils, a store of red earthen pottery, a stool or two for the children, a box for clothes or other petty valuables, a mud granary in which the grain supply of the household is stored. In the house of the yeoman or small proprietor the only obvious difference is that brass pots are in greater abundance and the women folk own more heavy silver jewelry, in which, in default of banks of deposit, the surplus income is invested. If the owner has a few spare rupees he piles them in an earthen cup and hides them in a hole of the mud wall or under the place where he does his cooking. The village banker does the same as far as he can, for he is in constant dread of thieves who cut away his mud walls with a chisel during the moonless nights and clear off all his moveables.

In the house itself the carpentry and masonry are of the very rudest kind. The use of the arch is uncommon, and the lintels consist of weak, unseasoned wood which collapse under the weight of the superstructure and in a short time bring the whole building to ruin. Glass windows, except in the towns, are practically unknown; there is nothing in the shape of artistic furniture or articles of elegance and beauty such as the Japanese provide with such unerring taste. It is only in the larger towns, and particularly those like Agra, Mathura, or Mirzapur, which are close to good quarries, that the fine stone-carved decorated arches, balconies, or porticoes are to be seen. In the village house there is no such thing as art decoration or painting, except perhaps a rude lithograph of one of the gods hung in the room in which worship is done, or a coarse caricature of the guardian deity, or of a European soldier with musket and cocked hat which scares evil spirits from the household.

Another striking point is the utter absence of inventiveness as applied to domestic or industrial life. The plough and other agricultural implements are of the traditional form which have been used for a thousand or ten thousand years. Labour-saving tools and appliances are useless to a people where labour is a drug. The shape of the spinning-wheel, the flour mill, the curry pounder, the loom, the tools of the blacksmith or carpenter never changes. It is only when the craftsman is trained under European influence that he adopts the improved methods.

So, there is no periodical change of fashion in dress. The woman's skirt, mantle or bodice never vary in form, and the lady of the West, with her inventiveness in the way of millinery, is quite beyond the ken of the Oriental woman. All that contact with western civilisation has given them is a greater variety of material, a wider and brighter range of colour. The men wear the turban, loin cloth, and jacket of coarse cotton cloth, which we know from the monuments has been unchanged for nearly twenty centuries. So, in the poorer household the variety of food is very limited, and the people never seem to crave a change of dishes or seasoning. A little pepper and turmeric, a few common spices, exhaust the list of relishes. In a wealthier family the range of delicacies, in the form of curries and sweetmeats, is much greater. In the nutritiousness and variety of his food the Musalmân has a great advantage over the Hindu, particularly on a journey, when the latter must confine himself to parched grain, greasy sweets or cakes.

The chief signs of change in rural life are the general use of lucifer matches and umbrellas, the substitution of kerosine for vegetable oils. In urban life, of course, things are different, and watches and cutlery, petty trumpery of all kinds, mostly of French or German manufacture, are largely sold.

The prevailing note of village life is the absence of domestic privacy and the publicity amidst which the people live.

Life is largely spent in the open air, and there is none of the isolation of the family which is the predominant feature of Western civilisation of the higher type. Hence there is an utter lack of seclusion, except for the women of the higher classes, and even among them isolation from the outer world is much less stringent than is commonly supposed. Even behind the gloomy enclosure of the Zanâna the wife and mother crave for gossip, and little that goes on outside escapes their vigilant ears. In the general management of the household they exercise wide influence and control. This is more marked in the family of the peasant, where the wife is a true helpmate, works side by side with her husband in the fields, or toils all day long cooking, spinning, or tending the cattle.

But, living in a narrow ill-fenced house, with no provision for the segregation of the sexes, or for the requirements of common decency, the peasant woman, like her sister of the London slum, loses much of the reticence and modesty of pure womanhood. Under the influence of excitement she will break out in a flood of the coarsest ribaldry. She will objurgate her neighbour in a storm of cursing if a cow trespass in her field or a strange brat boxes the ears of her child. All her domestic affairs are common property, and should her husband be vicious or extravagant, she will appeal for an hour at a time in the shrillest tones to all the viragoes of the quarter, and never dreams of veiling her grievances under a wise reticence, or she will abuse her co-wife in public till the whole village rings with the recital of her wrongs. Her husband is much calmer and less emotional, and during an incident like this will sit and smoke quietly till the storm of her passion exhausts itself. He pays little heed to her flirtations, unless his easy-going tolerance is interrupted by some public scandal, when he will chastise her that all may see, or he will convoke the council of elders and turn her out of house and home if any impropriety is established against her. If he appears in the Criminal Court to prosecute her paramour, he is less regardful of his honour than of the jewelry which she removed on her elopement. But in some cases a scandal will rouse him to a state of mad passion, and he will slay her as she stands before him, and wait quietly till the policeman hales him to prison.

A scandal of this kind is one of the few interludes in the general stagnation of existence. It is discussed in detail by the women at the well and by the men at the village meeting house. The monotony of life is broken by incidents such as these. Quite as important is a burglary in the money-lender's storeroom, when the red-turbaned police assemble, the chief officer sits in lordly fashion on a cot and accepts a pipe and light refreshments. The whole population is convoked; the criminals and ne'er-do-wells of the vicinity are interrogated. Or, perhaps, on a cold weather morning, the village receives a visit from an English officer, who harries the watchman for negligence in registering births, or stirs up that dignified functionary, the accountant, for failure to correct his map, and the stagnant village life is wakened with a temporary excitement. Every one turns out to wonder and speculate on the strange manners of the visitors—the curious dress of the lady, the puny baby, the dogs, horses or elephants, the white tents in the mango grove. Every house-top is crowded with interested girls, and the urchins congregate round the camp all day long. Every one bows in reverence to the restless Sâhib, who sniffs about the manure heaps or blames the foul surroundings of the water supply. The elders grin acquiescence in his remarks, and promise to carry out the needful reforms; once he has left the neighbourhood the old apathy and squalor are as intense as ever.

Amusement in the village there is little. There is no circus, which we know, on good authority, the English yokel prefers to a meeting of the Parish Council. There is no cricket on the green, and it is only the ne'er-do-wells who collect round the dirty shed, where the Kalwâr doles out tots of well-watered spirits; but it does not in any way answer to the English beer-house, the poor man's club. The children have their games, but, like their seniors, they take their pleasures sadly. Sometimes the young men wrestle in the evenings; but the ordinary peasant is too dull, too tired, to get much pleasure out of his life. The only real stir is when the banker's daughter is married, amidst a discordant blare of trumpets and a display of fireworks, or when a convoy of laughing girls and awe-stricken bumpkins start to bathe at Hardwâr or Benares, in a lumbering cart, dragged by the patient oxen over many a long mile of glare and dust.

The really important point for the peasant is what he shall eat and wherewithal he shall be clothed. His talk, if you listen to him as he marches along the roads, is always of pice and food.

Let us see what he usually eats. Thus, in Bareilly, to follow the very careful report of Mr Moens[1]—the rustic eats two meals, at mid-day and after sunset. For seven months of the year rice in the north of the district and to the south the Bâjra millet are the staple diet; for the remaining five months those who are comfortably off eat wheaten flour, the rest barley. With their cakes they eat pulses or lentils of various kinds and occasionally a few pot-herbs, peas and chillies, and a little ghi and oil. The young shoots of the gram plant and a wild weed called Bathua are largely consumed. In the hot season the farinaceous diet is often supplemented by various preparations of sugar and treacle. Sweets of many kinds are largely eaten; a family of five will eat, including festivals, rather over two cwt. of sweet stuff. Mr Moens estimates the average consumption of food per head at 1·81 lbs. of grain, ·29 lb. of pulses, and 142 grains of salt. This is rather higher than the jail dietary, where there are no infants, and where extra food is needed to counteract the effects of confinement, regular labour and depression of spirits. According to the best medical opinion 100 grains of salt daily are sufficient to keep a native in health. The consumption of salt in India, exclusive of Burma, rose from 32¼ million maunds (82$\frac{2}{7}$ lbs.) in 1885-86, to 34 millions in 1893-94, and the income derived from the State monopoly was in the latter year Rx. 7¾ millions. The present price of salt in the Cawnpur market is about 3½ rupees per maund, or about 4⅘ rupees per cwt. It would appear that the consumption is fairly keeping pace with the increase in population and this is practically the only

[1] *Settlement Report*, p. 53 sq.

tax which touches the lower classes. There seems no evidence that the existing supply is below the needs of the human population: for the cattle it is probably insufficient.

The food of the low caste Hindu, like the Chamâr, and of the Musalmân, is more varied and nutritious than that of the higher classes, because he adds to it a considerable amount of coarse meat; the better class Hindu supplies the nitrogenous elements wanting in his daily diet by the use of ghi and oil.

The amount of clothing, not its fashion, varies with the means of the peasant. The yeoman always has a blanket or coverlet for the winter, and this is the only addition he makes to his raiment as the seasons change. The state of the poor is very different, and young children run about entirely unclad, a cause which must largely contribute to the excessive infant mortality. Mr Neale, writing of Etâwa in the Central Ganges-Jumna Duâb, says[1]—"The very poorest have not even a blanket, which costs about a rupee and a half, but are obliged to protect themselves from the cold by a mere cloth into which they stuff cotton if they can get it. I remember asking a Chamâr how he passed the night with so little clothing. He said he slept till the cold awakened him, when he lit a few sticks and warmed himself till the fire went out, when he went back to his cot; and he repeated these proceedings at intervals till the sun arose." When he can get it, the poor man lays a pile of straw on the floor of his hut and huddles inside with his family until daybreak, when he cowers over a smoky fire of rubbish or suns himself beside a sunny wall facing eastwards. This lack of clothing is doubtless the chief cause of the deadly pneumonia which follows fever as autumn changes into winter.

Mr Moens in Bareilly calculates that a man's clothing costs Rs. 2-9-3 per annum; that for a woman Rs. 2-11-1; that for a child Rs. 0-9-0. Thus a man, his wife and three children would spend in a year on clothes about Rs. 7, or eight shillings. This does not leave much margin for dressmakers' and tailors' bills. Climate, of course, makes all the difference, and probably the poorest Indian labourer does not suffer the

[1] *Gazetteer, North-West Provinces*, iv. 288.

same privation from want of clothing as is experienced by the destitute classes in English cities. For one thing, he needs little shoe-leather: while want of boots is the sorest trial to the poverty-stricken European.

The same is to some extent the case with food. Want of food is more terrible in western lands, where it is aggravated by the lack of fire and clothing. At the same time, Europe happily never witnesses the awful suffering which accompanies drought in India. No one who has had practical experience of a famine camp can ever forget the emaciated forms, the starving children, the ghastly varieties of disease which follow a failure of the harvest. What proportion of the people habitually suffer from want of food it is very difficult to determine. It is quite certain that throughout the Province many of the menial labouring class are in a state of abject poverty, hardly raised above the point of starvation. This is clearly shown by the rapid increase of petty theft as the stocks of one crop are exhausted and the new harvest is beginning to ripen. That much of the theft of standing crops is due to sheer want is quite certain; and when such cases come for trial it only needs inspection of the members of the "criminal's" household to be convinced of the fact. Among such people want would be much more urgent were it not that the fields offer a quantity of herbs eatable as pottage, and there are many jungle fruits and roots in addition to the village mango crop which, innutritious as they are, are readily consumed. Above these absolute paupers there is, again, a large but ill-defined class of petty cultivators, field labourers and artizans whom the occurrence of drought drives at once into distress.

The condition of this residuum of the people has, it is needless to say, frequently attracted the attention of the Government. In 1888 an elaborate enquiry was made into the subject, and the official view, apt though it be to prove decidedly optimistic, may be quoted[1]—"The officers conducting the enquiry have approached the subject from different points of view: some evidently predisposed to think a con-

[1] *Administration Report, North-West Provinces*, 1888-89, p. 11.

siderable section of the people insufficiently fed; others with contrary conceptions. It is impossible, however, to mistake the consensus of opinion that the people generally are not underfed. It is equally clear that being for the most part an agricultural people, dependent on the seasons and holding small areas of cultivation, or dependent (if artizans) for the disposal of their handiwork on those who hold such areas, they have little reserve in hand, and that in the event of a failure of the rains and of high prices, many of them are soon reduced to a position in which food is obtainable either in insufficient quantities or not at all—in other words, to the point in which the Government intervenes and provides famine labour for their relief. We can see them in ordinary times consuming the produce of their fields, adding to it in season green herbs or leaves, such as those of the gram, or fruit or other accessories. We find them in possession of cattle, of which they drink the milk or consume the butter; fish and flesh are eaten by them, though not by all of them. The day labourer and the tenant of a small holding are those who are most exposed to the chance of insufficient food; but the artizans and the more respectable tenants are in ordinary circumstances raised above want. The succession of pictures drawn for us is in a great measure identical with those which were furnished in 1877-78 to the Famine Commissioners' Report. One caution, it should be noted, applies to all evidence on this subject. So far as these Provinces are concerned, when an officer speaks of the more indigent class of the people under enquiry as being always on the verge of starvation, this must not be understood to mean that they are always living on insufficient food, but that they always run the risk, in view of a failure of the rains, of finding themselves in the position where employment will not be forthcoming, and where consequently food will be difficult to obtain. It is not, in other words, that they are habitually underfed, but that if a calamity should arise at any time from a bad season, owing to the failure of the rains, they will have insufficient means of securing an adequate maintenance."

This official commentary certainly does not minimise the

dangers of the present situation, with a population multiplying almost without restriction and closely trenching on the available means of support. It is true that the recent rise in the price of grain, though the petty tenant has far from realised his fair share of the advantage, has somewhat improved his position; on the other hand, the day labourer, unless he is paid in kind, has suffered.

No part of the country is worse situated in this respect than Oudh. In Faizâbâd,[1] "the tenant's profits are probably just what they are in other parts of Oudh—just enough to pay for his labour and for the keeping up of his stock. In recent years, owing to the rise in rent, the bad seasons and cattle murrain, they have not reached this standard." Mr Irwin,[2] a good authority, if perhaps slightly pessimistic in his views on the land question, goes so far as to write that "even now, taking the Province as a whole, it is scarcely too much to say that a large proportion of cultivators have neither sufficient food to keep them in health, nor clothes sufficient to protect them from the weather; that their cattle are miserably thin and weak from underfeeding; that they are hardly ever out of debt for twelve months together, though in good seasons they can pay off their debt within the year, while in a bad one it accumulates; and that, except in specially favourable seasons, they are dependent on the money-lender for their food for from two to six months in the year." And this, it must be remembered, is written of the tenant and not of the landless labourer.

At the same time, there is some evidence that the condition of the tenant class is in some places improving. Thus, in Bareilly[3] "since the last Settlement, the earthen vessels, which were almost universal, have entirely been replaced by brass or other metal. According to Lâla Gulzâri Lâl, a retired Deputy Collector, who has been in the district since 1828, the improvement in this respect is extraordinarily great. Formerly, he says, hardly any cultivator had more than a blanket and a very small loin-cloth. Now every cultivator

[1] *Oudh Gazetteer*, i. 427.
[2] *Garden of India*, p. 38.
[3] *Settlement Report*, p. 55.

dresses like a Brâhman or a Zamîndâr of the old days. Most of the headmen have a small cart to ride in when they go abroad, or at least a pony. And some of them since last Settlement have been able to save money and buy villages for themselves. The houses, though all with mud walls and thatched roofs, are, as a rule, tolerably good; many are neatly plastered outside. I doubt much whether the cultivating class will ever be much better off than they are now. The Rent Law which was meant to protect the cultivator in Bengal is a curse to him here, by the power it gives the landlord to enhance the rents. Population is rapidly spreading, and with it a fierce competition for land must set in, as in Bareilly we have nearly reached the limits of cultivation." The evidence of Mr Neale from Etâwa is much to the same effect.[1]

To sum up this discussion, it may be said that there is a considerable residuum, which even at the best of times is only one degree removed from destitution, and which even a slight failure of the rains drives on the parish: that above these there is a class of petty tenants deeply in debt, and with no resources in reserve to enable them to resist famine: that in personal comfort and in the general amenities of life there has been some improvement among the better yeoman class, though here civilisation has produced fresh needs and more temptations to extravagance. On the other side of the case we have shown that the tendency to a rapid increase in the population is not so marked as has generally been supposed, and that prudential restrictions do to some extent operate to keep down its numbers. There are, then, no clear reasons for anticipating in the immediate future any striking aggravation of the existing condition. There will always remain a depressed class which, though it suffers in silence, does suffer to an extent which must command the sympathy of a paternal government.

The power of the State to relieve this mass of poverty is inevitably restricted by its financial necessities. That it can by any practicable methods permanently improve the con-

[1] *Gazetteer, North-West Provinces*, iv. p. 532.

dition of the depressed classes is the dream of an enthusiast. This can only be the result of a radical change in the habits of the people, of which they show no signs at present. If they would emigrate, as the Celts of Western Ireland did, if they would check the increase of their numbers as Frenchmen do, the case might be different. They must, in short, work out their own salvation for themselves. It is inevitable that this discipline must involve intense suffering—this is the lot of all creatures until they become adjusted to their environment. The last possibility is the discovery of some new agricultural methods which would suddenly increase the resources of the peasant class, or the appropriation of the areas now producing staples suitable for exportation to the growth of the coarser food grains. The first contingency is almost beyond the bounds of possibility: the latter would so seriously cripple the resources of the State as to make famine relief an intolerable burden.

It is for us, then, to provide against the danger of adding to the burdens of the peasantry by a rigid economy in administration: to check as far as possible the too prevalent tendency to add to these burdens by an adventurous foreign policy: to resist the desire to extend to a poor country an expensive system of elaborate government suited only to a much more advanced community. Lastly, it should be for us so to diminish the cost and fascination of litigation as to save the peasant from one of the chief causes of the difficulties which surround him.

These remarks, it must be clearly understood, apply only to the village day labourer, the small tenant, and the artizan. That the case is different with classes of a higher grade is sufficiently shown by the increased expenditure on house-building, particularly in cities, by the general erection of temples and mosques, by the increased use of the railway for purposes of pilgrimage and amusement, by an improvement in equipages and the larger use of horses, by the substitution of metal for earthen cooking vessels, of imported cloths for the coarse fabrics of the country, by the extension of the higher education, by the enormous absorption of the precious metals, and generally by a decided rise in the standard of comfort. This is especially observable among the commercial classes of the middle grade, and their example has encouraged a higher scale of expenditure among the landed proprietary classes, who arc not so well able to afford it, and have in consequence sunk more deeply into indebtedness.

CHAPTER VI

THE LAND AND ITS SETTLEMENT

THE foundation of the village communities of Northern India dates from those early times when the country was overrun by successive waves of invaders from the west. With the original form of the village among the Dravidian races we are imperfectly acquainted. Probably it took the nomadic form as we now find it along the Vindhyan range—small scattered collections of savages living chiefly by the chase or the collection of jungle produce, periodically burning down a fresh patch of forest and sowing a scanty crop of millets in the ashes.

The current theory of the origin of this class of tenure which has become popular through the writings of Sir H. Maine is that its basis was the undivided patriarchal family. He assumed that the Roman was the standard type of the primitive household, women as they married coming under the dominion of the *pater familias*, and a number of similar groups gradually forming around it and ultimately organising themselves into tribes. Subsequent investigations have, however, thrown doubt on the correctness of this analysis. It fails to account satisfactorily for the growth of the agnatic bond, or for the forms of early marriage, such as the Beena or polyandrous type: nor does it explain the part which Totemism, however it may have originated, undoubtedly played in their evolution. It now appears probable that the sept is a more primitive form of organisation than the family, which was evolved from it when the rule of male kinship was established.

We can thus imagine the earlier stages of the colonisation of the country to have been carried out by small bodies of invaders, who occupied the most fertile clearings in the

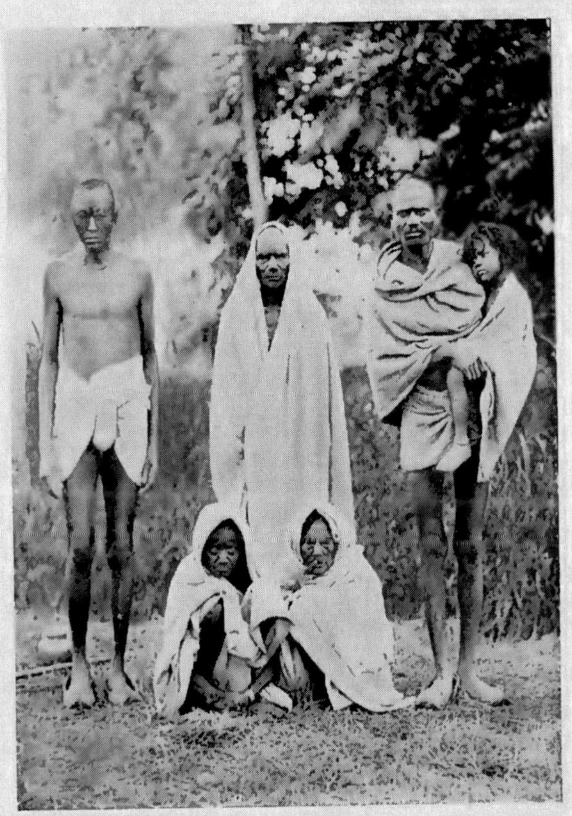

DHĀNGARS. MEMBERS OF DRAVIDIAN VILLAGE COMMUNITY, MIRZAPUR.

jungle, reduced to a state of serfdom the Autochthones, in many cases intermarrying with them, and thus producing the uniform craniological type which now prevails in Northern India. These bodies gradually threw off other groups, which divided the country between them, and thus formed the village as we see it now.

The traces of this early form of colonisation may be observed to the present time in the local subdivisions of the Pargana and Tappa, which correspond to the baronial or hundred subdivisions of some of our English and Irish counties. These probably represent the areas originally occupied by the invading septs. The Tappa, for instance, as in Gorakhpur, corresponds with the natural divisions formed by rivers or other natural features. This was a characteristic of the Râjput settlements, where the various colonising bodies are separated from each other by rivers, the chief ethnical frontiers of the early times. So far is this the case that it is most unusual to find the same tribe occupying both banks of the stream. Though subsequent migrations and transfers have done much to wear away this primitive form of tribal settlement, we still find a decided tendency of many septs to occupy well-defined local areas, such as the Bais of Baiswâra in Southern Oudh, the Dikhits of Dikhtiyâna, and so on. A typical instance of this is that of Bamiâri in Farrukhâbâd, which is the headquarters of a Sombansi house of Râjputs, comprising five hundred members, and occupying sixteen contiguous villages, which are divided into six branches, three of them holding respectively a half, a third, and a sixth of the parent village, an arrangement which has naturally been productive of constant litigation.

We must also recollect that the definition of fixed rights in the land has been mainly the work of our revenue system. First of all the tribe or clan seems to have settled on one or more fertile spots, holding a large tract in common. By and by, as cultivation extended from each centre, boundaries were gradually demarcated, and separate estates were formed, within which part of the area was still held in common. But up to our times no one held an indefeasible right in the land which he cultivated. He merely held so many Biswahs or "twentieths," annas or "sixteenths," ploughs, or whatever the shares were called in the original estate or some division of it. In many cases the old ancestral rights had become modified as more powerful members of the community usurped the rights of their weaker brethren, as desertions through the pressure of war or famine occurred, as the place of the absentees was taken by outsiders, who were admitted as new settlers. The annals of such a village tell a tale of constant modification in the constitution of the proprietary body. There is no actual evidence that the practice of the periodical redistribution of lands took place; but these changes possibly point to the existence of such a custom at an earlier date.

Under our reorganisation of the district, this Pargana and Tappa division has fallen largely into decay. The more ancient units have been grouped into Tahsîls or revenue subdivisions, of which some five or six usually constitute a Collector's charge; but the boundaries of the Parganas have been largely modified tò suit the needs of our administration, so that in many cases all that remains of the ancient division is its name.

We find, again, survivals of the original grouping in the local areas supposed to be held by the brethren of a single sept. Such are the Chaurâsi, or division of eighty-four villages, the Satâsi of eighty-seven, the Biyâlisi of forty-two, and the Tera of thirteen, which is the traditional number of villages presented by Jay Chand of Kanauj to the bodies of Râjput colonists who settled under his auspices. These, too, have passed through the melting-pot of the Civil Courts and the Sale Laws, and little more than the old title survives to our day.

But we are now more concerned with the village, or, as it is technically called, the Mauza, into which the whole land is divided. That the whole country is thus divided among proprietors or joint communities must be insisted on as an answer to those writers who suppose that the Indian Government in this part of the country has at its disposal large areas of waste or common land, which might under a more liberal system be colonised, and produce crops such as cotton for the benefit of Lancashire mill-owners. After the suppression of the Mutiny it is true that the State had at its disposal considerable areas of confiscated lands; but these were all conferred as rewards for loyal services. Except the State lands reserved as forests there is now no public waste; what waste there is is attached to the existing villages, and over this the State has no more authority than the British Government possesses over a grouse moor in the Highlands or over an Irish peat bog.

In the village as it now exists we have only faint survivals of the three primitive Marks, as they appear in the Teutonic form of the institution. We can, perhaps, recognise in the village site the original township or village where the right of selecting positions for houses is carefully restricted: in the cultivated area the Arable Mark, and the Common Mark in the Ûsar Plains and coarse, unculturable tracts where the village cattle graze. But this commonage is the property of the owners of the village, or of the section to which it is attached, and co-sharers have the right to break it up on condition of accounting for the income derived from it at the annual distribution of profits. The primitive custom of the redistribution of the arable lands at periodical intervals has quite disappeared.

The village, then, as we see it now, is a definite surveyed area, with well-marked boundaries, these sometimes following the line of some natural feature, such as a rivulet or a ravine, at others being merely a line drawn on a map. The city or town is a much newer creation. Every town was founded from considerations of politics or trade in the lands attached to one or more villages; these are still recognised, separately demarcated, and assessed to revenue.

In all, the Province contains no less than 106,200 villages of varying size. This gives an average area of somewhat more than a square mile to each village; in other words, about five Indian villages would go to a parish in Great Britain. There is, or was up to quite recent times, a village in the Hamîrpur district of Bundelkhand with an area of 28½ square miles, and when it was necessary to collect the revenue a drum was beaten on an adjoining hill to assemble the co-sharers, who numbered 379. But this is quite exceptional. All over the Province one-third of the agricultural population live in villages of less than 500 souls; there are 43,000 villages with less than 200; two-thirds live in villages of over 500, of whom two-fifths occupy centres of more than 1000 inhabitants.

There is a steady decrease in the size and population of villages as we pass from West to East—a result, as we have already remarked, of the long reign of peace along the Bengal frontier, which has encouraged the wider dispersal of the people over the village area. Thus, in Meerut each village has an area of 1·42 square miles and a population of 669, which decrease all along the course of the Ganges till we come to Basti, where the average area is only ·403 of a square mile and the population 260.

The same rule of distribution applies to hamlets. As a rule, the high caste peasant, the Brâhman, and the Râjput, who possesses resources derived from the ownership of the soil, and is less industrious than his lower caste neighbours, clings to the parent settlement; while the low caste man, who, either like the currier or sweeper, practises occupations and ways of life offensive to those in his vicinity, or devoted, like the market-gardener tribes, to petite culture in its most elaborate form, prefers to live close to his field and have his ploughmen and manure supply close at hand. On the other hand, to the West this minute kind of husbandry does not so widely prevail, and the exigences of defence in the days of trouble which accompanied Muhammadan, Sikh, or Marhatta raids have forced him to live close to his brethren in more powerful communities. This tendency has produced a noteworthy economical effect. The closely-knit organisation of the Western districts is more potent to resist the entry of a capitalist purchaser, or to fight the landlord if he embarks on a campaign to enhance rents, than the weaker groups to the East of the country.

Before we speak of the organisation of these village bodies, it must be pointed out that, in one respect at least, the landed system of Oudh differs widely from that of the sister Province. The former is the land of the Râj and the Taluka, which are hardly found beyond the limits of Oudh.

It is in the sub-Himâlayan districts that we find the Râj in its most perfect form. This tract was, up to recent times, a waste of jungle and savannahs of grass and reeds. Probably none of the bodies of original colonists here obtained such a degree of fixity of tenure as to permit of any system of collective property, much less any recognition of individual ownership. Hence at the head of rural society stood the ruling Râjput or Muhammadan families, and beneath them was a mass of tenant farmers with no proprietary rights. Some of these clans, like the Bisen Râjputs, organised themselves on a democratic footing, all the brethren being equal in position and receiving their portion in the joint-inheritance. In most cases, however, the monarchal constitution was preferred, the representative of the ruling branch being, as Râja, vested with supreme authority over the whole ancestral domain, and the younger branches provided for by arbitrary assignments for their support The Râja had the right of collecting the Government share of the produce where it had not been alienated to a cadet of the house; he governed the foreign policy of the sept; made levies for war or repair of the central fort; he exercised the power of judge in deciding disputes among his subjects, and in repressing crime.

But the important point to notice in this connection is that the peasant tenures under the Râja were the creation of his grants, not in the form of a village community built up on the nucleus of the colonisation of the soil by a body of associated brethren. When the country came under the rule of the Court of Oudh, this condition of things continued; the Râja paid as little as he could to the ruling power; he often achieved practical independence, and the coercion of these refractory chieftains became a regular part of the duty of the Administration. It was not till our stronger Government took these chieftains seriously in hand that they were brought under the rule of law, and the Queen's writ began to run in their estates.

This condition of things, again, tended to the feudalisation of the country; in other words, to the rise of the Taluka. In these isolated tracts the overlord was enabled in those unquiet times to absorb the weak, straggling village communities, many of whom accepted his authority as a means of protection from the extortion and oppression of the ruling power. This process of feudalisation took various shapes. In some cases grants of waste lands were made to some enterprising soldier or courtier, who was from the first practically independent, and all cultivators settled by him were his villeins, destitute of any rights except what he chose to grant or could be induced to sell. In other cases, again, the ruling power would delegate its authority to some officer, like a Turkish Pasha, who was able to enforce his control over the lawless elements of this semi-savage society. He would at the outset be invested with authority only for his single life; but it is easy to understand how many a lord of the marches would hand down his authority to his successor.

Another form was the grant by the State to some influential local magnate, devoted to its interests, of the right to a percentage of the revenue over wide tracts of country. To this he gradually added the right of settling the waste and bringing it under the plough to his own advantage.

Sometimes, too, the same result followed from dissension among the members of a coparcenary community. This ended in the devolution of authority to some able leader, who gradually consolidated his power over the remainder of the brethren. Or, again, in some cases the harassed village proprietors bartered their inheritance for the protection and support of some local magnate, who alone was competent to stand between them and the State harpies.

Gaining authority by one or more of these varied modes, was developed the Talukdâr or overlord, who is such a prominent personage in Oudh politics. Round his rights or usurpations has raged a fierce controversy, which is still going on.

At the annexation of Oudh, in 1856, the Government of the time was under the influence of that school of revenue officers of whom Mr Thomason was the leader. They were pledged to the support of the village community, which they regarded as the only element in the country which deserved to be maintained; they looked on the Talukdâr as a grasping interloper, a danger to the State, a curse to the people themselves. The first move of the new Government was to do what its predecessors would have done had they dared—to settle the land, independently of the overlords, with the people themselves. This was done, and the first Oudh Settlement left the Talukdârs deprived of the greater part of their property.

How far this measure was a promoting cause of the Mutiny of the following year is not quite certain. But the result of its suppression was a conviction that the situation must be reconsidered. In the end a new Settlement was made under the auspices of Sir C. Wingfield, by which, in the main, the condition of things as we found it on annexation was maintained, and the Talukdârs, as they accepted our supremacy and surrendered, were confirmed in the lordship of their estates by virtue of Sanads or title deeds, conferred by the British Government. From the point of view of the opponents of this measure, a body of peasant proprietors was made over, bound in chains to the mercy of their hereditary oppressors. By the disciples of the other school this *volte face* was justified as an act of simple justice to a body of landowners, who deserved our sympathy and protection, and who formed the only stable basis on which the future prosperity and maintenance of peace in the Province could be founded.

Taking a calmer view of this famous controversy, now that the lapse of a generation has somewhat cooled the passion of the disputants, it may perhaps be said that both policies were too sweeping. The rights of the village communities might have been safeguarded without wholesale confiscation: the re-establishment of the overlords should have been limited by much more stringent provisions for the protection of the peasantry. Until the Oudh tenant is as perfectly protected as his neighbour in the sister Province, until his rent is definitely fixed for a period long enough to encourage expenditure of capital and labour on the land, the claims of the cultivating body will remain a thorn in the side of the Government, and it will be beyond its power to avert the impoverishment of the people.

The result is that we have at present about two-thirds of the soil of Oudh held by less than three hundred gentlemen, whom it is not very easy to classify. To adopt Mr Irwin's analysis,[1] they comprise the old feudal chiefs, mostly Râjputs, some of whom have embraced Islâm; mushroom Talukdârs, generally officials of the Oudh Court; lastly, loyal grantees, mostly Panjâbis, who were granted estates by our Government in consideration of Mutiny services. Mr Irwin, though he condemns the system under which they were invested with nearly absolute control over a large part of the soil of Oudh, does not take a generally unfavourable view of them. "They are," he writes, "probably the most fortunate body of men in India. And, taking them as a whole, one may gladly admit that, considering all things, they have done quite as much in return for the favours they have received as there was any reasonable ground of expecting from them. Though often culpably indifferent to the welfare of their tenantry, they are seldom actively oppressive. They are entitled to the credit, and it is no small praise, of having generally refrained from any marked abuse of the almost unlimited powers conferred upon them by our legislation. Improving landlords, or regenerators of agriculture, they are not, but that was not to be expected."

So much for Oudh, the land of great landlords, and a depressed peasantry. A few figures will show the difference of the revenue system of the two Provinces. Premising that Oudh has one-fourth of the population, and less than one-fourth of the area of the North-Western Provinces, the revenue payers in both may be thus contrasted—

[1] *Garden of India*, p. 8.

	North-Western Provinces.	Oudh.
Paying more than R.x. 5,000 . .	2321	113
Paying between R.x. 5,000 and R.x.500	39,157	4578
Paying between R.x. 500 and R.x. 10 .	1,448,837	8374
Paying less than R.x. 10 . . .	951,965	160,125

In short, while the landed proprietary in the larger Province is essentially composed of petty yeomen, in Oudh this class is practically non-existent.

Let us turn from this picture to the most instructive example of a peasant proprietary. We have the sub-division of Kosi, on the western bank of the Jumna, in the Mathura district, where fifty-five per cent. of the cultivated area is held by Jâts; except a few resident shopkeepers and menial servants here every one is to some extent a proprietor. The revenue is realised by the headmen, and in the whole tract there is not a single land-holder of any social position. Here we find a distinctly low level of social life. The land is held by a mass of peasants, devoted to a career of rather sordid drudgery. There are none of those amenities which we are prone to associate with civilisation. There is no man head and shoulders above his neighbours; no Talukdâr, with his showy equipages, his ill-devised rambling house, adorned with European furniture and gaudy French pictures; no half-educated swashbuckler, who frequents cities and loves to attend Darbârs; no horde of tawdry menials. On the other hand, the wealth derived from the soil is more evenly distributed. There is a more general average of comfort, less grinding poverty; steady, laborious industry is devoted to agriculture, in a land where the seasons are less propitious and the fields of less abundant fertility. But the race is more manly and robust, the tone of daily life more free, honest and self-reliant. And when times grow hard, the heavens withhold the rain, the hail sweeps over the ripening fields, the Jât somehow manages to brave the storm of trouble, while the Oudh serf sinks into beggary.

It has been the habit to speak of these village communities as if they were the ideal form of land tenure. And indeed when we compare them with the serfage of Oudh they have much to recommend them. The evolution of these proprietary bodies is part of the gradual change which we have witnessed in Europe—"the slow breaking-up of that military type of society which reached its highest development in, though it did not disappear with the Roman Empire"; "the story of political and social enfranchisement of the masses of the people hitherto universally excluded from participation in the rivalry of existence on terms of equality."[1]

The great advantage of this form of tenure is that the income is not spent to humour the extravagance of some magnate, who has no capital to spend on developing the resources of the country and no real desire to aid in the improvement of the condition of the people. Whatever is gained from the annual harvests is spent in securing the rude comfort of hundreds of industrious households. The peasant here has a future of prosperity before him; the petty holding, barren and irresponsive to his labour though it may be, is yet his own. If he can save he devotes his capital to widening the bounds of his heritage. He will endure a life of ceaseless labour and the most grinding economy if he can add but one rood to his birthright. He will sink the savings of years in building a well which is the only form of stable improvement in which he has confidence. He is learned in the tending of cattle; he loves the great white cow and his pair of sleek oxen as if they were his children, and he will starve himself rather than that they should lack their daily provender. In almost every farm is the brood mare whose produce he sells year by year at a profit. Drought may wither the crops, famine and disease may ravage the household: war may destroy the accumulations of generations, and the fields may lie barren for a season. But when the storm of calamity blows over the yeoman returns to his homestead and starts

[1] Kidd, *Social Evolution*, pp. 150 ff.

afresh his meagre farm supported by the help and sympathy of his brethren. The best example of this recuperative power of the peasant classes is shown in Colonel Baird Smith's celebrated Report on the famine of 1860, where he proves that by that time all trace of the disaster of 1837-38 had quite disappeared in the western Duâb.

At the same time it would be incorrect to attribute this rapid recovery altogether to the village system. The peasant of the Upper Duâb recovered his position so rapidly mainly because his wants were so few and his appliances so limited. The chief danger to him in time of drought is the loss of his plough cattle. The rain seldom fails for two seasons in succession, and if he can save his oxen or purchase a new team he can easily borrow a small supply of seed grain. Then he at once restores his ruined hut, sets his plough to work, and after a year or two he is nearly as well off as he ever was before.

But even admitting that the village organisation does to some extent tend to assist in the revival of agriculture after one of those disasters to which husbandry in Oriental lands is always exposed, it brings other evils in its train. Our system of administration is framed to vindicate the rights of the individual to protection for himself and his property, and the growth of private rights is inconsistent with the theory of the communal organisation. In particular, fairly accessible and tolerably equitable Courts of law encourage that spirit of litigation which is the besetting sin of the small proprietor. The sharer in a joint estate lives in an atmosphere of wrangling and suspicion; there is constant squabbling over the disposal of the waste, over the partition of tenants, over the annual scrutiny of the accounts. Communal life thus tends to become sordid and unkindly: every man's hand is against his brother; ancestral feuds are actively fostered, and once a stranger forces his way into the community by purchase of a share, he spends his time devising schemes whereby he may absorb more and more of the estate. Meanwhile the old co-sharers loathe him and spare no pains to work him injury. The estate of a widow is a favourite source of disputes of this kind, and once the pettifogging lawyer is called into consultation, the fate of the community is sealed. Often, too, the passion for the land shows itself in wild outbursts of revenge. There is still many a village where a Banya who has purchased a share dares not enforce his rights. He might go to shear and perchance come away shorn.

But it may be said that such local quarrels are equitably settled by the council of greybeards who sit under the old pîpal tree. This, it may be feared, is only an idyllic picture. The lower castes, it is true, have their tribal councils which sit in judgment on unfaithful wives, girls light o' love, and culprits who have violated the Draconian code of caste or in some way offended Mrs Grundy. Many cases of this kind they settle fairly enough. There is little pretence of hearing evidence or arriving at a judicial decision. The members are compurgators, not jurymen. Village life has so little of repression or reticence that the seniors know fairly well by general repute how the rights of the matter lie. But even here there is much chicanery and partiality. A case of this kind often gives a good opportunity of paying off old scores, of putting down some upstart whose prosperity is an eyesore in the opinion of his neighbours. Often the women folk of a substantial man, who can afford to pay a smart fine and can be compelled to give a series of feasts to the brethren, are more hardly judged than the sluttish quean who is the helpmate of a pauper.

It is our law which has sapped the authority of the village council. There is no finality about their decisions, and an aggrieved suitor in the face of a hostile decree hastens to the nearest court for redress. Where faction runs so high as it does in these communities, the difficulty of securing impartial arbitrators is very great, and it is the experience of most judicial officers that it is almost hopeless to refer anything like a tangled dispute to the decision of arbitrators. In order to avoid odium they are most averse to give a definite decision. They will potter over minor issues, they will yield a trifle here, clip and pare a little there, but at the end no principle has been established, and the dispute is as far from settlement as ever. Hence most people now-a-days prefer the judgment of the young English officer to that of the village tribunal. He may be sometimes hasty, he may be imperfectly acquainted with the local patois or with rural custom, but at any rate he is honest, and if his ruling be wrong at least the suitor has had good value for his money: he has asserted his independence, and his social importance is enhanced in the eyes of his neighbours by his enterprise in bringing a Sâhib to the spot to survey his disputed boundary, or to decide how half a dozen mango trees can be equitably divided. If the claimant fail, all that can be said is that fate was too strong for him and the great gods unkind.

Influences such as these have for some time been tending to lower the position of the village headman, the pivot on which the whole institution works. It is all very well to be a headman so long as you command general respect, so long as your decrees have the binding force of law. For this it is even worth standing the pressure of the native revenue collector when the instalment is due, to be haled off by the Tahsîldâr, even to lose hard cash over a defaulting co-sharer. But as soon as some envious neighbour or some menial serf whom you have hitherto despised begins to flout you, and perchance drags you to the Court on some trivial charge, the office is hardly worth the having.

It is the post office, however, of all things in the world which seems likely to give the village system its final blow. Not long since it came into the head of some bustling official that it would save the sharer a long march to the distant headquarters and the douceur which he must pay to the native accountant if he could remit his revenue instalment through the post. This was all very well, and in some cases the new arrangement was an obvious convenience. But this is not the view of the headman. It suited him that all payments should be made through him alone, and it detracted from his importance that the revenue demand should be discharged without his intervention. Hence it is becoming more and more difficult to find suitable persons to discharge duties which have been shorn of much of their old dignity. It rather looks as if we were tending more and more to what will be practically a ryotwâri system, where the State deals direct with every petty proprietor. What the end of this may be it is difficult to forecast. One thing is quite certain—if we have to keep the separate accounts of fifty co-sharers in place of one headman, the present revenue establishment must be very largely reinforced.

In other ways, too, the communal system has become weakened under our administration. Our definition of individual rights in the land and the protection of them which we have guaranteed all tend in the same direction. It is naturally the interest of any man who is cursed by a body of quarrelsome, impecunious co-sharers to get his own property separated from the common stock. He knows exactly what he has and how much revenue he is bound to pay. At one time it was the rule that the creation of no new revenue unit was to be approved unless it was of adequate size. This was intended to limit the amount of partition and save the State from the worry of a mass of trivial accounts. It is much easier to realise a hundred pounds a year from one or two solvent headmen than from a host of embarrassed sharers. But a check like this could only be temporary, and now in practice any man can demand that even a minute share should be divided.

Another bond which united the sharers was the common responsibility for the revenue demand. The old theory was that if any sharer failed to pay his instalment, the amount might be realised from the headman or some solvent sharer, who was left to recoup himself as best he could by suit against the defaulter. Our milder system has tended to check what was often a cause of crying injustice. At present it is only in the most exceptional cases that the communal responsibility is enforced. The Collector will distrain the goods of the defaulter, arrest him, lease his share for a time to some one else; but he hesitates before he compels a neighbour to discharge his arrears.

Thus, by the gradual influence of our administration and changes in practice tentatively introduced, the bond which held the village community together has been seriously weakened, and there has not been for generations any stress of war or rapine which would enforce combination to resist the general enemy. It may be well that the State should deal directly with each proprietor: it may be that the communal arrangement is effete. The danger is that we should drift into a new policy for which we are not prepared, and find ourselves exposed to difficulties which will profoundly affect our revenue system. At any rate, it is quite time to realise the direction in which we are moving, and if the village organisation be worth preserving, to do something to prop it up before it be too late.

It has seemed worth while describing the modern development of an institution which has aroused widespread interest among European sociologists. We must now attempt to explain what is the actual village organisation of which we have been speaking, and to see what a Settlement and a Record of rights really mean. And here, in the first place, we must draw a distinction. When we speak of a "village" we generally think of a definite area with its site, cultivated fields, wells, tanks, and groves. But it is not of the Mauza or village that the revenue officer thinks: it is of the Mahâl or assessment unit. The Mahâl is the unit which is separately assessed to revenue. There may be only one Mahâl in a village: there may be a dozen. When a village is partitioned one or more new Mahâls are formed, each of which, so far as revenue matters are concerned, is quite distinct from the others. The map of a village which has undergone partition into half a dozen new Mahâls is a curious sight. You cannot take a ruler and mark off one corner to A, another to B, and so on. To begin with, the Mahâls may be of various sizes—one may be one-third, another one thirty-third of the whole estate. Each of these must have its proper share of the best and worst lands, of the wells, tanks, groves, cultivated area, and waste, not to speak of the village site. So the map in its final form is a mass of apparent confusion—splotches of red and green and blue all over the surface represent the fields which have been allotted to each Mahâl.

How it ever comes to be done is a standing wonder. To the casual visitor only the broad distinctions between the different classes of soil are apparent. He sees that one belt is loam, another sand, one side watered, the other dry. But the keener eye of the peasant trained from boyhood to watch every individual field recognises minute differences of fertility, superiority of position and so on, which are not readily apparent. One field catches the warmth of the morning sun which a grove or belt of trees shuts out from another. The slope of one facilitates the labour at the well: one is grazed by the village cattle as they return from pasture, another is ravaged by pigs or monkeys or deer. So, before a partition can be made there must be many palavers, arguments which go on for days at a time, the wails or imprecations of some disappointed claimant, here a little to be yielded to one, a fragment to be lopped from another, till resignation to the award, not contentment, which is out of the question, is finally secured. Each man, of course, keeps his ancestral fields if it can possibly be so arranged. But it is when he has to surrender a scrap of ground he has ploughed since he was a boy, or has to give up the tree under which his children play or the corner where he stalls his cow, that the real struggle comes, and his emotional nature finds relief in a wild passion of tears, execrations or appeals to the universe at large, if he thinks or chooses to imagine that he has been wronged.

The theory on which the land system was originally based, one which we inherited from our Musalmân predecessors, was that the sovereign was absolute owner of all the land in the country, and that all property in land existed only by his sufferance. "The Muhammadan theory and the corresponding Muhammadan practice had put out of sight the ancient view of the sovereign's rights, which though it assigned to him a far larger share of the produce of the land than any western ruler has ever claimed, yet in nowise denied the existence of private property in land. The English began to act in perfect good faith on the ideas which they found universally prevailing among the functionaries whom they had taken over from the Muhammadan semi-independent viceroys dethroned by their arms. Their earliest experiments, tried in the belief that the soil was theirs, and that any land law would be of their exclusive creation, have now passed into proverbs of maladroit management."[1]

This conception that the State is the owner of the soil still occasionally appears. Thus, the Famine Commissioners write[2]—"The expression 'ownership of land' when used with reference to India must be used in a sense differing in some important respects from that in which it is commonly used in England. In India the immemorial and unquestioned custom of the country is that the landholders do not own the land in the sense in which ownership is understood in England, but merely certain limited rights to it. Originally the occupant of the land possessed the right to hold and till it subject to the payment of a part of the produce to Government; and the Government possessed the correlative right to a share of the produce of the land, known as the land revenue."

The controversy whether Government really owns the land or not has become in a great measure academic. The State does reserve the right that its demand is to have precedence of all other claims, and theoretically at each revision of settlement asserts its power of refusing to renew the engagement with the landholder in possession; or it may secure the same end by fixing his revenue on a scale which leaves him no margin of profit, and at which he declines to re-engage. But this right has practically fallen into abeyance. As a matter of fact, the refusal of the Government to recognise the holder in possession or to assess a reasonable demand upon him is as rare as the rejection of the terms of resettlement by the proprietor. All the substantial authority of an owner has been conferred upon him. He can sell and mortgage, he can settle tenants on the waste, he can cut down the trees, he can raise his rents so far as he is not restricted

[1] Maine, *Village Communities*, p. 104. [2] *Report*, Part ii. p. 110.

by special law. If his land is appropriated by the State for a Canal or Railway, he will receive equitable compensation.

Whether we have been wise in conferring these extensive powers upon a proprietary in this social stage is another matter. What the result has been is clear from the case of Jhânsi. Here we have the most backward, least fertile part of the country, the portion of the Province most exposed to drought, worst protected by artificial irrigation, the proprietors less intelligent than in other parts, less completely dissociated from the traditions of the wild life which characterises Central India. Such people would probably be much happier if they possessed only a limited tenure in the soil and were unable to sell and mortgage their property. As it is, partly from unfavourable economic conditions, partly from their natural boorish simplicity, they have fallen into the hands of the money-lender, and it became necessary not long since to introduce special measures for their relief. A Court was established for the purpose of arranging a compromise between debtor and creditor; but it is more than doubtful if such measures are likely to have any permanent effect.

Under the Hindu rule, as we have seen, the country was divided into a number of semi-independent communities, each of which through its headman paid the Râja a recognised share of the produce. In this state of society the land was the only source of the public revenue. It is only at a later stage that the evolution of industries of the commercial and industrial type open up new sources of revenue. Hence came the theory that the land was the property of the State, that the occupant was the tenant of the ruling power, and that if one despot chose to confer his rights on a favourite minion, his successor was perfectly entitled to resume the grant. Theoretically the demand had no limit but the expenses of cultivation and the margin on which the peasant could live. But this was a limit which under existing circumstances could never be attained. The demand might be excessive, but it could never be recovered with regularity. If the peasant community or the local chieftain under whose protection they lived could keep their ragged militia in tolerable efficiency, they might hope for a time to baffle the Collector altogether; but sooner or later the deficiency was realised in a fierce raid, when the torch was applied to the thatched roofs, and the community extirpated for a time.

It was Shîr Shâh who first, with the prescience of genius, saw the urgent need of leaving a margin between the profits of cultivation and the demand of the State, and conferring this, or, to use the technical phrase "settling" it with a middleman who would act as an intermediary between the Government and the peasant, and having a secured proprietary interest in the soil, would see his advantage in encouraging agriculture, settling new tenants under his protection, and bringing the abundant waste under the plough.

Hence the vocabulary of our land system dates from the Mughal era, and is of Persian origin—Zamîndâr, the landholder; Mauza, the corporate village; Mahâl, the revenue unit. It is needless to enter on a discussion of the stages by which the rights of these Zamîndârs were established. Some of them were mere upstarts, creatures of the Court to whom certain lands were assigned; they were mere tax-gatherers, who paid a portion of their collections into the Treasury. But in other cases the Mughals recognised the local Hindu Râja, or the leading man of the village community, as the representative of the peasantry, and in this way the continuity of the traditional regime was to some extent maintained.

It was under Shîr Shâh that Todar Mall, the Thomason of the Musalmân period, was trained. To him is due a remarkable reform—the substitution of Persian for the Hindi script in which up to his time the village records were maintained. The object of this seems partly to have been to make the system intelligible to the bureaucracy at the capital; but he had also a patriotic feeling in thus inducing his countrymen to acquire the language of their conquerors and qualify themselves for public employment. The Hindus in the sixteenth century applied themselves so zealously to the new learning that before another hundred years had passed they were fully equal to the Muhammadans in literary acquirements.

What we are told that Todar Mall, the first Settlement officer, did, was to carry out a detailed survey, classifying the land into that which was waste, fallow, or cropped. When it was cultivated in vetches, cereals, or oil seeds, the Government assessment was at the rate of one-third of the gross produce, the remaining two-thirds being left to the middleman and tenant. At the same time, in regard to the more valuable crops, such as cotton and sugar-cane, the custom of cash assessments was introduced, and the principle, hitherto unknown to the jurisprudence of Islâm, that the believer and the unbeliever were to be taxed alike, was finally established.

We could have spared much of the details in the Aîn-i-Akbari devoted to the account of the royal elephants and His Majesty's wardrobe for a more particular account of his revenue system. The cursory way in which it is referred to indicates that even then its supreme importance was not fully recognised. In fact, among those scholars who have devoted most time to the study of the records of the later Musalmân Empire, the conviction is gradually growing that too much reliance has been hitherto placed on the traditions of the revenue settlement, that it was far from being as general or detailed as is commonly supposed, and that the assessment, wherever it was really made, was an ideal to be worked up to rather than a methodical definition of the rights of the State, the proprietors and the tenantry.

What Akbar appears to have done was to take the average produce of the best, of the middling, of the poorest classes of soil in all the chief varieties of crop. Of this, one-third was set aside as the amount of the revenue demand. Statements of price current were then prepared, and on these were based the commutations of the assessment in kind for a cash payment. As Abul Fazl explains, this commutation was made for the convenience of the cultivators and the soldiery. This Settlement was at first annual, but was subsequently made for periods of ten years.

This Settlement, then, so far as we are acquainted with the details, had one point of contrast with, and one of resemblance to, our most modern Settlements. The Settlement

Officer of our day has given up troubling himself to ascertain the actual amount of produce. He makes, it is true, occasional enquiries and experiments in this direction as a check on his work, but what he assesses on is the rent, which is the best measure of the fertility of the soil, and much more easily ascertained than the produce of individual fields. Unlike the Settlement Officer of our earlier period, he bases his revenue demand on the actual assets without speculating to what extent the estate might be expected to develop between one survey and the next. This is, as will be seen, the principle to which we have now reverted, after close on a century of experiments in revenue administration.

The variations of tenure within the Mahâl are most numerous. M. Thiers is said to have asked Lord Palmerston to give him in half-an-hour an account of the British Constitution. A short sketch of Indian land tenures is likely to be quite as misleading.[1]

We find, first, the Zamîndâri form, in which the whole land is held and managed in common, the profits being thrown into a general fund and periodically divided among the sharers, whose interests are recorded in fractions of the rupee or bîgha, the local unit of land measure. This form of constitution as a rule works smoothly only where the sharers are close relations and few in number.

More numerous are the forms of what is called the Pattidâri tenure, in which the estate is held in severalty by the co-sharers, each of whom is responsible for his due share of the revenue. This is supposed to be paid through a headman, and theoretically the whole estate is liable for the default of any co-sharer, a penalty which, as has been already said, is very seldom enforced. The varieties of this tenure are infinite. In one form, for instance, only the home farm of the proprietors is held separately, while all else is divided. This is not very usual. In another form the greater part of the cultivated area, the menial cultivators or artisans, and

[1] For complete information on a most intricate and difficult question, the various forms of the village Constitution, the reader may be referred to Mr Baden Powell's *Land Systems of British India*.

some of the waste and manorial dues—income from jungle, fishing, market dues, and so on—may be divided, while the rest is common to all. The case becomes still more complicated where the Mahâl has been divided into Pattis or sections, and in this constitution we find land held severally by individual households, land held in common by certain households, land held in common by the households constituting the main Patti, and land held in common by the sharers of the original Mahâl. The welfare of such a complex organisation as this, and the absence of wasteful litigation, depend on the skill with which, at the periodical Settlements, the interests of the individual sharers have been defined, and the care with which the code of rules regulating their position has been prepared.

It is this work of entry of the interest of each co-sharer and the preparation of a village constitution, with the determination of the tenures of the cultivators, which constitutes the Record of Rights. Its basis is a field map in which every minute plot is numbered and entered in an index with the name of the tenant, the area he holds, the crop he plants, the rent he pays, the status he enjoys. Next comes the series of rent accounts, and lastly, those which prescribe the distribution of the surplus among the co-sharers after the Government revenue and other general village charges have been paid.

Few Englishmen have any conception of the elaborate form which this system of village accounts has assumed, gradually developed, as it has been, by the labours of one generation of officials after another. The accounts are prepared in the first instance by the village accountant or Patwâri, and above him is a regular chain of supervisors, ending with the Collector himself. These officers, field map in hand, trudge day after day through the wide expanse of cultivation, testing and checking, comparing and verifying, in the presence of the parties concerned, a certain proportion of entries regarding these multitudinous plots. It is an irksome, monotonous task, but one of prime importance to the welfare of the peasantry. These records form the basis of a mass of agricultural statistics, such as perhaps no other Government in the world has at its disposal.

The value of this mass of statistical information it is difficult to overrate. If drought be threatened, an order flashes from the desk of the Collector to a myriad of accountants, and in a few days he has before him complete details of the area sown in crops threatened by ruin, and he is thus in a position to make a trustworthy forecast of the situation. Early in each season he is able to publish an estimate of the coming harvest, which is of the greatest value to the local trader and exporter.

Even more valuable are these statistics for the purposes of the periodical revision of the Settlement. In olden days, the officer in charge of this work was obliged to prepare all these figures for himself. He began with a survey and a new map; then he drew up a rent-roll, and so proceeded to fix the fresh demand. Now he finds the maps kept up to date, the annual corrected rent-rolls to hand, the changes of ownership regularly recorded; and, with a certain amount of checking and analysis of the figures, he is able, in a comparatively limited time, to draw up his scale of rates, and proceed to announce the amount of revenue which he proposes to assess.

It is only because the British public is so ignorant of Indian affairs, so confident that its officers are alive to their duties and responsibilities, that more attention has not been paid to what, in its way, is about the greatest work done by Englishmen in the present generation.

When the Record of Rights, and more particularly the corrected rent-roll, have been prepared, the way is open for the assessment. The next question is, whether this assessment is to be for a limited period, or whether it is to be permanent? This is not the place to discuss a matter of Imperial interest—the advantages and disadvantages of the Permanent Settlement. It is sufficient to say that the opinion of all competent authorities is decidedly opposed to its extension to northern India; that under its operation Bengal pays much less than its due proportion of the public burdens; and that there the main arguments in its favour—the expectation that it would lead to the agricultural development of the country, that the Zamîndâr could be converted into the Oriental equivalent of the English country gentleman, that exceptional benefits conferred upon the landlord class were not inconsistent with the protection of the peasantry from extortion and oppression—have all been disapproved by experience.

At present in this Province the area under the Permanent Settlement is inconsiderable. In the early days of our rule, about 10,000 square miles to the East were permanently settled. To this have been added about 2000 square miles permanently settled in Oudh, as a reward for Mutiny services. In all, 11,830 square miles, or 11 per cent. of the total area, is permanently settled, and this, about the richest part of the Province, pays 9 per cent. of the total revenue.

What is less generally known is that it was only through a fortunate accident that a large part of the Province was, since the Mutiny, saved from a permanent assessment. There must be a special form of thanksgiving prepared for the daily use of modern finance members of Council that this project was overruled.[1]

In his famous Resolution of 1861, Lord Canning enunciated his views on two vital questions—one was "the sale of waste lands in perpetuity, discharged from all prospective demand on account of land revenue"; the other, "permission to redeem the existing land revenue by the immediate payment of one sum equal in value to the revenue redeemed." His Excellency in Council "finds that the ablest and most experienced public officers very generally concur with private parties interested in land, in the expectation that substantial advantage will follow the adoption of both these measures." As to waste lands, he concluded, "there could be no question." He had still less doubt as to the beneficial results of permitting a redemption of the land revenue. "He believes that increased security of fixed property, and comparative

[1] For a complete review of the whole question, see Sir A. Colvin's *Memorandum on Settlements in the North-Western Provinces.*

freedom from the interference of the fiscal officers of the Government, will tend to create a class which, though composed of various races and creeds, will be peculiarly bound to the British rule; whilst under proper regulations the measure will conduce materially to the general revenue of the Empire."

These proposals did not meet with the approval of the Home Government, and just then came the commercial boom, resulting from the demand for cotton during the American war. So the question was for a time laid aside.

When it came again under consideration, the conditions on which a tract might be permanently settled were thus formulated—the actual cultivation must have reached 80 per cent. of the culturable area; Government was to receive 60 per cent. of the existing assets. "Districts in which agriculture is backward, population scanty, and rent not fully developed, were to be exempted from permanent settlement. Fully developed districts were to be permanently settled; comparatively backward estates in forward districts were to be permanently settled, if the proprietors accepted a demand assessed at 80 per cent. of the culturable area, but not falling at a rate higher than 60 per cent. of the assets existing at the time of settlement. No assessment was to be made on the strength of unreclaimed land, under any circumstances, until the assessing officer should have personally examined the soil, and assured himself that it might easily and profitably be brought under tillage. The addition to the assessment, it was added, was invariably to be within the full estimate of public improvement. In every permanent settlement the initial was to be the permanent demand. No progressive assessments would, under any circumstances, be allowed in a settlement made in perpetuity. All estates not susceptible of permanent settlement under the prescribed conditions would be subject to a temporary settlement for a term of thirty years." To this later on was added another condition—"that no permanent settlement shall be concluded for any estate in which canal irrigation is, in the opinion of the Governor-General, likely to be extended within the next twenty years, and the existing assets would be thereby increased by 20 per cent."

The final blow to these proposals for a Permanent Settlement of the land revenue was struck by the revelations of the results in the Bâghpat subdivision of Meerut and in the Bulandshahr district. The conditions of this district were peculiar. The settlement, commenced before the Mutiny, was interrupted by the disturbances; just about that time the conditions of the tract were greatly changed by the introduction of canal irrigation; it possesses a body of landlords stronger than in any other part of the country, who have been notorious for a determination to force up rents and to disguise their real profits, with a view to evade enhancement of the demand. The settlement itself was far from satisfactory. To use the words of the official resolution—"The settlement, which has now been revised, was made in the year 1865. From various causes its operations were unusually protracted. Though the work was begun before the Mutiny, and resumed in 1858, final orders were not passed till 1871, by which time it had been ascertained that the assessments reported in 1865 were inadequate, and involved the sacrifice of the just rights of the State. Immediately after the settlement there was a very substantial increase in the recorded cash rental. Part of this increase was real, and due to the enhancements made after the announcement of the assessment. Part was nominal, and represented assets existing at the time of settlement which had been concealed and not brought to record. Little or no regard was paid to the declared rentals, the village rent rolls were usually left untotalled, and the Settlement Officer scarcely professed to consider actuals. The assessments were based on valuation rates, and there was a failure to gauge the real rent-paying capacity of the district. The valuation rates were inadequate, mainly because they were applied to inaccurate areas of classification. The irrigated area was much understated. Owing to the adoption of a single set of rates for large tracts, containing villages of very varying fertility, the revenue fell heavily in bad estates and very lightly in good ones. But under the rapid increase in material prosperity, which set in soon after the settlement, the demand even in the worst cases became fair or even moderate."

It was a settlement thus conducted which, under the new rules, would have become permanent. It was soon found that Bulandshahr was not the only case in which the revenue was inadequate. It was perhaps well that this was so. After the disasters caused by the Mutiny, particularly in the western districts and Oudh, the imposition of a moderate demand was prescribed by all considerations of policy and justice. But to make such a demand permanent—in the face of the rapid revival of the country, the spread of railways and canals, the development of industries and commerce—was seen to be out of the question. The Imperial finances suffered for a time, but the moderation of the demand bore its natural fruit in the general prosperity and contentment with the new Government, which assured peace to the country. It was left to the present generation to reap the harvest. It has been possible, under the revision now in progress, to make large enhancements of the revenue without encroaching on the resources of the people. Thus we have in Gorakhpur, after thirty years, an increase of 45 per cent.; in Basti 46; in Bulandshahr 50; while in Jhânsi, where the progress has been less striking, the increase was only 13 per cent. The total land revenue of the joint Provinces has increased by about half a million since 1875.

The case of Bulandshahr and other districts also directed attention to the principles on which the revision of the assessment should be conducted. We have seen that in the case of Bulandshahr nearly fifteen years elapsed between the beginning of and the final orders upon the settlement. So in Azamgarh, the work lasted twelve years, and cost R.x. 70,000. The recent revision in Bulandshahr, of which the area is 1913 square miles, as compared with 2147 in Azamgarh, was completed in three years, at a cost of about R.x. 20,000.

"These facts," writes Sir A. Colvin, "are significant to those who know what the settlement of a district means—the value of property depreciated until the exact amount of the new assessment is declared; credit affected; heart-burning and irritation between landlord and tenant; suspicion of the intentions of Government; a host of official underlings scattered broadcast over the vexed villages. I can conceive nothing more beneficial than a prompt assessment of the public demand, with a speedy adjustment of rents and of proprietary rights. But nothing can equal the injury inflicted by a slow, uncertain settlement, dragging its length along, obstructed by conflicting orders, harassed by successive Administrations, and finally threatened with annihilation at the moment when it seemed to have nearly finished its course. Little wonder that we hear of the land needing rest."

It would be unjust to the former generation of Settlement Officers to blame them in any way for this result. The difference between the old and the new methods of assessment depends almost altogether on the degree to which the existing village records were capable of utilisation for the purpose of ascertaining the rental assets. The modern system of supervision has secured much more accuracy and completeness in these records. The accountants by whom they are prepared are now more fully trained and more closely controlled. The field maps are now annually revised, and thus the need of a fresh survey at each revision of settlement no longer exists. The large increase in rents, due to a rise in the value of produce, leaves such an ample margin for enhancement of the revenue that the assessing officer is no longer required to make such minute inquiries. He knows that an immediate doubling or trebling of the demand is out of the question. A landlord, like any one else, becomes accustomed to a certain scale of expenditure and comfort, and if his income be suddenly reduced by half he is forced either to make a sudden reduction in his establishment or to fall into debt. It is perhaps more difficult for such a man to retrench his expenditure, to reduce his outgoings on entertainments, charity or household expenditure, than it is for an Englishman to dispense with the services of his coachman or his cook. Still harder is the case of the yeoman, to whom the loss of a sovereign a month means penury in lieu of moderate comfort. The old Settlement Officer had to speculate how much he could take without undue pressure upon the resources of the village; his successor puzzles his head by thinking what plausible reasons he can suggest for holding back his hand, how to reconcile the moderation of his demand with the traditional right of the State to something like half the rental.

Hence in former days the investigation was much more searching and minute. Every man's hand was against the official; not a penny more, so every one told him, could be screwed out of an indigent peasantry; another straw would break the tenant's back. The village records were fabricated with intent to deceive him; all sources of trustworthy information were closed. So perforce he had to go on patiently dividing the villages into groups of average fertility; breaking up each village into belts of uniform soil—first class, second and third, clay and loam, and sand, irrigated and dry, fields that bore wheat or rice, millets or garden crops; here extracting some information from a solitary peasant in his field, there utilising the envy, hatred, and malice of one discontented sharer to match the wiliness of another. It was a thankless, irritating duty; the wonder is that it was on the whole done so well.

Even now the work of the assessing officer is one of extreme difficulty. He finds sometimes, as in Bulandshahr, a class of powerful landlords banded together to resist him, with one set of rent rolls for private use, another for settlement purposes. But here he is aided by the growing independence and self-reliance of the peasant. It requires a slavish and depressed tenantry to secure full compliance with the landlord's aims. The unjust steward himself must have been backed up by people who dealt in the mammon of unrighteousness; and the tenant soon comes to see that the advantage is all one way if he gets a receipt for half-a-crown an acre and pays five shillings for the next thirty years. So, as was the case in Bulandshahr, the fraud recoils on those who planned it, and sooner or later comes the time when it must be disclosed.

It is to avoid this form of misrepresentation that the Settlement Officer must still frame average rates; but he uses them not as the sole basis of assessment, but as a check on fraudulent concealment of assets. When he once obtains a fairly trustworthy rent roll his work is nearly done. He has to apply tenant's rates to the landlord's home-farm, which is usually entered in the papers at a nominal rent, and to plots held rent-free or at small rents by the village Brâhman or barber. Thus he arrives at a tolerably trustworthy account of the rental income, and out of this he deducts the proportion due to the State, and distributes the surplus over the shares of the coparceners.

The case of the smaller village communities requires special consideration. It is obvious that a sudden enhancement of revenue, which can be borne by a great landlord, will press unduly on the resources of a body of yeomen. But this is only one side of the case. As the Government puts the matter in its review of the last Shâhjahânpur settlement—"While unquestionably the principle of the Government order, that proprietary cultivating communities should be assessed leniently is right, especially if an assessment at full rates would involve a great enhancement of the previous demand, there is a limit to the indulgence with which they should be treated. Pushed to an excess, it would imply that no assessment should be imposed when the community had multiplied to such an extent, and property become so subdivided that individual holdings no longer yield a sufficient income for bare subsistence. Apparently, if subdivision go on until holdings are too small to furnish full employment for the proprietor and his family, any leniency encouraging it and tending to increase the burden upon the land is a mistaken policy."

We now come to consider the proportion of the rental assets which the State claims as its share. It is extremely difficult to compare the proportions taken by the State in Hindu and Muhammadan times with those of our settlements. The value of silver, the conditions of social life, the standard of comfort have all greatly changed, and we have no adequate materials for comparing the economical position of the people now with what it may have been five or ten centuries ago. It may be assumed also that the old settlements were to a large extent ideal, in other words, the revenue was fixed as a maximum, and the assessment was probably very different from the actual realisations.

The old Hindu rule is said to have been that the State share was one-fourth of the produce. Manu lays down that the Râja may take an eighth, a sixth, or a twelfth, and his commentator adds that this is according to the difference of the soil and the labour necessary to cultivate it. It is very doubtful if the rule was ever distinctly formulated, and it must be remembered that all Governments, prior to ours, enforced the obligation to provide a militia from which the people are now relieved.

Under Akbar's, the first attempt at a scientific settlement, the State took one-third of the gross assets. Mr Thomas has made calculations showing that, all round, Akbar's revenue was about treble that of the British Government. This seems almost incredible, for, as we have seen, there were enormous areas of waste in his time. In Bareilly it is said that the land tax levied by Akbar, the Rohillas, and that of our last settlement was respectively R.x. 53,468; 194,100; 207,512. Calculating 40 Dâms to the rupee, Budaun paid in the time of Akbar 26 lakhs of rupees; our last settlement was 10¼ lakhs. But it must be repeated that these figures furnish no accurate basis for a calculation of the pressure of the assessment.

It is more important to ascertain the incidence of the revenue on the gross produce. An apparently careful calculation made during the last settlement of Etâwa, estimates the State share at between one-ninth and one-eleventh of the gross produce. But with such calculations, except in those few tracts in which the rent is paid in kind, the modern settlement officer has no concern. His business is to discover, as best he can, what the average rents are, and then out of this he takes about half as land revenue.

We do know accurately the incidence of the demand in

the temporarily and permanently settled tracts. This amounts respectively to Rs. 1-2-4 and Rs. 0-15-3 per acre on the total area; Rs. 1-12-7 and Rs. 1-8-10 per cultivated acre; Rs. 1-10-9 and Rs. 0-14-9 per head of the population. The incidence is thus, as might have been expected, considerably lower in the tract permanently settled as compared with that under the thirty years' period. This is only natural, considering the great rise in prices and spread of agriculture since the permanent settlement was concluded. It might have been anticipated that side by side with this difference in assessment the condition of the people would be much superior under the lighter demand. This is not so. There are no districts in which population presses more closely on the resources of the soil, and in which poverty is more apparent, than in some of the permanently settled districts, like Jaunpur and Ghâzipur; no tract is more prosperous than Meerut under a temporary settlement. Nor is this confined to the small tenant or field labourer class. Among the proprietors there is no evidence of greater wealth as shown in houses, dress, or the general average of social comfort, and there the money-lender is as much, or perhaps more, the master of the situation than is the case towards the west of the Province.

Hence some careful observers have not hesitated to conclude that to bring out the best qualities of the Indian peasant, to encourage thrift and self-reliance, a periodical revision of the demand provides a healthy stimulus. On the other hand, here racial and physical facts influence the situation. The Jât, with abundance of canal water, will thrive almost anywhere, and will make a living where the less sturdy eastern peasant will starve.

Whilst, then, our modern assessments have been studiously moderate, the reverse was undoubtedly the case in the earlier years of our rule. The Company was always anxious to recoup the money spent on its conquests; the natural course of events necessitated large military expenditure; the first officers who were posted to the Province were naturally ignorant of local conditions, and were compelled to rely on a grossly corrupt native staff. Sufficient consideration was not given to the fact that the country had been desolated by a century of misrule and internal disturbance.

Thus, in Allahâbâd we began by exacting R.x. 10,000 more than had been paid to the Oudh Government, to which we succeeded. The result was that immediately one-fifth of the revenue-paying lands of the district was brought to the hammer. In Cawnpur the Board of Commissioners wrote at the time: "The district, we have reason to apprehend, was over-assessed at the first triennial settlement, and it is still suffering, we fear, from the consequences of that injurious proceeding. Much too great an anxiety was manifested in this and other instances to draw from the country suddenly the utmost revenue which it could be supposed to yield. Large reductions became necessary in consequence at the second settlement; but even after these concessions were made, the assessment in particular estates was far from moderate."

Evidences of this reckless severity in taxation are constantly found in the earlier reports. The result was that native underlings took advantage of the situation and bought up wholesale the estates of these luckless proprietors. Some efforts were made to restore them as soon as the Government realised the facts; but immense and irremediable mischief had already been worked, and there are many estates to this day in alien hands, which survive as evidences of the widespread ruin caused by well-meaning but inexperienced officials.

Much the same evils have characterised our rule up to the present time. Every year more and more of the ancestral landed property is being brought to sale under the orders of the Civil Courts. There can be little doubt that this was one of the prime causes of the Mutiny, and since then the question has been debated almost *ad nauseam* without any tangible results, and still auctions have gone on merrily all the same.

The fact is, briefly, that it is only under our rule that the proprietor has possessed or exercised the power of alienating the land in perpetuity. There seems to have been under the native Government a principle known as Damdupat, by which interest beyond double the amount of the original loan could not be recovered. We ourselves did try a form of usury law, but with the natural result. It was evaded wholesale by necessitous debtors, and the simple device was adopted of tacking on the prohibited interest to the original loan.

With our notions based on the sanctity of contract, we have always, wisely or unwisely, steadily resisted any attempt to go behind the letter of the bond. Be the terms iniquitous or reasonable, our Courts have enforced them. It has not availed to urge that the debtor, pressed to marry his daughter or to perform the rites which ensure to his late father entrance into heaven, is practically in a state of duress, and must borrow, and must accept any terms which Shylock chooses to enforce. To this it is answered that the borrower is neither a minor nor a lunatic, and must be supposed to understand what he signs. All we have done is to set up the Collector, who conducts all sales ordered by the Civil Court, as a sort of conciliator between the parties. It is his duty to call them before him and arrange a compromise if possible. But he has no power of enforcing payment by instalments, or any arrangement of a similar nature, of doing anything, in fact, except giving sage advice; and as the property has usually been sucked dry before the matter comes before him, his interference is generally futile. He feels like a surgeon who has to deal with a limb distorted by an ignorant bonesetter, or a physician with a patient whose constitution has been irretrievably ruined by quacks.

Just now the question has reached one of its periodical acute stages, and the wise men of the land have taken it again under consideration. A native ruler of the old type would probably begin by putting half a score of usurers to death by slow torture; but this is not our way, nor would it in this case do much good except to check money-lending for a season. We are on the horns of a dilemma. We believe in the sanctity of contract, but we loathe Shylock and writhe at seeing the peasant come shorn out of his clutches. But we know too well that any drastic remedy is out of the question.

One remedy has been often suggested and seems at last to be seriously considered. Nothing in our rule has been on the whole better done than what is called the Court of Wards—a sort of Encumbered Estates Court. It takes over the property of the widow and orphan or lunatic, and administers it for a time. We have in this way not only rescued a number of properties from ruin, but we have in many cases made them model estates. We have built wells, planted trees, done, in fact, what a liberal English landlord habitually does, and we have preferred to sink the accumulations of a minority in the land than leave a fund for some dissipated youth to squander when he comes of age. This institution has also provided an admirable training school for many of our young officers in the practical management of the land. But hitherto its benefits have been showered on Dives, not on Lazarus. A really large estate it has been always possible to manage with a considerable measure of success; but the Court will have nothing to do with Naboth and his vineyard; it is too small a business, and not worth the trouble. This principle will now, it may be hoped, finally disappear. There is no reason why such an institution should not be established in each district, using the surplus funds of solvent properties to pay off the demands of the usurer. It would be a troublesome business, full of worry and difficulty, but this it would be worth risking if we could only do something to save the sturdy, patient yeomen from ruin.

The new system of the assessment of the land revenue which has been described was not arrived at without protracted discussion. One plausible proposal was that the new demand should be based on the rates of produce. It was, for instance, suggested that if the staple produce of a district had risen within the period of the settlement by twenty-five per cent., the existing demand should be enhanced to a proportionate extent. To this there are obvious objections. It would involve a general rateable increase over large tracts or districts, and would therefore operate with great inequality in cases where the initial assessment had been unfairly distributed, or had since it was imposed become unfair in consequence of the varying rates of progress made by neighbouring villages.

To quote the official comment[1]—"An investigation into the actual incidence of the existing demand showed that in a very large number of estates it was already as high as they could afford to pay; and as a uniform rate of enhancement must be calculated on a consideration of what the worst and lowest units of assessment could bear, the proposed measure would virtually amount to the abandonment of the right of the State to a share of the increase of the rental, which in many estates was very great, and which there was no reason to forego. The selection of the staples of produce and the periods on which a calculation of a rise in prices should be based presented considerable difficulties, and the whole system was much too indefinite and loose to sustain the hope that any declaration of any principle of the kind would reassure the minds of the landowners, or give greater security to agricultural enterprise by making known with some degree of exactness the conditions and limitations of future assessments. It was found that rents were very generally determined by custom, and bore no recognisable relation to the variation of prices; so that in order to permit the adoption of any scheme of assessment by prices, it would be necessary to invest Government with extensive powers for the regulation and assessment of rents. A careful enquiry into the relations which existed between landlords and tenants showed that no such action was required for the protection of the latter; while the magnitude of the proposed undertaking and the manifest objections to a general interference with long-established rights, which had not been abused by their owners, made any such measure altogether undesirable. The proposal was therefore abandoned; but the enquiries of which it was the occasion resulted in the establishment of the following principles:—Tracts or districts which were in a backward condition when the existing assessments were framed, or where the subsequent process of development has produced inequalities so great and so

[1] *Administration Report, North-Western Provinces*, 1885-86, pp. xvii. ff.

numerous as to make the application of a general uniform rate of enhancement inadvisable or unfair, must be left for regular assessment. In other localities a general rate of enhancement is to be determined on the basis of a summary enquiry into the conditions and resources of the area under settlement."

These controversies also led to various useful results.

It was one of the most time-honoured of fallacies that with a moderate settlement the yeoman saved money in a good year, and was thus able to pay in a bad season. To interfere when times were poor was supposed to be the best means of discouraging thrift and self-reliance. As a matter of fact few of them can or do lay by for a rainy day, and when the crop fails, if the tax-gatherer presses his claims, the peasant must resort to the money-lender. All these ideas are now quite out of date. It is admitted all round that when the strain commences no time should be lost in suspending the whole or part of the demand, the suspension to be converted into remission if the pressure become more severe. The arrangements proposed to meet the famine now anticipated have been based on this principle.

Again, the question of the taxation of improvements has been disposed of, and it has been made quite clear that a man who has been enterprising enough to build a well must not be taxed on the profits of his undertaking until he has at least been recouped the initial cost of the work.

Thirdly, opportunity has been taken to arrange the dates at which the revenue instalments are claimed so as to make the payment least irksome. Some villages depend on the autumn, some on the spring crop; in some the revenue is paid from sugar, in others from wheat, cotton or poppy. The dates have now been arranged so as to suit the convenience of the peasantry, and a great deal of useless loss and inconvenience has been avoided.

But the most valuable reform has been the assertion of the principle that the assessment is based on the actual rental assets, not on possible future profits. The Settlement Officer of old days used to speculate what the village rental might be ten years hence, how much waste would be brought under the plough, and so on. Now he has only to find out what is really paid. Thus, to take the important question of culturable waste, Mr Moens, one of the ablest of the former generation, thus dealt with it in Bareilly[1]—"Where there was a large proportion of waste land I treated it according to the population and circumstances of the neighbourhood. If the land was of fair quality, the village inhabited and the neighbourhood well populated, I then assessed such an amount of the waste at full rates as would bring the cultivation up to the average of the neighbouring villages. Under similar circumstances, when the waste was poor, I took into account only its actual value as a waste for grass or grazing." This with the uncertain conditions of cultivation was obviously risky. No demand of the kind can now be made; none but actual assets are taken into account in assessing the revenue.

To sum up the matter, we have now arrived at a fairly workable method of fixing the burdens assessed on the land. Whether this demand be a rent or a land tax does not make any practical difference. Out of a revenue raised within the Province of about nine millions, two-thirds are provided from this source by a mode familiar to the people and collected without any appreciable amount of friction. But the success of a highly elaborate system such as this depends altogether on the efficiency of the staff by which it is controlled. The danger at present is that the district staff tends to become a mere machine working under the orders of a central bureau, by which all power of initiative is lost, and the local officer, immersed in judicial work and the bonds of a heavy correspondence, becomes simply an agency for the collection of statistics and the compilation of voluminous reports. The Collector has less time than his predecessors to sit and chat with the village greybeards at the well, to wander through the fields and watch the crops and the cattle, and pick up in this way a practical knowledge of the people, their wants and their prejudices.

[1] *Settlement Report*, p. 156.

What the peasant of the village likes best is the patriarchal form of rule. He wants some one with time and patience to listen to his complaints, and even if he fail to obtain redress for the actual grievance of the moment, it is something to have had a chance of explaining what he wishes. Above all he wants something done at once, and when the answer comes that his representations will be considered, that his case will be referred to the higher powers, that when sanction comes from some distant office his swamp will be drained or canal water brought into his village, he looks on all this as so much purposeless babble, and he is sure that when a new king comes to rule him who knows not Joseph the whole business must be gone through afresh.

The obvious remedy for this state of things is wider decentralisation, a strengthening of the hands of the local officer, to free him from much of the work of the desk, and give him more time to study the people for himself and gain his experience at first hand. No code, no digest of rules will furnish him with this kind of knowledge, and without it all the best laid schemes of land revenue administration must remain ineffective.

CHAPTER VII

THE PEASANT AND THE LAND

WE now come to consider the relation of the peasant to the land from which he draws his support; and here it will be necessary to give some figures showing the general distribution of the people.

In the first place, out of a total population of 47¾ millions, those wholly or partially dependent on agriculture for their support amount to nearly 35 millions, of which about 4 millions are proprietors, 25 millions agriculturists, and nearly 6 millions labourers. The persons, then, who derive the whole or a large part of their means of subsistence from the soil form about 74 per cent. of the people. In other words, about three out of every four souls in the Province are dependent on the land.

Next comes the distribution of the people between the urban circles and the rural tracts. Of every 100 souls, eleven live in towns and eighty-nine in villages. Excluding the Hill tracts and those districts, like Lucknow and Benares, where the city population is predominant, we find that, owing to the influence of the Imperial Government at Delhi, the proportion of the urban to the country dwellers is greater towards the west than in the east of the Province. Thus, while in the Meerut division about 19 per cent., or one-fifth of the people, live in towns, in the Central and Lower Duâb from 15 to 13 per cent. are urban; in Rohilkhand 16 per cent. But in the Benares division to the extreme east the proportion falls to 12 per cent., and in half the Oudh districts and Gorakhpur to less than 5 per cent.

The predominance of agriculture is thus the primary social fact which must never be forgotten. Agriculture is the really vital industry of the people : with it are most closely linked all the other local industries. It is on its development that all hope of raising the status of the people depends ; in comparison with it all other industries take a lower room.

The next vital point for consideration is the pressure of this agricultural population on the resources of the soil. Here, though the density of the people on the whole area is a material factor, what is much more important is the distribution on the cultivated area and the reserve of land which is available to meet its increasing needs.

Throughout the whole Province the population on each square mile of cultivation is 677 ; in other words, each individual has to make his living out of less than one acre of tillage. But here, as in most cases, the conditions vary enormously in different parts of the country. The Azamgarh peasant, with 1244 souls to a square mile of cultivation, has to subsist on about half an acre; in the Meerut division to the extreme west each person has about an acre and a half; in Oudh about three-quarters of an acre. But in parts of thinly peopled Bundelkhand the average cultivated area per head rises to nearly two acres.

The same result may be arrived at from a comparison of the average holding and the area cultivated by each plough. Thus, to contrast Sahâranpur and Azamgarh—in the former there are nearly twelve acres to each plough : in Azamgarh only five and a quarter. The difference of condition between the east and the west is, as has been already shown, reflected in the forms of husbandry.

Next comes the question what room there is for extension of tillage in the future. Including new fallow, the actual proportion of the total area under cultivation is 51 per cent. in the North-Western Provinces and 60 in Oudh. This would seem to imply that at least 40 per cent. is still open to the plough. But from this uncultivated margin large deductions must be made. There is, in the first place, 12 per cent. which is occupied by forests. The remaining portion includes the Ûsar or salt plains, the roads, the beds of rivers, the inhabited sites, the village groves. Besides these there is the large area of rough grazing land, the rugged slopes of the Hill tract, the marshes and savannahs of the Tarâi—all of which are essential for the support of the cattle.

Most of the recent settlements have shown that the area still available for cultivation is small. All through the western districts the only land uncultivated which could be farmed with advantage is that covered with jungles of the Dhâk tree. But if these were destroyed the supply of fire-wood and fodder would be seriously reduced. In Oudh and the eastern districts the case is even worse, and here a congested population working largely by spade labour has extended cultivation to what is practically its highest limit. In some districts there has been in recent years an actual reduction of the cultivated area. It would seem that in some cases land has been brought under the plough which could not be tilled with a profit. The highest estimate of the margin available for cultivation is 10 per cent. of the culturable area, or say 3½ million acres, which would support about as many additional souls.

"Whilst, however," says Mr Baillie,[1] "the cultivated area has been at a standstill, there has been a considerable increase of late years in the cropped area owing to the increase in the practice of double cropping the best land. During the rains in the beginning of the Indian agricultural year the cultivator of the North-West Provinces grows millets, pulse, rice, maize or cotton over nearly 59 per cent. of the cultivated area. In the cold weather, again, he grows wheat, barley, gram, peas or other spring crop over about 60 per cent. of the area, in addition to certain of the rain crops which stand through both harvests. In the hot weather less than 1 per cent. grows melons or vegetables. In all, 20 per cent. of the cultivated area in the North-West Provinces of late years grows two crops, whilst a part of the richest land near towns or large villages grows three crops year after year. In Oudh the proportion of double cropped land is still higher, and in two of the Oudh districts it exceeds 40 per cent. of the actually cropped area."

[1] *Census Report*, p. 82.

There can be no question that with a well-regulated system of double cropping, the success of which depends altogether on skill in husbandry, and in particular on careful conservation of manure, a much larger supply of food might be raised from the soil. For the poorer cultivator what is chiefly wanted is something which will carry him over the month or two of leanness, when the stocks of one harvest are approaching exhaustion and the new crop is still unripe. There are many vegetables, such as carrots, which would be most valuable at such seasons. It is to this failure to utilise what may be called the by-products of his land that the Indian peasant owes half his troubles. Everywhere the bonds of caste or custom prevent him from using articles of food which are nutritious and easily produced. It is hardly too much to say that 50 per cent. more Chinamen would live and thrive on the same area.

Next comes the question whether these congested areas can be relieved by dispersion, either vertically by the development of new industries and occupations or laterally by emigration.

We know what has occurred in England, where the emigration of the agricultural population to the towns, as a result of the depression in the farming industry, has become a very serious social problem. We have now to see whether there has been any similar movement in this Province. It must be remembered that the definition of "a town" is very elastic—any area under any form of Municipal constitution and any tract continuously occupied by groups of houses with an aggregate population of not less than 5000 souls. These areas are constantly undergoing change by administrative order, and it is not very easy to make a comparison between the results of the last and the present Census. It would appear from the figures that the urban population has increased in ten years from 9·7 to 11·3 per cent. The enumeration in the urban is likely to be much more complete than in the rural tracts, and so far there does not seem to be any decided tendency towards changing a country for a town life. The Indian conditions, again, present no analogy to those of

England. While in England 53 per cent. of the people reside in 182 towns with a population of 20,000 or upwards, in India, though there are 227 such towns, only 4·84 per cent. of the people dwell in them.

The conditions of city life have been so well described by Mr Baines that his remarks deserve reproduction.[1]—"In the minds of the great majority of the masses, city life and its attractions are no more than a 'nebulous hypothesis,' and the town might just as well not be in existence. To the upper classes it is distasteful, saving to a native chief in his own capital, of which more anon. The local magnate in his own domains is a Triton among minnows, by hereditary right; but in the city the equality of all before the law, a feature in British administration which he despises, is at its full height, and liberty lords it over birthright. Thus the field is left open to the trader, the professional and business man generally, and under the influence of railways and foreign commerce his horn has been greatly exalted, to the prejudice of others, into whose presence, a few generations back, he could not hope to be admitted. There is also to be considered the stimulating presence of the foreign element found in the centres of trade, which is thrown into the scale in favour of the middle classes. On the whole, then, the main factors in the development of the cities of the present day, such as the seaports, Presidency towns, and the few trading and manufacturing centres in the interior, have been foreign capital administered by foreigners, and the scope given to the talents of the native trading classes."

And he goes on to point out that "in former times, whatever the theory in practice, the State existed for the maintenance of the chief, and his duties began at the outer edge of the frontier. The public revenue was sucked into the treasury, and the expenditure was limited to the army and the personal tastes of the Chief, or the embellishment of his palace and capital."

Hence came the growth of cities, like Delhi and Agra, which were really little more than overgrown military can-

[1] *Indian Census Report*, p. 45.

tonments. This was not so much the case in the cities ruled by the smaller Râjput chiefs. But even here the most lucrative trade was in arms, ornaments, fine fabrics, and the other requirements of a small, luxurious aristocracy, which could not, once the temporary Court stimulus was removed, form the basis of a sound commercial industry.

The ornamentation of these great cities, with stately buildings, was also not a genuine sign of their prosperity. Tavernier tells us that the royal eunuchs used to build splendid tombs for themselves in their lifetime, because, when they had amassed fortunes, they were not allowed to go on pilgrimage to Mecca, and, as they knew that their property would escheat to the Crown on their death, they built splendid mausolea, so as to leave at least some monument to posterity.

There seems then no reason to believe that the congestion of some of the rural tracts is likely to be relieved by emigration to the towns. The urban industries are not in so flourishing a condition as to attract much surplus labour, and there is no pressing demand for unskilled workmen.

It remains to be considered whether the congestion can be relieved by vertical or lateral extension—that is to say, the development of new occupations or by emigration. Lastly, the question of possible improvement in the methods of agriculture must be specially discussed.

As to new outlets and fresh industries, the prospect is not encouraging. The growth of new handicrafts is checked by the guild or occupational castes, in which, under a rigid rule, the son follows the business of his father, and the entry of outsiders is actively restricted. This is exactly what prevailed in Egypt and Sparta, where, Herodotus tells us, the musician is the son of a musician, the cook of a cook, the herald of a herald. It may be admitted that under our rule these restrictions have been much relaxed, and the occupational castes are ever undergoing re-organisation; but, at the same time, it tends to act as an efficient check on the industrial progress of the nation.

The rise of new industries is again checked by the want

of the prime necessaries of an industrial life—a cheap supply of coal and other minerals. Labour is extraordinarily cheap and tolerably effective, and at places, like Cawnpur and Agra, has been enlisted in the service of machinery of the most modern type. But, on the whole, the prospects that occupations, such as those of cloth, leather, or paper-making, will do much service in absorbing the surplus rural labour do not seem encouraging.

There remains the possibility of relief in the congested districts from emigration, either within or without the Province. In spite of modern facilities for communication, the results have been so far very disappointing. The fact is that the Hindu has little of the migratory instinct, and all his prejudices tend to keep him at home. As a resident member of a tribe, caste or village, he occupies a definite social position, of which emigration is likely to deprive him. When he leaves his home, he loses the sympathy and support of his clansmen and neighbours; he misses the village council, which regulates his domestic affairs; the services of the family priest, which he considers essential to his salvation. Every village has its own local shrine, where the deities, in the main destructive, have been propitiated and controlled by the constant service of their votaries. Once the wanderer leaves the hamlet where he was born, he enters the domains of new and unknown deities, who, being strangers, are of necessity hostile to him, and may resent his intrusion by sending famine, disease, or death upon the luckless stranger. The emigrant, again, to a distant land, finds extreme difficulty in selecting suitable husbands for his daughters. He must choose his sons-in-law within a narrow circle, and if he allows his daughter to reach womanhood unwed, he commits a grievous sin. Should he die in exile, he may fail to win the heaven of the gods, because no successor will make the due funeral oblations, and no trusted family priest be there to arrange the last journey of his spirit. So he may wander through the ages a starving, suffering, malignant ghost, because his obsequies have not been duly performed.

BRÂHMANS WITH REGISTERS OF THEIR CLIENTS. HARDWÂR.

All this will to some extent explain why there is so little movement among the people. We may first consider the internal migration. Some of this is due to economic or climatic causes. Thus, during harvest time in Bundelkhand there is some movement of labour from tracts where the crop is late in ripening to others where it is early; in the same way Irishmen from Connaught cross the Channel to northern England. The same is the case in the northern hilly tract, where peasants move into the lowlands of the Bhâbar and Tarâi when the stress of malaria is reduced, or others are driven by the pressure of the snow from the higher levels to the more sheltered valleys.

There is, again, another form of migration based on religious or industrial considerations. Besides the great bathing fairs and the constant stream of pilgrims to the holy places, many of the wealthier classes in their old age move to the neighbourhood of shrines like those of Benares or Mathura, death within these sacred precincts being a sure entrance to eternal happiness. And on the purely industrial side, Oudh in particular supplies a considerable number of recruits to the army and police, house servants, grooms and the like, as educational centres like Allahâbâd, Benares or Agra furnish clerks and tutors, Pandits or Maulavis to rural districts. The railway and the Post Office, commercial entrepots like Cawnpur, large public works or the chances of employment in Settlement Offices or the like add to the number of emigrants of this kind.

But, curious to say, it is chiefly women who contribute to this stream of internal migration. Every Râjput, for instance, is bound to find a husband for his daughter in a sept superior to his own. The bluest blood is found among tribes like the Chauhân and Râhtaur of the Central Ganges-Jumna Duâb; hence the well-known rule—"Marry your daughter to the West and your son to the East." With the bride from a distance often come her servants or dependents or poor relations, who hope to better their condition under her auspices.

This feeling also acts beyond the boundaries of the Province. Bihâr is distinguished by its large number of women

—there are 1005 women to 1000 men, while in the North-Western Provinces there are only 923. Hence there is little attraction for women to emigrate into a tract already overstocked, and Bihâr sends some of its surplus girls further west.

For foreign emigrants from outside its borders there is naturally little room. At the last Census 89 per cent. of the people were enumerated in the district of their birth, and no less than 98 per cent. were born somewhere within the Province. Only 62 per cent. of Londoners are born there; the proportion in Cornwall, the most stay-at-home of our English counties, is the same as that in this Province.

As regards foreign emigration, the Province sends criminals to the Andamans, coolies to the tea gardens of Assam, recruits to distant cantonments, servants or porters to Calcutta. Along the Nepâl frontier there is a constant flux and flow. New settlers move backwards and forwards, criminals or bankrupts fly to the shelter of a strange Government to avoid the police or the bailiff. On the whole we rather lose in this way; but on the other hand we gain in numbers by the inroad of the Bengal Bâbu, the Mârwâri trader from Central India, the Kashmîri Pandit, the Afghân horse dealer, the Pârsi shopkeeper.

Beyond India the movement is inconsiderable. Some few, of course, leave their homes of whom we have no account. The most important outlet is the State-aided emigration to Natal or the West Indies. But this relieved us of only about 90,000 persons between 1881 and 1891.

Emigration has thus done something, but not very much, to relieve the congestion. The Hindu, like the Irishman in the States, is very loyal to his kinsfolk at home, and many a struggling peasant in Oudh and the eastern districts is helped to pay his rent or appease the money-lender by a remittance from abroad. But striking the balance between immigrants and emigrants, the Province was in the last ten years' period relieved only to the extent of 590,000 souls. These figures are truly insignificant when we remember that between 1853 and 1888 six millions of our people emigrated to America, and while Chinamen have been flocking to the Malay peninsula and the islands of the tropical seas the Hindu has preferred to work out his salvation at home.

We have heard much lately of the prospects of a movement of the people of India to Africa. So far there seems no probability of the peasantry of the north seeking new homes beyond the ocean. Those nearer the coast at Bombay or Madras are more migratory, and a movement of this kind started from those parts of the country might eventually react on the inland population.

We thus arrive at these conclusions—up to the present the relief of the pressure in the congested tracts from emigration has been and in the immediate future is likely to be inconsiderable; secondly, the vast bulk of the people are and must remain dependent on agriculture for their support, and that too within an area where there is little room left for the extension of cultivation. The next question is—how far are the existing methods of agriculture efficient; to what extent can it be improved so as to provide a larger supply of food. Coupled with this is the enquiry—one of vital importance for the future wellbeing of the people—whether the soil does or does not show signs of exhaustion.

First, as to the efficiency of the present system of cultivation, there can be no better testimony than that of a European expert like Dr Voelcker. Most men of this class come with preconceived impressions of the superiority of European to Indian methods; some come, like Balaam, prepared to curse and remain to bless. Of all recent students of the subjects none is better informed, none more cool and impartial than Dr Voelcker.

"On one point," he writes,[1] "there can be no question that the ideas generally entertained in England, and often given expression to even in India, that Indian agriculture is, as a whole, primitive and backward, and that little has been done to try and remedy it, are altogether erroneous. It is true that no matter what statement may be made, as deduced from the agriculture of one part, it may be directly contradicted by reference to the practice of another part; yet the conviction

[1] *Report*, p. 10 sq.

has forced itself upon me that, taking everything together, and more especially considering the conditions under which Indian crops are grown, they are wonderfully good. At his best the Indian cultivator is quite as good and in some respects the superior of the British farmer; whilst at his worst it can only be said that this state is brought about largely by an absence for facilities for improvement which is probably unequalled in any other country, and that the peasant will struggle on patiently and uncomplainingly in the face of difficulties in a way that no one else would."

And he goes on to say—"To take the ordinary acts of husbandry, nowhere would one find better instances of keeping land scrupulously free of weeds, of ingenuity in device of water-raising appliances, of knowledge of soils and their capabilities, as well as of the exact time to sow and to reap, as one would in Indian agriculture, and this not at its best alone, but at its ordinary level. It is wonderful, too, how much is known of rotation, the system of mixed crops, and of fallowing. Certain it is that I, at least, have never seen a more perfect picture of careful cultivation, combined with hard labour, perseverance and fertility of resource, than I have seen at many of the halting places in my tour."

This is indeed high praise from a very competent authority. But no one who is familiar with the best types of Indian farming, the broad style of the western Jât, the more minute methods of the eastern Kurmi, will hold it to be undeserved. At the same time, there is plenty of slovenly, indifferent husbandry among Brâhmans who are too proud to touch a plough, or Gûjars whose proper business is cattle rearing combined with stealing their neighbours' beasts.

There are two stock charges which are commonly laid against the Indian farmer, both of which are to a large degree undeserved. One is his so-called stupid reverence for traditional methods: the other, that he will only scratch the surface instead of properly ploughing his field.

First, as to his caution and lack of enterprise, it is true that an appeal to the customs of his ancestors never fails to impress him; but, on the other hand, his methods are based on an amount of inherited experience which few European farmers possess, and in the absence of books his practice is regulated by tradition and a mass of saws and rural rhymes which are ever on his lips. He is cautious: but caution is enforced for him by the conditions under which he lives. The climate is always rigorous and often very uncertain. He is dependent on the amount and timeliness of the annual rainfall, which in many parts of the country is very precarious. His crop is exposed to many disasters—a day or two of fierce sunshine, a few hours of drenching rain, frost and hail, locusts, and many other forms of insect life or blight, a bout of fever attacking him at some critical time, murrain which is endemic in the land seizing his plough cattle. And when the crop is ripe, a night snatched for rest may let in the thief, the wild boar, the antelope, or one morning of neglect may set the green parrots tearing down the ears. Such are some of the many risks to which he is exposed. His capital is narrow in the extreme and he is often obliged to borrow his seed grain. A man like this dares not make experiments. Life is much too serious to permit him to leave anything to chance. Still less can he afford to listen to the ill-instructed censors who presume to criticise his methods when they should be at school themselves. His attitude when he is preached at and admonished is rightly that of the old Pindâri—

> "Then comes a Settlement Hâkim, to teach us to plough and to weed,
> (I sowed the cotton he gave me, but first I boiled the seed),
> He likes us humble farmers, and speaks so gracious and wise,
> As he asks of our manners and customs; I tell him a pack of lies."

It is, again, a mistake to say that the cultivator is absolutely destitute of enterprise and opposed to all improvement. In fact he is quite ready to cultivate new staples, if they suit his land and modes of tillage and are likely to be profitable. Thus, during the American war, he turned his attention to cotton, and in quite recent times he has largely extended the culture of crops, like sugar, potatoes, indigo and opium, the advantages of which have been made apparent to him.

It is true that he has adopted, on an extensive scale, only one modern machine, the iron roller sugar mill; but, as regards most of the other machines which a well-meaning but ill-instructed zeal has endeavoured to force upon him, he can show reasonable grounds for his disapproval. They are in some cases too expensive for his narrow means, too intricate and incapable of repair by the unskilled village artisan; their object is often to save labour, an important gain to a farmer in the Western States, but unnecessary here, where labour is a drug on the market, or, like the plough, they offend the first principles of the science which he has received from the wisdom of his ancestors. He looks on a modern threshing machine or scarifier with amazement, but without any enthusiasm. They are inventions, like the engine on the railway, entirely beyond his practical experience, suitable enough for wealthy Sâhibs who can afford to buy and work them, but useless to a poor man like himself.

And even in his affection for his ancient plough, which is still only one stage ahead of the stake with which the savage scratches up the soil, he is not without some reason on his side. Anything heavier will be beyond the strength of his half-starved cattle, anything that goes deeper and turns over the clods equally offends him. It may bring sterile sand or clay to the surface; the damp slice turned over and exposed to the power of the relentless sun gets baked like a brick, and it is beyond his power to pulverise it; it will not give him the fine tilth, which absorbs every drop of the precious dew or other moisture falling upon it; it may bury the noxious weeds instead of bringing them to the surface, where they can be collected or burnt. But his great complaint is that it widens the area to be manured. His present scanty supply barely suffices to fertilise the thin, topmost layer of the upper soil; what will become of it, he thinks, when a foot or more of the sub-soil, which has never been aerated or manured, is suddenly brought to the surface? Arguments, such as these, may seem crude and meaningless to the capitalist farmer with ample means, abundance of manure and haulage power at his disposal; but they are very real and forcible to the peasant whose resources are extremely limited.

Dr Voelcker realises this when he writes[1]:—"I cannot help suspecting that the system of shallow ploughing, as practised by the native, and his aversion to ploughs that turn over a broad slice and form a wide furrow, may have something to do with this matter of the retention of moisture, and that the effect of deep ploughing would too generally be to lose the very moisture the cultivator so treasures."

From arguments such as these it is not pretended to assert that the Indian style of farming is perfect, or that the peasant has nothing to gain from the discoveries of western science. His omissions are not a few, his commissions are many. But it is not just to say that from the self-confidence of ignorance he sets his face against all progress. What he understands, and rightly understands, is that he cannot afford to make experiments, that he dare not endanger one harvest, on the produce of which he must pay his rent and live, on the chance that a year or two hence his crop may improve. The conditions under which he works, and in particular his lack of capital, which he can provide only by borrowing on usurious terms, enforce upon him the most extreme economy. In his own business he is anything but a fool, and any suggestions for the improvement of his methods must be based, not on theoretical views, but on practical considerations of what he can afford, and, in spite of his narrow means, utilise to advantage.

The most effective charge against him is his method of conserving manure. Night-soil, the most valuable of all, he refuses to employ. It is only in the neighbourhood of some towns that the market-gardener class are beginning to understand its value. But caste considerations as yet bar the adoption of this potent fertiliser, without which the crowded masses in the great China plain could not live. Bones he also for the same reason will not use and it is sad to see them exported in large quantities to Calcutta from the land which

[1] *Report*, p. 43.

sorely needs them. As to the ordinary manure from his cattle shed and the sweepings of his house, he leaves it in an open heap exposed to wind, sun and rain. At last he throws it on his field when much of the valuable constituents have been lost, and even then he is in no particular hurry to plough it in. Green soiling he will have nothing to do with, as with his frugal mind he cannot see the advantage of sacrificing one crop to secure a doubtful increase in its successor.

But even here he is not quite without an excuse. He will put no manure on his field before it is thoroughly decayed, because he fears the ravages of the white ant, and if he is a bad hand at conserving the best part of his farmyard manure he simply replies that he has no stuff available for litter, that any scraps of stalks or straw which he possesses he must use to burn with most of his manure because he has no other fuel, and that he dare not risk an outbreak of foot-rot among his cattle by allowing any dampness in the stall. At the same time there is all the difference in the world between the practice of a good and bad cultivator. The Jât, for instance, makes a pit in the corner of his field and systematically collects manure: the Gûjar hardly troubles his head about it.

Is the soil of Upper India becoming exhausted or not? The Indian cultivator, like the farmer all over the world, is prone to take a despondent view of the situation; and here this feeling is strengthened by the uncertainty of the conditions under which his industry is carried on. In addition to this, the fact that the revision of the settlement is likely to add to the revenue which he is called on to pay makes it to the landlord's interest to underestimate his profits. Thus, tenants are all agreed in asserting that the land now yields much less than it did in former years; but in support of these assertions no distinct evidence is forthcoming. This much may be admitted that within the present generation there has been a cycle of unfavourable seasons in which the annual rainfall was so insufficient as to cause drought or famine, or so excessive as to result in disastrous floods. It is also true that the cultivation of inferior soils and double cropping have reduced the average out-turn over the whole cropped area. This, again, is the case with the poorer soils as they come under the influence of canal irrigation. In their natural state such lands are usually cropped with the coarser millets; when artificial irrigation is provided they are sown often twice a year with more exhausting crops, the manure supply is insufficient and they lose the relief afforded by periodical fallows. For a time they respond to the new stimulus, but after a while the out-turn falls off.

On the other hand, a much larger amount of labour is now devoted to the land and there is no evidence that the number of cattle maintained has lessened; in fact, the reverse is probably the case. There is also no evidence that in former times fallows were more general in the area permanently cultivated, and where the fields remained unsown, this was often due to the ravages of war and social disturbances from which in modern times the peasantry have been totally relieved. Such a condition of things as prevailed in the period immediately preceding our rule must have resulted in a much lower standard of agriculture.

The question could, of course, be definitely solved if we had at our disposal a continuous series of agricultural statistics, including both the period of native rule and that of our own administration. But we have no materials for estimating the condition of the peasantry in ancient times; and it is only quite recently that any attempt has been made to collect statistics of the actual produce.

One fact seems tolerably well established from the Woburn experiments—that unmanured land will for a long series of years produce crops with but small diminution of out-turn. But though when once a certain level of exhaustion has been reached deterioration does go on very slowly, the returns show that it does go on.

The case is thus summed up by Dr Voelcker[1]—"The real answer to the question whether the soil of India is becoming exhausted or not, seems to me to lie in the fact of the small produce annually removed. In England with its 28 or 30

[1] *Report*, p. 41.

bushels per acre, what is removed over and above the yield of the unmanured land is due to what is put into the land in the form of manure: India's 10 bushels, on the contrary, represent almost entirely what is taken out of the soil itself. The extra crop in England is, in other words, the produce of what is added to and not, as in India, the produce of what is taken out of the soil. Nevertheless the powerful sun of India, aided by moisture, or by water (where it is applied artificially) exercises, I believe, a far more rapid and powerful influence in decomposing and bringing into an assimilable condition the constituents of the lower layers of the soil and of the stones and rocks which go to produce soil than is the case in England; and why no decline is noticed, after a certain level has been reached, may be due to there being just enough fresh material decomposed and brought into active condition annually to produce the requisite small yield. It must not be forgotten, it is true, that the wheat crop of England is generally a nine months' crop, that of India only a five months' crop; but I believe that the influences named above are the most potent factors in causing the differences of yield. Were demand, however, made upon the soil for a greater yield, the soil could no longer supply it, and it would have to be met by outside sources, in other words, by manure."

The produce of the land of Upper India is much below that of high-class farming in European countries. Thus, while wheat here yields on an average 10 bushels per acre, in the United Kingdom the produce is 28, in Germany 18, and in France 17 bushels. The produce in Canada is 14 bushels, in the United States 12½, in Australia 11, and in Russia it falls to 9, less than the Indian average.

The question then remains—whether it is within the power of the State by any measures to secure a higher out-turn from the soil than it gives at present. And here it must be remembered that among writers on the rural economy of India there is a tendency to confound two quite distinct things—an improvement in the condition of the tenant, and an increase of the produce of the land. The former may perhaps be secured by a modification of the system of land tenure, by a relief of the burden of taxation, or of the demands of the money lender, by checking wasteful litigation or reducing its cost. But such measures, valuable as they may be, will not add one bushel to the produce of the land or render it better able to support an increasing population.

The climate of the country, though the peasant hardly as yet realises the fact, is, of course, quite beyond the influence of State control. We can to some extent check the ravages of famine by artificial irrigation. But it is by an improvement of the quality or increase of the amount of the manure supply that the general fertility can alone be enhanced. Hence we return to the question of fuel and fodder on which the whole matter depends. If we could relieve the peasant from the necessity of using most of the manure of his cattle as fuel, or if the existing supplies could be more efficiently conserved, there would be a certain increase in the produce.

As has been already pointed out, it is very doubtful if it would be expedient to take up large areas of culturable land and convert them into fuel and fodder reserves. These, if properly farmed, would yield a larger supply of artificial fodder than can be supplied by the natural grasses; and, with the existing humanitarian feelings of the people, the provision of open pasture grounds would almost certainly only result in the increase of useless, half-starved cattle.

There are large areas of poor land which might be planted with advantage. The State has given a powerful inducement to the extension of arboriculture by remitting the revenue on grove land so long as the plantation is maintained and extensive avenues have been planted at the public cost along the roads and canals. There is also a strong sentiment in favour of tree planting among the people themselves, who have raised the formation of a grove to the level of a religious duty. At the same time, the shade of trees is in India most injurious to the crops exposed to it, and the large multiplication of fuel reserves would lead to a great increase in the number of wild animals and birds which even now do considerable damage and impose on the cultivator the arduous task of field watching.

Nor have efforts been wanting to encourage the utilisation of night-soil. The villager to some degree attains this object in an indirect way by planting a patch of thick crops near the village site, but beyond this he will not move in the matter. His more intelligent brethren near some of the larger towns have been more prompt to recognise the value of this fertiliser, and it is now largely used in the production of potatoes, garden crops and sugar cane. Bones are still under a stringent taboo which will not be lightly abandoned.

Short, then, of the sudden discovery of some new and cheap fertiliser within the means and not opposed to the prejudices of the peasant, it does not appear reasonable to expect any immediate increase in the manure supply.

There remains to be considered the question of irrigation.

Of canal irrigation we have already spoken. It is possible that the next famine in Oudh, such as that now impending, will bring the Sârda canal within the range of practical politics. The water system in the Ganges-Jumna Duâb is being steadily developed, and there are large tracts where water is abundant and at a moderate depth from the surface where the construction of wells might be still further encouraged. It is not long since a vast scheme, the construction of State wells, was launched by the Government of these Provinces: but it hardly survived the criticism of Sir Andrew Clarke.[1] He pointed out that every acre irrigated by the Ganges canal represented a cost of about Rx. 3½, and that, according to the best authorities, the cost of irrigating from wells, is no less than thirteen times that of the canal. But this assumes that an actual money price can be put upon the labour of the peasant and his household which possesses, as a rule, little or no market value.

It seems clear, that any scheme, such as that which we are now discussing, which proposed to make the construction of wells compulsory, is impracticable. In fact, any plan for widespread protection from famine by the wholesale construction of wells is out of the question. There are many places where the common clay well, with its sides protected

[1] *Report, Famine Commission, Appendix*, v. p. 104.

by fascines when it passes through friable strata, can be cheaply and easily constructed. But there are some tracts where the character of the soil and the depth of the water from the surface make this impossible. It has long been the habit for the Government to make advances at a low rate of interest for the building of masonry wells. But the scheme has not been a complete success. The grant of the loan has been hedged round by vexatious restrictions, too much enquiry is required, too many douceurs have to be paid to menial officials, the instalments have been sometimes realised with too little regard to the temporary difficulties of the debtor, and the native officials on whom falls the burden of collecting the advances, detest the trouble involved in this mass of petty detail and do nothing to encourage the system. There is, lastly, the influence of the local money lender, who actively resents any interference of the Government in what he considers his legitimate domain.

Many proposals have been made for the establishment of agricultural banks to meet the wants of the peasants. This is hardly a business in which Government can engage with advantage. It is only a man on the spot who has personal knowledge of the circumstances of each tenant who can make such advances with confidence. Here the best chance of improvement seems to lie in a system of local or village co-operation for which the existing caste guild offers a suitable basis. But, as has already been pointed out, the main difficulty lies in the suspicion and internal squabbles which are the result of this communal organisation.

The same is the case with the provision of seed grain. The cultivator is quite aware of the advantage of selecting his seed, and he does so whenever he is able to afford it. But a man in a normal condition of indebtedness must take whatever the banker chooses to give him. Enquiries made in this connection vividly illustrate the scantiness of the resources of the peasant. Thus Mr Moens, one of our best authorities, took ninety-three villages at random from every part of the Bareilly district, and he found that out of 4741 cultivators, 3169, 66 per cent., or in other words, two out of every three were forced to borrow their seed grain. Here, as in many other places in Upper India, most of the grain is made over to the village banker at harvest time and he doles out occasional advances for food and sowing. The arrangement does not involve that depth of grinding want which a similar state of things in any other country would imply; but it obviously prevents careful selection of seed, and to this extent affects the produce.

But here it must be clearly stated that no State department can undertake the duty which these village bankers discharge. Let us take a single district, that of Bareilly, from which the previous remarks were quoted, and we find that irrespective of cultivating proprietors, many of whom are hardly better off than the tenantry, there are nearly a quarter of a million of tenants. Taking an average of five to a household, this represents the population of New South Wales, and they cultivate about a million of acres, the area of Hampshire. And this district is only one out of fifty-one similar units. It is quite obvious that the existing staff is quite inadequate to conduct the banking business of this host of peasants. It would need an army of highly paid officials to investigate the solvency of these million of borrowers, and the public finances are quite unable to bear the enormous demands if a State bank were to attempt to oust the money lender.

Before we deal more in detail with the indebtedness of the peasantry, we must refer to the remarkable rise in the value of food grains within the present generation. A movement like this which must involve far-reaching effects has so far passed almost unnoticed by English critics of the economics of India. Since the great famine of 1837-38 the market price of wheat has risen by 42 per cent., and harvest prices, which more particularly affect the peasant, by 55 per cent. At some of the last revisions of settlement the tenant was found to be receiving half as much again for his produce as was the case thirty years before. In more recent years the case is even stronger. Thus, in Cawnpur, by the last returns, the rise in prices in thirty years was as much as 90 per cent.:

in Bulandshahr, 90·9 per cent. To quote Mr Stoker, the officer who revised the assessment of the latter district[1]—"Not only have quinquennial averages run high, but prices have never on any occasion sunk to the low point they used to attain. This is a matter of the first importance, having perhaps even more effect on rents than the high prevailing quinquennial and decennial averages. Under the old order of things, prices rose to a high point when the local harvests failed and the cultivators had little or no surplus which they could sell at the profitable rate. But in good years, when the yield was bountiful and large surplus stocks available, prices fell so low that profits were still small. The persons who gained were grain dealers, who laid in large stocks in the cheap seasons and sold at high profit when the crops failed. But with the introduction of railways and telegraphs, a better commercial system and large export trade, things have changed. Prices still go up when there are bad years, but the depression is caused not merely by local failure, but by short crops in other parts of India, or even in other parts of the world. In good seasons prices still remain comparatively high and the cultivators sell their surplus stocks to such advantage that they gain large profits which with ordinary prudence would carry them through bad years. They, in fact, secure much of the profits which used to be absorbed by the local grain dealers."

The causes of this startling rise in the prices of food grains are not far to seek. It is clear that it cannot be due, as the native universally believes, merely to foreign exportation. When trade with Europe was at its highest point, only one per cent. of the total food grains and one-tenth of the whole wheat crop left the country. Such an amount of export could not raise prices all round nearly 100 per cent. The really potent cause is the improvement of communications which has made the price practically uniform throughout Northern India. It is seldom that the seasons are uniformly favourable throughout this enormous tract, and the variety of crops sown is so great that it usually happens that every year some one staple at

[1] *Bulandshahr Settlement Report*, p. 36.

least is in deficiency in some part of the country. To illustrate the comparative stability of prices which this new system of commerce has produced, between 1861 and 1876 the highest and lowest prices of wheat were respectively 7 and 45 pounds to the shilling; between 1877 and 1891 the range was only from 12 to 27.

With this enormous rise in prices, rents have not increased in anything like the same proportion. Thus, in Bulandshahr, with an aristocracy of rack-renting landlords, though, as we have seen, the rise in prices was 90 per cent., the rise in recorded rent was between 65 and 70 per cent. Again, in Cawnpur, a rise of 42 per cent. in the price of wheat before the last settlement was found to have practically no effect on rent. This curious fact was thus explained by the Settlement Officer—"The effect of a rise in prices ordinarily tells in some such sequence as this—first, the good prices of one year induce competition for home-farm lands to let; these fetch high rents and have the effect of raising to some degree the rents of all lands held by tenants-at-will. When once the general standard is raised ever so little, the landlord is encouraged to go into Court against the tenant with rights of occupancy, and by arbitration, as often as not, gets a compromise in the way of an enhancement given by arbitrators to make one party satisfied without injuring the other. Thus, at a long interval, the rise in prices affects the rent rate of the whole tenantry; in the meantime prices may have fallen and the temporary gain be even lost to the landlord."

That rents respond slowly to the stimulus of a rise in prices is certain. In fact, over a large part of the country rents are hardly at all based on prices. What is paid is the customary rate which has always been paid in the village, and the rent is not economical, but dependent on custom, which, particularly in India, is very slow to change.

It may well be asked how with prices largely increased and rents rising at a much lower rate there can be any peasant problem in Northern India. We have here all the conditions which go to make a people prosperous. And it cannot be denied that it has had a considerable effect in improving their

A BANYA GRAIN MERCHANT.

condition. The higher class of cultivator certainly lives better, travels more, and has more spare cash for amusement and ordinary expenditure than was the case a generation ago.

At the same time the amount of indebtedness among this class is very serious.[1] In the greater part of the Agra district it was found at the last settlement that 78 per cent. of the tenantry were in the hands of the money lender; in the Fatehâbâd subdivision the average rose to 89 per cent. Of two selected subdivisions of Cawnpur, in one 26 per cent. of the cultivators were never in debt; in the other 47 per cent. declared that they had never been borrowers; the proportion of those who might be considered permanently involved was in the former 20 and in the latter 12 per cent. In the Bârabanki district of Oudh it was found that the small farmers, men with from 3 to 15 acres owed as a rule from R.x. 4 to R.x. 10.

It would be easy to add to instances of this kind. It is in the opinion of the most competent authorities not an exaggeration to say that three-fourths of the tenantry are indebted to the amount of a year's rent at least. To find a parallel to this state of things in Europe we have to go as far as Greece, where, we are told, three-fourths of the landed property is mortgaged for its full saleable value.[2]

Once a man gets into the hands of the money lender it is easy to understand how his difficulties increase. The following account of the system prevalent in Azamgarh is from the pen of the Settlement Officer, Mr J. R. Reid[3]—"The rate of interest charged by the Mahâjan is nominally 25 per cent., but is in fact a great deal more. Accounts are settled between him and his constituents in the summer or autumn, usually after the refined sugar of the year has been disposed of. Any balance is then struck in his favour; if not paid off it is debited as a fresh advance to his constituent. Upon it and upon cash payments made by him during the succeeding season he assesses interest at the rate of 25 per cent., credit, of course, being given by him for the value of all produce made over to him by his constituent. The price rate, how-

[1] *Gazetteer, North-Western Provinces*, vii. 548; *Oudh Gazetteer*, i. 239.

[2] *Reports on Tenure of Land in Europe*, p. 27.

[3] *Settlement Report*, p. 144.

ever, at which the Mahâjan values his constituent's sugar produce is not the full price rate of the open market at the time of its delivery. In that he makes a deduction of from 5 to 10 per cent., and moreover he weighs the produce at delivery considerably to his own advantage. There are agriculturists, of course, who are able to sell their sugar produce in open market; but these are probably themselves Mahâjans *in esse* or *in posse;* and the great bulk of the agricultural population loses part of the value of the sugar produce in the manner above described."

We have next to consider the main causes of this large indebtedness. The popular explanation is the extravagance of the peasant. On the whole perhaps too much has been made of his occasional foolish lavishness in the marriage of his children, the rites for deceased relations and other ceremonies. Mr Moens in Bareilly found that the average expenditure on marriages among the cultivating classes was R.x.4 per marriage. This it is true is a large amount for men of this position to spend: but it is made up for by a lifetime of the most rigid economy or even penuriousness. All over the world the peasant class are given to outbreaks of lavishness on such occasions. We see it among the Irish Celts, who will often seriously embarrass themselves in providing marriage portions for their daughters and all our lower class habitually spend more than they can afford on the interment of the dead.

Another and perhaps nearly as serious a cause of indebtedness is the litigious habits of the people. Whatever a man's difficulties may be he seems always able to afford money for a lawsuit. In many cases considerable sums have been levied among the tenant class to resist enhancement of rent or other law proceedings which affect their interests. In 1893 the number of revenue and criminal cases decided, in the great majority of which the parties are drawn from the peasant class, amounted to 682,936, of which revenue suits accounted for more than a third. The minor forms of revenue suits amounted in the same year to 168,433, and the number has about doubled since 1881. This litigation is all of the most trivial kind. The amount in dispute in 22,376 civil and

61,854 revenue suits was under R.x. 1; and in 70,265 civil and 75,095 revenue cases did not exceed R.x. 5. We have already seen that much of the increase in this kind of litigation is due to the gradual break-up of the village organisation. But in addition to this the litigious instincts of the peasantry are encouraged by a horde of ill-educated, astute legal practitioners who, with their touts and agents, throng the purlieus of our Courts of Justice. While native practitioners of the higher grade are, as a rule, men of some learning and position, this is not the case with those who conduct most of the peasant litigation. Many of these disputes might and ought to be disposed of by the village council of elders. But this body has under our legal system become so much discredited that it is very doubtful if any attempt to reconstitute it can now be successful. The boasted simplicity of our Codes has been overwhelmed in a mass of judicial precedents, and the system of justice is yearly becoming more elaborate and expensive. Besides the time lost in attending distant Courts as parties or witnesses, money is never wanting for the conduct of this trumpery, vexatious litigation which is gradually becoming a more and more serious burden upon a class ill fitted to bear it.

This is not the place to attempt a history of the measures which have been taken by the State for the protection of the peasant. So far as we know the position of the tenant under the old village constitution, a clear distinction which we have ignored, seems to have been drawn between the man who was resident and held land in his own village and he who farmed beyond the limits of his village. The latter appears to have been left to make the best terms with the alien community into which he chose to enter. The resident tenant, on the other hand, seems to have had the right to hold his field safe from disturbance so long as he paid the customary rent payable in the locality. It would have been well if this rule had been kept clearly in view by our legislators.

The Rent Code, originally passed in 1859, has been gradually revised, until in its final form it provides a fairly simple and on the whole adequate body of law regulating the relations of landlord and tenant.

To discuss, first, the main provisions of the law in force in the North-Western Provinces—it deals with four modes in which rent may be collected—by division of the ripe crop; appraisement of the landlord's share; fixed rents on special crops, such as sugar-cane or cotton; cash rents paid in a lump-sum, or on some measure of area. Payment in kind, the primitive form of rent collection, has in most places given way to cash rents. Much has been written on the results of this change of system. On the one hand, as in the Metayer system of Europe, when the landlord receives a fixed share of the produce, he is more directly concerned in the welfare of the tenant; there is an absence of the competition which tends to enhance rent; the rent is self-adjusting to meet vicissitudes of the season, and the landlord is more ready to advance seed grain and give other aid to his tenantry. On the other hand, the tenant is not so directly interested in devoting his skill and labour to the improvement of the land; he is tempted to embezzle the grain as it ripens; the landlord, if he be hostile, may cause him loss by delay in appraisement; there is extra cost and friction in watching the produce until it is divided; lastly, it gives a roguish landlord a better chance of concealing his income and evading payment of his due share of the revenue.

The law next deals with four classes of tenants. The first class is known as "tenants at fixed rates," which are found only in those districts to the east of the Province where a Permanent Settlement was introduced, as in Bengal, in the early days of our rule. Tenants whose land has been held since the Permanent Settlement (twenty years holding raising a presumption of a fixed rate tenure) by themselves or their predecessors in interest at the same rate of rent, are called "tenants at fixed rates," and are entitled to cultivate at such rates. Their rents may only be enhanced or reduced on account of a change in the area of their holdings by alluvion, diluvion or otherwise. These rights are hereditable and transferable, a concession which has naturally led to much loss of the interest by sale or mortgage.

Next come the classes known as occupancy or ex-proprietary tenants. Those whose land has been continuously occupied or cultivated for twelve years by themselves, their fathers, or those from whom they inherit, are called "occupancy tenants." Persons who lose or part with their proprietary rights have been secured the right of occupancy in their Sîr or home-farm which they held at the time of transfer and pay a rent twenty-five per cent. below that payable by tenants-at-will for similar lands. These are called "Ex-proprietary tenants." No tenant can acquire a right of occupancy in land which he holds from an Occupancy tenant, or from an Ex-proprietary tenant, or from a Tenant at fixed rates or in home-farm land, or land held by him in lieu of wages, or by including any term during which he has held under a written lease.

The rent of Occupancy tenants can be enhanced only by a written agreement duly registered, or by the order of a Settlement Officer, or of a Revenue Court, and then only under certain prescribed conditions of change in the area or value of the holding. The right of occupancy is hereditable like land; but collaterals can inherit only if they were co-sharers during the lifetime of the last incumbent. It is transferable only by voluntary transfer between co-sharers in the right and therefore cannot be sold in execution of a decree.

Such a tenant can be ejected by suit on proof of any act or omission detrimental to the land, or inconsistent with the purpose for which it was let, or which by law, custom or special agreement involves the forfeiture of the right. Any of these protected tenants may be ejected for decreed arrears of rent remaining due after the close of the year, if after receiving notice the arrear be not discharged within fifteen days.

Below these are the great masses of the unprotected tenants, the tenants-at-will, who can be summarily ejected by notice served before the beginning of the agricultural year.

In Oudh the condition of the tenant class is far less satisfactory. The strong landlord body of Talukdârs have been always opposed to any definite measures for their protection. The present Rent Law of Oudh, which is in the manner of a compromise, was introduced only after protracted negotiation between the Government and the landed interest, and can be regarded only as a temporary arrangement.

Here the ordinary tenants, who form a large proportion of the peasantry, have been so far protected that their rent cannot be enhanced for seven years after the first occupation of the holding, and then if the tenant pays a cash rent, the enhancement cannot exceed 6¼ per cent.; or if the rent be payable in kind, more than the customary rates prevailing in the locality. It is only when the landlord himself effects an improvement that he can claim an increased rent during the statutory period. But the tenant is liable to ejectment if he fail to pay his rent, sublet all his holding, use it in a way that makes it unfit for the purposes of his tenancy, or without cause, if he pays in kind, diminish the produce below the local standard.

Other elaborate provisions have been devised for the protection of those classes who possessed proprietary or sub-proprietary rights in villages which were subsequently absorbed into the great Talukdâri estates.

The following table shows the striking differences between Oudh and the sister Province as regards cultivating tenures:—

Forms of Cultivating Tenure.	Proportion of Cultivated Area.	
	North-Western Provinces.	Oudh.
Home Farm, various forms	22·5	10·3
Held with sub-proprietary or privileged rights	3·3	4·2
Held with occupancy rights	33·1	1·3
Held by proprietary and occupancy tenants without occupancy rights in addition to privileged holdings	6·7	1·4
Tenants—at will or statutory	32·8	79·7
Held rent-free or in lieu of wages	1·6	3·1

From this it is clear that the protection of the Oudh tenant is much less satisfactory than in the North-Western Provinces.

It has often been asserted that the North-Western Provinces have been the scene of a constant struggle between landlord and tenant, the one interested to prevent and the other to secure occupancy rights. This assertion is mistaken. Careful enquiries, made in 1885, showed after a review of the complete statistics that there had been a net increase of 7 per cent. in the area held by such tenants at the last settlement; that more than half the land held by tenants of all classes was protected by rights of occupancy; and that landlords generally were not seriously opposed to the accrual of such rights. Where the occupancy tenant enjoys an advantage over the tenant-at-will lies in the protection from disturbance and from constant enhancement of rent. All round, the land which he holds is of the superior class, but he pays a lower rent. In the North-Western Provinces he pays Rs. 3-14-10 per acre as against Rs. 3-14-5 paid by tenants-at-will for inferior land. In Oudh the contrast is even greater, the two classes paying respectively Rs. 2-6-0 and Rs. 4-12-10 per acre.

Sooner or later, Government must nerve itself to fix the rent with the revenue at the periodical revisions of the settlement. When the share of the produce to be paid by the landlord to the State for thirty years is definitely fixed, there seems no logical reason why the same boon should not be conferred upon the tenant. The objection always raised has been the multitude of these petty holdings and the difficulty of disposing of such a mass of litigation in a limited time. This is only a question as to the judicial establishment required. The final settlement of rents for a fairly long period would prevent the ceaseless litigation and heart-burning which result from these cases, and would free the district staff from a mass of irksome work which occupies time to the neglect of more important matters. The words of Mr Hume, written soon after the great Mutiny, are as true now as ever—"I am convinced that nothing would benefit the country at large more than the fixation of rents for a long term of years. Such a measure would do more to prevent famine and misery than all the waters of the rivers of India could they be poured over the country in the canals. The more I see the landowners of this country, the stronger is my conviction that they are not fit to be entrusted with the power and licence which have been given to them under our system. It mattered little as long as the competition was for tenants and not for the land. But for the last fifteen years the competition is the other way, and the result must be the impoverishment of the land, which is already a general complaint, and the abandonment of the mass of the people to a hopeless poverty that will always embarrass the Government and retard the progress of civilisation."

It will, in short, come to something like a ryotwâri settlement which has not been beyond the power of Provinces like Madras and Bombay.

The necessity for such a measure is emphasised by the recent revelations of the proceedings of the landlord class in Bulandshahr, and by what we know of the condition of serfage which prevails in other places. This is what Mr Smeaton, the Settlement Officer, writes of part of Rohilkhand [1]—"The peasantry of Hasanpur in Morâdâbâd are living virtually in a state of serfage. Generally speaking, as long as the tenant submits unconditionally to the will of the landlord, does not hanker after independence, does not seek to have his rent commuted into money, and cultivates his holding diligently, he may live in peace, keep his free grazing, use (but not sell) the timber on the waste, and cut as much thatch as he needs for his house and sheds. But the moment he seeks to assert his independence, dares to aspire to money rents, or to claim timber or thatch as his right, the landlord looks on him as renegade and seldom fails to crush him." Up to quite recent times a custom prevailed in northern Oudh, where people in consideration of a small advance became the bond slaves of their creditors. It was common to meet men whose fathers had incurred these

[1] *Gazetteer, North-Western Provinces*, ix. (2) p. 191.

obligations and who still laboured to discharge them, though they were well aware that the servitude could not be enforced.[1]

Many attempts have been made to frame a budget of the income and expenditure of the average cultivator. The point on which all such estimates fail is the difficulty of assigning a money value to the labour of the peasant and his family, which in most places is not a marketable commodity; secondly, it depends on individual circumstances whether the cultivator is in a position to dispose of his produce at the most opportune time, or is compelled to make it over to the village banker on more or less inadequate terms. Most of these estimates, too, were made before the era of high prices of cereals.

Thus, it was calculated at Aligarh that a five acre holding was equivalent to wages at Rs. 5 *per mensem;* in Muzaffarnagar that it would take five acres of very good land to support an ordinary family; in Cawnpur that a low caste tenant will make a profit of Rs. 46 out of the same area, a market gardener Rs. 90 out of eight acres, a really good cultivator Rs. 135 out of fifteen acres. All these estimates must be received with much caution. Agriculture and many of the village industries are very closely connected—the potter spends part of his labour in the field; the Chamâr or currier will in addition to his special work do day labour, cultivate, and so on. What the wife and children contribute to the common stock either by independent labour or by the herbs and wild fruit, fuel, or manure that they can collect is always a variable quantity, and the factors are so diverse that any precise calculation is impossible.

They do exist and multiply on most minute areas—so much is certain. To bring this fact out accurately from the Census figures is not easy, because the occupation of agriculture cannot be readily separated from other industries. With this qualification, comparing the number of persons who have an "interest in land" with the net area cultivated, we find that in Aligarh the land per head is 2·1 acres; in

[1] *Oudh Gazetteer*, i. 145.

Bareilly 1·4, and in Ballia to the extreme east ·9 of an acre.

The information as to the size of the average agricultural holding is more precise. This is in Aligarh 9 acres; in Bareilly each occupancy tenant holds 4·7 acres, each tenant-at-will 2·3 acres; in Cawnpur each cultivator holds 3½ acres. We have to go to Belgium to find any analogy to these figures. There out of every hundred farmers, 43·24 per cent. hold less than fifty acres; 12·3 per cent. less than one hectare (2 acres, 1 rood, 3½ perches); and 28·99 per cent. land not exceeding 5 hectares; only 8 per cent. cultivate more than 10 hectares. On this M. Lavelaye remarks[1]—"The subdivision of land is not quite an ideal to propose to modern society, for it demands of man redoubled exertion and labour but little compatible with the development of his intellectual faculties; but it can be affirmed that up to this time the results in Flanders have proved advantageous, at least as far as production and rents are concerned."

Why the condition of the peasant of Northern India is so much below that of his Flemish brethren is perhaps mainly due to the fact that the latter combine with farming other industries, such as dairy management, fruit growing, and the rearing of poultry, which, with the English market close by, must be exceedingly profitable. This combination of industries does not prevail in Indian farming. Dairy work is confined to the making of Ghi, and no pains are taken to prepare a superior article; it is sold as it is made to the village Banya or even the produce is mortgaged in advance. The fowl is regarded nearly as impure as the pig, and the rearing of both is confined to the menial castes; here, again, there is no pretence of care or scientific breeding. The growth of fruit or vegetables is hardly an industry of the ordinary peasant; it is specialised by the market gardener castes. Even the neighbourhood of a city gives little healthy stimulus to this petite culture; it merely attracts to the bâzâr fuel and fodder which would be used to more real advantage at home. The strings of women and children with their bundles of grass

[1] *Report on Tenure of Land in Europe*, pp. 107, 110.

or fuel cakes whom one sees plodding along the dusty roads near the towns imply the gradual exhaustion of their lands. But the chief distinction between the Indian and the Flemish peasant is that the one possesses capital and has savings to invest in land and other speculations; the other lives from hand to mouth: if he has a rupee to spare he invests it unproductively in jewellery or simply hoards it.

The only real improvement ever carried out is the building of wells and the excavation of tanks. Of the latter we have already spoken. The former represents a large expenditure in labour and capital. We can realise this from the case of Oudh. Here there are no artificial canals, but still 21 per cent. of the cultivated area is irrigated as compared with 24 per cent. in the sister Province. The peasant believes in the superior value of well water as compared with canal irrigation, and here, as in many other instances, scientific investigation has shown the soundness of his faith. "Repeated applications of well water are equivalent to a manuring with readily soluble salts, such as nitrate of soda, carbonate of soda, common salt, and salts of magnesia."[1] It is not easy to realise the extent to which wells have been constructed. In one district, that of Azamgarh, there are twenty-four thousand masonry wells, half of which are used for irrigation. Each well irrigates fourteen acres. But this does not fully represent the degree to which they are used in seasons of scanty rainfall. In such years the lever well worked by human labour alone approaches that average, while the area watered from buckets drawn by oxen is probably little less than twenty-five acres.

The village well is the chief centre of social life. All through the morning hours it is thronged by crowds of merry girls in bright dresses and glittering jewels, who laugh and chatter, flirt and gossip, while the boy sings to his oxen as they wearily descend the slope and the rough pulley creaks and the water splashes in the sunshine, and the pure stream trickles into the thirsty fields, where a woman diverts the current from one tiny patch to another. Here comes the wandering beggar to drink, and tells the news of far distant

[1] Voelcker, *Report*, p. 78.

lands, and accompanied by her friends the mother, safe over the troubles of maternity, brings her brown baby and reverently walks round the platform in the course of the sun, smearing the brickwork as she goes with splashes of vermilion. There the Brâhman bathes amid the noisy crowd and draws a little water which, with a few flowers, forms his daily offering to the neighbouring lingam shrine.

While, then, among the more advanced cultivating tribes this petite culture provides much moderate prosperity over a considerable area, among the less industrious races its evils are apparent. It needs a peasantry of stronger fibre than many of the inhabitants of the great Indian Plain to practise that stern economy and unceasing industry, that power of utilising all the products of the soil, which makes it so successful a social institution in Belgium and France, that our statesmen long to see it extended to the rural districts of Great Britain and Ireland. But small farms, except under the most favourable conditions, where choice products can be grown for a profitable market, must in the long run fail to secure for the tenant more than a mere subsistence. The Jât or Kâchhi makes his little plot pay, because the one grows the finest wheat and sugar and keeps a brood mare or two; the latter, because he produces opium and vegetables. Without the advantage of such industries the ordinary tenant must waste labour on growing comparatively unremunerative corn crops for food; he must work with inferior machines and half-starved cattle. The true blessing of the best form of peasant proprietary can never fall to his lot.

The problems before the statesmen of Europe and India are thus essentially different. The former aims at restoring a social state which has almost disappeared; to re-establish the yeoman in his cottage and thus check the emigration of rural labour to the towns. The other has the peasant farm, the three acres and a cow, ready made. What he wants to secure is more protection to the yeoman from the oppression of the landlord and from the stress of rents forced up by competition; to develop a more intelligent rule of trade, by which the produce can be disposed of direct without the intervention of that shark, the Banya middleman; to free the yeoman from the bondage of the usurer, and divert more of the capital of the country, at easier rates, into the cultivation of these little five-acre plots.

The first steps towards attaining these ends must be to make tenure, particularly in Oudh, more secure; to limit the enhancements of revenue at the periodical revisions of settlement; to devise means for fixing rents *pari passu* with the revenue assessments; to lose no opportunities of spreading a more scientific knowledge of agriculture, and, in particular, of the conservancy of manure among the masses; to reduce the cost and attractiveness of litigation; to popularise State advances; and, by improvement of the police and revenue establishments, to relieve the people from petty forms of oppression. The peasant, with his pair of lean oxen and rude plough, is the pillar of the Empire, and our task in India is only half done as long as we neglect any feasible methods for advancing his interests.

INDEX

INDEX

INDEX

INDEX

INDEX

A CATALOGUE OF BOOKS AND ANNOUNCEMENTS OF METHUEN AND COMPANY PUBLISHERS : LONDON 36 ESSEX STREET W.C.

CONTENTS

NOVEMBER 1896

NOVEMBER 1896.

MESSRS. METHUEN'S ANNOUNCEMENTS

Poetry

RUDYARD KIPLING

THE SEVEN SEAS. By RUDYARD KIPLING. *Crown 8vo.* 6*s.*

150 copies on hand-made paper. *Demy 8vo.* 21*s.*

30 copies on Japanese paper. *Demy 8vo.* 42*s.*

The enormous success of 'Barrack Room Ballads' justifies the expectation that this volume, so long postponed, will have an equal, if not a greater, success.

GEORGE WYNDHAM

SHAKESPEARE'S POEMS. Edited, with an Introduction and Notes, by GEORGE WYNDHAM, M.P. *Crown 8vo.* 3*s.* 6*d.*

[*English Classics.*

W. E. HENLEY

ENGLISH LYRICS. Selected and Edited by W. E. HENLEY. *Crown 8vo. Buckram.* 6*s.*

Also 15 copies on Japanese paper. *Demy 8vo.* £2, 2*s.*

Few announcements will be more welcome to lovers of English verse than the one that Mr. Henley is bringing together into one book the finest lyrics in our language. The volume will be produced with the same care that made 'Lyra Heroica' delightful to the hand and eye.

'Q'

POEMS AND BALLADS. By 'Q,' Author of 'Green Bays, etc. *Crown 8vo. Buckram.* 3*s.* 6*d.*

History, Biography, and Travel

CAPTAIN HINDE

THE FALL OF THE CONGO ARABS. By SIDNEY L. HINDE. With Portraits and Plans. *Demy 8vo.* 12*s.* 6*d.*

This volume deals with the recent Belgian Expedition to the Upper Congo, which developed into a war between the State forces and the Arab slave-raiders in Central Africa. Two white men only returned alive from the three years' war—Commandant Dhanis and the writer of this book, Captain Hinde. During the greater part of the time spent by Captain Hinde in the Congo he was amongst cannibal races in little-known regions, and, owing to the peculiar circumstances of his position, was enabled to see a side of native history shown to few Europeans. The war terminated in the complete defeat of the Arabs, seventy thousand of whom perished during the struggle.

S. BARING GOULD

THE LIFE OF NAPOLEON BONAPARTE. By S. BARING GOULD. With over 450 Illustrations in the Text and 13 Photogravure Plates. *Large quarto.* 36*s.*

This study of the most extraordinary life in history is written rather for the general reader than for the military student, and while following the main lines of Napoleon's career, is concerned chiefly with the development of his character and his personal qualities. Special stress is laid on his early life—the period in which his mind and character took their definite shape and direction.

The great feature of the book is its wealth of illustration. There are over 450 illustrations, large and small, in the text, and there are also more than a dozen full page photogravures. Every important incident of Napoleon's career has its illustration, while there are a large number of portraits of his contemporaries, reproductions of famous pictures, of contemporary caricatures, of his handwriting, etc. etc.

It is not too much to say that no such magnificent book on Napoleon has ever been published.

VICTOR HUGO

THE LETTERS OF VICTOR HUGO. Translated from the French by F. CLARKE, M.A. *In Two Volumes. Demy 8vo.* 10*s.* 6*d. each. Vol. I.* 1815-35.

This is the first volume of one of the most interesting and important collection of letters ever published in France. The correspondence dates from Victor Hugo's boyhood to his death, and none of the letters have been published before. The arrangement is chiefly chronological, but where there is an interesting set of letters to one person these are arranged together. The first volume contains, among others, (1) Letters to his father; (2) to his young wife; (3) to his confessor, Lamennais; (4) a very important set of about fifty letters to Sainte-Beuve; (5) letters about his early books and plays.

J. M. RIGG

ST. ANSELM OF CANTERBURY: A CHAPTER IN THE HISTORY OF RELIGION. By J. M. RIGG, of Lincoln's Inn, Barrister-at-Law. *Demy 8vo.* 7*s.* 6*d.*

This work gives for the first time in moderate compass a complete portrait of St. Anselm, exhibiting him in his intimate and interior as well as in his public life. Thus, while the great ecclesiastico-political struggle in which he played so prominent a part is fully dealt with, unusual prominence is given to the profound and subtle speculations by which he permanently influenced theological and metaphysical thought; while it will be a surprise to most readers to find him also appearing as the author of some of the most exquisite religious poetry in the Latin language.

EDWARD GIBBON

THE DECLINE AND FALL OF THE ROMAN EMPIRE. By EDWARD GIBBON. A New Edition, edited with Notes, Appendices, and Maps by J. B. BURY, M.A., Fellow of Trinity College, Dublin. *In Seven Volumes. Demy 8vo, gilt top.* 8*s* 6*d each. Crown 8vo.* 6*s. each. Vol. II.*

W. M. FLINDERS PETRIE

A HISTORY OF EGYPT, FROM THE EARLIEST TIMES TO THE PRESENT DAY. Edited by W. M. FLINDERS PETRIE, D.C.L., LL.D., Professor of Egyptology at University College. *Fully Illustrated. In Six Volumes. Crown 8vo. 6s. each.*

Vol. II. XVII.-XVIII. DYNASTIES. W. M. F. PETRIE.

'A history written in the spirit of scientific precision so worthily represented by Dr. Petrie and his school cannot but promote sound and accurate study, and supply a vacant place in the English literature of Egyptology.'—*Times.*

J. WELLS

A SHORT HISTORY OF ROME. By J. WELLS, M.A., Fellow and Tutor of Wadham Coll , Oxford. With 4 Maps. *Crown 8vo. 3s. 6d. 350 pp.*

This book is intended for the Middle and Upper Forms of Public Schools and for Pass Students at the Universities. It contains copious Tables, etc.

H. DE B. GIBBINS

ENGLISH INDUSTRY: HISTORICAL OUTLINES. By H. DE B. GIBBINS, M.A. With 5 Maps. *Demy 8vo. 10s. 6d. Pp.* 450.

This book is written with the view of affording a clear view of the main facts of English Social and Industrial History placed in due perspective. Beginning with prehistoric times, it passes in review the growth and advance of industry up to the nineteenth century, showing its gradual development and progress. The author has endeavoured to place before his readers the history of industry as a connected whole in which all these developments have their proper place. The book is illustrated by Maps, Diagrams, and Tables, and aided by copious Footnotes.

MRS. OLIPHANT

THOMAS CHALMERS. By Mrs. OLIPHANT. *Second Edition. Crown 8vo. 3s. 6d.* [*Leaders of Religion.*

Naval and Military

DAVID HANNAY

A SHORT HISTORY OF THE ROYAL NAVY, FROM EARLY TIMES TO THE PRESENT DAY. By DAVID HANNAY. *Illustrated. Demy 8vo.* 15*s.*

This book aims at giving an account not only of the fighting we have done at sea, but of the growth of the service, of the part the Navy has played in the development of the Empire, and of its inner life. The author has endeavoured to avoid the mistake of sacrificing the earlier periods of naval history—the very interesting wars with Holland in the seventeenth century, for instance, or the American War of 1779-1783—to the later struggle with Revolutionary and Imperial France.

COL. COOPER KING

A SHORT HISTORY OF THE BRITISH ARMY. By Lieut.-Colonel COOPER KING, of the Staff College, Camberley. *Illustrated. Demy 8vo.* 7s. 6d.

This volume aims at describing the nature of the different armies that have been formed in Great Britain, and how from the early and feudal levies the present standing army came to be. The changes in tactics, uniform, and armament are briefly touched upon, and, the campaigns in which the army has shared have been so far followed as to explain the part played by British regiments in them.

G. W. STEEVENS

NAVAL POLICY: WITH A DESCRIPTION OF ENGLISH AND FOREIGN NAVIES. By G. W. STEEVENS. *Demy 8vo.* 6s.

This book is a description of the British and other more important navies of the world, with a sketch of the lines on which our naval policy might possibly be developed. It describes our recent naval policy, and shows what our naval force really is. A detailed but non-technical account is given of the instruments of modern warfare—guns, armour, engines, and the like—with a view to determine how far we are abreast of modern invention and modern requirements. An ideal policy is then sketched for the building and manning of our fleet; and the last chapter is devoted to docks, coaling-stations, and especially colonial defence.

Theology

F. B. JEVONS

AN INTRODUCTION TO THE HISTORY OF RELIGION. By F. B. JEVONS, M.A., Litt.D., Tutor at the University of Durham. *Demy 8vo.* 10s. 6d.

This is the third number of the series of 'Theological Handbooks' edited by Dr. Robertson of Durham, in which have already appeared Dr. Gibson's 'XXXIX. Articles' and Mr. Ottley's 'Incarnation.'

Mr. F. B. Jevons' 'Introduction to the History of Religion' treats of early religion, from the point of view of Anthropology and Folk-lore; and is the first attempt that has been made in any language to weave together the results of recent investigations into such topics as Sympathetic Magic, Taboo, Totemism, Fetishism, etc., so as to present a systematic account of the growth of primitive religion and the development of early religious institutions.

W. YORKE FAUSSETT

THE *DE CATECHIZANDIS RUDIBUS* OF ST. AUGUSTINE. Edited, with Introduction, Notes, etc., by W. YORKE FAUSSETT, M.A., late Scholar of Balliol Coll. *Crown 8vo.* 3s. 6d.

An edition of a Treatise on the Essentials of Christian Doctrine, and the best methods of impressing them on candidates for baptism. The editor bestows upon this patristic work the same care which a treatise of Cicero might claim. There is a general Introduction, a careful Analysis, a full Commentary, and other useful matter. No better introduction to the study of the Latin Fathers, their style and diction, could be found than this treatise, which also has no lack of modern interest.

General Literature

C. F. ANDREWS

CHRISTIANITY AND THE LABOUR QUESTION. By C. F. ANDREWS, B.A. *Crown 8vo.* 2*s.* 6*d.*

R. E. STEEL

MAGNETISM AND ELECTRICITY. By R. ELLIOTT STEEL, M.A., F.C.S. With Illustrations. *Crown 8vo.* 4*s.* 6*d.*

G. LOWES DICKINSON

THE GREEK VIEW OF LIFE. By G. L. DICKINSON, Fellow of King's College, Cambridge. *Crown 8vo.* 2*s.* 6*d.* [*University Extension Series.*

J. A. HOBSON

THE PROBLEM OF THE UNEMPLOYED. By J. A. HOBSON, B.A., Author of 'The Problems of Poverty.' *Crown 8vo.* 2*s.* 6*d.* [*Social Questions Series.*

S. E. BALLY

GERMAN COMMERCIAL CORRESPONDENCE. By S. E. BALLY, Assistant Master at the Manchester Grammar School. *Crown 8vo.* 2*s.* 6*d.* [*Commercial Series.*

L. F. PRICE

ECONOMIC ESSAYS. By L. F. PRICE, M.A., Fellow of Oriel College, Oxford. *Crown 8vo.* 6*s.*

This book consists of a number of Studies in Economics and Industrial and Social Problems.

Fiction

MARIE CORELLI'S ROMANCES

FIRST COMPLETE AND UNIFORM EDITION

Large crown 8vo. 6*s.*

MESSRS. METHUEN beg to announce that they have commenced the publication of a New and Uniform Edition of MARIE CORELLI'S Romances. This Edition is revised by the Author, and contains new Prefaces. The volumes are being issued at short intervals in the following order:—

1. A ROMANCE OF TWO WORLDS.
2. VENDETTA.
3. THELMA.
4. ARDATH.
5. THE SOUL OF LILITH.
6. WORMWOOD.
7. BARABBAS.
8. THE SORROWS OF SATAN.

M. A. OWEN

THE DAUGHTER OF ALOUETTE. By MARY A. OWEN. *Crown 8vo.* 6*s.*

A story of life among the American Indians.

RONALD ROSS

THE SPIRIT OF STORM. By RONALD ROSS, Author of 'The Child of Ocean.' *Crown 8vo.* 6*s.*

A romance of the Sea.

J. A. BARRY

IN THE GREAT DEEP: TALES OF THE SEA. By J. A. BARRY. Author of 'Steve Brown's Bunyip.' *Crown 8vo.* 6*s.*

JAMES GORDON

THE VILLAGE AND THE DOCTOR. By JAMES GORDON. *Crown 8vo.* 6*s.*

BERTRAM MITFORD

THE SIGN OF THE SPIDER. By BERTRAM MITFORD. *Crown 8vo.* 3*s.* 6*d.*

A story of South Africa.

A. SHIELD

THE SQUIRE OF WANDALES. By A. SHIELD. *Crown 8vo.* 3*s.* 6*d.*

G. W. STEEVENS

MONOLOGUES OF THE DEAD. By G. W. STEEVENS. *Foolscap 8vo.* 3*s.* 6*d.*

A series of Soliloquies in which famous men of antiquity—Julius Cæsar, Nero, Alcibiades, etc., attempt to express themselves in the modes of thought and language of to-day.

S. GORDON

A HANDFUL OF EXOTICS. By S. GORDON. *Crown 8vo.* 3*s.* 6*d.*

A volume of stories of Jewish life in Russia.

P. NEUMANN

THE SUPPLANTER. By P. NEUMANN. *Crown 8vo.* 3*s.* 6*d.*

EVELYN DICKINSON

THE SIN OF ANGELS. By EVELYN DICKINSON. *Crown 8vo.* 3*s.* 6*d.*

H. A. KENNEDY

A MAN WITH BLACK EYELASHES. By H. A. KENNEDY. *Crown 8vo.* 3*s.* 6*d.*

A LIST OF

MESSRS. METHUEN'S PUBLICATIONS

Poetry

Rudyard Kipling. BARRACK-ROOM BALLADS; And Other Verses. By RUDYARD KIPLING. *Ninth Edition. Crown 8vo.* 6*s.*

'Mr. Kipling's verse is strong, vivid, full of character. . . . Unmistakable genius rings in every line.'—*Times.*

'"Barrack-Room Ballads" contains some of the best work that Mr. Kipling has ever done, which is saying a good deal. "Fuzzy-Wuzzy," "Gunga Din," and "Tommy," are, in our opinion, altogether superior to anything of the kind that English literature has hitherto produced.'—*Athenæum.*

'The ballads teem with imagination, they palpitate with emotion. We read them with laughter and tears; the metres throb in our pulses, the cunningly ordered words tingle with life; and if this be not poetry, what is?'—*Pall Mall Gazette.*

"Q." THE GOLDEN POMP: A Procession of English Lyrics from Surrey to Shirley, arranged by A. T. QUILLER COUCH. *Crown 8vo. Buckram.* 6*s.*

'A delightful volume: a really golden "Pomp."'—*Spectator.*

"Q." GREEN BAYS: Verses and Parodies. By "Q.," Author of 'Dead Man's Rock,' etc. *Second Edition. Crown 8vo.* 3*s.* 6*d.*

'The verses display a rare and versatile gift of parody, great command of metre, and a very pretty turn of humour.'—*Times.*

H. C. Beeching. LYRA SACRA: An Anthology of Sacred Verse. Edited by H. C. BEECHING, M.A. *Crown 8vo. Buckram.* 6*s.*

'An anthology of high excellence.'—*Athenæum.*

'A charming selection, which maintains a lofty standard of excellence.'—*Times.*

W. B. Yeats. AN ANTHOLOGY OF IRISH VERSE. Edited by W. B. YEATS. *Crown 8vo.* 3*s.* 6*d.*

'An attractive and catholic selection.'—*Times.*

'It is edited by the most original and most accomplished of modern Irish poets, and against his editing but a single objection can be brought, namely, that it excludes from the collection his own delicate lyrics.'—*Saturday Review.*

E. Mackay. A SONG OF THE SEA: MY LADY OF DREAMS, AND OTHER POEMS. By ERIC MACKAY, Author of 'The Love Letters of a Violinist.' *Second Edition. Fcap. 8vo, gilt top.* 5*s.*

'Everywhere Mr. Mackay displays himself the master of a style marked by all the characteristics of the best rhetoric. He has a keen sense of rhythm and of general balance; his verse is excellently sonorous.'—*Globe.*

'Throughout the book the poetic workmanship is fine.'—*Scotsman.*

Ibsen. BRAND. A Drama by HENRIK IBSEN. Translated by WILLIAM WILSON. *Second Edition. Crown 8vo.* 3*s*. 6*d*.

'The greatest world-poem of the nineteenth century next to "Faust." It is in the same set with "Agamemnon," with "Lear," with the literature that we now instinctively regard as high and holy.'—*Daily Chronicle.*

"A. G." VERSES TO ORDER. By "A. G." *Cr. 8vo.* 2*s*. 6*d*. *net.*

A small volume of verse by a writer whose initials are well known to Oxford men.

'A capital specimen of light academic poetry. These verses are very bright and engaging, easy and sufficiently witty.'—*St. James's Gazette.*

F. Langbridge. BALLADS OF THE BRAVE: Poems of Chivalry, Enterprise, Courage, and Constancy, from the Earliest Times to the Present Day. Edited, with Notes, by Rev. F. LANGBRIDGE. *Crown 8vo. Buckram.* 3*s*. 6*d*. *School Edition.* 2*s*. 6*d*.

'A very happy conception happily carried out. These "Ballads of the Brave" are intended to suit the real tastes of boys, and will suit the taste of the great majority.'—*Spectator.* 'The book is full of splendid things.'—*World.*

Lang and Craigie. THE POEMS OF ROBERT BURNS. Edited by ANDREW LANG and W. A. CRAIGIE. With Portrait. *Demy 8vo, gilt top.* 6*s*.

This edition contains a carefully collated Text, numerous Notes, critical and textual, a critical and biographical Introduction, and a Glossary.

'Among the editions in one volume, Mr. Andrew Lang's will take the place of authority.'—*Times.*

'To the general public the beauty of its type, and the fair proportions of its pages, as well as the excellent chronological arrangement of the poems, should make it acceptable enough. Mr. Lang and his publishers have certainly succeeded in producing an attractive popular edition of the poet, in which the brightly written biographical introduction is not the least notable feature.'—*Glasgow Herald.*

English Classics

Edited by W. E. HENLEY.

'Very dainty volumes are these; the paper, type, and light-green binding are all very agreeable to the eye. *Simplex munditiis* is the phrase that might be applied to them.'—*Globe.*

'The volumes are strongly bound in green buckram, are of a convenient size, and pleasant to look upon, so that whether on the shelf, or on the table, or in the hand the possessor is thoroughly content with them.'—*Guardian.*

'The paper, type, and binding of this edition are in excellent taste, and leave nothing to be desired by lovers of literature.'—*Standard.*

THE LIFE AND OPINIONS OF TRISTRAM SHANDY. By LAWRENCE STERNE. With an Introduction by CHARLES WHIBLEY, and a Portrait. *2 vols.* 7*s*.

THE COMEDIES OF WILLIAM CONGREVE. With an Introduction by G. S. STREET, and a Portrait. *2 vols.* 7*s*.

THE ADVENTURES OF HAJJI BABA OF ISPAHAN. By JAMES MORIER. With an Introduction by E. G. BROWNE, M.A., and a Portrait. *2 vols.* 7*s.*

THE LIVES OF DONNE, WOTTON, HOOKER, HERBERT, AND SANDERSON. By IZAAK WALTON. With an Introduction by VERNON BLACKBURN, and a Portrait. 3*s.* 6*d.*

THE LIVES OF THE ENGLISH POETS. By SAMUEL JOHNSON, LL.D. With an Introduction by J. H. MILLAR, and a Portrait. 3 *vols.* 10*s.* 6*d.*

Illustrated Books

Jane Barlow. THE BATTLE OF THE FROGS AND MICE, translated by JANE BARLOW, Author of 'Irish Idylls,' and pictured by F. D. BEDFORD. *Small 4to.* 6*s. net.*

S. Baring Gould. A BOOK OF FAIRY TALES retold by S. BARING GOULD. With numerous illustrations and initial letters by ARTHUR J. GASKIN. *Second Edition. Crown 8vo. Buckram.* 6*s.*

'Mr. Baring Gould has done a good deed, and is deserving of gratitude, in re-writing in honest, simple style the old stories that delighted the childhood of "our fathers and grandfathers." We do not think he has omitted any of our favourite stories, the stories that are commonly regarded as merely "old fashioned." As to the form of the book, and the printing, which is by Messrs. Constable, it were difficult to commend overmuch.—*Saturday Review.*

S. Baring Gould. OLD ENGLISH FAIRY TALES. Collected and edited by S. BARING GOULD. With Numerous Illustrations by F. D. BEDFORD. *Second Edition. Crown 8vo. Buckram.* 6*s.*

'A charming volume, which children will be sure to appreciate. The stories have been selected with great ingenuity from various old ballads and folk-tales, and, having been somewhat altered and readjusted, now stand forth, clothed in Mr. Baring Gould's delightful English, to enchant youthful readers. All the tales are good.'—*Guardian.*

S. Baring Gould. A BOOK OF NURSERY SONGS AND RHYMES. Edited by S. BARING GOULD, and Illustrated by the Birmingham Art School. *Buckram, gilt top. Crown 8vo.* 6s.

'The volume is very complete in its way, as it contains nursery songs to the number of 77, game-rhymes, and jingles. To the student we commend the sensible introduction, and the explanatory notes. The volume is superbly printed on soft, thick paper, which it is a pleasure to touch; and the borders and pictures are, as we have said, among the very best specimens we have seen of the Gaskin school.' —*Birmingham Gazette.*

H. C. Beeching. A BOOK OF CHRISTMAS VERSE. Edited by H. C. BEECHING, M.A., and Illustrated by WALTER CRANE. *Crown 8vo, gilt top.* 5*s.*

A collection of the best verse inspired by the birth of Christ from the Middle Ages to the present day. A distinction of the book is the large number of poems it contains by modern authors, a few of which are here printed for the first time.

'An anthology which, from its unity of aim and high poetic excellence, has a better right to exist than most of its fellows.'—*Guardian.*

History

Gibbon. THE DECLINE AND FALL OF THE ROMAN EMPIRE. By EDWARD GIBBON. A New Edition, Edited with Notes, Appendices, and Maps, by J. B. BURY, M.A., Fellow of Trinity College, Dublin. *In Seven Volumes. Demy 8vo. Gilt top.* 8*s.* 6*d. each. Also crown 8vo.* 6*s. each. Vol. I.*

'The time has certainly arrived for a new edition of Gibbon's great work. . . . Professor Bury is the right man to undertake this task. His learning is amazing, both in extent and accuracy. The book is issued in a handy form, and at a moderate price, and it is admirably printed.'—*Times.*

'The edition is edited as a classic should be edited, removing nothing, yet indicating the value of the text, and bringing it up to date. It promises to be of the utmost value, and will be a welcome addition to many libraries.'—*Scotsman.*

'This edition, so far as one may judge from the first instalment, is a marvel of erudition and critical skill, and it is the very minimum of praise to predict that the seven volumes of it will supersede Dean Milman's as the standard edition of our great historical classic.'—*Glasgow Herald.*

'The beau-ideal Gibbon has arrived at last.'—*Sketch.*

'At last there is an adequate modern edition of Gibbon. . . . The best edition the nineteenth century could produce.'—*Manchester Guardian.*

Flinders Petrie. A HISTORY OF EGYPT, FROM THE EARLIEST TIMES TO THE PRESENT DAY. Edited by W. M. FLINDERS PETRIE, D.C.L., LL.D., Professor of Egyptology at University College. *Fully Illustrated. In Six Volumes. Crown 8vo.* 6*s. each.*

Vol. I. PREHISTORIC TIMES TO XVI. DYNASTY. W. M. F. Petrie. *Second Edition.*

'A history written in the spirit of scientific precision so worthily represented by Dr. Petrie and his school cannot but promote sound and accurate study, and supply a vacant place in the English literature of Egyptology.'—*Times.*

Flinders Petrie. EGYPTIAN TALES. Edited by W. M. FLINDERS PETRIE. Illustrated by TRISTRAM ELLIS. *In Two Volumes. Crown 8vo.* 3*s.* 6*d. each.*

'A valuable addition to the literature of comparative folk-lore. The drawings are really illustrations in the literal sense of the word.'—*Globe.*

'It has a scientific value to the student of history and archæology.'—*Scotsman.*

'Invaluable as a picture of life in Palestine and Egypt.'—*Daily News.*

Flinders Petrie. EGYPTIAN DECORATIVE ART. By W. M. FLINDERS PETRIE, D.C.L. With 120 Illustrations. *Crown 8vo.* 3*s.* 6*d.*

'Professor Flinders Petrie is not only a profound Egyptologist, but an accomplished student of comparative archæology. In these lectures, delivered at the Royal Institution, he displays both qualifications with rare skill in elucidating the development of decorative art in Egypt, and in tracing its influence on the art of other countries. Few experts can speak with higher authority and wider knowledge than the Professor himself, and in any case his treatment of his subject is full of learning and insight.'—*Times.*

S. Baring Gould. THE TRAGEDY OF THE CÆSARS. The Emperors of the Julian and Claudian Lines. With numerous Illustrations from Busts, Gems, Cameos, etc. By S. BARING GOULD, Author of 'Mehalah,' etc. *Third Edition. Royal 8vo.* 15*s.*

'A most splendid and fascinating book on a subject of undying interest. The great feature of the book is the use the author has made of the existing portraits of the Caesars, and the admirable critical subtlety he has exhibited in dealing with this line of research. It is brilliantly written, and the illustrations are supplied on a scale of profuse magnificence.'—*Daily Chronicle.*

'The volumes will in no sense disappoint the general reader. Indeed, in their way, there is nothing in any sense so good in English. . . . Mr. Baring Gould has presented his narrative in such a way as not to make one dull page.'—*Athenæum.*

A. Clark. THE COLLEGES OF OXFORD: Their History, their Traditions. By Members of the University. Edited by A. CLARK, M.A., Fellow and Tutor of Lincoln College. *8vo.* 12*s.* 6*d.*

'A work which will certainly be appealed to for many years as the standard book on the Colleges of Oxford.'—*Athenæum.*

Perrens. THE HISTORY OF FLORENCE FROM 1434 TO 1492. By F. T. PERRENS. Translated by HANNAH LYNCH. *8vo.* 12*s.* 6*d.*

A history of Florence under the domination of Cosimo, Piero, and Lorenzo de Medicis.

'This is a standard book by an honest and intelligent historian, who has deserved well of all who are interested in Italian history.'—*Manchester Guardian.*

E. L. S. Horsburgh. THE CAMPAIGN OF WATERLOO. By E. L. S. HORSBURGH, B.A. *With Plans. Crown 8vo.* 5*s.*

'A brilliant essay—simple, sound, and thorough.'—*Daily Chronicle.*

'A study, the most concise, the most lucid, the most critical that has been produced.' —*Birmingham Mercury.*

'A careful and precise study, a fair and impartial criticism, and an eminently readable book.'—*Admiralty and Horse Guards Gazette.*

H. B. George. BATTLES OF ENGLISH HISTORY. By H. B. GEORGE, M.A., Fellow of New College, Oxford. *With numerous Plans. Third Edition. Crown 8vo.* 6*s.*

'Mr. George has undertaken a very useful task—that of making military affairs intelligible and instructive to non-military readers—and has executed it with laudable intelligence and industry, and with a large measure of success.'—*Times.*

'This book is almost a revelation; and we heartily congratulate the author on his work and on the prospect of the reward he has well deserved for so much conscientious and sustained labour.'—*Daily Chronicle.*

O. Browning. A SHORT HISTORY OF MEDIÆVAL ITALY, A.D. 1250-1530. By OSCAR BROWNING, Fellow and Tutor of King's College, Cambridge. *Second Edition. In Two Volumes. Crown 8vo.* 5*s. each.*

VOL. I. 1250-1409.—Guelphs and Ghibellines.
VOL. II. 1409-1530.—The Age of the Condottieri.

'A vivid picture of mediæval Italy.'—*Standard.*

'Mr. Browning is to be congratulated on the production of a work of immense labour and learning.'—*Westminster Gazette.*

O'Grady. THE STORY OF IRELAND. By STANDISH O'GRADY, Author of 'Finn and his Companions.' *Cr. 8vo.* 2*s.* 6*d.*

'Most delightful, most stimulating. Its racy humour, its original imaginings, make it one of the freshest, breeziest volumes.'—*Methodist Times.*

'A survey at once graphic, acute, and quaintly written.'—*Times.*

Biography

R. L. Stevenson. VAILIMA LETTERS. By ROBERT LOUIS STEVENSON. With an Etched Portrait by WILLIAM STRANG, and other Illustrations. *Second Edition. Crown 8vo. Buckram.* 7*s.* 6*d.*

'The Vailima Letters are rich in all the varieties of that charm which have secured for Stevenson the affection of many others besides "journalists, fellow-novelists, and boys."'—*The Times.*

'Few publications have in our time been more eagerly awaited than these "Vailima Letters," giving the first fruits of the correspondence of Robert Louis Stevenson. But, high as the tide of expectation has run, no reader can possibly be disappointed in the result.'—*St. James's Gazette.*

'For the student of English literature these letters indeed are a treasure. They are more like "Scott's Journal" in kind than any other literary autobiography.'—*National Observer.*

F. W. Joyce. THE LIFE OF SIR FREDERICK GORE OUSELEY. By F. W. JOYCE, M.A. With Portraits and Illustrations. *Crown 8vo.* 7*s.* 6*d.*

'All the materials have been well digested, and the book gives us a complete picture of the life of one who will ever be held in loving remembrance by his personal friends, and who in the history of music in this country will always occupy a prominent position on account of the many services he rendered to the art.'—*Musical News.*

'This book has been undertaken in quite the right spirit, and written with sympathy, insight, and considerable literary skill.'—*Times.*

W. G. Collingwood. THE LIFE OF JOHN RUSKIN. By W. G. COLLINGWOOD, M.A., Editor of Mr. Ruskin's Poems. With numerous Portraits, and 13 Drawings by Mr. Ruskin. *Second Edition. 2 vols. 8vo.* 32*s.*

'No more magnificent volumes have been published for a long time.'—*Times.*

'It is long since we had a biography with such delights of substance and of form. Such a book is a pleasure for the day, and a joy for ever.'—*Daily Chronicle.*

'A noble monument of a noble subject. One of the most beautiful books about one of the noblest lives of our century.'—*Glasgow Herald.*

C. Waldstein. JOHN RUSKIN: a Study. By CHARLES WALDSTEIN, M.A., Fellow of King's College, Cambridge. With a Photogravure Portrait after Professor HERKOMER. *Post 8vo.* 5*s.*

'A thoughtful, impartial, well-written criticism of Ruskin's teaching, intended to separate what the author regards as valuable and permanent from what is transient and erroneous in the great master's writing.'—*Daily Chronicle.*

W. H. Hutton. THE LIFE OF SIR THOMAS MORE. By W. H. HUTTON, M.A., Author of 'William Laud.' *With Portraits. Crown 8vo.* 5*s.*

'The book lays good claim to high rank among our biographies. It is excellently, even lovingly, written.'—*Scotsman.*
'An excellent monograph.'—*Times.*
'A most complete presentation.'—*Daily Chronicle.*

M. Kaufmann. CHARLES KINGSLEY. By M. KAUFMANN, M.A. *Crown 8vo. Buckram.* 5*s.*

A biography of Kingsley, especially dealing with his achievements in social reform.
'The author has certainly gone about his work with conscientiousness and industry. —*Sheffield Daily Telegraph.*

A. F. Robbins. THE EARLY PUBLIC LIFE OF WILLIAM EWART GLADSTONE. By A. F. ROBBINS. *With Portraits. Crown 8vo.* 6*s.*

'Considerable labour and much skill of presentation have not oeen unworthily expended on this interesting work.'—*Times.*

Clark Russell. THE LIFE OF ADMIRAL LORD COLLINGWOOD. By W. CLARK RUSSELL, Author of 'The Wreck of the Grosvenor.' With Illustrations by F. BRANGWYN. *Third Edition. Crown 8vo.* 6*s.*

'A most excellent and wholesome book, which we should like to see in the hands of every boy in the country.'—*St. James's Gazette.*
'A really good book.'—*Saturday Review.*

Southey. ENGLISH SEAMEN (Howard, Clifford, Hawkins, Drake, Cavendish). By ROBERT SOUTHEY. Edited, with an Introduction, by DAVID HANNAY. *Second Edition. Crown 8vo.* 6*s.*

'Admirable and well-told stories of our naval history.'—*Army and Navy Gazette.*
'A brave, inspiriting book.'—*Black and White.*
'The work of a master of style, and delightful all through.'—*Daily Chronicle.*

General Literature

S. Baring Gould. OLD COUNTRY LIFE. By S. BARING GOULD, Author of 'Mehalah,' etc. With Sixty-seven Illustrations by W. PARKINSON, F. D. BEDFORD, and F. MASEY. *Large Crown 8vo.* 10*s.* 6*d.* *Fifth and Cheaper Edition.* 6*s.*

"Old Country Life," as healthy wholesome reading, full of breezy life and movement, full of quaint stories vigorously told, will not be excelled by any book to be published throughout the year. Sound, hearty, and English to the core.'—*World.*

S. Baring Gould. HISTORIC ODDITIES AND STRANGE EVENTS. By S. BARING GOULD. *Third Edition. Crown 8vo.* 6*s.*

'A collection of exciting and entertaining chapters. The whole volume is delightful reading.'—*Times.*

S. Baring Gould. FREAKS OF FANATICISM. By S. BARING GOULD. *Third Edition. Crown 8vo.* 6*s.*

'Mr. Baring Gould has a keen eye for colour and effect, and the subjects he has chosen give ample scope to his descriptive and analytic faculties. A perfectly fascinating book.'—*Scottish Leader.*

S. Baring Gould. A GARLAND OF COUNTRY SONG: English Folk Songs with their Traditional Melodies. Collected and arranged by S. BARING GOULD and H. FLEETWOOD SHEPPARD. *Demy 4to.* 6*s.*

S. Baring Gould. SONGS OF THE WEST: Traditional Ballads and Songs of the West of England, with their Traditional Melodies. Collected by S. BARING GOULD, M.A., and H. FLEETWOOD SHEPPARD, M.A. Arranged for Voice and Piano. In 4 Parts (containing 25 Songs each), *Parts I., II., III.,* 3*s. each. Part IV.,* 5*s. In one Vol., French morocco,* 15*s.*

'A rich collection of humour, pathos, grace, and poetic fancy.'—*Saturday Review.*

S. Baring Gould. YORKSHIRE ODDITIES AND STRANGE EVENTS. *Fourth Edition. Crown 8vo.* 6*s.*

S. Baring Gould. STRANGE SURVIVALS AND SUPERSTITIONS. With Illustrations. By S. BARING GOULD. *Crown 8vo. Second Edition.* 6*s.*

'We have read Mr. Baring Gould's book from beginning to end. It is full of quaint and various information, and there is not a dull page in it.'—*Notes and Queries.*

S. Baring Gould. THE DESERTS OF SOUTHERN FRANCE. By S. BARING GOULD. With numerous Illustrations by F. D. BEDFORD, S. HUTTON, etc. 2 *vols. Demy 8vo.* 32*s.*

This book is the first serious attempt to describe the great barren tableland that extends to the south of Limousin in the Department of Aveyron, Lot, etc., a country of dolomite cliffs, and cañons, and subterranean rivers. The region is full of prehistoric and historic interest, relics of cave-dwellers, of mediæval robbers, and of the English domination and the Hundred Years' War.

'His two richly-illustrated volumes are full of matter of interest to the geologist, the archæologist, and the student of history and manners.'—*Scotsman.*

'It deals with its subject in a manner which rarely fails to arrest attention.'—*Times.*

R. S. Baden-Powell. THE DOWNFALL OF PREMPEH. A Diary of Life with the Native Levy in Ashanti, 1895. By Lieut.-Col. BADEN-POWELL. With 21 Illustrations, a Map, and a Special Chapter on the Political and Commercial Position of Ashanti by Sir GEORGE BADEN-POWELL, K.C.M.G., M.P. *Demy 8vo.* 10*s.* 6*d.*

'A compact, faithful, most readable record of the campaign.'—*Daily News.*
'A bluff and vigorous narrative.'—*Glasgow Herald.*
'A really interesting book.'—*Yorkshire Post.*

W. E. Gladstone. THE SPEECHES AND PUBLIC ADDRESSES OF THE RT. HON. W. E. GLADSTONE, M.P. Edited by A. W. HUTTON, M.A., and H. J. COHEN, M.A. With Portraits. *8vo. Vols. IX. and X.* 12s. 6d. *each.*

Henley and Whibley. A BOOK OF ENGLISH PROSE. Collected by W. E. HENLEY and CHARLES WHIBLEY. *Cr. 8vo.* 6s.

'A unique volume of extracts—an art gallery of early prose.'—*Birmingham Post.*
'An admirable companion to Mr. Henley's "Lyra Heroica."'—*Saturday Review.*
'Quite delightful. The choice made has been excellent, and the volume has been most admirably printed by Messrs. Constable. A greater treat for those not well acquainted with pre-Restoration prose could not be imagined.'—*Athenæum.*

J. Wells. OXFORD AND OXFORD LIFE. By Members of the University. Edited by J. WELLS, M.A., Fellow and Tutor of Wadham College. *Crown 8vo.* 3s. 6d.

This work contains an account of life at Oxford—intellectual, social, and religious—a careful estimate of necessary expenses, a review of recent changes, a statement of the present position of the University, and chapters on Women's Education, aids to study, and University Extension.
'We congratulate Mr. Wells on the production of a readable and intelligent account of Oxford as it is at the present time, written by persons who are possessed of a close acquaintance with the system and life of the University.'—*Athenæum.*

W. M. Dixon. A PRIMER OF TENNYSON. By W. M. DIXON, M.A., Professor of English Literature at Mason College. *Crown 8vo.* 2s. 6d.

'Much sound and well-expressed criticism and acute literary judgments. The bibliography is a boon.'—*Speaker.*
'No better estimate of the late Laureate's work has yet been published. His sketch of Tennyson's life contains everything essential; his bibliography is full and concise; his literary criticism is most interesting.'—*Glasgow Herald.*

W. A. Craigie. A PRIMER OF BURNS. By W. A. CRAIGIE. *Crown 8vo.* 2s. 6d.

This book is planned on a method similar to the 'Primer of Tennyson.' It has also a glossary.
'A valuable addition to the literature of the poet.'—*Times.*
'An excellent short account.'—*Pall Mall Gazette.*
'An admirable introduction.'—*Globe.*

L. Whibley. GREEK OLIGARCHIES: THEIR ORGANISATION AND CHARACTER. By L. WHIBLEY, M.A., Fellow of Pembroke College, Cambridge. *Crown 8vo.* 6s.

'An exceedingly useful handbook: a careful and well-arranged study of an obscure subject.'—*Times.*
'Mr. Whibley is never tedious or pedantic.'—*Pall Mall Gazette.*

W. B. Worsfold. SOUTH AFRICA: Its History and its Future. By W. BASIL WORSFOLD, M.A. *With a Map. Crown 8vo.* 6s.

'An intensely interesting book.'—*Daily Chronicle.*
'A monumental work compressed into a very moderate compass.'—*World.*

C. H. Pearson. ESSAYS AND CRITICAL REVIEWS. By C. H. PEARSON, M.A., Author of 'National Life and Character.' Edited, with a Biographical Sketch, by H. A. STRONG, M.A., LL.D. With a Portrait. *Demy 8vo.* 10*s.* 6*d.*

'These fine essays illustrate the great breadth of his historical and literary sympathies and the remarkable variety of his intellectual interests.'—*Glasgow Herald.*
'Remarkable for careful handling, breadth of view, and thorough knowledge.'—*Scotsman.*
'Charming essays.'—*Spectator.*

Ouida. VIEWS AND OPINIONS. By OUIDA. *Crown 8vo. Second Edition.* 6*s.*

'Ouida is outspoken, and the reader of this book will not have a dull moment. The book is full of variety, and sparkles with entertaining matter.'—*Speaker.*

J. S. Shedlock. THE PIANOFORTE SONATA: Its Origin and Development. By J. S. SHEDLOCK. *Crown 8vo.* 5*s.*

'This work should be in the possession of every musician and amateur, for it not only embodies a concise and lucid history of the origin of one of the most important forms of musical composition, but, by reason of the painstaking research and accuracy of the author's statements, it is a very valuable work for reference.'—*Athenæum.*

E. M. Bowden. THE EXAMPLE OF BUDDHA: Being Quotations from Buddhist Literature for each Day in the Year. Compiled by E. M. BOWDEN. With Preface by Sir EDWIN ARNOLD. *Third Edition. 16mo.* 2*s.* 6*d.*

J. Beever. PRACTICAL FLY-FISHING, Founded on Nature, by JOHN BEEVER, late of the Thwaite House, Coniston. A New Edition, with a Memoir of the Author by W. G. COLLINGWOOD, M.A. *Crown 8vo.* 3*s.* 6*d.*

A little book on Fly-Fishing by an old friend of Mr. Ruskin.

Science

Freudenreich. DAIRY BACTERIOLOGY. A Short Manual for the Use of Students. By Dr. ED. VON FREUDENREICH. Translated from the German by J. R. AINSWORTH DAVIS, B.A., F.C.P. *Crown 8vo.* 2*s.* 6*d.*

Chalmers Mitchell. OUTLINES OF BIOLOGY. By P. CHALMERS MITCHELL, M.A., F.Z.S. *Fully Illustrated. Crown 8vo.* 6*s.*

A text-book designed to cover the new Schedule issued by the Royal College of Physicians and Surgeons.

G. Massee. A MONOGRAPH OF THE MYXOGASTRES. By GEORGE MASSEE. With 12 Coloured Plates. *Royal 8vo.* 18*s. net.*

'A work much in advance of any book in the language treating of this group of organisms. It is indispensable to every student of the Myxogastres. The coloured plates deserve high praise for their accuracy and execution.'—*Nature.*

Philosophy

L. T. Hobhouse. THE THEORY OF KNOWLEDGE. By L. T. HOBHOUSE, Fellow and Tutor of Corpus College, Oxford. *Demy 8vo.* 21*s.*

'The most important contribution to English philosophy since the publication of Mr. Bradley's "Appearance and Reality." Full of brilliant criticism and of positive theories which are models of lucid statement.'—*Glasgow Herald.*

'An elaborate and often brilliantly written volume. The treatment is one of great freshness, and the illustrations are particularly numerous and apt.'—*Times.*

W. H. Fairbrother. THE PHILOSOPHY OF T. H. GREEN. By W. H. FAIRBROTHER, M.A., Lecturer at Lincoln College, Oxford. *Crown 8vo.* 3*s.* 6*d.*

This volume is expository, not critical, and is intended for senior students at the Universities and others, as a statement of Green's teaching, and an introduction to the study of Idealist Philosophy.

'In every way an admirable book. As an introduction to the writings of perhaps the most remarkable speculative thinker whom England has produced in the present century, nothing could be better than Mr. Fairbrother's exposition and criticism.'—*Glasgow Herald.*

F. W. Bussell. THE SCHOOL OF PLATO: its Origin and its Revival under the Roman Empire. By F. W. BUSSELL, M.A., Fellow and Tutor of Brasenose College, Oxford. *Demy 8vo. Two volumes.* 10*s.* 6*d. each. Vol. I.*

'A highly valuable contribution to the history of ancient thought.'—*Glasgow Herald.*

'A clever and stimulating book, provocative of thought and deserving careful reading.'—*Manchester Guardian.*

F. S. Granger. THE WORSHIP OF THE ROMANS. By F. S. GRANGER, M.A., Litt.D., Professor of Philosophy at University College, Nottingham. *Crown 8vo.* 6*s.*

The author delineates that group of beliefs which stood in close connection with the Roman religion, and among the subjects treated are Dreams, Nature Worship, Roman Magic, Divination, Holy Places, Victims, etc. Thus the book is also a contribution to folk-lore and comparative psychology.

'A scholarly analysis of the religious ceremonies, beliefs, and superstitions of ancient Rome, conducted in the new instructive light of comparative anthropology.'—*Times.*

Theology

E. C. S. Gibson. THE XXXIX. ARTICLES OF THE CHURCH OF ENGLAND. Edited with an Introduction by E. C. S. GIBSON, D.D., Vicar of Leeds, late Principal of Wells Theological College. *In Two Volumes. Demy 8vo.* 7*s*. 6*d*. *each. Vol. I. Articles I.-VIII.*

'The tone maintained throughout is not that of the partial advocate, but the faithful exponent.'—*Scotsman.*

'There are ample proofs of clearness of expression, sobriety of judgment, and breadth of view. . . . The book will be welcome to all students of the subject, and its sound, definite, and loyal theology ought to be of great service.'—*National Observer.*

'So far from repelling the general reader, its orderly arrangement, lucid treatment, and felicity of diction invite and encourage his attention.'—*Yorkshire Post.*

R. L. Ottley. THE DOCTRINE OF THE INCARNATION. By R. L. OTTLEY, M.A., late fellow of Magdalen College, Oxon., Principal of Pusey House. *In Two Volumes. Demy 8vo.* 15*s*.

'Learned and reverent: lucid and well arranged.'—*Record.*

'Accurate, well ordered, and judicious.'—*National Observer.*

'A clear and remarkably full account of the main currents of speculation. Scholarly precision . . . genuine tolerance . . . intense interest in his subject—are Mr. Ottley's merits.'—*Guardian.*

S. R. Driver. SERMONS ON SUBJECTS CONNECTED WITH THE OLD TESTAMENT. By S. R. DRIVER, D.D., Canon of Christ Church, Regius Professor of Hebrew in the University of Oxford. *Crown 8vo.* 6*s*.

'A welcome companion to the author's famous 'Introduction.' No man can read these discourses without feeling that Dr. Driver is fully alive to the deeper teaching of the Old Testament.'—*Guardian.*

T. K. Cheyne. FOUNDERS OF OLD TESTAMENT CRITICISM: Biographical, Descriptive, and Critical Studies. By T. K. CHEYNE, D.D., Oriel Professor of the Interpretation of Holy Scripture at Oxford. *Large crown 8vo.* 7*s*. 6*d*.

This important book is a historical sketch of O. T. Criticism in the form of biographical studies from the days of Eichhorn to those of Driver and Robertson Smith. It is the only book of its kind in English.

'A very learned and instructive work.'—*Times.*

C. H. Prior. CAMBRIDGE SERMONS. Edited by C. H. PRIOR, M.A., Fellow and Tutor of Pembroke College. *Crown 8vo.* 6*s*.

A volume of sermons preached before the University of Cambridge by various preachers, including the Archbishop of Canterbury and Bishop Westcott.

'A representative collection. Bishop Westcott's is a noble sermon.'—*Guardian.*

H. C. Beeching. SERMONS TO SCHOOLBOYS. By H. C. BEECHING, M.A., Rector of Yattendon, Berks. With a Preface by Canon SCOTT HOLLAND. *Crown 8vo.* 2*s*. 6*d*.

Seven sermons preached before the boys of Bradfield College.

E. B. Layard. RELIGION IN BOYHOOD. Notes on the Religious Training of Boys. With a Preface by J. R. ILLINGWORTH. By E. B. LAYARD, M.A. *18mo.* 1*s.*

Devotional Books.

With Full-page Illustrations. Fcap. 8vo. Buckram. 3*s.* 6*d.*
Padded morocco, 5*s.*

THE IMITATION OF CHRIST. By THOMAS À KEMPIS. With an Introduction by DEAN FARRAR. Illustrated by C. M. GERE, and printed in black and red. *Second Edition.*

'Amongst all the innumerable English editions of the "Imitation," there can have been few which were prettier than this one, printed in strong and handsome type by Messrs. Constable, with all the glory of red initials, and the comfort of buckram binding.'—*Glasgow Herald.*

THE CHRISTIAN YEAR. By JOHN KEBLE. With an Introduction and Notes by W. LOCK, M.A., Sub-Warden of Keble College, Ireland Professor at Oxford, Author of the 'Life of John Keble.' Illustrated by R. ANNING BELL.

'The present edition is annotated with all the care and insight to be expected from Mr. Lock. The progress and circumstances of its composition are detailed in the Introduction. There is an interesting Appendix on the MSS. of the "Christian Year," and another giving the order in which the poems were written. A "Short Analysis of the Thought" is prefixed to each, and any difficulty in the text is explained in a note.—*Guardian.*

'The most acceptable edition of this ever-popular work.'—*Globe.*

Leaders of Religion

Edited by H. C. BEECHING, M.A. *With Portraits, crown 8vo.* 3 6

A series of short biographies of the most prominent leaders of religious life and thought of all ages and countries.

The following are ready—

CARDINAL NEWMAN. By R. H. HUTTON.

JOHN WESLEY. By J. H. OVERTON, M.A.

BISHOP WILBERFORCE. By G. W. DANIEL, M.A.

CARDINAL MANNING. By A. W. HUTTON, M.A.

CHARLES SIMEON. By H. C. G. MOULE, M.A.

JOHN KEBLE. By WALTER LOCK, M.A.

THOMAS CHALMERS. By Mrs. OLIPHANT.

LANCELOT ANDREWES. By R. L. OTTLEY, M.A.

AUGUSTINE OF CANTERBURY. By E. L. CUTTS, D.D.

WILLIAM LAUD. By W. H. HUTTON, M.A.

JOHN KNOX. By F. M'CUNN.

JOHN HOWE. By R. F. HORTON, D.D.

BISHOP KEN. By F. A. CLARKE, M.A.

GEORGE FOX, THE QUAKER. By T. HODGKIN, D.C.L.

Other volumes will be announced in due course.

Fiction

SIX SHILLING NOVELS

Marie Corelli's Novels

Crown 8vo. 6s. each.

A ROMANCE OF TWO WORLDS. *Fourteenth Edition.*

VENDETTA. *Eleventh Edition.*

THELMA. *Fourteenth Edition.*

ARDATH. *Tenth Edition.*

THE SOUL OF LILITH. *Ninth Edition.*

WORMWOOD. *Eighth Edition.*

BARABBAS: A DREAM OF THE WORLD'S TRAGEDY. *Twenty-fifth Edition.*

'The tender reverence of the treatment and the imaginative beauty of the writing have reconciled us to the daring of the conception, and the conviction is forced on us that even so exalted a subject cannot be made too familiar to us, provided it be presented in the true spirit of Christian faith. The amplifications of the Scripture narrative are often conceived with high poetic insight, and this "Dream of the World's Tragedy" is, despite some trifling incongruities, a lofty and not inadequate paraphrase of the supreme climax of the inspired narrative.'—*Dublin Review.*

THE SORROWS OF SATAN. *Twenty-ninth Edition.*

'A very powerful piece of work. . . . The conception is magnificent, and is likely to win an abiding place within the memory of man. . . . The author has immense command of language, and a limitless audacity. . . . This interesting and remarkable romance will live long after much of the ephemeral literature of the day is forgotten. . . . A literary phenomenon . . . novel, and even sublime.'—W. T. STEAD in the *Review of Reviews.*

Anthony Hope's Novels

Crown 8vo. 6s. each.

THE GOD IN THE CAR. *Seventh Edition.*

'A very remarkable book, deserving of critical analysis impossible within our limit; brilliant, but not superficial; well considered, but not elaborated; constructed with the proverbial art that conceals, but yet allows itself to be enjoyed by readers to whom fine literary method is a keen pleasure; true without cynicism, subtle without affectation, humorous without strain, witty without offence, inevitably sad, with an unmorose simplicity.'—*The World.*

A CHANGE OF AIR. *Fourth Edition.*

'A graceful, vivacious comedy, true to human nature. The characters are traced with a masterly hand.'—*Times.*

A MAN OF MARK. *Third Edition.*

'Of all Mr. Hope's books, "A Man of Mark" is the one which best compares with "The Prisoner of Zenda." The two romances are unmistakably the work of the same writer, and he possesses a style of narrative peculiarly seductive, piquant, comprehensive, and—his own.'—*National Observer.*

THE CHRONICLES OF COUNT ANTONIO. *Third Edition.*

'It is a perfectly enchanting story of love and chivalry, and pure romance. The outlawed Count is the most constant, desperate, and withal modest and tender of lovers, a peerless gentleman, an intrepid fighter, a very faithful friend, and a most magnanimous foe. In short, he is an altogether admirable, lovable, and delightful hero. There is not a word in the volume that can give offence to the most fastidious taste of man or woman, and there is not, either, a dull paragraph in it. The book is everywhere instinct with the most exhilarating spirit of adventure, and delicately perfumed with the sentiment of all heroic and honourable deeds of history and romance.'—*Guardian.*

S. Baring Gould's Novels

Crown 8vo. 6s. each.

'To say that a book is by the author of "Mehalah" is to imply that it contains a story cast on strong lines, containing dramatic possibilities, vivid and sympathetic descriptions of Nature, and a wealth of ingenious imagery.'—*Speaker.*

'That whatever Mr. Baring Gould writes is well worth reading, is a conclusion that may be very generally accepted. His views of life are fresh and vigorous, his language pointed and characteristic, the incidents of which he makes use are striking and original, his characters are life-like, and though somewhat exceptional people, are drawn and coloured with artistic force. Add to this that his descriptions of scenes and scenery are painted with the loving eyes and skilled hands of a master of his art, that he is always fresh and never dull, and under such conditions it is no wonder that readers have gained confidence both in his power of amusing and satisfying them, and that year by year his popularity widens.'—*Court Circular.*

ARMINELL: A Social Romance. *Fourth Edition.*

URITH: A Story of Dartmoor. *Fourth Edition.*

'The author is at his best.'—*Times.*

'He has nearly reached the high water-mark of "Mehalah."'—*National Observer.*

IN THE ROAR OF THE SEA. *Fifth Edition.*

'One of the best imagined and most enthralling stories the author has produced.' —*Saturday Review.*

MRS. CURGENVEN OF CURGENVEN. *Fourth Edition.*

'A novel of vigorous humour and sustained power.'—*Graphic.*
'The swing of the narrative is splendid.'—*Sussex Daily News.*

CHEAP JACK ZITA. *Third Edition.*

'A powerful drama of human passion.'—*Westminster Gazette.*
'A story worthy the author.'—*National Observer.*

THE QUEEN OF LOVE. *Fourth Edition.*

'The scenery is admirable, and the dramatic incidents are most striking.'—*Glasgow Herald.*
'Strong, interesting, and clever.'—*Westminster Gazette.*
'You cannot put it down until you have finished it.'—*Punch.*
'Can be heartily recommended to all who care for cleanly, energetic, and interesting fiction.'—*Sussex Daily News.*

KITTY ALONE. *Fourth Edition.*

'A strong and original story, teeming with graphic description, stirring incident, and, above all, with vivid and enthralling human interest.'—*Daily Telegraph.*
'Brisk, clever, keen, healthy, humorous, and interesting.'—*National Observer.*
'Full of quaint and delightful studies of character.'—*Bristol Mercury.*

NOÉMI: A Romance of the Cave-Dwellers. Illustrated by R. CATON WOODVILLE. *Third Edition.*

'"Noémi" is as excellent a tale of fighting and adventure as one may wish to meet. All the characters that interfere in this exciting tale are marked with properties of their own. The narrative also runs clear and sharp as the Loire itself.'—*Pall Mall Gazette.*
'Mr. Baring Gould's powerful story is full of the strong lights and shadows and vivid colouring to which he has accustomed us.'—*Standard.*

THE BROOM-SQUIRE. Illustrated by FRANK DADD. *Third Edition.*

'A strain of tenderness is woven through the web of his tragic tale, and its atmosphere is sweetened by the nobility and sweetness of the heroine's character.'—*Daily News.*
'A story of exceptional interest that seems to us to be better than anything he has written of late.'—*Speaker.* 'A powerful and striking story.'—*Guardian.*
'A powerful piece of work.'—*Black and White.*

Gilbert Parker's Novels

Crown 8vo. 6s. each.

PIERRE AND HIS PEOPLE. *Third Edition.*

'Stories happily conceived and finely executed. There is strength and genius in Mr. Parker's style.'—*Daily Telegraph.*

'Mr. Parker's latest book places him in the front rank of living novelists. "The Seats of the Mighty" is a great book.'—*Black and White.*

'One of the strongest stories of historical interest and adventure that we have read for many a day. . . . Through all Mr. Parker moves with an assured step, whilst in his treatment of his subject there is that happy blending of the poetical with the prosaic which has characterised all his writings. A notable and successful book.' —*Speaker.*

'The story is very finely and dramatically told. . . . In none of his books has his imaginative faculty appeared to such splendid purpose as here. Captain Moray, Alixe, Gabord, Vauban—above all, Doltaire—and, indeed, every person who takes part in the action of the story are clearly conceived and finely drawn and individualised.—*Scotsman.*

'An admirable romance. The glory of a romance is its plot, and this plot is crowded with fine sensations, which have no rest until the fall of the famous old city and the final restitution of love.'—*Pall Mall Gazette.*

Conan Doyle. ROUND THE RED LAMP. By A. CONAN DOYLE, Author of 'The White Company,' 'The Adventures of Sherlock Holmes,' etc. *Fourth Edition. Crown 8vo.* 6*s.*

'The book is, indeed, composed of leaves from life, and is far and away the best view that has been vouchsafed us behind the scenes of the consulting-room. It is very superior to "The Diary of a late Physician."'—*Illustrated London News.*

Stanley Weyman. UNDER THE RED ROBE. By STANLEY WEYMAN, Author of 'A Gentleman of France.' With Twelve Illustrations by R. Caton Woodville. *Eighth Edition. Crown 8vo.* 6*s.*

'A book of which we have read every word for the sheer pleasure of reading, and which we put down with a pang that we cannot forget it all and start again.'—*Westminster Gazette.*

'Every one who reads books at all must read this thrilling romance, from the first page of which to the last the breathless reader is haled along. An inspiration of "manliness and courage."'—*Daily Chronicle.*

'A delightful tale of chivalry and adventure, vivid and dramatic, with a wholesome modesty and reverence for the highest.'—*Globe.*

Mrs. Clifford. A FLASH OF SUMMER. By MRS. W. K. CLIFFORD, Author of 'Aunt Anne,' etc. *Second Edition. Crown 8vo.* 6*s.*

'The story is a very sad and a very beautiful one, exquisitely told, and enriched with many subtle touches of wise and tender insight. It will, undoubtedly, add to its author's reputation—already high—in the ranks of novelists.'—*Speaker.*

'We must congratulate Mrs. Clifford upon a very successful and interesting story, told throughout with finish and a delicate sense of proportion, qualities which, indeed, have always distinguished the best work of this very able writer.'—*Manchester Guardian.*

Emily Lawless. HURRISH. By the Honble. EMILY LAWLESS, Author of 'Maelcho,' etc. *Fifth Edition. Crown 8vo.* 6*s.*

A reissue of Miss Lawless' most popular novel, uniform with 'Maelcho.'

Emily Lawless. MAELCHO: a Sixteenth Century Romance. By the Honble. EMILY LAWLESS, Author of 'Grania,' etc. *Second Edition. Crown 8vo.* 6*s.*

'A really great book.'—*Spectator.*

'There is no keener pleasure in life than the recognition of genius. Good work is commoner than it used to be, but the best is as rare as ever. All the more gladly, therefore, do we welcome in "Maelcho" a piece of work of the first order, which we do not hesitate to describe as one of the most remarkable literary achievements of this generation. Miss Lawless is possessed of the very essence of historical genius.'—*Manchester Guardian.*

J. H. Findlater. THE GREEN GRAVES OF BALGOWRIE. By JANE H. FINDLATER. *Third Edition. Crown 8vo.* 6*s.*

'A powerful and vivid story.'—*Standard.*
'A beautiful story, sad and strange as truth itself.'—*Vanity Fair.*
'A work of remarkable interest and originality.'—*National Observer.*
'A really original novel.'—*Journal of Education.*
'A very charming and pathetic tale.'—*Pall Mall Gazette.*
'A singularly original, clever, and beautiful story.'—*Guardian.*
'"The Green Graves of Balgowrie" reveals to us a new Scotch writer of undoubted faculty and reserve force.'—*Spectator.*
'An exquisite idyll, delicate, affecting, and beautiful.'—*Black and White.*
'Permeated with high and noble purpose. It is one of the most wholesome stories we have met with, and cannot fail to leave a deep and lasting impression.'—*Newsagent.*

E. F. Benson. DODO: A DETAIL OF THE DAY. By E. F. BENSON. *Sixteenth Edition. Crown 8vo.* 6*s.*

'A delightfully witty sketch of society.'—*Spectator.*
'A perpetual feast of epigram and paradox.'—*Speaker.*
'By a writer of quite exceptional ability.'—*Athenæum.*
'Brilliantly written.'—*World.*

E. F. Benson. THE RUBICON. By E. F. BENSON, Author of 'Dodo.' *Fifth Edition. Crown 8vo.* 6*s.*

'Well written, stimulating, unconventional, and, in a word, characteristic.'—*Birmingham Post.*
'An exceptional achievement; a notable advance on his previous work.'—*National Observer.*

M. M. Dowie. GALLIA. By MÉNIE MURIEL DOWIE, Author of 'A Girl in the Carpathians.' *Third Edition. Crown 8vo.* 6*s.*

'The style is generally admirable, the dialogue not seldom brilliant, the situations surprising in their freshness and originality, while the subsidiary as well as the principal characters live and move, and the story itself is readable from title-page to colophon.'—*Saturday Review.*
'A very notable book; a very sympathetically, at times delightfully written book.—*Daily Graphic.*

Mrs. Oliphant. SIR ROBERT'S FORTUNE. By MRS. OLIPHANT. *Crown 8vo.* 6*s.*

'Full of her own peculiar charm of style and simple, subtle character-painting come her new gift, the delightful story before us. The scene mostly lies in the moors, and at the touch of the authoress a Scotch moor becomes a living thing, strong tender, beautiful, and changeful.'—*Pall Mall Gazette.*

Mrs. Oliphant. THE TWO MARYS. By MRS. OLIPHANT. *Second Edition. Crown 8vo.* 6*s.*

W. E. Norris. MATTHEW AUSTIN. By W. E. NORRIS, Author of 'Mademoiselle de Mersac,' etc. *Fourth Edition. Crown 8vo.* 6*s.*

'"Matthew Austin" may safely be pronounced one of the most intellectually satisfactory and morally bracing novels of the current year.'—*Daily Telegraph.*

W. E. Norris. HIS GRACE. By W. E. NORRIS. *Third Edition. Crown 8vo.* 6s.

'Mr. Norris has drawn a really fine character in the Duke of Hurstbourne, at once unconventional and very true to the conventionalities of life, weak and strong in a breath, capable of inane follies and heroic decisions, yet not so definitely portrayed as to relieve a reader of the necessity of study.'—*Athenæum.*

W. E. Norris. THE DESPOTIC LADY AND OTHERS. By W. E. NORRIS. *Crown 8vo.* 6*s.*

'A budget of good fiction of which no one will tire.'—*Scotsman.*

'An extremely entertaining volume—the sprightliest of holiday companions.'—*Daily Telegraph*

H. G. Wells. THE STOLEN BACILLUS, and other Stories. By H. G. WELLS, Author of 'The Time Machine.' *Crown 8vo.* 6*s.*

'The ordinary reader of fiction may be glad to know that these stories are eminently readable from one cover to the other, but they are more than that; they are the impressions of a very striking imagination, which, it would seem, has a great deal within its reach.'—*Saturday Review.*

Arthur Morrison. TALES OF MEAN STREETS. By ARTHUR MORRISON. *Fourth Edition. Crown 8vo.* 6*s.*

'Told with consummate art and extraordinary detail. He tells a plain, unvarnished tale, and the very truth of it makes for beauty. In the true humanity of the book lies its justification, the permanence of its interest, and its indubitable triumph.'—*Athenæum.*

'A great book. The author's method is amazingly effective, and produces a thrilling sense of reality. The writer lays upon us a master hand. The book is simply appalling and irresistible in its interest. It is humorous also; without humour it would not make the mark it is certain to make.'—*World.*

J. Maclaren Cobban. THE KING OF ANDAMAN: A Saviour of Society. By J. MACLAREN COBBAN. *Crown 8vo.* 6*s*.

'An unquestionably interesting book. It would not surprise us if it turns out to be the most interesting novel of the season, for it contains one character, at least, who has in him the root of immortality, and the book itself is ever exhaling the sweet savour of the unexpected. . . . Plot is forgotten and incident fades, and only the really human endures, and throughout this book there stands out in bold and beautiful relief its high-souled and chivalric protagonist, James the Master of Hutcheon, the King of Andaman himself.'—*Pall Mall Gazette.*

'A most original and refreshing story. James Hutcheon is a personage whom it is good to know and impossible to forget. He is beautiful within and without, whichever way we take him.'—*Spectator.*

'"The King of Andaman," is a book which does credit not less to the heart than the head of its author.'—*Athenæum.*

'The fact that Her Majesty the Queen has been pleased to gracefully express to the author of "The King of Andaman" her interest in his work will doubtless find for it many readers.'—*Vanity Fair.*

H. Morrah. A SERIOUS COMEDY. By HERBERT MORRAH. *Crown 8vo.* 6*s.*

'There are many delightful places in this volume, which is well worthy of its title. The theme has seldom been presented with more freshness or more force.'—*Scotsman.*

L. B. Walford. SUCCESSORS TO THE TITLE. By MRS. WALFORD, Author of 'Mr. Smith,' etc. *Second Edition. Crown 8vo.* 6*s.*

'The story is fresh and healthy from beginning to finish; and our liking for the two simple people who are the successors to the title mounts steadily, and ends almost in respect.'—*Scotsman.*

'The book is quite worthy to be ranked with many clever predecessors. It is excellent reading.'—*Glasgow Herald.*

T. L. Paton. A HOME IN INVERESK. By T. L. PATON. *Crown 8vo.* 6*s.*

'A distinctly fresh and fascinating novel.'—*Montrose Standard.*

'A book which bears marks of considerable promise.'—*Scotsman.*

'A pleasant and well-written story.'—*Daily Chronicle.*

John Davidson. MISS ARMSTRONG'S AND OTHER CIRCUMSTANCES. By JOHN DAVIDSON. *Crown 8vo.* 6*s.*

'Throughout the volume there is a strong vein of originality, a strength in the handling, and a knowledge of human nature that are worthy of the highest praise.' —*Scotsman.*

J. B. Burton. IN THE DAY OF ADVERSITY. By J. BLOUNDELLE BURTON. *Crown 8vo.* 6*s.*

'Unusually interesting and full of highly dramatic situations.'—*Guardian.*

'A well-written story, drawn from that inexhaustible mine, the time of Louis XIV. —*Pall Mall Gazette.*

H. Johnston. DR. CONGALTON'S LEGACY. By HENRY JOHNSTON. *Crown 8vo.* 6*s.*

'The story is redolent of humour, pathos, and tenderness, while it is not without a touch of tragedy.'—*Scotsman.*

A worthy and permanent contribution to Scottish creative literature.'—*Glasgow Herald.*

Julian Corbett. A BUSINESS IN GREAT WATERS. By JULIAN CORBETT. *Crown 8vo.* 6*s.*

'In this stirring story Mr. Julian Corbett has done excellent work, welcome alike for its distinctly literary flavour, and for the wholesome tone which pervades it. Mr. Corbett writes with immense spirit, and the book is a thoroughly enjoyable one in all respects. The salt of the ocean is in it, and the right heroic ring resounds through its gallant adventures.'—*Speaker.*

C. Phillips Woolley. THE QUEENSBERRY CUP. A Tale of Adventure. By CLIVE PHILLIPS WOOLLEY, Author of 'Snap,' Editor of 'Big Game Shooting.' *Illustrated. Crown 8vo.* 6*s.*

'A book which will delight boys: a book which upholds the healthy schoolboy code of morality.'—*Scotsman.*

'A brilliant book. Dick St. Clair, of Caithness, is an almost ideal character—a combination of the mediæval knight and the modern pugilist.'—*Admiralty and Horseguards Gazette.*

Robert Barr. IN THE MIDST OF ALARMS. By ROBERT BARR. *Third Edition. Crown 8vo.* 6*s.*

'A book which has abundantly satisfied us by its capital humour.'—*Daily Chronicle.*

'Mr. Barr has achieved a triumph whereof he has every reason to be proud.'—*Pall Mall Gazette.*

L. Daintrey. THE KING OF ALBERIA. A Romance of the Balkans. By LAURA DAINTREY. *Crown 8vo.* 6*s.*

'Miss Daintrey seems to have an intimate acquaintance with the people and politics of the Balkan countries in which the scene of her lively and picturesque romance is laid. On almost every page we find clever touches of local colour which differentiate her book unmistakably from the ordinary novel of commerce. The story is briskly told, and well conceived.'—*Glasgow Herald.*

Mrs. Pinsent. CHILDREN OF THIS WORLD. By ELLEN F. PINSENT, Author of 'Jenny's Case.' *Crown 8vo.* 6*s.*

'Mrs. Pinsent's new novel has plenty of vigour, variety, and good writing. There are certainty of purpose, strength of touch, and clearness of vision.'—*Athenæum.*

Clark Russell. MY DANISH SWEETHEART. By W. CLARK RUSSELL, Author of 'The Wreck of the Grosvenor,' etc. *Illustrated. Fourth Edition. Crown 8vo.* 6*s.*

G. Manville Fenn. AN ELECTRIC SPARK. By G. MANVILLE FENN. *Second Edition. Crown 8vo.* 6*s.*

'A simple and wholesome story.'—*Manchester Guardian.*

R. Pryce. TIME AND THE WOMAN. By RICHARD PRYCE, Author of 'Miss Maxwell's Affections,' 'The Quiet Mrs. Fleming,' etc. *Second Edition. Crown 8vo.* 6*s.*

'Mr. Pryce's work recalls the style of Octave Feuillet, by its clearness, conciseness, its literary reserve.'—*Athenæum.*

Mrs. Watson. THIS MAN'S DOMINION. By the Author of 'A High Little World.' *Second Edition. Crown 8vo.* 6*s.*

Marriott Watson. DIOGENES OF LONDON. By H. B. MARRIOTT WATSON. *Crown 8vo. Buckram.* 6*s.*

'By all those who delight in the uses of words, who rate the exercise of prose above the exercise of verse, who rejoice in all proofs of its delicacy and its strength, who believe that English prose is chief among the moulds of thought, by these Mr. Marriott Watson's book will be welcomed.'—*National Observer.*

M. Gilchrist. THE STONE DRAGON. By MURRAY GILCHRIST. *Crown 8vo. Buckram.* 6*s.*

'The author's faults are atoned for by certain positive and admirable merits. The romances have not their counterpart in modern literature, and to read them is a unique experience.'—*National Observer.*

E. Dickinson. A VICAR'S WIFE. By EVELYN DICKINSON. *Crown 8vo.* 6*s.*

E. M. Gray. ELSA. By E. M'QUEEN GRAY. *Crown 8vo.* 6*s.*

THREE-AND-SIXPENNY NOVELS

3/6

Crown 8vo.

DERRICK VAUGHAN, NOVELIST. By EDNA LYALL.
MARGERY OF QUETHER. By S. BARING GOULD.
JACQUETTA. By S. BARING GOULD.
SUBJECT TO VANITY. By MARGARET BENSON.
THE MOVING FINGER. By MARY GAUNT.
JACO TRELOAR. By J. H. PEARCE.

AUT DIABOLUS AUT NIHIL. By X. L.

THE COMING OF CUCULAIN. A Romance of the Heroic Age of Ireland. By STANDISH O'GRADY. *Illustrated.*

THE GODS GIVE MY DONKEY WINGS. By ANGUS EVAN ABBOTT.

THE STAR GAZERS. By G. MANVILLE FENN.

THE POISON OF ASPS. By R. ORTON PROWSE.

THE QUIET MRS. FLEMING. By R. PRYCE.

THE PLAN OF CAMPAIGN. By F. MABEL ROBINSON.

DISENCHANTMENT. By F. MABEL ROBINSON.

MR. BUTLER'S WARD. By F. MABEL ROBINSON.

A LOST ILLUSION. By LESLIE KEITH.

A REVEREND GENTLEMAN. By J. M. COBBAN.

A DEPLORABLE AFFAIR. By W. E. NORRIS.

A CAVALIER'S LADYE. By Mrs. DICKER.

HALF-CROWN NOVELS 2/6

A Series of Novels by popular Authors.

1. HOVENDEN, V.C. By F. MABEL ROBINSON.
2. ELI'S CHILDREN. By G. MANVILLE FENN.
3. A DOUBLE KNOT. By G. MANVILLE FENN.
4. DISARMED. By M. BETHAM EDWARDS.
5. A MARRIAGE AT SEA. By W. CLARK RUSSELL.
6. IN TENT AND BUNGALOW. By the Author of 'Indian Idylls.'
7. MY STEWARDSHIP. By E. M'QUEEN GRAY.
8. JACK'S FATHER. By W. E. NORRIS.
9. JIM B.

Lynn Linton. THE TRUE HISTORY OF JOSHUA DAVIDSON, Christian and Communist. By E. LYNN LINTON. *Eleventh Edition. Post 8vo.* 1*s*.

Books for Boys and Girls 3/6

A Series of Books by well-known Authors, well illustrated.

1. THE ICELANDER'S SWORD. By S. BARING GOULD.
2. TWO LITTLE CHILDREN AND CHING. By EDITH E. CUTHELL.

3. TODDLEBEN'S HERO. By M. M. BLAKE.
4. ONLY A GUARD ROOM DOG. By EDITH E. CUTHELL.
5. THE DOCTOR OF THE JULIET. By HARRY COLLINGWOOD.
6. MASTER ROCKAFELLAR'S VOYAGE. By W. CLARK RUSSELL.
7. SYD BELTON: Or, The Boy who would not go to Sea. By G. MANVILLE FENN.

The Peacock Library

A Series of Books for Girls by well-known Authors, handsomely bound in blue and silver, and well illustrated. 3/6

1. A PINCH OF EXPERIENCE. By L. B. WALFORD.
2. THE RED GRANGE. By Mrs. MOLESWORTH.
3. THE SECRET OF MADAME DE MONLUC. By the Author of 'Mdle Mori.'
4. DUMPS. By Mrs. PARR, Author of 'Adam and Eve.'
5. OUT OF THE FASHION. By L. T. MEADE.
6. A GIRL OF THE PEOPLE. By L. T. MEADE.
7. HEPSY GIPSY. By L. T. MEADE. 2*s.* 6*d.*
8. THE HONOURABLE MISS. By L. T. MEADE.
9. MY LAND OF BEULAH. By Mrs. LEITH ADAMS.

University Extension Series

A series of books on historical, literary, and scientific subjects, suitable for extension students and home-reading circles. Each volume is complete in itself, and the subjects are treated by competent writers in a broad and philosophic spirit.

Edited by J. E. SYMES, M.A.,
Principal of University College, Nottingham.

Crown 8vo. Price (with some exceptions) 2s. 6d.

The following volumes are ready:—

THE INDUSTRIAL HISTORY OF ENGLAND. By H. DE B. GIBBINS, M.A., late Scholar of Wadham College, Oxon., Cobden Prizeman. *Fourth Edition. With Maps and Plans.* 3*s.*

'A compact and clear story of our ndustrial development. A study of this concise but luminous book cannot fail to give the reader a clear insight into the principal phenomena of our industrial history. The editor and publishers are to be congratulated on this first volume of their venture, and we shall look with expectant interest for the succeeding volumes of the series.'—*University Extension Journal.*

A HISTORY OF ENGLISH POLITICAL ECONOMY. By L. L. PRICE, M.A., Fellow of Oriel College, Oxon. *Second Edition.*

PROBLEMS OF POVERTY: An Inquiry into the Industrial Conditions of the Poor. By J. A. HOBSON, M.A. *Third Edition.*

VICTORIAN POETS. By A. SHARP.

THE FRENCH REVOLUTION. By J. E. SYMES, M.A.

PSYCHOLOGY. By F. S. GRANGER, M.A., Lecturer in Philosophy at University College, Nottingham.

THE EVOLUTION OF PLANT LIFE: Lower Forms. By G. MASSEE, Kew Gardens. *With Illustrations.*

AIR AND WATER. Professor V. B. LEWES, M.A. *Illustrated.*

THE CHEMISTRY OF LIFE AND HEALTH. By C. W. KIMMINS, M.A. Camb. *Illustrated.*

THE MECHANICS OF DAILY LIFE. By V. P. SELLS, M.A. *Illustrated.*

ENGLISH SOCIAL REFORMERS. H. DE B. GIBBINS, M.A.

ENGLISH TRADE AND FINANCE IN THE SEVENTEENTH CENTURY. By W. A. S. HEWINS, B.A.

THE CHEMISTRY OF FIRE. The Elementary Principles of Chemistry. By M. M. PATTISON MUIR, M.A. *Illustrated.*

A TEXT-BOOK OF AGRICULTURAL BOTANY. By M. C. POTTER, M.A., F.L.S. *Illustrated.* 3*s.* 6*d.*

THE VAULT OF HEAVEN. A Popular Introduction to Astronomy. By R. A. GREGORY. *With numerous Illustrations.*

METEOROLOGY. The Elements of Weather and Climate. By H. N. DICKSON, F.R.S.E., F.R. Met. Soc. *Illustrated.*

A MANUAL OF ELECTRICAL SCIENCE. By GEORGE J. BURCH, M.A. *With numerous Illustrations.* 3*s.*

THE EARTH. An Introduction to Physiography. By EVAN SMALL, M.A. *Illustrated.*

INSECT LIFE. By F. W. THEOBALD, M.A. *Illustrated.*

ENGLISH POETRY FROM BLAKE TO BROWNING. By W. M. DIXON, M.A.

ENGLISH LOCAL GOVERNMENT. By E. JENKS, M.A., Professor of Law at University College, Liverpool.

Social Questions of To-day

Edited by H. DE B. GIBBINS, M.A.

Crown 8vo. *2s. 6d.*

2/6

A series of volumes upon those topics of social, economic, and industrial interest that are at the present moment foremost in the public mind. Each volume of the series is written by an author who is an acknowledged authority upon the subject with which he deals.

The following Volumes of the Series are ready:—

TRADE UNIONISM—NEW AND OLD. By G. HOWELL, Author of 'The Conflicts of Capital and Labour.' *Second Edition.*

THE CO-OPERATIVE MOVEMENT TO-DAY. By G. J. HOLYOAKE, Author of 'The History of Co-operation.' *Second Edition.*

MUTUAL THRIFT. By Rev. J. FROME WILKINSON, M.A., Author of 'The Friendly Society Movement.'

PROBLEMS OF POVERTY: An Inquiry into the Industrial Conditions of the Poor. By J. A. HOBSON, M.A. *Third Edition.*

THE COMMERCE OF NATIONS. By C. F. BASTABLE, M.A., Professor of Economics at Trinity College, Dublin.

THE ALIEN INVASION. By W. H. WILKINS, B.A., Secretary to the Society for Preventing the Immigration of Destitute Aliens.

THE RURAL EXODUS. By P. ANDERSON GRAHAM.

LAND NATIONALIZATION. By HAROLD COX, B.A.

A SHORTER WORKING DAY. By H. DE B. GIBBINS and R. A. HADFIELD, of the Hecla Works, Sheffield.

BACK TO THE LAND: An Inquiry into the Cure for Rural Depopulation. By H. E. MOORE.

TRUSTS, POOLS AND CORNERS: As affecting Commerce and Industry. By J. STEPHEN JEANS, M.R.I., F.S.S.

THE FACTORY SYSTEM. By R. COOKE TAYLOR.

THE STATE AND ITS CHILDREN. By GERTRUDE TUCKWELL.

WOMEN'S WORK. By LADY DILKE, MISS BULLEY, and MISS WHITLEY.

MUNICIPALITIES AT WORK. The Municipal Policy of Six Great Towns, and its Influence on their Social Welfare. By FREDERICK DOLMAN.

SOCIALISM AND MODERN THOUGHT. By M. KAUFMANN.

THE HOUSING OF THE WORKING CLASSES. By R. F. BOWMAKER.

MODERN CIVILISATION IN SOME OF ITS ECONOMIC ASPECTS. By W. CUNNINGHAM, D.D., Fellow of Trinity College, Cambridge.

Classical Translations

Edited by H. F. FOX, M.A., Fellow and Tutor of Brasenose College, Oxford.

Messrs. Methuen are issuing a New Series of Translations from the Greek and Latin Classics. They have enlisted the services of some of the best Oxford and Cambridge Scholars, and it is their intention that the Series shall be distinguished by literary excellence as well as by scholarly accuracy.

ÆSCHYLUS—Agamemnon, Chöephoroe, Eumenides. Translated by LEWIS CAMPBELL, LL.D., late Professor of Greek at St. Andrews. *5s.*

CICERO—De Oratore I. Translated by E. N. P. MOOR, M.A., Assistant Master at Clifton. *3s. 6d.*

CICERO—Select Orations (Pro Milone, Pro Murena, Philippic II., In Catilinam). Translated by H. E. D. BLAKISTON, M.A., Fellow and Tutor of Trinity College, Oxford. *5s.*

CICERO—De Natura Deorum. Translated by F. BROOKS, M.A., late Scholar of Balliol College, Oxford. *3s. 6d.*

LUCIAN—Six Dialogues (Nigrinus, Icaro-Menippus, The Cock, The Ship, The Parasite, The Lover of Falsehood). Translated by S. T. IRWIN, M.A., Assistant Master at Clifton; late Scholar of Exeter College, Oxford. *3s. 6d.*

SOPHOCLES—Electra and Ajax. Translated by E. D. A. MORSHEAD, M.A., late Scholar of New College, Oxford; Assistant Master at Winchester. *2s. 6d.*

TACITUS—Agricola and Germania. Translated by R. B. TOWNSHEND, late Scholar of Trinity College, Cambridge. *2s. 6d.*

Educational Books

CLASSICAL

TACITI AGRICOLA. With Introduction, Notes, Map, etc. By R. F. DAVIS, M.A., Assistant Master at Weymouth College. *Crown 8vo.* 2s.

TACITI GERMANIA. By the same Editor. *Crown 8vo.* 2s.

HERODOTUS: EASY SELECTIONS. With Vocabulary. By A. C. LIDDELL, M.A., Assistant Master at Nottingham High School. *Fcap. 8vo.* 1s. 6*d.*

SELECTIONS FROM THE ODYSSEY. By E. D. STONE, M.A., late Assistant Master at Eton. *Fcap. 8vo.* 1s. 6*d.*

PLAUTUS: THE CAPTIVI. Adapted for Lower Forms by J. H. FREESE, M.A., late Fellow of St. John's, Cambridge. 1s. 6*d.*

DEMOSTHENES AGAINST CONON AND CALLICLES. Edited with Notes, and Vocabulary, by F. DARWIN SWIFT, M.A., formerly Scholar of Queen's College, Oxford; Assistant Master at Denstone College. *Fcap. 8vo.* 2s.

GERMAN

A COMPANION GERMAN GRAMMAR. By H. DE B. GIBBINS, M.A., Assistant Master at Nottingham High School. *Crown 8vo.* 1s. 6*d.*

GERMAN PASSAGES FOR UNSEEN TRANSLATION. By E. M'QUEEN GRAY. *Crown 8vo.* 2s. 6*d.*

SCIENCE

THE WORLD OF SCIENCE. Including Chemistry, Heat. Light, Sound, Magnetism, Electricity, Botany, Zoology, Physiology, Astronomy, and Geology. By R. ELLIOT STEEL, M.A., F.C.S. 147 Illustrations. *Second Edition. Crown 8vo.* 2s. 6*d.*

'Mr. Steel's Manual is admirable in many ways. The book is well calculated to attract and retain the attention of the young.'—*Saturday Review.*

'If Mr. Steel is to be placed second to any for this quality of lucidity, it is only to Huxley himself; and to be named in the same breath with this master of the craft of teaching is to be accredited with the clearness of style and simplicity of arrangement that belong to thorough mastery of a subject.'—*Parents' Review.*

ELEMENTARY LIGHT. By R. E. STEEL. With numerous Illustrations. *Crown 8vo.* 4s. 6*d.*

ENGLISH

ENGLISH RECORDS. A Companion to the History of England. By H. E. MALDEN, M.A. *Crown 8vo.* 3*s.* 6*d.*

A book which aims at concentrating information upon dates, genealogy, officials, constitutional documents, etc., which is usually found scattered in different volumes.

THE ENGLISH CITIZEN: HIS RIGHTS AND DUTIES. By H. E. MALDEN, M.A. 1*s.* 6*d.*

'The book goes over the same ground as is traversed in the school books on this subject written to satisfy the requirements of the Education code. It would serve admirably the purposes of a text-book, as it is well based in historical facts, and keeps quite clear of party matters.'—*Scotsman.*

METHUEN'S COMMERCIAL SERIES.

Edited by H. DE B. GIBBINS, M.A.

BRITISH COMMERCE AND COLONIES FROM ELIZABETH TO VICTORIA. By H. DE B. GIBBINS, M.A., Author of 'The Industrial History of England,' etc. etc. 2*s.*

COMMERCIAL EXAMINATION PAPERS. By H. DE B. GIBBINS, M.A. 1*s.* 6*d.*

THE ECONOMICS OF COMMERCE. By H. DE B. GIBBINS, M.A. 1*s.* 6*d.*

A MANUAL OF FRENCH COMMERCIAL CORRESPONDENCE. By S. E. BALLY, Modern Language Master at the Manchester Grammar School. 2*s.*

A FRENCH COMMERCIAL READER. By S. E. BALLY. 2*s.*

COMMERCIAL GEOGRAPHY, with special reference to Trade Routes, New Markets, and Manufacturing Districts. By L. W. LYDE, M.A., of the Academy, Glasgow. 2*s.*

A PRIMER OF BUSINESS. By S. JACKSON, M.A. 1*s.* 6*d.*

COMMERCIAL ARITHMETIC. By F. G. TAYLOR, M.A. 1*s.* 6*d.*

WORKS BY A. M. M. STEDMAN, M.A.

INITIA LATINA: Easy Lessons on Elementary Accidence. *Second Edition. Fcap. 8vo.* 1*s.*

FIRST LATIN LESSONS. *Fourth Edition. Crown 8vo.* 2*s.*

FIRST LATIN READER. With Notes adapted to the Shorter Latin Primer and Vocabulary. *Second Edition. Crown 8vo.* 1*s.* 6*d.*

EASY SELECTIONS FROM CAESAR. Part I. The Helvetian War. 18*mo.* 1*s.*

EASY SELECTIONS FROM LIVY. Part I. The Kings of Rome. 18*mo.* 1*s.* 6*d.*

EASY LATIN PASSAGES FOR UNSEEN TRANSLATION. *Third Edition. Fcap. 8vo.* 1*s.* 6*d.*

EXEMPLA LATINA. First Lessons in Latin Accidence. With Vocabulary. *Crown 8vo.* 1*s.*

EASY LATIN EXERCISES ON THE SYNTAX OF THE SHORTER AND REVISED LATIN PRIMER. With Vocabulary. *Fourth Edition. Crown 8vo.* 2*s.* 6*d.* Issued with the consent of Dr. Kennedy.

THE LATIN COMPOUND SENTENCE: Rules and Exercises. *Crown 8vo.* 1*s.* 6*d.* With Vocabulary. 2*s.*

NOTANDA QUAEDAM: Miscellaneous Latin Exercises on Common Rules and Idioms. *Second Edition. Fcap. 8vo.* 1*s.* 6*d.* With Vocabulary, 2s.

LATIN VOCABULARIES FOR REPETITION: Arranged according to Subjects. *Fourth Edition. Fcap. 8vo.* 1*s.* 6*d.*

A VOCABULARY OF LATIN IDIOMS AND PHRASES. 18*mo.* 1*s.*

STEPS TO GREEK. 18*mo.* 1*s.*

EASY GREEK PASSAGES FOR UNSEEN TRANSLATION. *Fcap. 8vo.* 1*s.* 6*d.*

GREEK VOCABULARIES FOR REPETITION. Arranged according to Subjects. *Second Edition. Fcap. 8vo.* 1*s.* 6*d.*

GREEK TESTAMENT SELECTIONS. For the use of Schools. *Third Edition.* With Introduction, Notes, and Vocabulary. *Fcap. 8vo.* 2*s.* 6*d.*

STEPS TO FRENCH. *18mo.* *8d.*

FIRST FRENCH LESSONS. *Crown 8vo.* *1s.*

EASY FRENCH PASSAGES FOR UNSEEN TRANSLATION. *Second Edition.* *Fcap. 8vo.* *1s. 6d.*

EASY FRENCH EXERCISES ON ELEMENTARY SYNTAX. With Vocabulary. *Crown 8vo.* *2s. 6d.*

FRENCH VOCABULARIES FOR REPETITION: Arranged according to Subjects. *Third Edition.* *Fcap. 8vo.* *1s.*

SCHOOL EXAMINATION SERIES.

EDITED BY A. M. M. STEDMAN, M.A.

Crown 8vo. *2s. 6d.*

FRENCH EXAMINATION PAPERS IN MISCELLANEOUS GRAMMAR AND IDIOMS. By A. M. M. STEDMAN, M.A. *Sixth Edition.*

A KEY, issued to Tutors and Private Students only, to be had on application to the Publishers. *Second Edition.* *Crown 8vo.* *6s. net.*

LATIN EXAMINATION PAPERS IN MISCELLANEOUS GRAMMAR AND IDIOMS. By A. M. M. STEDMAN, M.A. *Fourth Edition.* KEY issued as above. *6s. net.*

GREEK EXAMINATION PAPERS IN MISCELLANEOUS GRAMMAR AND IDIOMS. By A. M. M. STEDMAN, M.A. *Third Edition.* KEY issued as above. *6s. net.*

GERMAN EXAMINATION PAPERS IN MISCELLANEOUS GRAMMAR AND IDIOMS. By R. J. MORICH, Manchester. *Third Edition.* KEY issued as above. *6s. net.*

HISTORY AND GEOGRAPHY EXAMINATION PAPERS. By C. H. SPENCE, M.A., Clifton Coll.

SCIENCE EXAMINATION PAPERS. By R. E. STEEL, M.A., F.C.S., Chief Natural Science Master, Bradford Grammar School. *In two vols.* Part I. Chemistry; Part II. Physics.

GENERAL KNOWLEDGE EXAMINATION PAPERS. By A. M. M. STEDMAN, M.A. *Second Edition.* KEY issued as above. *7s. net.*